Hans Conried

Hans Conried

A Biography; With a Filmography and a Listing of Radio, Television, Stage and Voice Work

by Suzanne Gargiulo

McFarland & Company, Inc., Publishers
Jefferson, North Carolina, and London

Frontispiece: CBS Television publicity portrait of Hans Conried circa 1956. The sardonic arched eyebrow and world-weary gaze became Hans' trademark during the late 1950s. The photograph was taken by celebrity photographer Ben Polin.

Library of Congress Cataloguing-in-Publication Data

Gargiulo, Suzanne, 1961–
Hans Conried : a biography; with a filmography and a listing of radio, television, stage and voice work / by Suzanne Gargiulo.
     p.   cm.
Includes bibliographical references and index.

ISBN-13: 978-0-7864-1338-6
softcover : 50# alkaline paper ∞

1. Conried, Hans. 2. Actors—United States—Biography.
I. Title.
PN2287.C5825 G37   2002
792'.028'092—dc21   2002006895

British Library cataloguing data are available

©2002 Suzanne Gargiulo. All rights reserved

No part of this book may be reproduced or transmitted in any form or by any means, electronic or mechanical, including photocopying or recording, or by any information storage and retrieval system, without permission in writing from the publisher.

Manufactured in the United States of America

Cover photograph: Hans Conried as Dr. Terwilliker in a Columbia Pictures publicity photo for the 1953 film *The 5000 Fingers of Dr. T*

McFarland & Company, Inc., Publishers
Box 611, Jefferson, North Carolina 28640
www.mcfarlandpub.com

Acknowledgments

It is hard to know where to start. One big reason for that is the way this book developed from just an idle curiosity on my part into a full-fledged manuscript. I only wish I had kept better notes at the beginning! I have been struck over and over again by the generosity and kindness of the many people I spoke to and corresponded with over this long process. People I had never met before urged me to stick with it and publish this book no matter what the odds—and there were some formidable ones. It is important that I try to thank them all. If I have left anyone out, please know that it wasn't intentional, and your help was greatly appreciated.

The most difficult part of researching this book was compiling the log of Hans Conried's radio work. After struggling with it for a short while, it dawned on me why no one had endeavored to attempt such a foolish thing before. I gave up on my dream of finding every single show he ever spoke a word on, and settled in to make, at the very least, the best log of Hans Conried's work that is humanly possible. I believe I succeeded, but not without a substantial amount of much needed help. Martin Grams, Jr., the noted radio historian, worked early on to flesh out my meager framework of shows and has provided continued support throughout. His help has been invaluable. And so have the Herculean efforts made by my good friend Michael L. Campbell. Mike went above and beyond the call of duty for "The Cause" (as it came to be known), and sacrificed countless hours collecting information, burning CDs, and generally keeping my spirits up. Mike provided hundreds of radio shows so I could experience them firsthand, and often he would send "mystery" CDs with possible Hans material to listen to and make a decision on. We managed to find some hidden treasures that way. The radio log would not be nearly as comprehensive if it weren't for him. I can assure you, Mike has earned his place in heaven.

I am especially thankful to James Karen, who spent a good deal of time talking to me on the phone providing information as well as encouragement. He gave me the push I needed early on to forge ahead. The Conried family has been very patient and kind. Trilby and Hans, the younger, have gone out of their way to be accessible, and I was very grateful for their unique insights. Without the generous help of Mike Wallace, I would not have been able to rescue a copy of his 1959 television interview with Hans Conried from the UCLA archives where the negatives were rapidly deteriorating.

The following individuals have also contributed something, be it large or small: Janet Aycock, Harry Bartell, Conrad Binyon, Peter Blau, Angela Cartwright, Jennifer Childs (BibNet), Norman Corwin, Burnie and Ruth Craig, William Davies, Dorothy Dybisz, Larry Dobkin, James F.

Engelhardt, Ray Erlenborn, John Fink, June Foray, Lydia Franklin, MaryAnn Gibson, Ormly Gumfudgin, Phil Gries, Buddy Hackett, Gordon Kelley, Mrs. Stanley Kramer, Marietta LaFargue, Stu Levin, Marjorie Lord, Hal Kanter, Dick Moore (Dick Moore & Assoc.), John Moore, Mike Murray, Mike Ogden, Bill Owen, Gary Owens, Joe Ponazecki, Tony Randall, Elliott Reid, Jimmy Roberts, Dr. Nathan Rosenbloom, George Sanchez, Keith Scott, Jan Schilling, Tom Shelton, Dana Snow, Lynne Stuart, William Stout, Charles Ulrich, and a few others who wished to remain anonymous.

The Boston University Department of Special Collections became something of a home-away-from-home for me. I spent countless hours in their Researcher's Room poring over tiny scraps of newsprint until my eyes could no longer focus. I am indebted to Sean D. Noel and J.C. Johnson, as well as Dr. Herman Gotlieb and others on the B.U. staff, for their patience and assistance. Other institutions and organizations were instrumental in gathering the information for this book:

• Academy of Motion Picture Arts and Sciences, Margaret Herrick Library, Beverly Hills CA: (Kristine Krueger and Barbara Hall).

• The Lilly Library, Indiana University, Bloomington, IN—The Orson Welles Collection (the letter to Welles from Hans Conried written from the Philippines in 1945)

• Thousand Oaks Library, Special Collections, Thousand Oaks CA (Brad Bauer)

• Museum of Radio and Television, New York NY (Jane Klain and Michael Buening)

• New York Library of the Performing Arts, New York NY

• UCLA Film and Television Archives, Hollywood CA (Howard Hays)

• Maryland State Archives, Annapolis MD

• Los Angeles Public Library, Los Angeles CA (Robert Anderson)

• Marin County Public Library, San Rafael CA

• Sonoma County Public Library, Santa Rosa CA (Julie Johnson)

• Boston Public Library, Boston MA

• Wichita State University, Special Collections, Wichita KS (Michael Kelly)

• SPERDVAC, Los Angeles CA (Larry Gassman)

• Pacific Pioneer Broadcasters, Los Angeles CA (Marty Halperin)

• AFTRA and Actor's Equity Association

I would like to thank my brother, Shane Gargiulo, for listening to me drone on about Hans Conried, the book, and all the associated trials and tribulations. The same appreciation goes out to other family and friends (you know who you are).

Last, but certainly not least, I feel the need to thank Hans Conried. If he had not been such a packrat, all of those wonderful little bits of newspaper and other memorabilia would not have been available for someone like me to work with. Mr. Conried, your efforts (and mine) were not in vain.

Contents

Acknowledgments v
Foreword by Leonard Maltin 1
Introduction 3

I. Radio and Motion Pictures

1. The Early Years 9
2. A New Life as a Radio Actor Begins 17
3. Motion Pictures, Marriage, and More Radio 24
4. The Army Years 44

II. The Death of Radio

5. Sergeant Conried Returns 55
6. *Peter Pan, The Twonky,* and *Dr. T* 78
7. *Can-Can* and the Brink of Oblivion 92

III. Jack Paar and the Call of the Road

8. A "TV Personality" Is Born 105
9. The Road Show Begins 124
10. The Business of TV Guest Spots and Jay Ward 138

IV. The Final Years

11. "One with the Gypsies, the Charlatans, the Rogues, the Vagabonds" 153
12. Winding Down: The End 165

V. Appendices

A. Radio Log   183
B. Filmography   197
C. Television Log   206
D. Stage Work   211
E. Voice Work   215

Bibliography   221
Index   225

Foreword
by Leonard Maltin

I have been lucky enough to interview scores of actors over the years, many of them big stars, some of them pop-culture icons. But one of the memories I cherish most is from an encounter very early in my career with an actor who never became a star.

I was nineteen years old, publishing a magazine for old-movie buffs, and desperate to get interviews with veterans of the "golden age" of Hollywood. I had no clout and few connections, but I lived near a theater on the venerable straw-hat circuit, a stomping ground for older actors who took plays on the road, and I had a tip that it wasn't hard to get backstage.

So it was that I attended the opening night of Herman Shumlin's *Spofford!* at the Playhouse on the Mall in Paramus, New Jersey. Hans Conried was playing the title character, which had been created on Broadway by Melvyn Douglas.

Following the performance, I timidly (or was it boldly?) ventured backstage, and found the star's dressing room. I knocked, and Mr. Conried himself came to the door. I introduced myself and pressed some copies of my magazine into his hands, explaining that I would be honored if he would grant me an interview about his film career.

"My dear boy," he said, flipping the pages with interest, "we cannot delude someone as young as yourself into believing that I had anything resembling a 'film career.'"

I was undaunted, and he readily invited me to come backstage an hour before curtain on Monday night. I arrived with tape recorder in hand and was regaled with wonderful stories about his adventures as a young actor in Hollywood. He said, more than once, that he hadn't thought about these things in years, and I'm sure it was true. By this time, he was a fixture on the TV talk-show circuit, but hosts like Jack Paar seldom if ever asked about his earlier career. What recognition he had at the time came mostly from playing Uncle Tonoose on *The Danny Thomas Show*. (Many years later, in trying to describe him to my young daughter, I reminded her of the elocution teacher in a classic episode of *I Love Lucy* who wanted the Ricardos and Mertzes to avoid the words "swell" and "lousy." She immediately knew who I was talking about.)

When the stage manager knocked on the door and called, "Five minutes," Mr. Conried finished his modest preparations for his performance and asked if I'd like to return the following night. Would I!

I spent the next two evenings in his company, not only soaking up anecdotes and observations, but also marveling at his eloquence and erudition. I'm sorry to say we never met again, although we did speak on the telephone after he had recovered from a stroke and hit the boards once more.

I've since learned that nothing short of

a piano falling on his head could have kept him off the stage, or screen, or away from the microphone. In the course of researching a book on radio history, Hans' name was mentioned on a regular basis by his many colleagues behind the mike, and always with fondness.

One of his peers, the late Gale Gordon, told me, "He was an actor-holic. I'm sure that Hans' idea of heaven would be to do a play that had thirty characters, men and women, and that he would do them all."

As I continue to listen to vintage radio shows, I often hear his voice—sometimes masked by an accent, other times instantly recognizable—and I never fail to smile. I believe Hans Conried's joyful approach to acting was, and is, contagious.

Whether you know him best from radio plays, television series, talk shows, or movies, I'm sure you're going to enjoy getting to know him better in the pages of this book.

Leonard Maltin is best known for his long tenure as film critic and correspondent on television's Entertainment Tonight. *He is also the author of many books on film, including the popular annual reference* Leonard Maltin's Movie & Video Guide.

Introduction

> "Make this a downgrading, backbiting kind of article, please. People don't enjoy reading praise of others that much. Whereas, if you sort of pick on me, they'll like me. Underdogs are very popular."
>
> —*Hans Conried to a reporter in 1968*

Hans Conried was a complex soul who preferred the realm of Shakespeare, yet thrived on making people laugh. And that he did—by any means at his disposal, from perfectly tuned facial expressions to brazenly displaying brightly colored, mismatched socks at just the right moment. He once said, "I'm a big ham. Give me a laugh on-stage, and I am like a tiger who has just tasted blood." A versatile, intelligent actor, he could handle all aspects of his craft with equal aplomb. The well-known Hollywood gossip columnist Hedda Hopper once described him as a "high-strung, droll fellow, plagued by a multitude of talents."

Hans confided to a friend towards the end of his life that he was just too damn talented for his own good. This may sound like arrogance, but it was very close to the truth. In a world that loves specialists, he was a generalist. The Hollywood machine is no different from our society at large, and seeks to compartmentalize and categorize everything and everybody. Hans Conried's versatility worked against him and made it more difficult to find a niche as an actor. Near the end of his life, he commented, "I've never been, so to speak, typed. But is this good? The big ones, the Gables, the John Waynes, the Cary Grants, were all typed, as it were. It does beat having always to put on another hat and false face."

At the height of World War II during the early 1940s, if a studio needed someone to play a Nazi for 60 seconds in a picture, Hans Conried was their man. Or a waiter, or hotel clerk. One early RKO Pictures publicity biography starts off with "If you see a picture these days in which the part of a waiter, a hotel clerk, or a tailor stands out, you can just about be sure that the actor who makes it so is Hans Conried." Every actor has to start somewhere, but this certainly wasn't the kind of "push" that would launch a young actor's career into the stratosphere. It is no wonder, then, that Hans played so many hotel clerks and waiters in motion pictures. He did manage to advance to headwaiter in a few films. The work must not have been very challenging for an actor fresh from doing Shakespeare on the radio.

Of all the media he worked in—and he did just about everything an actor can do—Hans Conried loved radio the most. He referred to it as the "best of all possible worlds." For an actor as in love with acting as he was in those early days, one can imagine the wide-open possibilities of radio. "Ah, radio," he once sighed. "Once it was the theater of the mind, a stage where the rubies were always big and flawless." Radio gave an actor the opportunity to play just about any character imaginable; there were no limitations based on physical appearance, age, or ethnicity. Hans' well-documented prowess with foreign dialects and diction found an environment that didn't care if he was "too tall, thin, and Adam's-appled." He was supremely confident of his acting ability, but harbored some misgivings about his physical appearance. No doubt he was told many times over the years (probably none too tactfully either) by various executive types that he just didn't have the looks they were after. He was therefore relegated to the category of "character actor" when his time came to test the celluloid waters.

In motion pictures, Hans Conried was a good utility character actor (he usually referred to himself more pejoratively as a "bit player"). The majority of his films were produced between 1941 and 1953, with the period between 1941 and 1943 being the most prolific. With only a few exceptions—*Blondie's Blessed Event* (1942), *The 5000 Fingers of Dr. T* (1953), and *The Twonky* (1953)—the average time Hans spent on the screen was so brief, you scarcely had time to take a bite of popcorn before he disappeared. His part very often was a memorable one, though, like the cocky young hotel clerk with the thick New York accent in *A Date with the Falcon* (1942), or the sweet natured but lethal Cockney assassin in *Behave Yourself!* (1951). So many little moments that are sadly brief, but give a glimmer of the potential of this unique individual. But only a glimmer. The vast majority of Hans Conried's best work, ultimately, was ephemeral, and never recorded on film. Many of the old television shows from the 1950s and early 1960s were taped over. Unless there is a video in private hands somewhere, it appears that none of his college lectures (he did hundreds of them) were ever recorded. The same can be said of his thousands of stage performances on Broadway, and the seemingly endless stock company tours. A relative handful of the myriad radio shows he worked on during the 1940s and 1950s are on tape, but it is nearly impossible to experience those shows the way they were meant to be heard. Virtually all that is left are the films, and some of the television shows he did guest appearances on.

This predicament—the idea that the bulk of Hans Conried's work may soon be completely forgotten—was one of the reasons why I felt so strongly about putting this book together to record his accomplishments and preserve his memory. There is nothing wrong with being remembered only for a cartoon voice (Snidely Whiplash) and a cartoonish character like Uncle Tonoose. That is more than many actors have to their credit. Hans Conried was so much more than that, and even these two claims to fame are fast fading from our collective memory. How many people today remember *The Danny Thomas Show*?

The seeds for this book were actually planted many years ago. They came to full germination one day when I was watching the incomparable "Do-Me-Do-Duds" scene from *The 5000 Fingers of Dr. T* for what must have been the twentieth time. It hit me that I had no idea who this guy Hans Conried really was. What else had he ever done? I remembered him vaguely as the host of the TV series *Fractured Flickers* in the early 1960s. I can still remember sitting on the floor very close to the TV set thinking that old man on the screen was really funny (yes, I was quite young then). That was about the extent of my knowledge. My inquisitive nature led me to comb the Internet and local libraries for information. I was disappointed to find the few sources available were either woefully incomplete, or contradictory. By now my curiosity was sufficiently piqued, and I set off on this long, arduous journey to discover the "real" Hans Conried. I can't say I ever found him, but, then again, that is probably the way he would have wanted it. I would like to believe, though, that I did manage to peek—if ever so briefly—behind the facade. Along the way I have developed a deep admiration and respect for this gifted human being, who was also quite a mensch. It seemed only natural to want to share what I have learned with other fans, and those who knew and loved him.

Hans Conried's world was an interesting, vibrant place to be. He loved to share his knowledge of acting, life, and the universe, and would do so freely, without bias or snobbery. The few who found him smug or intimidating probably never made it beyond the imposing facade (granted, he was a rather imposing figure at almost 6'3" tall). Some said he had a way of "looking down his nose" at people that could rattle one's confidence. Most of the initial stern demeanor and his erudite British sounding accent were just the first line of guards he had posted outside his fortress. When asked about his accent he replied, "Hah! So that impresses you, does it? Well, it's meant to. But it's a theatrical accent, not British. Call it an affectation, if you will." Once the drawbridge was lowered, the genial, genteel, impeccably dressed bon vivant would appear armed with his favorite weapon—humor. "Humor is not a light bulb I can turn on and off," he explained. "It is my insulated armor coat against an often absurd world." Hans Conried's armor may have suffered its fair share of scrapes and dents over the years, but it served him very well during his lifetime.

Hans Conried was never able to realize the lofty dreams he had as a young actor for his career, and in some ways, did not quite fulfill his personal dreams either: "Of course you're entirely dramatic when you're young. You have all kinds of dreams. No one in this business ever imagined himself doing walk-ons. We all imagined ourselves playing Hamlet or Lear. But one must be realistic. One's life changes, and I suppose that, somewhere, the intelligent man makes his compromise."

The idea of "compromise" was a recurrent theme in many of the interviews Hans was to give over the years. It is interesting to note the severe change in tone that occurred in his retelling of how he became an actor. Early on, it was the only thing he ever wanted to do, and he passionately felt the need to act. Much later, and with a distinct note of bitterness, he would snap, "That's all it is. It's just a job... a rigorous one, and a way to earn a living." He went from describing his enthusiasm over his early stage work, and first radio job in early interviews, to saying he just sort of "drifted into the theater" during the depression, and only then decided it was for him. Quite a disconcerting change of heart, I would say. Maybe the sense of humor that early on was described as having a "tinge" of the sardonic mutated later in life into full, Technicolor cynicism.

Whatever the case may be, Hans Conried forged ahead no matter what sort of uncharted territory he may have been treading upon. Like his great-uncle Heinrich before him, his motto could very well have been "Immer Vorwärts" ("Always Forward"). He had an inexorable, and honorable, sense of responsibility, and he never let himself stray too far from the straight and narrow (at least, no one ever caught him). One of the accomplishments that instilled the most pride in him was the fact that in all the years he worked as an actor, he never had to stand in line at the unemployment office. As with many people who grew up during the Great Depression, providing all of the physical comforts for your family was indeed a great accomplishment. Hans' hard work was able to provide everything his wife and four children could want, save, perhaps, the one important thing he could only give sparingly—himself. Shortly before his death, when he had curtailed his extensive touring and settled into working closer to his home in Los Angeles, Hans was to tell a friend, "I'm enjoying not doing the road work. I want to get to know my widow."

If you heard him tell it, you would think Hans felt he had never been successful, and his career was ultimately a failure. "Self-effacing" was a term often used to describe his style of expressing his views regarding his career. There is one often-repeated quote from a 1959 publicity biography that must have been a personal favorite of his. He edited the original copy in red pencil, and had his annotated (and very funny) version copied and distributed. Just after the description of his break into radio in 1936 doing Shakespeare, it says (his added comments are in parentheses): "Conried (took the first of many subsequent steps downward and) developed less classical facets to his repertoire."

"The plums in life rarely fall to me," he would later say. Nonsense. He would always lament never having the chance to perform the "definitive King Lear," but he was anything but a failure. Even when his favorite medium, radio, died in the 1950s, he had the fortitude to re-invent himself, and forge ahead where many other radio actors simply could not make the transition. He would later proudly refer to himself as a "survivor." Hans had to put his youthful aspirations in his back pocket and take a more realistic, somewhat mercenary approach to finding work. Maybe acting did start feeling like "just a job" to him at this point, but his sense of humor, intelligence, and exquisite command of his craft made even the humblest of assignments a gem to behold. Most of them were, anyway.

Hans' sharp, playful intellect loved to wrap itself around any subject that caught his fancy, and he used each acting job as an opportunity to learn something new. Besides acting, Hans posed for print ads hawking everything from Honeywell thermostats to Seagram's Gin to haberdasheries, as well as doing radio spots for local businesses in the towns he would pass through during one of his summer stock tours. He even made a special commemorative recording extolling the virtues of "dynamic Denton, Texas." Then there is the anonymous work he did dubbing the voices of actors for foreign films. No matter. Hans took it all in stride. At least that is what he wanted people to think, and for the most part he did.

Hans once told a reporter, "The curtain will always be down on my private life." Rarely did he ever discuss his family in interviews, and preferred to keep them out of the whole "celebrity" lifestyle as much as possible. I would have loved to have seen the Jack Paar show where Paar stunned Hans by asking him to discuss his wife's pregnancy on live TV! I am sure he was able to find a dignified way out of that one.

I have attempted to paint, using the words of this book, a full-length portrait of Hans Conried. My style is somewhat impressionistic—meant to suggest, rather than define. There are gaps in the story I had no model for and was obligated to fill in as best as I could. It is very regrettable that Margaret Conried—Hans' wife of 40 years—was not able to provide her unique voice to this book due to her advanced illness. Shortly after his death, personal journals were discovered amongst his papers. Margaret had them destroyed in the belief that no one should ever read them, not even his family. Given that Hans was a fiercely private person, maybe it is best that the most intimate parts of his life are left unknown.

Hans had more than his fair share of adversity and disappointments in his life and career. In spite of it all, he lived a good life—a relatively short life (he died 3 months short of his 65th birthday), but one that sparkled with the vibrant spirit of a truly unique, intense individual.

So go out and rent a copy of *The 5000 Fingers of Dr. T*, or *Blondie's Blessed Event*. Both films offer the best opportunities left to us to catch a glimpse of the comedic genius, and fiery artistic energy Hans Conried possessed. There will never be another quite like him.

Part I
Radio and Motion Pictures

1

The Early Years

Before there was Hans Conried, the man, there was little Hans Conried, the boy. Even though it is hard to imagine a "little" Hans Conried, he was once an infant, with two loving parents. His father, Hans Georg Conried, Sr., was a high-spirited young man who early in life caused his family no small amount of consternation. His restless nature made holding any one job for long rather a difficult task. Hans Sr. was an intelligent boy growing up in an affluent household in Vienna, Austria, around the turn of the 20th century. His conservative parents found his inability to grasp the finer points of steady employment a bit of an embarrassment. Something had to be done to put their boy on the right track, and keep him out of trouble. They must have been very concerned for his welfare, for their solution was to ship Hans Sr. across the ocean to New York to live with his successful émigré uncle Heinrich Conried. Surely, Heinrich could teach him a thing or two about life, and help the younger Conried find a career for himself in America.

Heinrich Conried had acting in his blood from an early age, and became a professional actor in Vienna at the age of eighteen (after a brief attempt to learn the family trade of weaver). He came to America around 1878 to manage the Germania Theatre in New York City. Heinrich was a colorful figure with a forceful personality (that's the polite way of saying it) who seemed to be able to make things happen by the sheer strength of his will. His early productions for his own Conried Opera Company were considered quite elaborate for their time, and he had a keen ear for up-and-coming new talent. As impresario for the Metropolitan Opera House (1903-1908), he is credited with introducing the great Italian tenor Enrico Caruso to American audiences. Heinrich was also an excellent self-promoter who presented lectures on the subject of opera as a way to gain interest in his company's performances. One major criticism of Heinrich was that he was a businessman more interested in making profits than fine art. The jury is still out on that issue, but no one would deny he managed to forge a place for himself in the annals of Opera history.

It is not known precisely when Hans Sr. lived with his Uncle Heinrich, but it probably was around 1903. Heinrich's serious illness (which was diagnosed as sciatic neuritis) forced his resignation as impresario for the Met in 1908. Shortly thereafter he left America with his wife Augusta and son Richard to return to Austria in an attempt to regain his health. He died there the following year on April 27th.

With the probable help of his uncle, Hans Sr. was able to find employment in the field of theatrical publicity and program publishing. He was doing well at his new career in New York, and met and married a young lady named Flora. They had a son, Edwin, but their relationship was a stormy one. Shortly after their son's birth, the couple divorced. It must have been a very bitter affair. Hans Sr.'s letters went unanswered, and eventually his ex-wife left town, taking their young son with her. He never saw her or his son again. Hans Sr. spoke about Edwin often over the years, and it was clear to all who knew him that the pain of this separation never subsided.

The theatrical publishing business kept Hans Sr. busy and constantly on the move. While in his early thirties, he met a lovely young woman from New Canaan, Connecticut, named Edith Beyr Gildersleeve. Her family was from sturdy Pilgrim stock, and she must have been just the sort of calming influence he needed in his troubled life. Edith had grown up on a farm, and was probably swept off her feet by this dashing Continental character who was far more worldly than she. It wasn't long before they were married in Bridgeport, Connecticut.

In April of 1917, the Conrieds were traveling through Maryland on one of Hans Sr.'s many business trips. Edith was well into the ninth month of her first pregnancy by now, and she was beginning to have contractions. Her son was anxious to make his entrance onto this grand stage, and nothing was going to stop him. The couple had to make a quick change of plans and find a hospital — any hospital. They were in Baltimore at this time, and luckily found the Maryland General Hospital at the corner of Linden and Madison. Hans Georg Conried Jr. was born at 9:25 A.M. on April 15th. His birth certificate lists the date of his birth as April 14th. Hans Jr. and his family always gave the 15th as the correct date. No doubt the birth was recorded incorrectly.

There is a little matter that needs to be clarified before we go any further: Hans Georg Conried, Junior, is Conried's full, legal name ("I would have changed it to this?!" he would later quip). His name was not, and never had been, "Frank Foster." The origins of this bizarre rumor can be traced to the 1972-1973 summer stock season when Conried was appearing in a stage production of *How the Other Half Loves*. His character in the play was named Frank Foster. The character's name appeared in parentheses besides Conried's own name in the blurb about him that was printed in the theater program. A quick glance at the program may make you may think the name in the parentheses was there to show his "real" name. It would appear that a newspaper reporter for the *Denver Post* named Ralph Albi thought he had discovered Conried's secret, for he published this "real name" in 1972 as a part of his "Hans Conried Trivia Quiz." Somehow, this error was picked up time and time again over the years, and it can still be found in various publications and on the Internet to this day.

While we are on the subject of "real" names, Conried is not a real surname. The name was changed a few generations before Hans Jr. as a way to disguise the family's Jewish heritage. Being a Jew in Austria or anywhere in that vicinity left a person vulnerable to the whims of history. Conried's ancestors felt that changing their family name, Cohn, would make life more comfortable. Some sources say that Heinrich Conried was the first to use the "Conried" name. His biography states he was born "Heinrich Cohn" in 1855. Hans Sr. was born in 1883, and by all indications, he used the Conried name. Heinrich had two brothers, and they apparently went by Cohn. There is also the theory that the family name was not Cohn, but Cohen: the difference of one vowel. The only Conrieds left today are descendents of Heinrich and Hans Sr. To further confuse genealogists, the name Conried is often misspelled — an act guaranteed to ruffle Conried's feathers. When asked about his career goals by a reporter in 1960, among other things, Conried sited "having people spell my name right. It's 'I ... E ... D,' you know."

Back to Baltimore, Maryland, in the spring of 1917: The Conried family stayed

Hans Georg Conried, Jr., at 2 years of age.

old standing in front of a gas station in Los Angeles with his stuffed monkey doll. There is no indication how long his family lived in California. One biography written for Columbia Studios' publicity department mentions that Conried's schooling was constantly being interrupted. Another bio for Paramount mentions that he attended "eight elementary schools in eight years." This did not give the young Conried much time to develop friendships, or even have a pet dog. His whole world revolved around his parents, and he was their "golden boy." Conried was a model student (when in school), and even a boy scout for a time. Conried said of himself as a boy, "I was not a 'cut-up' in school. I was a bookish sort, dull as dishwater... I tried to soak up knowledge like a sponge soaks up water. Because of the necessity of my parents' constant moving, I had much less time than I desired in school, and had to make the most of my opportunities... I remember all I did on in Baltimore for a short time while Edith recovered, and Conried grew strong enough to travel. Conried claimed to have never returned to the state of his birth, for one reason or another. To quote Conried from 1967: "Born in Baltimore—but left as a babe of six weeks. So they can't claim me. Claim me? They don't even want me. I've never been back, and I've heard no public outcry to have me return to place my feet in cement...."

The Conrieds moved from place to place across the Eastern Seaboard, living in residential hotels. The family even ventured out west at least once before their permanent move in the 1930s. There is a remarkable article cut out of a newspaper and glued into a scrapbook that Conried kept from the time he was about seventeen until around age thirty-three. It is dated 1937, and shows on the right side a photo of Conried as a twenty-year-old performing in a radio studio, and on the left as a three-year-

A dapper, 4-year-old Hansel outside his family's residential hotel.

was study. Nineteen or twenty hours a day... I had a hard time of it." Conried was so intense about his studies that he would often automatically wipe his slate clean at the end of the evening, forgetting that his homework was on it. He would then have to do his work all over again the next day.

In 1925, when Conried was eight years old, his mother gave birth to another son, Alfred. They were living again on the East Coast, and though his business was doing well, Hans Sr. was beginning to have the health problems that would soon curtail his hectic lifestyle. Little Alfred never really had much of a chance in life. The boy contracted whooping cough and wasn't strong enough to fight the ravages of the disease. He died at five years of age. Conried's parents were devastated with the loss of Alfred, and Mrs. Conried would become especially protective of her surviving son. H.C rarely talked about his grief or his loneliness as a child. It wasn't until Conried was a man of about sixty years of age that he had a chance to meet his half-brother, Edwin. They were to meet only one time.

Conried's interest in the theatre started early in life. It is easy to imagine his father's theatrical publicity business—and the free passes he received—afforded a window into that magical world that must have caught his imagination. From all accounts, Con-

Hans with his father, H.G. Conried, Sr., circa 1936 (notice where Hans' left hand is positioned). From the Hans Conried Collection, Department of Special Collections, Boston University.

ried was a sensitive, weedy lad, with thick, dark brown hair, who was well liked, but didn't have many close friends. Many years later, Conried wrote of his early love of the theatre: "I wanted to be an actor all my life; not once have I regretted that all my baseball-playing time was spent in darkened theatres watching matinees. Then—as now—I wanted nothing except to spend as many hours as possible in that lovely, magic darkness."

There was a residue of anti-German sentiment during the late 1920s and early 1930s stemming from the First World War. The Germanic name "Hans" brought a bit too much negative attention. Throughout most of his school years, his schoolmates knew the younger Conried as "Jack." His father usually answered to the more authoritative sounding "H.G.."

It was during his early school days that he took the big plunge and acted in his first play. Very fittingly, it was a production of Shakespeare's *Hamlet*. Conried was twelve years old, and tall for his age, and was able to play the roles written for much older actors. Even so, it's hard to imagine such a youth playing the aged Polonius—the role he played in his first *Hamlet*. Conried explained, "I later attended an exclusive boys school.... There wasn't much opportunity for dramatics. Nevertheless, they did have a little drama group."

The Great Depression hit everyone hard in the early 1930s, and Hans Sr.'s theatrical publishing business was especially vulnerable. Money was increasingly tight, and Conried did a few odd jobs to help ends meet. It may have been around this time that Hans Sr. felt it was important his son learn a trade of some kind. Conried was enrolled in a vocational high school—The High School of Commerce—in New York. He did very well in his studies there, and was able to serve four consecutive terms in the school's Arista League for those students who excelled in "character, service, and scholarship" (it was later called the Arista Society). During this time, his passion for acting started to firmly take root in him. Possibly he had been inspired by stories of his Great Uncle Heinrich, or the many trips to the theater he made with his parents over the years. Somewhere along the way, this gangling teenager fancied himself a Shakespearean actor, and couldn't conceive of doing anything else. Conried joined the school's Dramatic Club, and worked in all aspects of putting on each show. One particular play was called *Commerce on the Air*, and was co-written by the aspiring young thespian, "H.G. Conried, Jr." It was a good-natured parody of the school and the drama department.

His father, apparently, did not see a future for his son in acting, and encouraged Conried to develop his interest in commercial art. As one publicity biography put it: "He studied to become a commercial artist, but the desire to act was predominant within him." To this, Conried penciled in the margins, "This is nonsense. I couldn't draw, and had few other artistic talents. In a word, I flopped!" Consistent with his self-effacing personality, Conried was being unduly hard on himself. He possessed a strong artistic talent, and created a wonderful "self-portrait" caricature that was used instead of a photo in a 1941 radio actor's directory. Conried would have tried to make a go of it as a commercial artist, but the hard truth was, there were no jobs for new illustrators during the Depression. Besides, as Conried would later confide, acting seemed like the best option at the time considering "there wasn't much else for a big, gawky kid who could read well."

He continued on with acting in school productions, and eventually began performing in community summer stock theatre. During the summer months, he would often go to Connecticut with his mother to visit her family. The only record of his early acting experience is from the snapshots and local news clippings he meticulously saved and glued into his scrapbook. In 1934 he appeared with the Birmingham Players in productions of *Plus the Press* and *Brigham Young*. Conried would say of *Plus the Press*: "I was a reporter in this play and I counted the words I had to say. Those twenty-five words were very important to me, and I gave them everything I had."

One snapshot from a Roxbury Theatre production of *The Forest Rose* shows a sixteen- or seventeen-year-old Conried dressed as a farm hand (wearing too much make-up), and looking like he's getting ready to do a jig of some kind. Shyness does not seem to have been a part of his personality, and the usual teenage awkwardness appeared to melt away for those rarified moments he stood on that big stage.

The year 1935 was a turning point in the Conried family's life. There are differing accounts of the story of why Hans Sr., Edith, and Conried packed everything up, got on a bus, and headed out to California. At this time, Conried was working days, and attending the Columbia University's extension program studying theatre arts a couple of nights each week. He was a member of the Columbia Laboratory Players—the campus theatre group—and appeared in a variety of works from Shakespeare, Sheridan, and Goldsmith. Columbia had an arrangement with the Roxbury Theatre in New Milford, Connecticut, and many of the "Lab" students—Conried included—would perform there during the summer months.

The most influential of his Columbia performances was *The Tempest*, which took place at the McMillin Academic Theatre on May 2nd, 3rd, and 4th of 1935. A grainy photo from this time shows an eighteen-year-old Conried dressed for the role of Sebastian, and looking much older with false moustache and goatee.

Hans Sr.'s health was continuing to fail. His blood pressure was high, and there were serious problems with his heart. His doctor

Dressed as Sebastian for the Columbia Laboratory Players production of *The Tempest*: May of 1935. From the Hans Conried Collection, Department of Special Collections, Boston University.

at the time gave him a grim prognosis, and it was recommended that he seek out the milder climate and more relaxed environment of California. Some romanticized accounts of the events that followed include a story about how Conried's parents, recognizing his gift for acting, unselfishly gave up everything to establish their son's career in Hollywood. They did love him very much, but Conried was anything but happy about the move west. To him, acting was the "legitimate" theatre, and Broadway was the place to be. Hollywood?! "You understand, of course," said Conried, "that a drama student at Columbia in 1935 thought of the movies as a business somewhat [more] like a sardine cannery than a branch of the theatrical arts. You told yourself 'There are the films, of course,' followed this with a long, choking gasp, and looked for greener pastures."

There is no exact date recorded when the Conried family left New York, but there are a few clues. In July of 1935, Conried was appearing in productions of *Lady Windermere's Fan, The Discovery,* and *The Taming of the Shrew.* On August 2nd and 3rd he portrayed Randy Fleming in *The Green Bullet* at the Roxbury. By November of that year, Conried was already auditioning for a part in the Santa Monica Civic Theatre production of *A Doctor in Spite of Himself* that opened the day after Christmas. It certainly didn't take Conried long to find an outlet for his passion amongst the "sardine factories."

Out on the West Coast, the family moved into an apartment building on S. Normandie in a working class neighborhood of Los Angeles. Though Conried was devoted to becoming a professional actor, the burden of supporting his family was beginning to shift on to his slender shoulders. He needed to find a "regular" job, and was fortunate to obtain employment—this was still during the depression when jobs were scarce—with a firm that manufactured sporting goods. Conried's job was to go around to various department stores and demonstrate their equipment. One humorous attempt to put a more colorful spin to this detour from acting was written by one of Conried's publicity men many years later: "He sought work in allied fields where he could learn by observing human nature." "Actually," Conried explained, "I sold basketballs and demonstrated punching bags." This was no ordinary punching bag, though. It was a revolutionary design that required Conried to wear a headband to which the bag was attached by a heavy rubber band. It took a great deal of skill to use this device without ending up black and blue. For all his effort, Conried earned a whopping $2.00 per day. "I wonder how many stage-struck eighteen-year-old kids start out every year wanting nothing but to play *Hamlet*—uncut—and settle for the equivalent of a punching bag! There ought to be a law...."

Conried never lost his hope of finding a way to fulfill his acting ambitions, and never stopped dreaming of his big break: "Broadway was still 3,000 miles away, and I was bruised and a little punch drunk from the daily tussles with the punching bag. There must be, I thought, some way an actor could make a living at his craft in Southern California." A clever Conried used the department store demonstrations as a forum to display his acting prowess: "I developed what I consider a rather erudite patter in my best Shakespearean voice. I thought my performance was rather good, and always felt my audience failed me. They stopped, looked, and listened, but never bought the things."

Another romanticized story of Conried's entrance into the world of radio comes from those resourceful publicity people: "He had tough sledding at first, spending the 1935 Christmas season demonstrating a punching bag in a Hollywood department store. A loudspeaker blared away in the adjoining radio department. An announcement came through the receiver that a local broadcasting station was casting Shakespeare's *The Tempest*, and Hans, who had performed in the play at Columbia University, applied for a role and was accepted." It kind of happened that way, but not with *The Tempest*, or at the department store. Conried described it this way: "I had never thought of radio, not even long enough for one of my long, choking shudders. I had one of the things, used mainly for hearing the symphonies on Sunday and for keeping up with the news. But as an art form? I was amazed—and immediately broke out with an idea—when my favorite station, KECA, announced a revolutionary program change. Henceforth, in addition to its traditional twelve hours a day of sustained classical music and news, it planned an experiment with radio drama. And KECA—after all, it called itself 'The Aristocrat of the Airways'—meant Drama! All of the plays of Shakespeare, uncut! With a little luck at this point, I could see that I might elude the punching bag. I hurried over to KECA, braced Forrest Barnes—who was producing the Shakespearian series—in his office, whipped out samples of *Hamlet*, *The Tempest*, and the *Merry Wives of Windsor*, and stood there panting. 'Why sure', Barnes said, giving me my first taste of radio's casual approach, 'I think we can use you, kid.' The next day the cast—nearly everybody except me was a reputable, established actor with years of experience behind him—did *Othello*. Right out of the book, without cutting a word! We all doubled up on parts, of course. I found myself with a hatful—the First Gentleman, the Second Senator, and the First Musician. How, on the air, could I make them distinguishable? I made the musician a comic low Dutchman for a start. After the broadcast, Lindsay MacHarrie, who had played *Othello*, pulled me aside. 'You have a coupla voices, son', he said. 'How would you like to make a few dollars with them?'"

And so, on January 14, 1936, Conried embarked on the long, wonderful journey through the "best of all possible worlds." It may not have been Broadway, but the air was ripe with possibilities, and he had all the hopefulness of youth. Surely, his big break was just around the corner.

Hans dressed in form-fitting military garb for an early stage role (1936). From the Hans Conried Collection, Department of Special Collections, Boston University.

2

A New Life as a Radio Actor Begins

Conried managed to avoid the punching bag after all, and by 1936 he was performing professionally as a radio actor. Radio in the early 1930s was dominated by powerful advertising agencies that not only helped to write many of the network shows, but also had control over which talent was hired. Many people tuned in for the music, news reports, or a favorite comedy program. Radio drama had not yet found its core audience, though more and more dramatic programs were being experimented with. Due to the stranglehold the sponsors had on radio programming, the dramatic shows being produced were not generally considered of high quality. The actors employed were mainly hired to read their lines and collect their paychecks (not always easy in the days before unionization). Merrill Denison of the *Theatre Arts Monthly* wrote in 1933: "While other fields of radio have interested men qualified to serve them, few workers from the theatre have given to radio [drama] any attitude but that one of contemptuous superiority with which the theatre first approached the motion picture. Neither the playwright, the director, nor the actor has attempted to understand, much less master, the difficulties and opportunities of a medium that, for all its aesthetic limitations, has certain imposing quantitative advantages."

With the influx of such high-powered creative talent as Irving Reis, Arch Oboler, Norman Corwin, and Orson Welles, it wasn't long before dramatic radio productions were attracting well-known stage and motion picture personalities. Conried was also striving to develop an identifiable personality, as a reporter for the *Hollywood Lowdown* would report in 1936: "Barely nineteen, Hans Conried ... is the newest actor to enter local radio, and one of the most versatile. In such programs as *Calling All Cars*, *Annals of the Ages*, and *It Happened Today*, he has to jump from one to any of his twenty polished dialects."

It Happened Today was a Hal Styles produced news program that was on the air five nights a week. Conried was frequently called upon to play numerous parts, and once played eighteen different roles in one night for a total fee of 50 cents! This program, Conried was to recall later, "tried to make it so newsy that we only got two or three pages of script at a time, and these were on those gelatin transferals—you know, you used to get them in a Kosher delicatessen when you knew all you wanted was a pastrami sandwich, but the waitress would hand you one of these slimy gelatin menus just the same. Well, we slipped and slid our way through all these scripts—there were four of us on the show; three guys and a doll—we'd get two more pages just as we were finishing the last, several pages would slide to the floor, and as we picked them up we sounded something like Floyd Collins. One of the other guys was a young fellow named Alan Ladd. He staged a revolution and quit because we were getting paid only 50 cents a show. We thought he was crazy. But he's done all right, I hear. The girl got out of the profession. She married a producer—if you can call that getting out of the profession—and I hear she's gone straight ever since. The sponsor of the show was a very wealthy man, but he was partial to girls. Of course, I have nothing against girls, as such, but this joker used to love to take them out on his yacht for the weekend. Now I also have nothing against that, as such. But he used to get so partial that he'd forget to pay us our $2.50. We used to starve all weekend until he got unpartial."

A reporter for the *Hollywood Citizen News* preserved in print a snapshot of one day in March of 1937 when she sat in on a rehearsal of the "Spring in Kansas" episode of *The First Nighter* radio series starring Barbara Luddy and Don Ameche: "Several pictures stand out. One is of Hans Conried, tall, slender, young, supple, with Barbara's almost child size umbrella, walking along the edge of the foot light mask as though it were a tight rope or wire... Another was the huddle for the final cuts in the script ... part of the cast sat, or crouched on the floor... And then there was the position taken on the floor by Hans as he marked his script. It was natural to him, but I would like to see anyone but a contortionist try it." The reporter went on to describe a war scene in which Conried was rehearsing with another actor: "'Get the laugh out of your voice', was the command Ted Shuderman, NBC Producer, gave to Hans, 'Isn't war glorious anymore?', asked the young actor, 'No, it stinks', was the prompt and sharp answer."

Conried would become a regular on *The First Nighter* for a season. He described the series as being "stylish," and remarked how each episode was performed in front of a live audience: "It was very formal, you know. The ushers were turned out in handsome uniforms, and everyone on the set had to wear tuxedos."

A few months later, Conried would be involved in an important episode of the dramatic series, *Thrills*, re-enacting the triumphant return to the stage of Edwin Booth after his brother's assassination of President Abraham Lincoln. Conried was a regular on *Thrills* for its entire run, and received a good deal of positive press related to this program and his growing power as a radio actor.

In 1937, NBC's *Streamlined Shakespeare* series provided Conried with the opportunity to meet and work with the great John Barrymore. The legendary actor was well past his prime by now, but still a commanding presence. Barrymore was deeply impressed with Conried's natural affinity for acting. The elder actor would select Conried as his double to take over for him when he was "indisposed" for one reason or another. Barrymore selected Conried to perform with him on his *John Barrymore Presents* series, in a modern play titled *Accent on Youth*. Dazzled by Conried's performance, Barrymore raved: "[Hans Conried] is one of the most versatile actors I have ever seen. It is nothing short of amazing how a boy like Conried can step from serious Shakespearean roles into a modern character like Dickie and do credit to both." Barrymore was to become his mentor, and provided the sort of professional guidance he needed. Conried would later mention how patient Barrymore was with him, and how he went out of his way to help an inexperienced, young actor: "At a beardless 20, I saw Barrymore through youthful eyes, and he seemed the greatest mortal I'd ever encountered. He set a mark, a target, for everyone. He—was —an—Actor!" Conried was so touched by Barrymore's magnanimity, that he would name his first child—a daughter—Trilby, in honor of his mentor's performance as Sven-

Resplendent in his flamboyant plaid suit, Hans reads for NBC's "Accent of Youth" (1937) with unidentified announcer (left). The radio play starred John Barrymore. From the Hans Conried Collection, Department of Special Collections, Boston University.

gali in the play adapted from the George Du Maurier novel.

The famous crooner with a megaphone, Rudy Vallee, was another important influence on the young Conried. Vallee was very popular on the radio, but felt uncomfortable in a sterile studio environment. He felt he needed the feedback of an audience to perform to his full potential. In the late 1930s, a special recording system was set up at the Victor Hugo supper club in Beverly Hills, where Vallee and his band had a lengthy engagement, to broadcast the live entertainment. In 1939, Vallee decided to try a new format that incorporated live dramatic readings to create a unique diversion for the guests of the club, as well as the listeners at home. According to Vallee: "It was simply a reading by some of the best Hollywood radio personalities of some of our Barrymore Sealtest scripts. We put long, low portable foot lights on the floor, and read the radio scripts just as we would in the radio studio. At the time, Hans Conried was more than willing to perform for me, and since he did an excellent imitation of John Barrymore, we had much fun with these beautifully written scripts in addition to several other acts of the typical nightclub genre. Barrymore came in one night and seemed to enjoy Hans Conried's characterization of the 'Great Profile'."

Reverently pasted into Conried's scrapbook is an autographed photo of Rudy Vallee inscribed with high praise for the young actor. He also saved a magazine article describing Vallee's palatial estate high in the Hollywood hills complete with swimming pool and tennis court. The description of this magnificent home, and how the maddening maze of narrow streets in the hills provided a security barrier against unwanted visitors, may have been what inspired Conried to purchase his own mansion nearby many years later.

Radio acting posed a difficult challenge

to "legitimate" actors, as Merrill Denison was to describe: "On the air, there can be neither scenery, gesture nor action. The significance and importance of the play can only be conveyed through dialogue and the use of occasional sound effects. Even the meaning of the latter must often be explained by words. So it is that the play depends finally on the actor's voice. It alone can create the desired effect on the listener. The author may write brilliant, moving dialogue; the director may help with intelligent, imaginative guidance; but it is upon the actor that the final and most important burden rests... By means of [his voice, the actor] must not only create character, but through some intangible quality of voice and delivery, build an objective world in which his created character has its being. He cannot count on the attention of his scattered listeners; he must first fight for it, and then hold it if he can." Conried not only held the attention of thousands of listeners, but quickly distinguished himself as one of the top radio actors of his time. Those early days were fraught with their trials and tribulations, though, as in any fledgling career.

Conried never minded the long hours, or pitifully small wages. He welcomed each new assignment as a chance to perfect his craft, and genuinely basked in the sheer joy of acting. He loved every minute of it, and would jump at the chance to explore and expand his range by playing any type of part or dialect. What he didn't know, he was eagerly willing to bluff. He once remarked that if a director had asked him if he could do an Eskimo with a harelip, he would have emphatically said "Yes!" As Conried explained, "If we couldn't do the accents, or at least fake them, we didn't work. So we had to learn them all. You do it by ear—but I can't imitate actual people, though."

For a young man of twenty, he was ahead of the game by further developing his personal, as well as professional style. He became somewhat infamous for wearing loud (some described them as "obnoxious"), brightly colored (often plaid) suits with a fire engine red tie. He developed an anachronistic style that included waistcoats, watch fobs, and large neckwear. When he could afford it, Conried had his clothes specially made for him, and later fancied jackets that were cut high at the waist with long tails, reminiscent of Edwardian fashion. There was a definite method to Conried's madness. The affected British-sounding accent and garish clothing turned his 6'2½" frame into a walking billboard advertisement for himself that was not easy to ignore. Many years after his death, those wild clothes—complete with red and green mismatched socks—were one of the things people who knew him during that time remembered the most vividly.

In radio, Conried also found a sort of extended family and friends he had missed growing up: "I remember my first years of radio stock-playing as an experiment in collective living, full of just as much frenzy, and just as much fun. We all spent our social lives with the same gang with whom we worked on the air... We loaned one another money and clothes, coached one another, beefed about one another, without ever really meaning it. For one series of programs, which ran daily at a station fifteen miles from where most of us lived ... we managed by paying Clayton Post, the one fellow who had a car, ten cents apiece to transport us. The thirty cents carfare would have made doing the show a luxury we couldn't afford. I say we got by. Sometimes it was by the squeakiest margin. Lots of days, I had nothing to eat but one of those foot-high milk shakes—ten cents, and you had to cut it with a knife and fork. Lots of nights, I—and a lot of other 'great actors with small funds'—found in people like Verna Felton (you know her as Red Skelton's grandma) and Lee Millar friendly sort of people ... who always had room at their dinner table for one or two more. It was a great period. And it was exciting."

As many young people do, Conried was experimenting with being an independent adult, and learning to rely less and less on his parents. Up until his marriage in 1942, Conried lived with his parents and helped to support them as much as possible. His father's health prevented him from working, but Papa Conried (as Hans Sr. was known) must have had a nest egg of some kind to allow them to pay the rent and afford other necessities during their son's lean years. Conried continued to support his parents until they passed away—Hans Sr. in 1957, and Edith in 1970. They were both a strong influence in Conried's life, and provided the stabilizing force he needed. One touching item Conried pasted into his big scrapbook was a card he had specially designed and printed for his mom on Mother's Day in 1940. The picture on the front shows Conried dressed as a bespectacled old woman sitting in a rocking chair, and knitting a large, red sock. Inside is printed: "To the Best Friend a Boy Ever Had."

Papa Conried took an active interest in his son's career, and took care of some of the business details his son loathed. Conried, it appears, didn't have much of a head for numbers, so his father handled his financial affairs, and balanced the books. Papa Conried was an outgoing, diminutive fellow who loved a good joke. Many times he accompanied his son to parties at the recording studio, and often managed to grab all the attention telling funny stories in his thick Austrian accent (that was heavily tinged with Yiddish).

After having shared the same air space with the legendary John Barrymore, Conried felt certain that stardom was just around the corner. He wasn't exactly a "star" just

1940 Mother's Day card designed by Hans. Inside it reads: "To the Best Friend a Boy Ever Had." From the Hans Conried Collection, Department of Special Collections, Boston University.

yet, but his work was drawing the attention of influential individuals in the motion picture industry. There was a casting call at MGM for a large number of young actors and actresses for their new production, *Dramatic School*, starring the winsome Viennese actress Luise Rainer. Conried described his experience during a 1970 interview with Leonard Maltin: "There were an awful lot of us; they had about twenty young persons in that film: Alan Hale Jr., Dick Haymes, Lana Turner—who still had a schoolteacher on the set, an unbelievably beautiful young lady—some very promising young people. It was a story with as much reality as was required in those days, each age feeling that its subsequent theater is the most realistic.

We thought it touched on the very heart of matters; indeed it was just tinsel and puffery, as were most of the things then, and as our children will feel about most of the pictures we make now... Luise Rainer, with this marked Viennese accent, was a Parisian gamin who worked in a gas-meter factory at night, and apprenticed herself to the theater, in which before our movie was over she established herself as a famous star. And they required some other young people to surround her. When one thinks back—you know, the best efforts today, the most dramatic efforts, hardly entail more than two or three leading actors, and then the other people are little more than atmosphere ... people apprehended on the street, rolling drunks or stripping cars. Here, I cannot tell you how many exquisitely dressed and handsomely presentable persons, who indeed in private life were probably unfrocked Russian grand dukes, as extras were in those days, were standing around in evening clothes doing these marvelous scenes—that was typical of that era. My beginning salary, as I recall, was $100 a week, which was rather less than a man would get who swept off the stage, but we all felt we were part of motion pictures—my first movie job, which was pretty exciting. In that picture, Rand Brooks was one of the kids, Virginia Grey... We were all madly in love with one another, but primarily with ourselves, I fancy, as young actors are."

Conried played the role of a self-absorbed dramatic student named Ramy, who (in the end) wasn't such a bad sort after all. His best scene was when Ramy was called upon to judge a contest a couple of female students were engaged in to decide who had the best legs. Ramy offered his services with the curious line, "My pulse is normal, and I shall not be swayed biologically." Perhaps female legs were not what raised Ramy's blood pressure. Ultimately, Ramy could not choose a winner, saying he would "have to wait for absolute perfection." One other scene had some of the student's toasting with champagne and divulging what it was they wished for. Ramy's wish was for "a sweetheart as beautiful as Helen of Troy, as rich as Croesus, and..."—here he was interrupted by a female student who looked derisively at him and added, "as blind as a bat." Conried's character would pop in and out of a few more scenes, but he only had a line or two more of dialogue. A portent of things to come in his motion picture career, you might say.

The young cast of *Dramatic School* wanted to end their time together in a big way, and also honor their leading lady, Luise Rainer. An elaborate party was arranged at the home of Eddie Price for October 16, 1938, and announcements were printed and distributed that followed the "school" theme. They called their production the "MGM Dramatic Asylum," and the party was to be their "graduation" ceremony. Conried was chosen as the "valedictorian." A reporter noted "the guests played games and at midnight, gathered at the edge of the barbeque pit for a feast... Highlights of the evening were Luise Rainer's badminton and ping-pong games, and Hans Conried's valedictory at the 'commencement'...."

Conried was to make two more films for MGM in 1939: *It's a Wonderful World*, starring Claudette Colbert and James Stewart, and an unbilled performance in *On Borrowed Time*. *It's a Wonderful World* is a very funny, sadly overlooked film that had Conried playing a small part as a stage manager in a summer stock theater. Conried said his part was something "about which I had a lot of experience, since I had been in summer theater just a season or so before." As for *On Borrowed Time*, Conried recalled, "I worked for the first time in that [film] with a gentleman for whom we all had enormous respect, Cedric Hardwicke. And Lionel Barrymore played the part that Dudley Digges had done on Broadway. But Lionel always got those parts... Right at the very beginning I was a consumptive boy, who wanted to give Mr. Death [*sic*] (Hardwicke) a lift, and he said 'Not yet' very wisely, and the audience knew immediately what he meant, and I coughed my way out of the scene. That was the sort of stellar role I enjoyed for a number of years."

As 1939 drew to a close, Conried was no doubt dreaming of great things for his career in Hollywood. He was working nearly non-stop now, but found the time to privately indulge himself in what would be the first of many collections to come. Conried enjoyed collecting exquisitely detailed toy soldiers, and already had acquired hundreds of models with the increasing wealth he was accumulating. Collecting interesting military themed items, books, and *objets d'art* would later become a consuming passion of his, and help him intellectually to branch out into diverse fields of study.

Conried seemed to harbor a sense of shame that he did not have a college degree, and read voraciously as if to compensate for any lack of knowledge he felt others may perceive in him. It wasn't enough for him to just know about a subject. He had to know everything about it — inside and out. Many people who knew Conried would later in life refer to him as a "walking encyclopedia." The young Conried took most things quite seriously in his private life, though always maintaining that quick wit and dry sense of humor.

On the radio, the years 1936–1939 heard Conried lending his versatile voice to many different programs, including *Short Story Playhouse, One Man's Family, Hollywood Hotel, Texaco Star Theater, Signal Car-*

Relaxing between radio shows with his toy soldier collection (1937). The huaraches seem out of place. From the Hans Conried Collection, Department of Special Collections, Boston University.

nival, and *Tuesday Night Party.* Conried was primarily doing straight dramatic roles. His comedic depths had not yet been fully explored, but were beginning to rise to the surface at the close of the 1930s by working on such whimsical programs as the "Blondie" series in 1939. The early 1940s would provide fertile ground for Conried to build his comedy repertoire in both radio and motion pictures, and establish himself as a strong comedic character actor.

3

Motion Pictures, Marriage, and More Radio

It was impossible to ignore the news reports in the late 1930s and early 1940s about the ominous events in Europe and Japan, and the malevolent change in the way Adolf Hitler exerted his ever increasing power. The United States was being soothed by FDR's "fireside chats," but the possibility of American's fighting in another world war loomed on the horizon.

This uncertain and volatile period of time in America's history was also the most prolific for Conried's acting career. The early 1940s are considered the Golden Age of radio, and Conried worked constantly, sometimes ten hours a day or more, going in and out of recording studios. The major motion picture studios were also making use of Conried's ample talent in small—mainly unbilled—roles in films and short subjects.

In 1940, the threat of war was on everyone's mind, and Hollywood fed the nation's collective fears with picture after picture depicting the grim prospects of another world war. One very popular MGM series of short subjects was based on the predictions of the mysterious sixteenth century prognosticator, Nostradamus. The first "Nostradamus" short was so successful that a second film, *More About Nostradamus*, was quickly prepared. These shorts were mainly thinly veiled anti–Hitler propaganda. Hans had about twenty seconds of screen time as the young monk who would much later become Pope Sixtus V. There is only one quick close up of Conried made up as the aged Pope. He probably sat in the make-up chair for hours for that one take.

The twenty-three-year-old Conried also appeared in the full-length motion picture *Dulcy* as the playwright Vincent Leach and had a bit part in the Technicolor Noel Coward musical extravaganza *Bitter Sweet*, with Nelson Eddy and Jeannette MacDonald.

Dulcy provided some memorable moments for Conried, who was to recall many years later, "In *Dulcy* I had no lines, although I remember the word 'saturnine' was used to describe me in the script. I was a writer, and I sat typing in a canoe, in a lake, and Dulcy, in her comedic efforts at rambunctiousness, took a motorboat on to the lake, and created enough of a wave to overturn my boat. And that was a big laugh, to see a man of some dignity and scholarly bent thrown in the water. That was a big joke. Well, in order to get out of the picture, they used it again; this time she runs out onto the lake again in her boat, and you see this writer again, and she runs by and again I am thrown over, but on this occasion I am in a kayak, and I turn around and come upright, still typing. So although it was a very small part, people laughed and remember it as the picture faded out. Now that effect, I must confess to you, was done with the

kayak on an axle, with wagon wheels at both ends; manually these wheels were turned and I was brought up. Well, it was a cold morning, and we shot out of doors, and a minor actor is not too important, and I was noticeably cold... [My] work having been done, my unimportant efforts having been noted on film, I was dismissed pretty much from the attention of everyone but this generous character actor, Roland Young, who invited me into his dressing room to get warm... [He] gave me a marvelous whiskey, which I did not appreciate and probably to this day would not appreciate since I am not a drinker, but his Christian efforts were noted and remembered by this young actor."

In radio, Conried was quickly building a reputation as a top-notch radio actor in dramatic productions on *Gulf Screen Guild*

Top: Hans as the young monk who is prophesied to become Pope Sixtus V in *More About Nostradamus* (MGM: 1940). From the Hans Conried Collection, Department of Special Collections, Boston University.
Bottom: Publicity shot for *Unexpected Uncle* (RKO: 1940), with Anne Shirley and Charles Coburn.

Theater, Lux Radio Theatre, and *Arch Oboler's Plays.* Conried's first chance to work with the eccentric genius of Arch Oboler was in 1939 with a patriotic program called "This Precious Freedom." Oboler's ego demanded all to give it a wide berth, and he created a persona for himself of the avant-garde artist in his rumpled dungarees and equally rumpled hat. His talent as a writer was undeniable in the early 1940s, and he was ranked second only to Orson Welles in genius at the time. Like Welles, he failed to live up to his earlier promise, but never produced a definitive work to seal his place in cinematic history like Welles' *Citizen Kane.* Oboler was impressed with the young Conried, and would feature him in many different radio productions during the 1940s. In 1949, Oboler chose Conried to star in the first episode of his short-lived television series on ABC—*Arch Oboler's Comedy Theatre*—called "The Ostrich in Bed." In 1953, Oboler would dip into the pool of radio actors to cast his ill-fated motion picture, *The Twonky,* and hired Conried as the star.

Conried also made a big impression on Orson Welles, and the two would develop a personal, as well as professional relationship. Conried often said over the years that he had been a member of Welles' Mercury Theater troupe, but that isn't entirely accurate. It was inherent to Welles' personality to consider anyone who worked with him, even if it was only briefly, to be part of the Mercury Theater "family." Conried wasn't a full-fledged member, but he did work with Welles often enough to earn that honorary status.

Conried first worked with Welles on his 1941 series, *Orson Welles Theater,* sponsored by Lady Esther. Welles and Conried performed in a sketch titled "An Irishman and a Jew." The two would meet again the following year when Welles took the helm of a series dedicated to the war effort called *Ceiling Unlimited.* The title was chosen to highlight the way the series focused on stories related to the various aircraft that made such an important contribution to our military forces (the sponsors were Lockheed and Vega). It was an imaginative, well-acted series that gave Conried the opportunity to take center stage once in a while, as in the amusing episode, "Espionage Report." Welles brought in Conried to help with the dramatics on *Ceiling Unlimited* as of the premiere episode on November 9, 1942, and he remained as a regular in the cast.

Welles would again make use of Conried's talents later that month as a regular on another series: *Hello, Americans.* This project was spawned from Welles' ill-fated movie making trip to Brazil to film *It's All True.* The film was never finished (due to well publicized budget problems), but Welles was allowed to produce a radio show extolling the wonders of the Americas. Conried portrayed the legendary conquistadors, Pizzaro and Cortez, as well as a number of other colorful characters. *Hello, Americans* ended its run on January 31, 1943.

In January of 1944, Welles was given another chance at radio with his *Orson Welles Radio Almanac* series. Quite often, it was a veritable mess of a show where the flubs generally received the most laughs. To his credit, Welles displayed an excellent sense of humor, and frequently made fun of the mistakes along with the audience. Conried performed regularly on the series. Another frequent co-star, and Mercury Theatre alumna, was the gifted actress Agnes Moorehead.

Legendary sound effects man Ray Erlenborn summed up the general consensus of Conried's peers during this time by colorfully describing his "humorous, ludicrous, preposterous, farcical, absurd, outlandish, eccentric demeanor." Erlenborn went on to say, "When I entered a studio ... and spotted the mischievous countenance of Hans Conried sitting there with the rest of the cast, wearing one red sock and one green sock, and smiling at me with a capricious look in his eyes, I knew I should get ready (I was used to playing stooge to his antics which always garnered laughter from all those assembled). So as I wheeled my sound effects table into position, I stubbed my toe on a mike stand base, and did one of my pratfalls. Hans immediately sprung to my assistance and grabbing a whiskbroom from my prop table, he helped me up and began brushing me off. He was never reluctant to use an old gag: 'Have a nice trip?' he asked (No! The whiskbroom was not a set up. There was a Pullman Porter in the script)."

Reporter Jerry Kelly of the *Hollywood Shopping News* commented on how "Hans is one of the best actors, but sometimes he appears to be a bear rug. Much of the time he's to be found lying flat on his back, in the middle of the floor, smoking a huge pipe, with a far away look in his eye." Other startled visitors to the studios noted another one of Conried's unusual ways of relaxing between shows: "Between bits at rehearsals, Hans, double-jointed, sometimes relaxes by wrapping one leg around his neck and contorting himself into other grotesque positions." The earliest reference to this peculiar habit was found in the *Hollywood Citizen News* in an article from April of 1939: "Hans Conried, the gifted young actor wearing the brightest of red socks... can get himself into the weirdest positions of any person I ever saw. One would think his bones were made of rubber." It is hard to say whether or not the young Conried was actually practicing Yoga, but he did enjoy showing off how limber he was, as many publicity photos will attest.

The *Hollywood Citizen News* reported in 1940 that during a rehearsal for an episode of the KECA radio series *Promising Priscilla*, Hans snatched a white "wrap your own" turban belonging to one of his female colleagues, and ran out of the room. "When he came back, he had the turban on his head and a fire extinguisher. He proceeded to sit cross-legged on the floor, and put the extinguisher's hose in his mouth as if he were smoking an Indian hookah."

Conried was not only a talented actor, but he undoubtedly inherited some of the flair for showmanship his famous Uncle Heinrich had exhibited in his attempts to gain publicity and fame. His wild collection of haberdashery caught the eye of a young journalist, Ann Comar, one day in March of 1944: "Through the door of *Radio Life's* office the day of our interview came a belted beige raincoat, gunmetal gray suit, white shirt, brown and white checked vest, crimson tie, cherry red plaid scarf, wool socks—in still another red tone—, and brown 'lazy loafers,' with Conried more or less carelessly inserted therein." This, no doubt, was one of his "conservative" outfits of the day. The article continues on to say, "[Conried] was seldom seen in an ensemble lacking some item in red. 'I'm almost superstitious about that color. It makes me feel more confident of good luck. But blue—the other way. Once I had a beautiful blue costume and I blew up in my lines as high as a kite. But maybe it was just because I kept thinking, 'This isn't going to be good!' A less vivid personality would be completely drowned out by raiment of such neon-like brilliance as Conried's. But in conversation with this thespian, the vibrant-hued duds are forgotten. Watching the fast-changing succession of expressions [that] play across his countenance is like looking at the sky on a day when storm clouds and sunshine alternately vie for dominance. He impatiently sweeps back the strands of long hair that fall over his face and his long, slender artist's hands shoot out as he talks. On 'the boards' and off, he's ever and always the actor."

Miss Comar went on to ask Conried, "'If you couldn't be an actor, what vocation would you choose? Do you like business and money matters?' [Conried] almost shouted, 'NO! I loathe them! ... If I weren't in this work, I don't know what I'd choose. It's the only way of earning a living that ever interested me.'"

"Scene stealer" Hans with Arthur Lake in a publicity shot for *Blondie's Blessed Event* (Columbia: 1942).

Conried's popularity on radio garnered him quite a bit of attention from young female listeners as early as 1940. The young bachelor caught the attention of an entire girl's school. They read in the fan magazines of his fascination with military paraphernalia and sent him some sort of missile as a gift (it was a dud, fortunately), and a letter gushing about how he looked like John Barrymore. As of 1941, Conried was receiving a significant amount of fan mail and gifts.

Though extremely successful as a radio actor, Conried felt he was a failure in motion pictures. Possibly, it was the pictures that failed him. For an actor as in tune with the reactions he was eliciting from his audience—any audience—Conried was lost in front of a cold camera, surrounded by a myriad of technical people checking the lighting, sound and other seemingly unrelated aspects of his craft. His performance was in a vacuum of sorts, and it made him somewhat inhibited. Conried inhibited? It does appear he was uncomfortable in front of the camera, and seemed too preoccupied with where to stand, and what his next line was. Conried commented on how an audience's reaction was "a vital supplement which keeps up an actor, and helps him with his performance."

When the conditions were right—and, sadly, that didn't happen too often in films—Conried could give into his inner "ham" and let loose a marvelously broad, comedic performance that gives one a hint of what he was capable of. Take for instance his first big "break" as the down-in-his-luck playwright and actor George Wickley from the 1942 Columbia Pictures production of *Blondie's Blessed Event* (the working title was *Blondie Greets a Guest*).

This feature originally envisioned the part of the playwright as being "an imposing man in his late forties." The director, Frank Strayer, must have recognized Conried's potential for explosive hamminess, and cast him instead in this important part, though he was a mere twenty-five years old. The newspaper reviews enthusiastically lauded his performance. A large still from the film showing Conried and Arthur Lake orating in the hotel hallway was printed in one newspaper with the caption: "Picture Stealer Caught Red Handed!" Rail thin, with long hair swept to one side, Conried looked every bit the starving "artiste." Another review stated that the film "proves definitely that Hans Conried has a flair for comedy." *Blondie's Blessed Event* provided Conried with the most substantial film role he would have until his starring roles in *The Twonky* and *The 5000 Fingers of Dr. T* in 1953.

A hungry George Wickley (Hans) prepares to dig into Dagwood's (Arthur Lake) snack, while a waiter (Don Barclay) looks on in disgust. From *Blondie's Blessed Event* (Columbia: 1942).

Irving Reis had been very impressed with Conried's young talent as a radio performer, and vowed to use him in some way in every motion picture he would direct. The Reis directed "Falcon" films do use Conried's talents, though sparingly most of the time. As the first "Falcon," George Sanders was the epitome of the calm, cool, suave bon vivant, and was so at home in front of the camera he often looked like he was in danger of falling asleep. Combined with his enormous size, Sanders made the youthful Conried seem like a nervous stick figure in comparison. Conried did manage to elicit a fine performance alongside Sanders in the 1941 film *A Date with the Falcon*. Here he played a slimy clerk at the Federal Hotel with slicked back hair, speaking in heavy New Yorkese. His part was brief—less than five minutes of screen time—but memorable. In *The Gay Falcon* (1940), he had a small part as Herman, the high-strung police sketch artist, and was (if only briefly) the nefarious Lindsay Marriott in *The Falcon Takes Over* (1942).

Legendary voice artist Mel Blanc, a close friend of Conried's, noted, "Hans was so serious about acting that he cracked me up. I thought he was the funniest man I had ever met." It was hard for the young man with dreams of performing blank verse drama to make the transition to comedy, but Conried was realistic enough to admit, "You can't play Shakespeare exclusively and eat too."

At times, a young man's fancy—even Conried's—did turn now and then to love. By 1941, he was a bright, up-and-coming radio actor commanding a large salary—above scale at the time. He bought himself extravagant hand-made suits, and a car (a luxury few could afford in those days). All of this success gave him the courage to ask out the lovely girl he saw each day behind

Top: Corny publicity photo (someone's script is still on the counter) for *A Date with the Falcon* (RKO: 1942). Hans is trying to "subtly" warn George Sanders that Wendie Barrie is lurking close behind.
 Bottom: Scene from *Something to Shout About* (Columbia: 1942) starring Don Ameche. Hans has a great pompadour going for him here. From the Hans Conried Collection, Department of Special Collections, Boston University.

the desk at NBC Studios on his way to work: "The boom times brought another and more important change in my life. With money in my pocket, I could do more than smile at the pretty girl behind the desk in the CBS [*sic*] production office. I could ask her to go to a movie with me. To dinner even. I was loaded. She was a nice girl. Her name was Margaret [Grant], and she didn't know a single dialect. She was tolerant of mine, so marriage was inevitable."

Conried and Margaret were the same age, and still living with their respective parents. They soon realized they were only residing a short distance from each other, so Conried began driving Margaret to work each day. It was a relaxed, non-threatening way for the couple to get to know each other better. Maybe "relaxed" isn't the best description for their ride, considering Conried's questionable driving ability. It was noted by another frightened passenger around this time that he "drives like mad, never permitting his job at the wheel to interfere with his expressive gesturing." Obviously, Margaret must have been too infatuated with this colorful young man to notice.

With the United States' entry into World War II after the bombing of Pearl Harbor on December 7, 1941, the whole country was thrown into a state of panic about the future. Many felt the end of the world was imminent. With this mindset, it was easy to see how Conried and Margaret were especially concerned about what might be, as it was a given that a young man like Conried would inevitably be drafted to fight. As the only surviving son, his conscription could be postponed, but not indefinitely. The couple decided to get married, and a modest wedding took place on January 29, 1942. There was no time for an elaborate honeymoon; Conried needed to get back to work.

Shortly before his marriage, Conried signed with an agent who was to help this ris-

Hans doing a good Basil Rathbone impersonation. Make-up test photo for role as a Nazi spy (also named Hans) in Universal's 1942 drama, *Nightmare*. From the Hans Conried Collection, Department of Special Collections, Boston University.

ing star manage his career. Sid Gold handled Conried's affairs throughout his long career. Conried jokingly commented years later on the timing of his marriage and finding an agent: "I have had the same agent for six months longer than I have been married... I am sure there is something terrible in that."

The couple moved into a cavernous square building in Westwood formerly used as a sorority house near the UCLA campus, and promptly set to work remodeling. They were able to turn this odd residence into a cozy home for themselves, as well as eight dogs and five cats. Conried was certainly making up for the pets he never had as a boy. Their new home would be the site of many lively parties for their growing circle of friends. Though their hosts did not drink (Margaret only had one drink on occasion) or smoke, guests to the Conrieds' home were provided whatever they wished.

Wardrobe test photograph for Dr. Graf (Hans) from *Hitler's Children* (RKO: 1942). Hans is wearing his favorite Patek-Phillippe watch. From the Hans Conried Collection, Department of Special Collections, Boston University.

Margaret ("Maggie" to her friends) probably didn't get a chance to see a lot of her husband in those early days. Conried's talents were being spread over two media now, and he had little time to enjoy his home and hearth. *The Citizen News* voted Conried to be "the most gifted character actor" in 1941, and another newspaper referred to him approvingly in 1942 as a "young Mischa Auer." Auer was known for his broad, comedic roles and heavy accent, and did look somewhat like Conried. One article also commented on Conried's "marked resemblance to Basil Rathbone." This latter resemblance is called to mind when watching his characterization of the Nazi spy (named "Hans") in the 1942 United Artists picture *Nightmare*. A publicity photo shows a very serious Conried dressed in a manner evoking Rathbone's "Sherlock Holmes," complete with pipe. Many years later, Conried received a letter from a fan who wanted him to state—in order to settle a bet with a friend of his—whether or not Conried was Basil Rathbone's son!

Between the years 1941 and 1944, Conried claims to have appeared—all unbilled performances—in hundreds of war related films as a Nazi of some sort or other: "No more sweet Viennese professors or lovely music masters," sighed Hans in 1942, "now I'm a nasty Nazi." Later he would explain, "The vogue for Nazi pictures came in, and my name being Germanic, it attracted attention, and I appeared then for every studio, in lesser pictures very often—in every possible Nazi uniform. I slept in a turtleneck sweater." The titles of these films by and large haven't been recorded for posterity, so it becomes a sort of "needle in a haystack" situation to attempt to uncover them. Conried often worked alongside other actors with Germanic names, such as Stefan Schnabel. Schnabel's father and Hans Sr. grew up together in Vienna, Austria. According to Conried, he and Schnabel had an agreement: Schnabel would play all the Nazis on the East Coast, and Conried would play all the Nazis on the West Coast.

The two most notable films where Conried portrayed a Nazi soldier are *Hitler's Children* (RKO: 1942) and *Hostages* (Paramount: 1943). Both are rather over-the-top propaganda films designed to show the cold-blooded, ruthless nature of the Third Reich. Even though Conried's performances were supposed to be dramatic, it's hard to look at them now without finding something unintentionally comical about them.

In *Hostages*, Conried portrays the young Lieutenant Glasenapp, who is in his cups at a tavern because the girl he had planned to marry has been conscripted to serve in one of Hitler's breeding camps. The

In *Hitler's Children*, Conried played one of the "villainous Nazis"—more specifically, Dr. Graf, the Minister of Education. Tim Holt was one of the young stars of this movie, and would appear again with Conried many years down the road—when both of their film careers were winding down—in *The Monster That Challenged the World* in 1957. As in many of his early films, Conried was trying to portray a much older man. References are made to Dr. Graf's many years of film begins with this tavern scene, and poor Lt. Glasenapp whining about his misfortune as he becomes increasingly despondent (and drunk). One of his lines in the film—a line the MPAA censorship office felt was a bit questionable—is: "I wouldn't be unhappy if she were unhappy ... but she's happy!" Glasenapp then proceeds to get sick to his stomach—another thing the MPAA office was concerned about: "We assume that the business of Glasenapp beginning to be sick to his stomach will be handled carefully, and inoffensively." Somehow he manages to make it down to the local river where he presumably commits suicide. Conried said of his role, "I was a pimply and weak Nazi; I always played pimply or weak Nazis, or mad Nazis, or cruel Nazis, or villainous Nazis, but there wasn't a human being among them." The film starred William Bendix and Luise Rainer. A special "movie edition" book of *Hostages* by Stefan Heym was published by Putnam to coincide with the movie release.

Top: Hans as the pathetic Lt. Glasenapp, with William Bendix from Paramount's *Hostages* (1943).
Above: Hans as a nasty, scar-faced Nazi from Columbia's *Underground Agent* (1942). From the Hans Conried Collection, Boston University.

service as if he was a man at least in his forties. At twenty-five years of age, Conried was not quite able to make himself seem that mature next to the very mature actor Otto Kruger. Conried did manage to hold his own, and turn out a good performance, though some of his facial expressions now seem more comical than they were likely intended to be.

Hitler's Children was quite sensational for its day, and was based on the book *Education for Death*, which was an exposé on the harsh training of "Hitler Youth." Publicity pieces for the film show images of an evil looking Gestapo agent menacingly holding a whip while an innocent looking young girl cowers on the ground with her blouse partially torn off: quite lurid, indeed. Edward Dmytryk (who would later be blacklisted during the McCarthy era) and Irving Reis (unbilled) directed the film.

A welcome change to all the depressing Nazi roles were a number of light, comedic parts that were occasionally sprinkled in between. I have already mentioned his most substantial comedic role of this period: *Blondie's Blessed Event*. In 1941, Conried played a churlish, upper crust houseguest named George in the MGM comedy *Maisie Was a Lady*—one of the many "Maisie" films starring the effervescent Ann Sothern. Conried would work with Sothern once again on the *Maisie* radio series that debuted in 1945. During one of his brief scenes in the film, Conried (as George) responds to a curt reproach from Maisie, while attending a poolside party, by diving into the swimming

Candid shot of Hans and Orson Welles taken in May of 1943. From the Hans Conried Collection, Department of Special Collections, Boston University.

pool, headfirst, fully clothed. Conried was to re-create this gag—in real life—by "accidentally" falling into the swimming pool while attending a party given in 1943 by Orson Welles and his then wife, Rita Hayworth. The guests debated whether the highlight of the event was the ravishing Rita's entrance in a stunning white gown, or Conried's fall into the pool. He probably hated to be upstaged, even by his lovely hostess.

In 1942, Conried played Joan Bennett's nutty Dutch husband, Hendrik Woverman, who was confined to a sanitarium (to dry out) in *The Wife Takes a Flyer* (working title: *Highly Irregular*); and Louie, the insipid headwaiter of a New York nightclub in *The Big Street* with Henry Fonda and Lucille Ball. Conried remembered Louie many years later as being "a rather disreputable, disgusting, repulsive man." He wasn't an entirely likable character, but that description seems a bit harsh. Louie was more of a jaded, unromantic character who didn't have the patience for some idealistic young pup. Conried recalled fondly that a review of the film by James Agee said in part, "[Hans Conried] packs so much cold, superb, style into his half minute that he makes everybody else's fun look forced...."

Also that year, Conried would appear in the mainly Orson Welles directed picture *Journey Into Fear* with Joseph Cotten (who later worked with Conried in radio on the popular *Suspense* series). Norman Foster directed Conried's brief appearance on the screen in place of Welles. Conried was barely recognizable in heavy makeup with moustache, goatee, and turban as the mysterious magician who is mistakenly shot and killed during his act. Welles and Cotten added this scene in their screenplay, which re-worked the original Eric Ambler story.

The comedy team of Olsen & Johnson released a vehicle for their brand of comedy in 1943 called *Crazy House* (a "shameful thing" according to Conried) that included many cameo performances. Conried played the eccentric, avant-garde artist, Trovatore Roco. Roco is enlisted by the comic duo to be their set designer. The name "Trovatore" only appears in the script, along with the majority of Conried's scenes. A wonderful scene was written for Conried's character that took the viewer to Roco's studio. When Olsen & Johnson arrive, they find the artist reclining on a divan, sniffing a rose, and painting blindfolded. Roco explains he is endeavoring to paint the scent of the rose — its very essence. Another scene has Roco offering the boys a cup of coffee, then pulling it out of a painting on the wall depicting the same. To their disgust, the liquid turns out to be paint. An unfazed Roco says, "I'm an artist, not a magician!" The finished film retained only fragments of Conried's performance, but he manages to shine, for the few moments he had to work with, in the courtroom scene at the end.

Conried's status as a sought after radio actor allowed him to achieve the "Guest Star" billing in the print ads for *Crazy House*. As Conried explained, "My constant

Make-up test photo, sans turban, for role of the magician in *Journey Into Fear* (RKO: 1942). This make-up is virtually identical to the way Hans was prepared for the role of the psychiatrist in *Song of Bernardette* (20th Century Fox: 1943). From the Hans Conried Collection, Department of Special Collections, Boston University.

employment in radio made me sufficiently independent to barter along with my agent; we were already in a bargaining position. If they wanted me for a small part, it was up to me to say which days I would be freest. Because I was already steadily employed in radio, I always had that to fall back on. Had I not had that, I would have been just more labor on the market. But I was in a position where the studios would say, 'Well, we can't get him; he's got a show that day. Can you get him the next day?' Also, there was the fact that they were bizarre parts, and I was young; there weren't that many bizarre, eccentric actors of my age. Plenty of splendid older ones, but if they wanted crazy younger people, you had to be a little tougher. And I guess I'd already proved I could sell a couple of lines, so my money was a little better. And then began 'Special Guest Star,'

Mugging it up as "Roco" from Olsen & Johnson's *Crazy House* (Universal: 1943). Hans referred to his part as a "shameful thing."

which was in lieu of money; to this day, if you see 'Also Starring,' you know the actor's in trouble." Conried was one of the very few actors who actually had clauses in their film contracts that read: "Conried must be off the set by 4:30 pm on Mondays because the schmo has to do a radio show then."

Also in 1943, Conried had a chance to play a more romantic lead (albeit a comedic one) in the John Wayne film: *The Lady Takes a Chance*—a.k.a. *The Cowboy and the Girl*. "I was a juvenile again," Conried would recall, "which was a rarity. I was one of three rebuffed suitors of Jean Arthur's; Grant Withers, Grady Sutton, and I made up the trio, but naturally, John Wayne walked off with the leading lady."

The year before, Conried had worked with John Wayne for the first time as a guest on Wayne's radio show *Three Sheets to the Wind*, which debuted on NBC on February 15, 1942. "I ... worked with [John Wayne] in a short-lived radio series called *Three Sheets to the Wind*, which was significant in its title for the general deportment of several members of its company—I don't include Mr. Wayne." Wayne genuinely liked Conried and would keep him in mind later on for other film roles.

Variety printed a small blurb on July 26, 1943, announcing that Conried and Fortunio Bonanova (who appeared in *Citizen Kane* as Mrs. Kane's music teacher) "are winding up roles in *Ali Baba and the Forty Thieves* at Universal, and immediately switch over to spots on ... *His Butler's Sister*." This article may have just been poorly worded, for Bonanova did appear in *Ali Baba and the Forty Thieves* (released in 1944), but not Conried. Then again, Conried can be seen in *His Butler's Sister* (released in 1943), but not Bonanova. The two actors did actually work together on the Warner Bros. feature *Mrs. Parkington* (1944).

Mrs. Parkington, starring Greer Garson and Walter Pidgeon, required Conried to once again play a character much older than his actual age. Mr. Ernst was the German, or Austrian, manager of a fussy Italian opera singer played by Bonanova. The exchanges between these two characters provide for some of the most entertaining moments in the film. Conried had a unique way of appearing to be something of a lightning rod, attracting kinetic energy while those around him in a scene generally remained static. He used his whole body to add expression to his words: a quick shrug and a slight nod—the hands always in motion. It was a style that was distinctly his own and allowed him to stand out from the rest even in the most fleeting of cinematic moments.

The second major motion picture to be released in 1944 was the dark, humorless World War II saga *Passage to Marseille*. The film boasted an all-star cast that included Humphrey Bogart, Sydney Greenstreet, Peter Lorre, and Claude Rains. Conried plays a young French lieutenant named

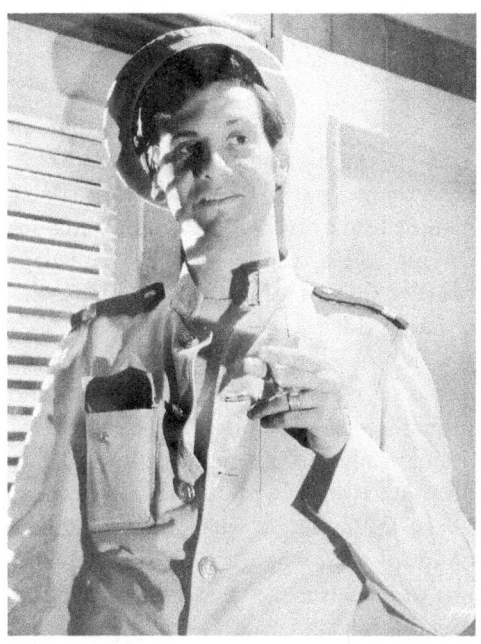

Moody publicity shot for *Passage to Marseille* (Warner Bros: 1944). Hans as the "treacherous youth," Lt. Jourdain.

Jourdain. Lt. Jourdain turns out to be considered a traitor by the rest of his mates (it seemed that he was only following orders, though), and spends a good deal of his screen time being used as a punching bag by Claude Rains. He was pummeled some more by George Tobias' character, who finally snapped his neck (off camera, fortunately).

On a much lighter note, Conried lent his voice to the Walter Lantz produced "Woody Woodpecker" cartoon "Woody Dines Out." This installment of Woody's misadventures featured a hungry Woody accidentally going into a taxidermist's shop thinking it is a restaurant. Conried voiced the character of the lugubrious feline taxidermist who dreams of the fortune he can make by stuffing a woodpecker just like Woody ("money ... women ... yachts ... women..."). Conried's vocal delivery is so slow, and low-key you can hardly recognize him (which may have been his intention). Conried and Walter Lantz would remain friends for many years.

Outside of motion pictures, Conried was still working constantly on the radio until his departure to Fort Knox, Kentucky, in 1944. Conried would frequently guest star on the famed dramatic series *Lux Radio Theatre*. This long running, critically acclaimed series was first broadcast from New York in 1934 using Broadway talent, but later turned to the rich bounty of Hollywood in 1936. The show began broadcasting from the Music Box Theater on Hollywood Boulevard. Legendary film director Cecil B. DeMille, who gave the series its sense of authority, introduced each episode. DeMille lost his job in 1945 over a dispute with the American Federation of Radio Actors union (he refused to pay a $1 fee for their war fund). The shows were performed on stage in front of an audience of 1000 lucky ticket holders, and attracted some of the top talent Hollywood had to offer until its final broadcast in 1955. Even though it was reported that many actors and actresses were terrified of the microphone, most of the major players of the day came to perform, including Marlene Dietrich, Claudette Colbert, Errol Flynn, Don Ameche, Fred MacMurray, Clark Gable, Humphrey Bogart, and many, many others. Conried's first appearance on *Lux Radio Theatre* was in 1941 in a production of *Rebecca*, starring Ronald Colman. He was credited as playing "The Doctor," but his voice can also be heard as the suspicious handyman.

In 1940, Conried had the opportunity to work again with Lionel Barrymore in a radio version of Dickens' *A Christmas Carol* in the role of Bob Cratchit. Lionel Barrymore, as Scrooge, would become a holiday tradition for radio listeners, and the show was produced year after year. Conried enjoyed lending his voice to either Bob Cratchit or Marley. Also in 1940, KECA radio gave Conried another chance to indulge his love of Shakespeare by performing in their production of *Romeo and Juliet* for *Woodbury's Hollywood Playhouse*.

Conried periodically made use of his early commercial art training by designing his own holiday cards. He created a delightful caricature of himself—stick thin and all nose, dressed in Shakespearean garb. Around this time, Conried briefly attempted to encourage people to just call him "Conried" for theatrical purposes, but that moniker fortunately did not catch on. He was listed this way, though, in a 1941 Radio Actor's Directory.

One Christmas card was carefully prepared for a special event involving Orson Welles, and some other radio personalities around 1941. They were all asked to submit special Christmas cards to a local newspaper for a charity event. The front of Conried's card shows his wonderful caricature, and is inscribed inside at the top with "Hans Conried Presents His Best Wishes." The card is designed to look like a theater program, and lists an imaginary holiday play with all the actors having the name Conried: Edwin Booth Conried, John Barrymore Conried, Orson W. Conried (as "The Man from Mars"), and the director is Dr. Max R. Conried.

Conried appeared for the first time in 1941 on the hit comedy series *The Great Gildersleeve*, starring Harold Peary (Peary had the lead until 1950). Conried had a recurring role as the insipid, sickly teenage boarder Olive Honeywell, complete with cracking voice.

Many radio shows were being produced to help out with the war effort, and provide either escapist entertainment or dramatically serious messages designed to illustrate tales of heroism and self-sacrifice. Often the messages were frightening scenarios of what would happen if the enemy was to take over the country, and the horrors that would ensue. Conried performed in many programs of this type during the early 1940s, such as *Radio Canteen* (1942), *Plays for Americans* (1942), *The World We're Fighting For* (1943), and *Everything for the Boys* (1944).

Plays for Americans and *Everything for the Boys* reunited Conried with the volatile Arch Oboler, whose patriotism moved him to give up more lucrative paying jobs and donate his time and talent to producing programs geared toward the nationalistic fervor surging through the country during that period of history. On *Plays for Americans*, Conried performed with the powerful German actor Conrad Veidt in the lurid, anti–Nazi themed drama "Hate," which was described by *Variety* as "a scalp-raising cry against a bar-

An intense Hans reading the part of Adolf Hitler for "Adolf and Mrs. Runyon" (*Plays for Americans:* 1942) as Arch Oboler looks on approvingly. From the Hans Conried Collection, Department of Special Collections, Boston University.

barous menace." Conried would also get a chance to perform a histrionic Hitler in the episode "Adolf and Mrs. Runyon" with Bette Davis. The plot was farfetched: Davis was a young newlywed who had just driven her soldier husband to the train station so he could be sent off to fight. On her way home, driving alone on a country road, she was so angry with Hitler and all the trouble he'd caused the world, she prayed to God for a chance to meet Hitler face-to-face so she could give him a piece of her mind. Lo and behold, there is a soldier in an odd uniform standing by the side of the road. Being patriotic, she stops to give him a lift. The "hitchhiker" turns out to be a very confused and agitated Adolf Hitler who thinks he is still back at Berchtesgaden! Davis' Mrs. Runyon coldy devises a plot to rid the world of her evil companion, while Conried has a field day as the hysterical, hapless Führer.

Radio Life magazine related a story connected with the "Adolf and Mrs. Runyon" broadcast: "Hans Conried, versatile young radio actor who played the part of Adolf (last name Schickelgruber) on Oboler's 'Adolf and Mrs. Runyon,' was paged for a telephone call immediately after the show went off the air. Into a booth in the Radio City lobby went Conried oblivious of the fact that Dick Ryan, a fellow actor, was in a booth directly across the hall, making with such conversation as 'If you ever play Hitler again on the radio, it will be at your own risk'. The 'gag' had a premature ending, when actor Ryan, who just couldn't act out his self-styled role of heckler, leaned against the door of his telephone booth, which was half ajar, and landed flat on his chuckle-creased face in the hall outside the booth Conried was using."

Actress Mercedes McCambridge recounted a story about one particular rehearsal, which involved Conried and director Oboler, many years later to host John Moore during an interview for his radio show based in Atlanta, Georgia. According to Moore: "Arch Oboler was in charge, and the cast included Hans Conried. [Mercedes] told me that Hans had obviously put a lot of work into the characterization he was doing... She said it was as if he had decided to create the characterization to end all others for that type of part. It was completely over-the-top... Whatever he was doing, it was too much, didn't fit the show, [and] didn't mesh with the other characters: it just didn't work. From the booth came the voice of Arch Oboler saying, 'Mr. Conried, I think it would be better if you would tone it down a bit'... He did, but it was still way too much. Again came the voice over the talkback, 'Mr. Conried, I'd appreciate it if you could tone things down some more for us.' The performance was still not making it, so again came the voice from the booth, 'Mr. Conried, it's just not working. Just forget all the characterization, and give us the REAL Hans Conried'... At that, [Hans] drew himself to his full height, nose in the air, and declaimed, 'My good man, there is no REAL Hans Conried!'"

Lights Out! was another Oboler helmed series Conried would be associated with. This series established Oboler's reputation as a top-notch writer-director after he had taken over the reins from the show's creator, Wyllis Cooper, in 1936. The first run of the series ended in 1938, but it was brought back to the air in 1942. Conried provided his vocal virtuosity to many episodes during this second incarnation. For one episode in particular—"The Flame," broadcast on March 23, 1943—Conried gave a chilling lead performance in the role of a man obsessed with fire worship, and the ancient evil he unwittingly unleashes. Conried's blood-curdling scream at the end, when the fire "goddess" consumes his character, is remarkable for its unrestrained emotion.

The year 1943 was pivotal for Conried, partly because of his debut on the long run-

Publicity shot for radio's *The Life of Riley* sitcom. Hans decided to paste on a moustache and wear a pince-nez for his "Uncle Baxter." (L-R: Conrad Binyon, William Bendix, Hans, and Paula Winslowe). From the Hans Conried Collection, Department of Special Collections, Boston University.

ning, highly acclaimed dramatic series *Suspense*, and also because of his emergence in what would prove to be his bread-and-butter work in situation comedies. Another program of note for 1943 was a production of *Casablanca* for the program *Lady Esther Screen Guild Theatre*. Humphrey Bogart, Ingrid Bergman, and Paul Henreid would re-create their 1942 MGM film roles, with Conried as Capt. Louis Renault.

Beginning with the audition show in July of 1943, Conried would work again with William Bendix in the very popular *Life of Riley* radio sitcom. Conried played Mrs. Riley's parasitic, but loveable, Uncle Baxter. Conrad Binyon, who was the first of many child actors who played Riley's son, Junior, recalled, "The first time I had the opportunity to work with Hans Conried, I noticed his different 'flair,' so to speak, his manner of dress, and the like. As I think of it, it was the only thing one could call different [about] him. He was soft spoken and his speech had a very soft accent, which I could only describe as 'Shakespearean'. But when he was called upon to be a Westerner from Topeka, Kansas, that's what he sounded like. He was very nice to be around, and included me in any of the exchanges that were carried on by any cast we happened to be on together. He often would exhibit various items of an intriguing nature during cast breaks. First of all was his elegant pocket watch, which he carried on a chain popped into his vest. As I remember, he also carried a key chain onto which was affixed his NBC Artist Entry plastic Pass Badge, which I thought strange he didn't just pin it on his coat. One day, he brought to a rehearsal a small case in which was an elegant stainless steel straight razor, part of a set he said he'd acquired from some source in Europe, I believe. It looked very menacing, and of course was very sharp. He said he [wanted] to learn how to shave with them so that he could have the full joy of owning them... I remember Hans as the nicest guy, and a jewel to work with."

Beginning in July of 1943, Conried worked with the self-styled "hillbilly" comedic actress Judy Canova on her *Judy Canova Show*. Though a very savvy lady, she knew a good thing when she saw it, and she used her country bumpkin shtick to her advantage over the years in radio and in motion pictures. Conried performed as Mr. Hemingway, the ill-tempered houseguest of Judy's Aunt Aggie, whose constant complaining was a comedic highlight. Hemingway was something of a frustrated actor, and allowed Conried to use his best Shakespearean affectations to their comedic hilt. Conried would also provide the voice on occasion for another character, Mr. Boswell. The cast included Mel Blanc as the Mexican gardener and chauffeur, Pedro, and Ruby Dandridge—who played Lucille Ball's maid in the 1942 film *The Big Street*—as the maid, Geranium.

The celebrated crime anthology series *Suspense* first aired on its own in 1942. Under the direction of the talented producer William Spier, *Suspense* quickly proved a favorite amongst listeners and actors alike. Spier's talent for helping to create the unusual sound effects for each episode heightened the chilling "suspense" until its shocking climax. *Suspense* was a goldmine of well-written material. As was the custom for supporting actors at the time, Conried rarely received credit for his performances. Content to work in relative anonymity, Conried would give voice to a large variety of characters in many different *Suspense* episodes—often two or three characters per show.

There is a widely circulated story about the infamous "Sorry, Wrong Number" episode that first aired on May 25, 1943, starring Agnes Moorehead in a tour de force performance as the tormented, disabled Mrs. Stevenson. Moorehead's amazing, physically draining, hysterical characterization would have been enough to provide high praise for the broadcast, but it was an actor's mistake that made this particular episode legendary. An improper cue was given to the actor who played the killer (the actor was not identified), and because of this missed cue the outcome of the story seemed to be left hanging, and it appeared that Mrs. Stevenson had actually been killed after all. The listeners were flabbergasted that there was no relief for the poor, tormented Mrs. Stevenson and the villains were never brought to justice. This particular show was heralded by many—Orson Welles included—as possibly the greatest show of all time, mainly for its defiance of the accepted formula of how good is supposed to triumph over evil. Evil got away with something in "Sorry, Wrong Number." Due to the large response from the public, the episode was redone and put on the air on August 21, 1943. This time, Conried took over the role of George, the killer (he had played the killer's boss in the first version), and the broadcast went off without a hitch. It would eventually be remade a total of seven times, and often reporters and photographers were invited to the sound stage to record Ms. Moorehead's histrionics.

Over the many years *Suspense* was on the air, Conried could be heard in over 70 episodes, making *Suspense* easily the most successful employment of his acting career. He would have the chance to work with such high-powered talent as Charles Laughton, Vincent Price, Cary Grant (Conried appeared with Grant very briefly in the 1942 film *Once Upon a Honeymoon*), Lucille Ball, Frederic March, Paul Muni, Gene Kelly, and Alan Ladd. "Dime a Dance," starring Lucille Ball, was a particularly masterful little tale with a twist ending. Conried's character, the manager of the dance club, appears to be a nice guy, but then again…

In addition to "Sorry, Wrong Number," another popular episode of *Suspense* was "Banquo's Chair." It would be produced at least three times, with Conried in the role of the callous nephew who murders his rich aunt and is brought to justice in a most unusual way. The part gave Conried the opportunity to play a confident, almost cocky, selfish young man who dissolves into a pool of hysterics by the tale's end.

Conried was a frequent performer on the mystery-thriller *The Whistler*, and starred in the February 21, 1943, broadcast of "Fool's Gold." Conried was adept at playing tightly wound characters, such as the embezzling bank teller, Herbert Lang, who eventually find themselves at the emotional and physical breaking point. It's no wonder that Conried later referred to this era of his radio career as his "emotional period."

After the flurry of activity in 1942, film roles would not be as forthcoming in 1943. Conried tested for the part of the psychiatrist for the film *The Song of Bernadette*, with Jennifer Jones and Vincent Price. A publicity photo exists of a scene with Conried, as the psychiatrist, examining Jones while Price looks on. The caption reads, "A Scene from the 20th Century Fox Picture, *The Song of Bernadette*," but the scene does not appear in the completed film. The finished film does contain a scene with a psychiatrist, but Alan Napier plays the role in an unbilled performance.

Conried's work would be cut short in 1944 by the arrival of an official looking envelope on February 22nd. The narrow slip of paper turned out to be a draft notice. Conried had until the end of August to put things in order at home, and then ship out to Fort Knox for basic training. Conried had always enjoyed playing with his toy soldier collection, and planning military strategies. Now he would be doing it for real. Margaret and his parents were understandably upset with the news, but Conried took the responsibility seriously (as he did most responsibilities), and tried to make the best of things.

The patriotic Conried was doing everything he could for the war effort. Besides being a regular blood donor, he participated in special broadcasts for enlisted men only. One such event was a ninety-minute program produced by Orson Welles that was broadcast live from the Fresno Air Service Training Command Center in May of 1944. Conried would fondly recall years later the "fraternal camaraderie" of those bus rides with Welles and the Mercury troupe.

By the time Conried was getting ready to report for duty as a private in the U.S. Army, his career as a radio actor was just reaching its zenith. Conried was so busy—he was known as the "busiest man in show business" at the time—*Radio Life* reported in their January 30, 1944, issue: "Last week it took a motorcycle escort to get Hans Conried to the premiere broadcast of ... *The Life of Riley* series... Much in demand, Conried is featured in another dramatic series over *Ceiling Unlimited* on Sunday morning at CBS, and doesn't get off the air until 11:30 a.m. That leaves him just thirty minutes to scramble from Sunset Boulevard to the Ebell Club across town where the *Life of Riley* goes on at [noon]."

Even though Conried was a "hot" property, and enjoyed one of the highest salaries allowed at the time, all of his hard-earned success would soon come to a screeching halt. Egon, the Chisler, Conried's character on *The Man Called X*, was made a regular on the show by popular demand in August of 1944. Unfortunately, Egon had to make a premature exit when Private Conried reported for military duty on August 30th.

By the time Conried would return to the States in 1946, the fate of radio was already sealed, and television was poised to move in for the "kill" and strike a deathblow to the medium he loved. Conried's departure to Fort Knox would mark the end of life as he knew it, and open the door to a new, sometimes uncertain, period in both his personal and professional life. Conried's world would never quite be the same again.

4

The Army Years

One of the requirements for entry into the service was the initiation ritual disliked by most young men: the haircut. Considering how fond Conried was of his long, unruly locks, this may have been one of the most traumatic aspects of his induction. Especially for the event, Conried had a photographer accompany him to the barbershop, and record his reaction to each inch of hair that was shorn. There is a poignant yet comical aspect to the photos Conried pasted in book fashion into his scrapbook. First you see him near tears as the first locks of hair come off; then the stunned look of disbelief as he views himself in a mirror at the end of his ordeal. Sadly to say, Conried's hair was another of those things that would never quite be the same again.

There was no special treatment for Conried, or any other actor, and he went through all of the basic training with the type of dedication he gave every task life handed him. While at Fort Knox, a reporter from the *Armored News* tried to interview Conried, but found him "quite reluctant to talk about himself for publication (can this be an actor?). Private Conried feels that he has left his movie career behind him for the duration, and wants to concentrate on the life of a soldier."

It was proving to be rather difficult to concentrate, though. Conried was miserable at first with the conditions of the Army camp, and the blatant racial prejudice he was witnessing firsthand within the ranks of new recruits and his superiors. Orson Welles sent his sad friend a gift of a gold bracelet about a month after his arrival at Fort Knox, and Conried took the opportunity to write his beloved mentor a poignant seven-page letter in his very best Elizabethan manner. He began with: "My very noble and approved good Master," and continued:

> I am here in the land of the Joseph Cotten, arrived by circuitous route and gross error of the War Dept., the gravity of the latter comparable only to that of Pearl Harbour [*sic*]. All this, in time, I know will be rectified; there will be courts martial, heads will roll, and I shall rise from this foul bewitched, uniformed husk, once more the magically liberated Prince. Until that happy day however, "they have tied me to a stake; I cannot fly, but bear-like, I must fight the course." I will do the State some service—and *I* will know it.

Next Conried profusely thanked "dear, good, kind generous Orson—lavish, extravagant, munificent Orson" for the bracelet. He went on:

> The bracelet, the only article of costume of which I must not divest myself prior to the bi-daily (or almost) genital inspection affords me still an opportunity to stand apart from my less favored fellows... Ft. Knox is an "Armored Training Replacement Center," so you see I am being groomed for a position in the Panzers. Certainly this is ridiculous, and since there

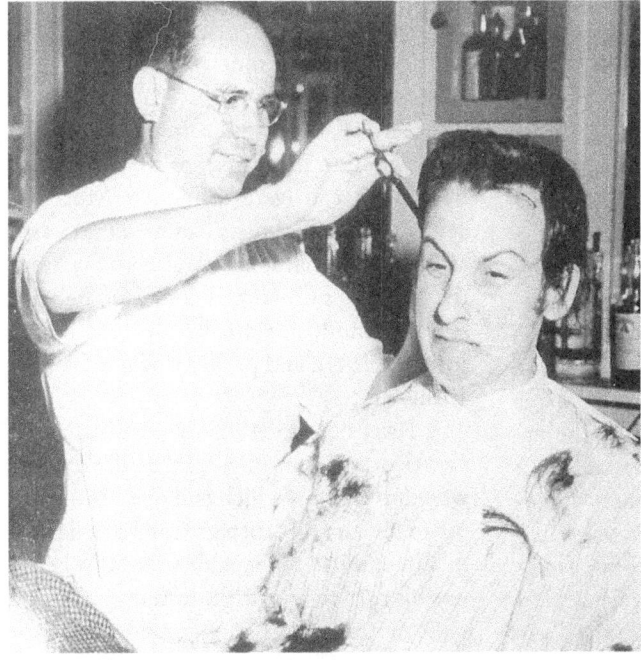

Top: Hans demonstrating the skills he thankfully never had to use as a "heavy mortar crewman" (circa 1946).
Bottom: A miserable Hans undergoing the dreaded haircut prior to departing for Ft. Knox, Kentucky to begin his Army training. (August of 1944). From the Hans Conried Collection, Department of Special Collections, Boston University.

has been, to now, no mention whatever, of the General Staff Corps, and since the wardrobe permitted me in this travesty, is of the cheapest stuffs and most unbecoming design, I confess I am not entirely happy with the situation into which God and my draft board have been pleased to place me.

So, dear friend and patron, should you, in your intercourse (what a lovely thought) with the bright free world outside, encounter anyone of military authority (but for your own sake, avoid them if you can)—"Absent thee, from felicity awhile, to tell my story...."—And now, farewell, I must away, for the Sergeant, an unhappy combination of Captain Blygh, Simon Legree, and an overplaying Christopher Sly, having just lunched on his own young (fortuitous loss) has flicked my bowed back with his barbed cat as an indication that I must go to the race discrimination class and lynching practice...."

Conried signed himself only as "#39727727."

After basic training, Conried was selected for specialized training as a tank driver. "Gawd knows why!" Conried would tell an interviewer in 1949, "I hate machinery! Nevertheless, they put me through practically the entire tank driving course before they reached the step where I was to be enclosed in my tank for a test run. Of course, they then discovered that, with me in it, the tank couldn't be closed! I was too tall! After all that! Naturally, I had to be transferred."

Private Conried was then given the title of "Heavy Mortar Crewman," and trained to operate the heavy mortar artillery from December of 1944 through March of 1945. Conried claims that he was sent to the Pacific because he told his superiors that he could understand German a little bit. He wasn't taken very seriously, as this story will tell: "My father was Viennese, but we never spoke German at home. In fact, I don't speak any foreign language... I was interviewed by an American soldier of German birth, who had a definite accent himself. He was considering how I could be of use to the Army, and he said to me 'Vell, ve could perhaps make you an interpreter—but only for prisoners who were very badly wounded.'"

Before too long, he landed in the Philippines, on the island of Luzon. "I was trained as a heavy mortar man in the armored division," Conried would recall, "but by the time I got to the Philippines, somebody had lost my papers and I bobbed up as a laborer in the engineers. This was not comfortable, and during a very fast leave I managed to maneuver through the lines into Manila, visit some old pals at the Armed Forces Radio Station, and arrange for a transfer to the AFRS."

Conried may not have ever known the full story behind his "lost" papers, and how he ended up with the AFRS. Radio actor Jack Kruschen was already in Manila when he read Conried had been drafted and was on his way to the front lines as a heavy mortar man. The mortality rate of mortar personnel was very high, and Conried's chances to make it out alive seemed slim. Kruschen went to his sergeant, and, with the help of three bottles of bourbon, was able to arrange for Conried's transfer to the AFRS station.

There was a mix up of sorts, and Conried didn't arrive on time. Out of the blue one day, he appeared at the station, and immediately asked the sergeant where his shovel was. For some reason, the sergeant didn't like the attitude of this odd-looking new guy wearing a "campaign" hat. The sarge roughly handed him the shovel and ordered him to dig a drainage ditch in back of the station. A short while later, Kruschen heard about the incident and went out back. Sure enough, there was Conried, knee deep in muck, digging a trench. Kruschen got the extremely grateful Conried out of the ditch, and found him a much better job in the radio station.

The WVTM studio in San Fernando was housed in the cistern of what had once been a large private residence. More recently, Japanese soldiers had used the cistern as a torture chamber. Paraphernalia from the building's brutal past could still be seen. A huge amount of dirt had to be dumped into the cistern and packed down to be used as the floor.

Kruschen noted many years later that Conried was the only man he'd ever met who didn't know which end of a hammer to use to hit a nail. It appears Conried's naiveté manifested itself in machinery too. When it was his turn to take the morning shift at the radio station, Conried managed to talk for over an hour before it was discovered that he didn't realize he had to turn a knob to start the transmitter first. Very clear operating instructions were written down and posted on the equipment, and there were no more problems.

Shelby Newhouse, an AFRS member at the time who would later serve under Conried in Japan, recalled a story told to him by Carl Cederberg. Cederberg was the Program Director of the AFRS station WVTM operating from the island of Leyte: "Hans Conried joined the station in Leyte. They had no idea as to how they might use this Hollywood actor. He was definitely too flamboyant to be an announcer. So, they decided to give him the morning record program. Today, we'd call him a 'disc jockey.' It didn't take long for complaints to come pouring in. Remember, this was the only radio station the troops could hear. It seems Hans had been playing records HE loved, not music of the day: not Glenn Miller, Artie Shaw or Tommy Dorsey, but CLASSICAL music. The GI's were waking up to Bach, Brahms, Beethoven, and Mozart! He was quickly pulled off the morning shift and given an assignment more suited to his talents ... reading the funnies! He read the cartoon strips doing all the voices as Mayor Fiorello LaGuardia did when there was a newspaper strike in New York in the 1930s!" This radio show was called *The Kilocycle Komics*.

Even with his lucky transfer to the AFRS, and his ability to work in radio again, Conried was experiencing a good deal of depression over his separation from his family and country. He wrote Margaret letter after letter describing his experiences, and undoubtedly, his longing to be home with her again soon. The following is part of a letter Conried wrote to Norman Corwin in June of 1945 from "Somewhere on Luzon" thanking him for a recent gift of the book, *On a Note of Triumph*. It gives a little snapshot into Conried's world at that time, and provides his own description of his entry into the AFRS:

> In all honesty, Norman, I am, in this, enormously indebted to you for an immeasurable stimulation to my slack spirits, or as military terminology will have it,

Hans, sporting a lush mustache, broadcasting from the AFRS station WVTM in Manila, the Philippines (1945). From the Hans Conried Collection, Department of Special Collections, Boston University.

> "moldering morale." It is heartening, really, to know that my name is, on occasion spoken "behind the scenes," and while here, touring in such far "provinces," I am thought of by my erstwhile fellows: "Thanks."
>
> My situation here, as a member of the staff of an Armed Forces Radio Station, is, circumstances considered, an excellent one. I have been trained in the mountain and bigoted fastnesses of Kentucky, for eight months, to take an *active* (Deus Misereatur) part in the machinations and machinery of the Armored Force; I was transported thence, labeled 'Driver, Halftrack — Crewman, Heavy Mortar', and having arrived here, set to work digging in this foreign strand, as a member of a Labor Battalion. With miraculous expedition,

Hans managed to find a traditional Korean outfit to wear while broadcasting from AFRS station WLFJ in Fusan, Korea. Hans is being assisted by an unidentified GI (1945). From the Hans Conried Collection, Department of Special Collections, Boston University.

may once again genuflect before the Moloch-microphone—my lot is not too mean.

I trust that this may find you in the best of health and spirits, Norman, and ask that you please extend, to all our mutual friends, my heartiest greetings—I am, again, with many thanks, which I hope to offer personally, in the not-too-distant future.

P.S. Should future situations permit, as far as proper production and casting are concerned, would I be free to make broadcasts to the troops of some of your things that have been published? My wife could send me my books and I should like to attempt something better.

however, I found myself recast within ten days, stationed in a lovely little town in the interior as "general utility" with this organization. With but very few exceptions, our broadcasts are recorded, having been processed for the purpose in Hollywood, and it is promised, within a short time, that there will be more live, dramatic shows. So, as you can see, now, for the first time in nearly a year, with clean hands I love, albeit in a somewhat wartorn temple of our art (generally, military regimen is restraining to, if not artistic freedom, then the freedom of the artist) I

Before long, Conried was back in his element, and he was beginning to enjoy his increasingly prominent role in producing AFRS radio broadcasts. He would say of his new experiences, "This could no longer be called war. With a unit of two officers and five men—I was a sergeant myself by this time—I went to Korea, and helped build and launch two radio stations, which was better than building landing fields under fire. It was cold—we wore paper-lined Japanese overcoats—and we had one bath in three months, but it was radio, and we knew how. At war, I'm not so expert." Conried was a member of the 40th Infantry Division in Fusan.

Conried couldn't help clowning around a bit, and had photographs taken of him and a couple other station mates (at WLKJ radio) wearing a traditional Korean outfit. He had another picture taken in this outfit sitting cross-legged smoking a long Korean pipe that was used on the front of a Christmas card he sent home to Margaret and his parents. Holidays were especially difficult. Conried commented on the Thanksgiving he spent huddled outside in the cold (there were no mess halls), eating his Army supplied turkey leg, and "my gob of dehydrated potatoes [that tasted] like cold cement."

The staff of Radio Tokyo—Tokyo, Japan—in 1946. Hans was now a sergeant, and the station's managing director. From the Hans Conried Collection, Department of Special Collections, Boston University.

Papa Conried was interviewed by *Radio Life* magazine out of Los Angeles during this time and was asked what he thought of his son's successful career in radio overseas. He replied with mixed emotions: "[Hans] has three programs of his own out there, and he is doing some producing. But I'd rather he had no programs of his own, and was doing no producing, and be back home!"

The usually dapper Conried resembled Arch Oboler a bit more these days, and had to make do with the ill-fitting, often grubby clothing. His hair was growing back, and he sported a rather lush mustache. The mustache was removed shortly after his transfer to Japan for the remainder of his service.

The end of World War II came officially on August 14, 1945—VJ Day. Conried wrote, "For a whole year after V-J Day, I was in Japan. It was wonderful work, and I had it—checking in at Radio Tokyo for fifteen minutes in the morning, whipping out instructions to a bunch of bewildered kids, fresh in from the States, and then to the open road in a Jeep, seeing that beautiful, beautiful country." Conried doesn't appear to have written down his reactions to the horrific atomic bombs that fell on Nagasaki and Hiroshima. He seems to have transcended all the pain and ugliness of war around him, seeing only the beauty of the culture and people of Japan. Here the seeds of Conried's intense passion for Japanese art—as well as art from China and Korea—were sown, and would blossom into a full blown obsession before long: "I began collecting, chiefly netsuke, the delicate and beautiful carvings no bigger than your thumb, which the Japanese use for costume adornment, and which people like me keep worshipfully under glass. I really saw the country, got to know the people. Because *His Butler's Sister*, a movie in which I had worked back home, was around, I had a certain stature as an actor. I even managed to get backstage at a production of the classical theater. I came home a rabid Japanophile."

Conried developed a friendship with a Mr. Hayashi, who ran one of the few surviving antique and curio shops in Tokyo along with his daughter. Conried would spend many hours discussing Japanese art and listening to stories about the development and training of actors for the Kabuki theater. Years later, after Mr. Hayashi passed away, his daughter sent Conried a few ukioy-e (wood block prints—often depicting Kabuki actors, or scenes from the theater) in remembrance of those earlier times.

Conried enjoyed a small amount of celebrity in Tokyo, and managed to have an article written about him for the *Nippon Times* in February of 1946. His 1943 film *His Butler's Sister* was the first American film made after the Pearl Harbor attack to be shown in Japan. He told the paper his role was not a substantial one, but he enjoyed playing opposite Deanna Durbin, who was quite popular in Japan at the time.

Shelby Newhouse was one of those "bewildered kids" Conried trained while director of Radio Tokyo: "When I worked with Sgt. Hans Conried in Tokyo, he was my boss, and the station's Program Director. WVTM was the key station of the eighteen Armed Forces radio stations in the Pacific. We were under the control of General Douglas MacArthur's Headquarter Staff... We were in the same facility as JOAK, the principal Japanese station. Indeed, we did many programs from a studio in which the infamous Tokyo Rose broadcast during the war. As I recall ... the building was about seven stories high and near the Emperor's palace. The city was about sixty percent destroyed during our firebombing. The famous shopping district, the Ginza, was a mass of rubble. Merchants and artists displayed their wares by clearing an area where once sidewalks and stores stood.

I bought a large and beautiful painting on silk for two cartons of cigarettes ... I knew Hans was interested in Japanese art, but at the time we worked together, living conditions didn't permit the acquisition of many pieces. Accommodations were very primitive. Beds, not army cots, had been dragged into hallways and large rooms to be used as living quarters. They must have been offices before the army of occupation took over. Privacy was at a premium, and storage space was virtually non-existent... In any event, Hans was a clever and resourceful guy... I well remember his sitting on his cot doing Yoga exercises and reciting the specifics (bargaining) concerning his latest art acquisition. I seem to recall Hans sending many pieces back home."

Poor Margaret now had to deal with the crate after crate of Japanese artifacts coming in on a regular basis. As usual, she took her husband's eccentricities in stride, and did her best to find a place for everything until he could return to sort it all out. The new, exquisite pieces of Japanese art would eventually clash with what Conried described as their "beer garden gothic" furniture.

Another GI who worked with Conried for Radio Tokyo was New York newspaperman Walter Kaner. In his "Kaner's Column" in the mid–1960s, he would recall of his days with Conried during WW II: "Conried would have no part of our plebian GI life in barracks. He set up housekeeping in a studio, equipped it with 'borrowed' Japanese furniture, and slept and ate Japanese style on a straw mat. Broadcasting details, such as giving the correct time, were mundane to Hans. Many's the time he put Army brass in a dither by announcing: 'The time is now ... it's getting to be ... no, it's past that ... oh, the heck with it. You know what time it is.' The last time [I] saw Conried, half the Tokyo police force was chasing him through the Ginza. Seems a Tokyo cop had stopped him for driving through a traffic light. That hurt Conried's dignity. So, he broke the cop's sword, and the chase was on."

Conried's year long "adventure" in occupied Japan during 1945 would have a profound effect on him. He yearned to settle down there and start a whole new life. Conried would remark many years later, "If I hadn't had a family, I would never have come home." In 1949 he exuberantly told a reporter, "I love [Japan]. It is a big piece of French pastry. And the people are wonderful, charming, gracious and kind, and are enduring much suffering. It is hard to know why we fought them."

This overwhelming love of Japan would spill over into every facet of Conried's life, as his youngest daughter, Edie, recalled: "[My father] told me had he not already been married to my mother, he probably would have found some nice Japanese woman, and somehow I would have been born Asian. If things could have been changed. Not that he didn't love my mom, but he was influenced by Japan, and so taken, and so enamored, he would have happily stayed if he hadn't been a married man and had ties here in the States. [His experience in Japan] definitely influenced the rest of his life. He got the collecting bug while stationed in Japan, and probably acting became secondary, and collecting art became the primary happiness in his life."

Conried produced a number of shows while director of Radio Tokyo, including *The Notebook*, and *Musical Mailbox*. The latter program was sort of forced on him, and he begrudgingly played the tunes requested by his fellow GI's, along with their dedications. A notice appeared in the AFRS Far Eastern Network newsletter titled: "The Sour Note in the Life of Corporal Conried." Supposedly, he was receiving about thirty-one letters a day, all requesting special tunes to be played for a special someone. Conried grumbled that he could only humanly play eighteen or nineteen tunes per day, and "he expects to go home sometime."

By the end of August 1946, it was time for Conried to board the ship that would carry him back home to the States, and back to his old life. In the short time he'd been away, radio broadcasting had reached the top of its popularity. A newcomer to the entertainment scene—television—was now seriously threatening radio's future. The first television broadcasts in the United States began as early as 1939 to an extremely small audience of those fortunate enough to have TV sets. By 1946, all the major networks—NBC, CBS, and ABC—could see the potential in this new technology, and were scrambling to get a piece of the pie. NBC would be the one to act as the pioneer network, and offer a limited number of shows (mostly light fare) to a small group of registered viewers, who received notice of the week's offerings via a postcard. The first dramatic series, *Kraft Television Theater*, would be broadcast in early 1947.

It is purely speculative, though potentially accurate, to suggest that Conried's military hiatus was detrimental to the positive forward motion of his acting career. One could argue that military service didn't hurt major stars like Jimmy Stewart, Clark Cable, or Cary Grant. But Conried wasn't a Stewart, or a Gable, or a Grant. Conried's success on radio had not translated itself to motion pictures, and yet there was a possibility he would have had more of a bargaining chip with the studios if his popularity had continued to rise as a radio actor. It's true that the studios were not giving him the big build-up that they afforded other actors, and never even offered Conried a contract. The fact that Conried had never been under a studio contract was inexplicably included in a 1959 publicity piece as if it were a positive achievement. Conried penciled in the comment, "Maybe this isn't anything to brag about." It wasn't really, and it meant that he didn't have the opportunity to work in a wider variety of roles. This situation may have changed if he had continued with his success as a radio actor a couple years longer, and been available for films. "Out of sight—out of mind" is a fair assessment of Hollywood's capricious attitude, and the fact that Conried was no longer in the pool of available talent meant that any possible breaks for his career were lost.

The times were changing rapidly, and as he sailed back to the States from Japan in September of 1946, he would soon have to use his wits (and wit) to keep afloat in this new world. Conried's experiences in the Pacific forever altered his perceptions of the world, and of himself. It was as if some of the wind had been taken out of his once majestic sails. There was a growing internal struggle to cope with the reality of what he wanted to be, and what he was expected to be. Once firmly on U.S. soil, Conried found that his unfailing sense of duty pointed him in the direction he needed to follow. Thankfully, he had made some good friends over the years who would later prove invaluable in helping to steer his career to safer shores.

Part II
The Death of Radio

5
Sergeant Conried Returns

"Not the flash of ticker-tape, nor the appearance of nylons and the disappearance of 'A' gas ration stickers on windshields, nor the return of men in uniform to civvies; not any of these things announced that the war was really over as does the cry that is echoing around radio row this week: 'Hans is back! Hey, have you heard? Hans Conried is back!'" So began an enthusiastic article that ran in *Radio Life*'s October 8, 1946, issue that put into words the hope of many fans to see Conried return to radio acting.

The transition from military to civilian life was a bit of a bumpy one, and initially, there were some tense moments wondering when the next job offer would come along. Fortunately for Conried, he wouldn't have to wait long to work again. Radio drama was still in great demand, but listeners were turning more and more to comedy as entertainment. With the war over, people wanted to forget their troubles, and laugh again. Conried always had a keen instinct for trends, and quickly picked up on the way the wind was blowing. It brought out a bit of insecurity in him, not just because he'd been away from Hollywood for so long, but because he had never felt comedy was really his forte: "Comedy became the rage. I felt inadequate. I never felt I had mastered the necessary timing for comedy."

Sid Gold was a competent manager, and Conried trusted him implicitly. It is debatable as to whether or not he worked as hard as he could have to keep Conried's name in front of the powers that be. Many of the more recognizable actors at the time—Stewart, Gable, Cooper—maintained a fairly high profile during the war. Their activities and exploits were routinely broadcast in newsreels and in the movie magazines. Stewart, an Air Force officer, was even able to fly in once in a while to do radio broadcasts. It may have been Conried's own choice to keep a low profile. As he said when he first went to Fort Knox, he wanted "to concentrate on the life of a soldier." Conried may have sabotaged his own Hollywood career to some extent by this decision to remain incommunicado. With so many major actors out of the way, lesser-known talent at the time (like Danny Kaye) was able to seize the opportunity and rise to star status during the War years. Kaye's popularity, for example, would only increase after the war. It was actually Conried's old friend Mel Blanc who helped him get back in front of the "Moloch-microphone" once again, and re-energized Conried's career. Blanc was given his own series (something Conried lamented that he never had), *The Mel Blanc Show*, in September of 1946, and urged Conried to join him in the cast. Conried put his misgivings about doing comedy aside, and joined the show as of the October 15th episode. At first he played the nosey mailman, Mr. Snoop, with the Midwestern drawl, but soon he took over the character of the blustery Mr. Cushing, the president of Mel's imaginary lodge;

"The Loyal Order of Benevolent Zebras." Conried recalled, "A friend of mine—Mel Blanc—had a comedy show, and asked me if I wanted to work. I told him I'd never been really successful at comedy roles, but he insisted. All at once I was 'hot.'" Conried would be a regular on the series until it went off the air in June of 1947.

Around the time Conried was hired by Mel Blanc, Orson Welles was gathering the cast for his motion picture version of Shakespeare's *Macbeth*. Welles wanted Conried to play the part of Macduff, and summoned him to his office. He informed Conried, very bluntly, that he felt Blanc's show was low comedy, and beneath Conried's dignity. Unfortunately, Welles wasn't able to offer as much money for the part of Macduff, and the entire cast would need to relocate to Denver, Colorado, temporarily to rehearse the play, and do a trial run before an audience before heading back to film in Hollywood. Once back in Hollywood, the film would require at least twenty-seven days to shoot. Conried pleaded with Welles, "Orson, look, I have to stay in town now; I have a job!" Conried felt he had to decline the role. The job with Blanc meant a regular paycheck and security for himself and his wife. After those long years in the Army, he felt that was more important than a wild ride with Welles for less money, even though he firmly believed Welles was a bona fide genius. Welles was furious; he angrily lashed out at Conried and ordered him to cut his hair, and stop wearing the attire of an artist. As far as he was concerned, Conried had forfeited his right to read the lines of the Bard, and should hire himself to a grocery store, or some such low profession. Conried suddenly found himself being thrown out of Welles' office.

The original long version (211 minutes) of *Macbeth* read in Scottish dialect did not go over very well with the public, so Welles shortened the film to eighty-nine minutes, and wanted all of the actor's parts dubbed in easier to understand English accents. A few weeks later, Conried received a three-page telegram from Welles directing him on how he would like a certain actor's part to be dubbed. Conried breathed a sigh of relief that he was now "gathered back into the fold." He may not have physically appeared in *Macbeth*, but his voice was heard when the dubbed version was released to the theaters.

Looking back, one can only try to make sense of what was going through Conried's mind to turn down such an opportunity as working on a motion picture version of *Macbeth* with someone like Orson Welles. Think of it; he turned down a chance to do Shakespeare on the big screen in favor of uttering "Ugga Ugga Boo Ugga Boo Boo Ugga" on *The Mel Blanc Show*! Obviously, there was a tectonic shift of priorities taking place deep inside Conried, and he was beginning to abandon his youthful dreams for the staid rewards of what was acceptable and secure.

It wouldn't be long before Conried was back in form again, and working constantly in radio. Between October and December of 1946, Conried performed in eight episodes of *Suspense*, co-starring with such celebrities as Rita Hayworth and Susan Hayward. He also did guest spots on *The Alan Young Show*, *The Bob Burns Show*, and a few other variety programs. Alan Young invited Conried to become a regular on his radio show as of the January 10, 1947, broadcast. Conried played a delightful ham actor named Jonathan Mildew, who became Alan's new tenant on the show. Young and Conried would meet again in 1949 on an early incarnation of the *Pantomime Quiz* television game show. Conried's association with Alan Young continued when he guest starred in 1962 on an episode of Young's popular sitcom, *Mr. Ed*.

It was in 1947 that Conried first performed as one of his most widely known and enduring characters, Professor Kropotkin, on the popular comedy series *My Friend Irma*. Conried originally used a very highborn Russian accent for Kropotkin (which was a distinguished Russian name), but it was felt to be a bit much for the character. He gave his dialect a Jewish flavor, and it proved successful. Marie Wilson was the ditzy Irma, and Cathy Lewis was her more levelheaded friend, Jane. John Brown was cast as Irma's love interest, Al. Brown worked with Conried before on the *Life of Riley* series as Digby (Digger) O'Dell, the undertaker. *My Friend Irma* officially premiered on April 11, 1947.

In an article for the *Radio-TV Mirror* in 1952, Conried recalled his days with the *My Friend Irma* crew, and Professor Kropotkin: "I love the character, but what's more, I love the gang of people who created and have sustained *My Friend Irma*. I fight with Cy Howard. A man of my insubordinate leanings just naturally fights with a fellow who gets himself billed as 'producer-creator-writer', but our arguments have more noise than substance. I think Cy is a terribly talented man, and he knows I think so. The writers—Parke Levy, Stanley Adams, and Roland MacLaine—are a bright bunch too. 'Irma' couldn't have zoomed from zero to the top of the heap the very first season it was on the air without them. As for the company, I wish all radio were populated with such congenial folk… Marie is as good as Irma, with native kindness and an instinctive sense of justice. But Irma is dumb. Marie is not dumb… Cathy is a little like Jane too—bright like Jane, but sure of herself… John Brown is not like Al. Is *anybody* like Al? So my neat little parallel breaks down at this point. And Gloria Gordon is no brassy Mrs. O'Reilly. A great woman she is, the greatest mitigating influence, oil-spreader-on-troubled-waters… 'Work, smile, be happy' she shouts at you in that wonderful voice, and then in a stage whisper, 'Aren't you getting paid?' I love her. Love 'em all, come to think of it. Love the show. Love radio. Who's Shakespeare?"

Indeed. Conried's Shakespearean days must have seemed far behind him at this point in his career. Conried spent seven years with the series on radio. One of the show's writers, Cy Howard, had this to say about Conried and *My Friend Irma* in an article for *Radio Mirror* (1949): "I was nutty about [Professor Kropotkin], and wanted to play him myself, which is why I was so hardboiled about finding the right man. One day I was rushing through the lobby at CBS when I spotted a great actor by the name of Hans Conried. He was so preoccupied that I swear he walked through the front door without opening it. 'Hey,' I exclaimed. 'Do you drink tea out of a glass with the sugar in your mouth?' He looked at me as though he'd be infinitely happy if I crawled back in the woodwork. Then he spoke in rumbling resonant tones: 'It is none of your business, Mr. Horowitz', he was deliberately lousing up my name, 'But as a matter of fact, I do drink tea out a glass with sugar in my mouth.' That makes two of us, and I knew we would enjoy insulting each other.

"Usually I get away with reading all the characters' lines the way they should be read, but my ambition is to play Professor Kropotkin on the air. This is the terrible cross that Hans has to bear. When I get to needling him, he suffers. Recently, he slammed down his script. 'If you can play this part better than I can', he demanded, 'why don't you do it?' 'What?' I returned in injured voice, 'and ruin your reputation in thirty seconds?' I should try to follow Hans Conried? I should fall over a corpse. That's a great man!"

A film was made in 1949 of *My Friend Irma* directed by George Marshall. Marie Wilson was initially the only member of the radio cast to be chosen for the film. Conried was too young at thirty-two years of age to portray an old man in his eighties on the screen, and he knew it. The part went to the veteran character actor Felix Bressart, who unfortunately died a short time into production. In a panic, the studio came to Conried to beg him to take over the role and save their production. "[It] was a shameful thing in which I only really half-appeared," Conried would recall many years later. "They wanted me for this part, which I had established to the delight of millions of radio fans. Well, I was so palpably wrong, that happily I had the integrity to say 'You're crazy, I can't play this eighty-year-old man.' It may have been only courtesy; my pride prompted me to think that they really wanted me. At any rate, very sensibly, they employed a fine character actor, Felix Bressart, who died in the middle of production. Then the producer, who was an old friend of mine, said 'Hans, you've got to fish us out.' So then I played the part; the close-ups are indeed little old me, very badly performed, I was so obviously made up. The best parts of that performance are the long-shots, in which Felix Bressart still crosses the camera field of vision."

Conried was being facetious here. He appeared as Kropotkin in all the shots—near and far. Yes, he was in heavy make-up, and employed the same heavy dialect that had endeared the character to radio audiences for years. There are only a couple very quick shots of Bressart far in the background of the scene. The continuity people didn't do a very good job, as there was no attempt to dress Conried's Kropotkin the same as the Bressart version in the scene. Possibly, the producers were hoping people would just think there was a Kropotkin look-alike lurking in the background, and not connect the two. In any case, Conried was right; it was a "shameful thing," but not entirely because of his performance (which wasn't that bad). The film was used as a vehicle for the comedy team of Dean Martin and Jerry Lewis.

When it came time to try out *My Friend Irma* as a TV sitcom in 1952, Conried and John Brown were not chosen to reprise their radio roles on the small screen. *Variety* magazine reported the reasoning behind this decision was that the "originals weren't used because of telegenic deficiencies." An audition show was recorded for a Cy Howard produced *My Friend Irma* spin-off that would have featured the two old sparing lovebirds, Professor Kropotkin and Mrs. O'Reilly, in their own show: *The Professor and Mrs. O'Reilly*. The recording was sent around to radio executives to preview the show in December of 1949, but it was never picked up.

In early 1948, writers Hal March and Bob Sweeney created a show especially tailored to Conried's talents called *There's Always the Guy*. Everyone involved invested a good deal of time and effort in the project by recording not one, but two audition shows for CBS. Even though the network had a willing sponsor—American Vitamin Company—CBS decided not to proceed with developing the show.

The late forties was a pivotal time in Conried's career. He had the opportunity to work with four friends who would prove to be influential in his life and career a few years down the road. In 1947, the successful radio writer Abe Burrows was given his own series on CBS. Known in the business as an accomplished musical satirist and wit, his show was critically well received, but lasted only one season. Conried performed in various guises as a semi-regular on the show, and developed a good rapport with Burrows. After his stint with radio, Burrows worked as a writer for television, and would later write for and produce some highly successful stage productions. One such production was the 1953 Broadway musical *Can-Can*, with Conried in the cast.

Another very influential association was with the enigmatic Jack Paar. Paar and Conried served in the same Army unit during World War II, but they didn't have the chance to meet until they returned to the States. Jack Paar had the good fortune to garner Jack Benny's special interest. It would be Benny who recommended Paar to take over for him on radio as a summer replacement in 1947. And so, *The Jack Paar Program* was launched on June 1st. The reviews were so favorable, the sponsor decided to keep the show on until the end of the year. Conried performed regularly on Paar's show in brief comedy parts that usually called for a heavy German, Austrian, or French dialect. An unfortunate personal incident caused Paar to lose his gig. A trade paper reported that NBC was going to give Paar another show, produced by Amusement Enterprises, which was to have been auditioned (or "waxed") on March 10, 1948. The report listed Paar, Leo Solomon, and Joe Quillan as the writers; Hy Averback as the announcer; and Florence Halop and Conried as regulars in the cast. NBC appears to have pulled the plug on that one, though a handful of shows may have been broadcast.

Paar had one other minor radio show that mainly employed him as a D.J. to spin records on the air. This show ran from July of 1956 to March of 1957. After that, it was another lucky break that he landed on *The Tonight Show* on television, and the rest, as they say, is history. Paar remembered his old buddy, Conried, and invited him to share in his good fortune. *The Tonight Show* was like a life preserver that was thrown to Conried just as his career was going down for the count. Not only did Conried survive, but he also went on to re-energize and expand his career in new directions.

The third friend was the very unusual, freethinking, talented fellow named Theodor Geisel—better known as Dr. Seuss. Geisel also served in the Army with Conried, but as with Paar, they didn't officially meet until after they returned to the U.S. Conried had been aware of Geisel's career as a cartoonist much earlier, though: "I first became aware of his efforts in the early 1930s when there was a campaign for the insecticide 'Flit.' He'd have funny-looking people in exotic-looking costumes, and one would be shouting, 'Quick Henry, the Flit!' He was a cartoonist, and his cartoons were signed 'Dr. Seuss.' He evolved to be the great children's book writer. I met him first after the War when I got back from Japan, it must have been 1946 or 1947. He had a picture to do, a documentary of edited captured Japanese film. The film was *Design for Death*, and he needed two voices (he'd written the film) to narrate the film, so he took Kent Smith to do the American voice, and I was to do the Japanese voice."

Design for Death was a short subject produced for RKO by Theodor Geisel and his first wife, Helen, and consisted mainly of confiscated Japanese newsreels and other bits of historical footage. After the war was over, many studios were making use of confiscated film that was being released by the government's Alien Property Custodian of the U.S. Customs Service to splice together for the information hungry post-war public (albeit in a rather lurid fashion). Marquees at the time were emblazoned with the teaser "The Story Behind Tojo." Conried was actually chosen over other Japanese actors to be "the voice of Japan." His natural affinity for picking up dialects proved useful during his yearlong stay in Japan, and he was able to speak in what sounded like fluent Japanese (it wasn't, but he knew quite a few words and phrases). Conried would comment later in life that possibly his version of a Japanese accent served the purposes of propaganda better than an authentic Japanese speaker. *Design for Death* was shown theatrically only five times in order to qualify the film for an academy award. It would go on to win for Best Documentary in 1948.

Dr. Seuss remembered Conried a few years down the road when he was given his one and only chance to create a full-length feature film for Columbia in 1953: *The 5000 Fingers of Dr. T*. Ted Geisel's work was

Cast of radio's *Life with Luigi*, circa 1948: L-R: Mary Shipp, J. Carrol Naish, Hans, Frank Nelson, and Ken Peters. From the Hans Conried Collection, Department of Special Collections, Boston University.

nothing short of amazing, but he wasn't prepared for the realities of working with a hardened studio system. His work was taken and mangled by people who didn't have a clue as to what his vision was for the film. It would end up being what he called "the worst experience of my life." It would be a very painful, disappointing episode in Conried's life as well.

In January of 1948, Conried worked with Danny Thomas for the first time on Thomas' own show as the improbable leader of the program's gimmick: an "All Girl Orchestra." It generally received very poor reviews, and would last only six months on the air. The *Hollywood Reporter* ran a review of it in their "Obituaries" column saying the show contained "the most hackneyed material ever to be assembled in one comedy script in many a year." The series didn't suffer from a lack of acting talent, and featured a strong supporting cast that included Jerry Hausner and Alan Reed.

Even though *The Danny Thomas Show* bombed on radio, Conried and Thomas hit it off very well on a personal level (in spite of the fact that Thomas fired Conried from his show shortly before it went under). Seven years later, Conried would appear on Thomas' television series, *Make Room for Daddy*. This would mark the beginning of a fourteen-year association with the show in its various manifestations, and the creation of one of Conried's most recognizable characterizations, Uncle Tonoose.

Conried was too busy to worry very much about losing a job, and quickly found gigs on other radio shows. In September of 1948, Conried became a regular on the popular *Life with Luigi* show, starring the talented J. Carrol Naish as Luigi. Conried played the grumpy old German, Mr. Schultz, who was enrolled in the same citizenship classes as Luigi. One of the things that Conried was well known for was his ability to "blow his top" (Gale Gordon and

Frank Nelson were probably the kings of "top blowers"). He was a master of the slow burn, and then the over-the-top tirade unleashed just at the right moment toward the object of his frustration. It was a performance guaranteed for a huge laugh, and he worked it whenever he could.

Although Conried had been quoted as saying no one becomes an actor without wanting to be a star, he appeared to be very content to play the supporting, character actor. In fact, supporting actors had the best thing going, according to a 1947 *Radio Life* interview with Bob "Jelly" Jellison, Frank Nelson, and Conried: "[They] prefer being carefree actors to shouldering the burden of stardom." According to Jellison, "I come to work, I read my lines, we do the show, and I go home. What more can a man ask? If I were a star, I'd probably be worrying about scripts all week, fretting myself into an early grave." Nelson added, "I make enough money to get along very nicely, but not so much I have to be a financial wizard as well as an actor, and work with one eye on the clock, and the other on the stock market reports." "And think of the production headaches!" Conried continued. "A star always feels completely responsible for the show, and he carries around the weight of the world, worrying about the budget, and Hooperratings, and rehearsal schedules, and competition, and writers, and producers, and everything!" "Jelly" summed it up by saying, "It's nice to be able to dodge worry the way we do." The article brought up the interesting fact that all three men were left-handed (something the reporter felt Freud should investigate).

Conried was able to return to some of the series he had worked with prior to his stint in the Army, such as *The Judy Canova Show*, and *The Life of Riley*. Conried would also perform as a semi-regular on *The Charlie McCarthy Show*, and did a few guest spots on *A Day in the Life of Dennis Day* (*The Dennis Day Show*), *Joan Davis Time*, *The Bud Abbott and Lou Costello Show*, and others. Conried would also work with George Burns and Gracie Allen on their *George Burns and Gracie Allen Show*, which in 1947 was called *The Maxwell House Coffee Time*.

Luckily for Conried, he found the opportunity to work in a little radio drama now and then for programs such as *Favorite Story*, *The NBC University Theater* (which ran programs for college credit), and *The*

The beleaguered psychiatrist, Dr. Miller (Hans), tries to diagnose the perky Gracie Allen. It looks like he needs to lie down! (1944) From the Hans Conried Collection, Department of Special Collections, Boston University.

Camel Screen Guild Players. The latter series was unique in that it donated all fees normally paid out to its high-powered Hollywood talent to a fund that built and maintained the Motion Picture Country Home, a special place where old and indigent former actors, and other film professionals, could go to spend their final days. Conried used to joke about the day he would be sitting around the old actor's home, waving yellowed notices of his past triumphs and sharing stories with his pals.

It was harder for Conried to get back into the motion picture business after his return from the Army. The old studio system had been quickly eroding over the course of a few short years, and events had already been set into motion that would forever alter the way films would be made. In particular, there were a series of rulings by the Supreme Court in 1948 and 1949 meant to destroy the monopoly the large studios had on the movie business. Independent filmmakers wanted a fair chance to make their pictures, and the courts found ample evidence of an unhealthy alliance of the big studios who actively sought to thwart the activities of any other, less influential studio.

This disintegration of the entire "studio system" in Hollywood, and the establishment of the House Un-American Activities Committee in 1945 which led to the first communist "witch hunt" in May of 1947, would mark one of the most volatile periods in movie history. Nothing would ever be the same again. Any hopes that Conried may have had about getting a contract with a studio after his return from the war were quickly dashed. No one was really getting a contract anymore. Many of the big name stars were finding it easy to work freelance now, and they could make more money forcing studios to haggle for their services.

The one major motion picture Conried was to be involved in was, ironically, a film that raised the ire of the House Un-American Activities Committee for what they felt was an "un-American" satire on politics and its cavalier attitude toward Communism. *The Senator Was Indiscreet* was the only film to be directed by the celebrated playwright and wit George S. Kaufman. Though Kaufman was active along with many prominent actors and writers as a member of the "Committee for the First Amendment" to fight against the HUAC, the film would prove his undoing in Hollywood. He was eventually blacklisted for his efforts.

The MPAA, which had originally approved the script, changed their minds after the film's release and banned it from being shown overseas. It is tragic to read how an entire country could seemingly lose its sense of humor, but that is what appears to have happened during those dark days of the anti–Communist fervor that swept the United States. Even *Variety* would say of the film, "This is such a broadly humorous lampoon of politico goings-on that it would be foolhardy for the most thin-skinned of our lawmakers to think the shoe fits."

Conried's character in *The Senator Was Indiscreet* was the surly, communist-sympathizing hotel room-service waiter who pops into the film now and again. The character's name was Karl (appropriately enough), though it is only spoken once in the film. His insubordinate attitude and heavy New York dialect make this character a memorable one. Karl was partial to vodka and would threaten to make a full report of any activity he disapproved of to Moscow. You could almost hear the HUAC's pencil's scratching away at that one. Conried would appear with Peter Lind Hayes, who was supposedly in his first film (he had actually appeared in over a dozen before this). He would work with Hayes again in *The 5000 Fingers of Dr. T*. William Powell did a superb job as the bumbling Senator Melvin Ashton.

Conried was never blacklisted, but did

end up on the "gray" list quite by accident. From what he understood, Conried aroused some suspicion when he and Margaret went to the Hollywood Hotel one day to pay a condolence call to the family of a friend who had passed away. It just so happened that it was the very same day an anti–McCarthy rally was being held down in front of the hotel, organized by many notable Hollywood actors. Supposedly, Conried was placed on the list to be questioned merely for being at the Hollywood Hotel at the same time the rally was going on. Fortunately, he never had to testify before the Committee. Whether or not this was to affect his career in motion pictures is not known. Conried would never achieve the prominence in films, or, at the very least, the quality of roles his considerable talent should have received.

The handwriting was on the wall, and it was becoming very clear to radio actors that if they wanted to continue their livelihoods, they would need to adapt themselves to the new technology—television. Conried was very shrewd in his ability to assess the current entertainment climate, and he found his way into several television productions, possibly as early as 1946. To be sure, he didn't go willingly into this new medium.

As television became more prominent in 1949, the FCC instituted a ban on "giveaways" that had long been popular with radio shows to encourage listeners. Without this powerful tool, radio programs would quickly see their fragile market share erode and blow away. *Radio and Television Life* printed an impassioned plea from Conried to reinstate the practice: "Ladies and gentlemen of sentiment: Desist, I cry! Radio, failing sadly these days often betrayed by us who should have loved her most, is now, indeed, breathing her last. Make not her dog's death meaner still by your fulsome fancy of 'something for nothing.' Let poor radio, trampled to the earth in the March of Progress, die in peace. But if you will not, and do persist till all the fair bonnets and truthful standards fall, even to the fearful end when the now green shoot of television (and I shudder at the word) springing from the gray stump of radio is itself infected for all its future verdant years—then tell me, tell me, a poor player, 'Pray—how can I get on a giveaway show?'"

One of Conried's first television appearances was in August of 1948 as a panelist on a local Los Angeles quiz show called *Pantomime Quiz*. Television pioneers Bernie Ebert and Mike Stokey developed the idea for the television version of the popular "charades" parlor game using Hollywood actors to act out quotes, songs, proverbs, and whatever else their audience could think of.

Pantomime Quiz first went on the air on KTLA-TV in Los Angeles in 1947. At the time, college kids were being used as contestants. A fortuitous visit to the set one afternoon by actor Roddy McDowall would inspire Mike Stokey to change the format of the show. Roddy was there mainly to see what all the commotion was about, but soon he got involved in the charades and became hooked. After that, the idea of using Hollywood celebrities came about, and they were divided into two teams: "Challengers" and "Champions."

The first sets consisted of metal folding chairs and a cardboard cutout "timer." The celebrity panel wasn't compensated very well—if at all—as Conried was to reveal to an interviewer years later: "We didn't get any money in the beginning. But in lieu of cash, the members of the panel were rewarded with cases of cigarette lighters. Also, a local mill company used to send six bags of its flour products to the show, so that the Conried household had a pantry full of macaroni, pancake mix, etc. We lost our figures for a while, until I started getting money for my appearances." One of Conried's early teammates was his good friend

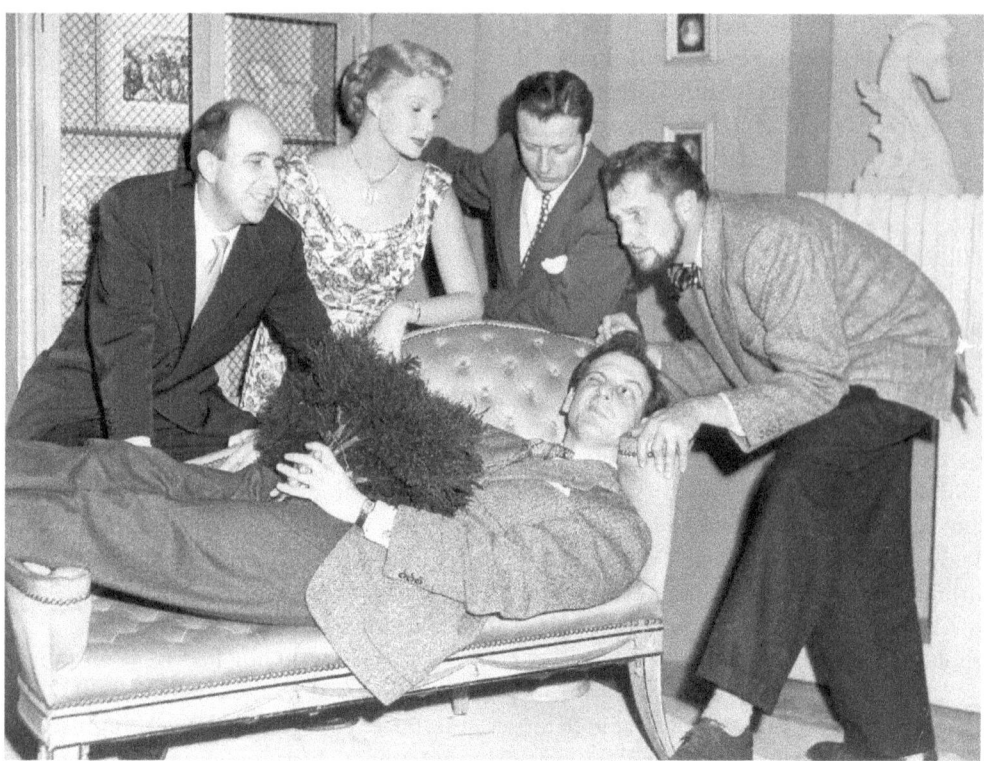

Silly publicity shot for the *Pantomime Quiz* TV show (1950): L-R: Frank DeVol, Adele Jergens, Mike Stokey, Vincent Price, and Hans (on the couch).

Vincent Price. Price won so many lighters that he pleaded with Stokey to please give him nothing until they were able to start paying cash!

Pantomime Quiz became a very popular summer replacement series, and went into syndication in 1950. Production was then moved to New York. The sets became a bit homier, and looked reminiscent of a casual living room. Conried would go on to be a regular during the 1950-1952, 1955-1957, and 1962-1963 (when the name was changed to *Stump the Stars*) seasons. He was so popular with the viewers that he was routinely flown in from the West Coast just for the show.

Conried's on-air "feud" with Vincent Price was one of the top reasons viewers tuned into the program in the early days of the show. Their verbal sparring was off-the-cuff (for the most part), and very funny to watch. On one memorable show, Stokey told the audience how Price had just been named "The Best Dressed Man" in Los Angeles. An outraged Conried is heard to say "What?! He isn't even the 'Best Padded Man'!" Stokey tries to continue by saying Price was awarded this honor by ... here Conried interrupts him, saying loudly off-screen, "His tailor!" Price is trying to disguise his amusement, and in feigned indignation growls, "Oh, you are so jealous, Hans Conried!"

Conried was very competitive, and took *Pantomime Quiz* quite seriously. In fact, it was noted by reporter Mina Wetzig that he took the game so seriously "he gets mad and won't speak to his team if they don't win. 'I'll do the next show alone' Mr. Conried has been known to announce. He also has been heard to state on the air: 'I'm a cheater. But I only cheat in front of 40 million Americans, and only to win.'"

The *Pantomime Quiz* television set circa 1950: L-R: Frank DeVol, Vincent Price, an unidentified L.A. police officer, Hans, Gale Robbins, Mike Stokey (standing), Carol Hughes, Elaine Riley, Scott Brady, and Lief Erickson.

Conried wasn't the only celebrity to get intensely infused with the competitive spirit. Though Mike Stokey enjoyed seeing his celebrity guests let their hair down, he never expected to witness what happened during a show involving Jackie Coogan. Coogan was so frustrated by his team's inability to guess "bald-headed man" that he ended up yanking off his toupee in desperation in order to win with only seconds to spare.

With the success of *Pantomime Quiz*, and another show, *Armchair Detective*, Ebert and Stokey developed the audience participation quiz show they called *Prime Ribbing* in 1949. Conried was given the job as the emcee. The sparse set featured a large picture of a steer that was divided into sections. Each section had a picture of a particular cut of meat. To claim their prize, the lucky participants would take a child's sized bow and shoot a suction-cupped arrow at the "steer." Whatever cut of meat they landed on would be their prize.

In a wonderful article titled: "Who's Afraid of Television?—Hans Conried!" written by reporter Bob Granger in 1949, television promoter Bernie Ebert and Conried talk about *Prime Ribbing* and television:

> "Most people nowadays like quiz shows," Bernie explained, "and on television they like good-looking girls. So we put Jane Adams on the new program as our Gibson Girl for the same reason that we have Sandra Spence on *Pantomime [Quiz]*." But that wasn't enough to give the planned program the desired "twist" to set it off from all others. "Finally, we hit upon it—prizes that no other show offers, prizes that people line up at counters to buy with hard-earned money ... choice cuts of steaks!"
>
> "Praise be, you didn't say hams, or somebody's nasty little mind would have made it a cue for my entrance!" Hans Conried's angular frame joined the group. We turned to greet the actor whose face and mannerisms have stamped him a

Top: Hans getting frisky with Jan Clayton during a break from *Pantomime Quiz* (1953). Jackie Coogan and Colleen Gray seem oblivious to the high jinks.

Bottom: At home in 1947: Margaret is on the left, sitting next to Hans' mother, Edith. Hans' father is standing.

"Shakespearean type" despite his jocular cavorting as emcee of *Prime Ribbing*. Conried held up a silencing hand; a pained expression fluttered lightly across his mobile face. "Don't!," he cried. "Please don't say it!"

"Say what?"

"That awful question everyone throws at me. To wit: how do you like working in television, Hans?"

"What's so awful about that question?" we asked innocently. "Matter of fact, it's one of our favorites!"

Conried snorted in true Elizabethan style. "Huh! Well, it's not one of my favorites!" He threw back his head, mental agony plainly reflected on his face. "How can anyone but a fool expect me to answer such a question?" "Can't you just answer that you like it or that you don't?" we asked foolishly. Hans collapsed into a nearby chair, obviously distraught by deep inner emotions. "What's the use? Everybody keeps badgering me ... no matter what I say."

We waited in respectful silence until the full drama of the moment had passed. "Well, just how do you like working in television?" we asked in sudden temerity. "Fine, just fine," Conried replied briskly. "There's only one catch—I don't think I can stand it much longer!" That stopped us—and just as we were getting off to such a good, sane start. We managed a cautious, "Huh?" But Conried ignored us, hunching his shoulders as he poked an inquiring finger at us. "What would you say if someone showed you gun powder for the first time and then asked how you like it?" He laughed, triumphantly. "See? There is no answer, is there? That's the way I feel!" This was fast becoming a merry-go-round; so we tried another question. "How do you like *Prime Ribbing* itself?" The dour expression on Hans' face gave way to full-throttle grin. "Wonderful!" he exclaimed. "Believe me, my wife is the best beefsteak cook in the world. Yes, I can honestly say I enjoy *Prime Ribbing*."

As the host of a television show, Conried was for the first time asked to simply portray "Hans Conried," a characterization he wasn't entirely comfortable with. This was a role he would be frequently asked to play with great success on television during the 1950s and early 1960s. But how was he to approach it? "Creating a character for yourself," Conried was to explain later, "is the worst job on earth. I was terrified at first. I had no mask to hide behind. All my career I had an accent, a wig, a beard—something to conceal the real me. Then, here I was being asked to go on these shows and be myself. I kept wondering how I should talk, what I should say. Should I lisp, or do an accent, wear a moustache, or maybe carry a cane? Naturally, you can't just be yourself. Nobody really wants to do that. So, you wind up playing it almost straight, but not quite."

Conried found television an untamed, uncharted territory that didn't require the meticulous preparation he was accustomed to. His way of describing the method employed by an actor on television game shows was "somebody plants his foot in the small of your back and propels you onstage, after which you ad lib for an hour hoping for an occasional chuckle." One can only imagine what must have been going through Conried's mind as he was handing the lucky winners on *Prime Ribbing* their prizes of frozen cuts of meat!

It was on early television shows like *Pantomime Quiz* that Conried first displayed his intellectual prowess and uncanny ability to remember almost every Shakespearean play he had ever read. Viewers would send in material to use for the show, and it became a favorite pastime to try to stump Conried by using the most obscure Shakespearean excerpt allowed. He astounded his teammates by almost always being able to come up with the correct quote. His erudite, though animated personality (he would frequently upset tables

Interesting portrait of Hans circa 1949. He still looks every bit the Shakespearean. From the Hans Conried Collection, Department of Special Collections, Boston University.

with his wild gesturing, and jump up on the couch) was very popular over the years, and helped to establish Conried as a "personality" in his own right.

The first real performance that Conried gave on television—portraying a character other than himself—was in 1949, in the premiere episode of his old friend Arch Oboler's new television series, *Arch Oboler's Comedy Theatre*. The program was called "Ostrich in Bed" and broadcast on ABC on September 26, 1949. Conried was in the lead as a young advertising man who, with his wife, was expecting an important prospective client for dinner. When the door is left open, an ostrich inexplicably comes in and makes itself at home in their bedroom. The comedy centers on their attempts to get rid of it before their guest arrives. *Variety* magazine said in their review, "Oboler drew his characters from radio, with an outstanding performance by Hans Conried, who played it straight without character or accent."

Arch Oboler had foreseen the demise of radio early on, and prophetically included at the end of his book of collected plays, *Oboler Omnibus* (published in 1945), a "Requiem for Radio": "A requiem written by a moving pencil of electronic rays conveying from a cathode tube. Television will eventually supplant 'blind' broadcasting even as sound pictures did away with the silent movies. To deny this is to whistle in the dark of wish-thinking."

Conried had a very small role as the headwaiter Francois in the Gene Kelly–Frank Sinatra Technicolor extravaganza *On the Town*. It was a routine role that only offered the challenge of a heavy French dialect. Another meager dialect role was given to Conried as the avant-garde European artist, Ladislav Ladi, in the Fred Astaire–Ginger Rogers musical *The Barkleys of Broadway*. In the latter film, Conried at least had a bit more material to work with, and managed to give Ladi a well-developed personality in his short time on the screen.

Though television was gaining fast, radio was still holding its own by 1950. Conried continued to perform as a regular on the long-running J. Carroll Naish series *Life with Luigi*, and as a semi-regular with Lucille Ball on *My Favorite Husband*. Conried first appeared on the *My Favorite Husband* series in the summer of 1948, and was heard in a wide variety of comical characters, including the neighbor, Mr. Woods, and a wacky psychiatrist, Rudolph Schweinkampf. The show had a talented star in the person of Ball, and fine writers, but the scripts now seem embarrassingly dated and unfunny. The antics of Ball's Liz Cooper often seem to be the workings of a childish and cruel mind, rather than the cute, mischievous wife her Lucy Ricardo would become. Conried was given a great deal of freedom to explore many different types of characters on the show, and his parts hold up very well in contrast to the rest of the episodes.

Conried's association with Lucille Ball would continue—with the help of friend Jess Oppenheimer—when Ball and her husband Desi Arnaz established their own television show, *I Love Lucy*, in 1951. This series was destined to become one of the most beloved television sitcoms of all time.

In the book, *Laughs, Luck ... and Lucy* published in 1999 with the help of his son Greg, Oppenheimer recalled a funny moment he shared with Conried while working on Edgar Bergen's radio show circa 1949: "We once did a sketch about Robert Fulton's invention of the steamboat. There was a scene in which the boat was leaving on its trip up the Hudson River and everyone was yelling good-byes. Hans, who played the commissioner of public works, came to me after the rehearsal and said, 'Jess, there's something that I've always wanted to do in one of these crowd scenes. Would it be all right with you if instead of 'Good-bye!' or 'Good luck!' I was to yell 'Mazel Tov'? Nobody would hear it over all of the other yelling. It would just be my own private joke.' I didn't see any harm in it, so I told him he could do it if he really wanted to. None of the other actors who made up the 'crowd' in the riverboat sketch had lines in the next scene. Unbeknownst to Hans and me, between the rehearsal and airtime, one by one, each of them asked and received permission to be excused as soon as the riverboat started to leave. So when the show aired, just as the sound-effects man played the sound of the giant paddlewheel turning as the riverboat pulled away from the shore, all the other actors turned to go instead of yelling their good-byes into the microphone. Hans, so keyed

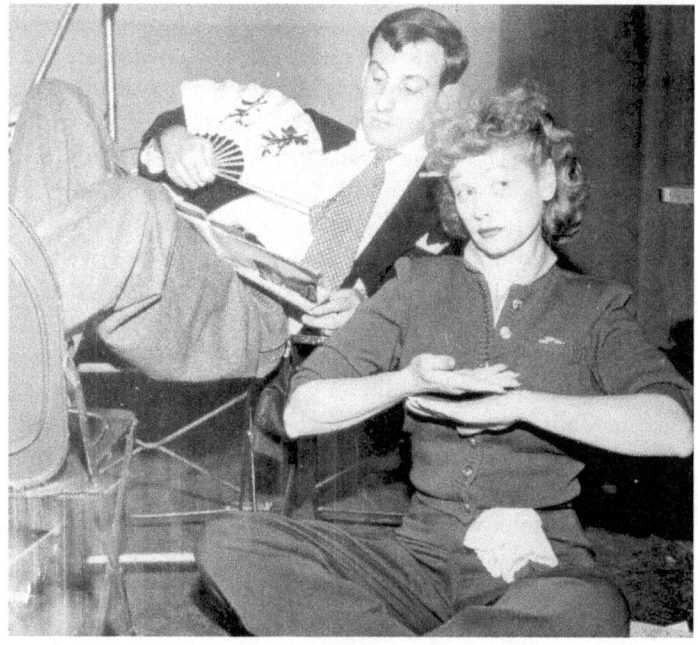

Top: Unusual Easter-themed publicity shot for a 1949 radio show.
Bottom: Relaxing on the sound stage of radio's *My Favorite Husband* sitcom starring Lucille Ball (pictured: circa 1950). From the Hans Conried Collection, Department of Special Collections, Boston University.

up that he failed to notice this, was left all alone, shouting Mazel Tov on coast-to-coast radio."

Jess Oppenheimer later developed a television series for Conried called *Hamilton the Great*. The pilot, which was filmed before a live audience in September of 1950, was written especially to showcase Conried's wide range of comedy skills and prowess as a dialectician. Unfortunately, the pace of the pilot was too frenetic, and the audience was not able to identify with, or even find a reason to like Hamilton. A wacky character that manages to get into a lot of comical trouble may work for a cute, female redhead, but it didn't work well for Hans. The series was never sold.

Several colleagues fondly remembered Conried from the late forties and early fifties. Writer Hal Kanter recalled, "In those days, Hans appeared on damn near everything that was on the air. I remember running into him one afternoon at NBC, and I said 'My God, Hans. I was very startled last night, I turned on the radio and listened to a show, and you weren't on it!' And immediately he said, 'You cad, you! You've been listening to the BBC again!'"

Radio actor Harry Bartell recalls an incident from his early days reflecting on Conried's kindness: "Although I was older than he, Hans started in radio long before I got to California. On my first network broadcast, I appeared at CBS a total stranger. This tall, lanky guy came over and said, 'I don't think we've met. My name is Hans Conried.' He then introduced me to all the cast members. For the balance of my time in radio, I remembered to do the same for newcomers who were strange to the show." Bartell would also add, "I always felt Hans was born a century too late. He was really meant for a career in the theater, and the theater of his lifetime would not allow that type of career for a man who loved a family."

Bill Owen, radio enthusiast and co-author of the book *The Big Broadcast*, remembered seeing Conried in the audience during radio broadcasts: "When I was a college student at USC from 1948 to 1953, I often visited the network radio studios in Hollywood to take in free broadcasts... Often in the morning hours, I would see Hans Conried doing the same thing, but carrying a small camera and taking many photos. Another difference between us was that he was an established radio performer, and seemingly enjoyed both performing and being a spectator. Strangers waiting in line with me would frequently comment that they saw him quite a bit."

As of 1950, with the decline of radio, Conried and Margaret had more time together to plan for the future. He had earned a good deal from his radio and film work over the years, and he felt it was time to purchase that dream house high in the Hollywood Hills, a house like he read his mentor, Rudy Vallee, owned. The Conrieds chose a beautiful Spanish style "castle" high in the hills with a balcony overlooking a rolling valley and Lake Hollywood. It was built in the 1930s, and was one of those California style, multi-leveled homes with a grand yard and a swimming pool. The confusing maze of roads leading to the home served as a deterrent to any unwelcome visitors so the Conrieds could enjoy the beautiful, peaceful surroundings. Conried would have the room now to display his burgeoning collections of Japanese art, stamps, military paraphernalia, oriental toys, and a library of books that numbered in the thousands.

Conried continued to be the main support for his elderly parents, and he made sure they would be close at hand in case of emergencies. He purchased a quaint bungalow for them in a quiet, suburban neighborhood of Burbank, less than five minutes away.

The 1950s started out with a healthy amount of work left to be done in radio for

Conried—including his first chance to direct. Conried was asked to direct episodes of the *Stars Over Hollywood* series beginning in January of 1950. The series first aired back in 1941 and managed to thrive in what was considered the worst possible time slot imaginable: Saturday mornings at 9:00. *Stars Over Hollywood* enjoyed a thirteen-year run and attracted many prominent Hollywood stars. As John Dunning noted in his book *Tune in Yesterday*: "The set was informal and loose, the clothes casual. Occasionally the stars arrived in robes and pajamas. But once on the air, it proceeded with all the precision of prime-time productions."

The opportunity to direct a radio program allowed Conried to discover what life was like on the other side of the glass. In his new role, Conried found himself in a happy position to employ many of his old friends. He had worked alongside many fine actors and actresses over the years, and he knew what each was capable of, and how best to use their talents. This part of the job was easy for Conried; it was the rest that presented a bit of a challenge. An article about the Conried directed *Stars Over Hollywood* series appeared in *Radio Television Life* describing this new experience:

> After five weeks of cue throwing, [Hans] has this to say. "I've learned things in the control room that I should have known years ago as an actor. You know, you should always look at the director before you go on." Hans told me how an actress (who didn't look at him before she went on) might have picked up the time on a show that was lagging had she looked, and that was one way he had come to realize the problems of the other side of the control room glass.
>
> MCA was the one to approach actor Conried to ask him if he would like to direct. He scoffed at the idea at first, then became enthusiastic when it presented a challenge. One of the great tricks in directing—casting a show—presents a minor problem to Hans because through years of working Hollywood radio shows, he pretty well knows his fellow supporting players and what they can do. One of his most successful *Stars Over Hollywood* programs was one starring Jack Paar, on whose show Hans used to play. Director Conried assembled some of the other Paar exes for this airing, calling on Hal March, Hy Averback, and Mary Jane Croft. Another time, not so good, was when he had to direct a girl who had never before faced a microphone and practically had to be shown where to stand.
>
> Naturally, Hans often restrains the wild urge to crash through the glass and take over a role. He squelches this feeling and also the one prompting him to show other actors how to do their parts by actually reading the lines. Hans feels that this changes the actor's interpretation too much and violates his thespian integrity. He and Jerry Hausner are old and good friends, and Jerry knows how Hans feels about this, so Jerry had a field day the first time he worked Hans' program. During rehearsal, he did all the things he could think of to infuriate Hans, like slumping in his chair and reading a magazine, missing cues and feigning nonchalant oblivion while rehearsal surged on. Hans retaliated by changing one of Jerry's parts from Swedish to Hungarian, but Jerry did it so well Hans was almost envious. Finally, the time came for the director to come out of the control room and make his final comments to the cast. This Hans did, reserving Jerry until last. Jerry bristled and waited, daring Hans. Hans turned to him, "And you, Jerry," he said ... "You be ... better!" Jerry got such a kick out of this that he is the one who is telling the story around Radio Row. Hans, being a very modest and gallant fellow, naturally depreciates his prowess at directing and credits network producer Dale Harper, soundman Jack Dick, Alex Alexander, Harry Essman, Rex Koury, and all the others working *Stars Over Hollywood*. Claims Hans, "All I do is point."

The "Be Better" story took on a life of its own, and has been repeated numerous times, in many different variations, over the years. When asked about the incident in 1970, Conried recalled that his dear old pal Jerry was "an iconoclast, and disrespectful, and he didn't seem to feel the deep responsibility that I felt for my situation and the dignity and prominence to which I'd risen. And he was ragging me, frankly. That's not ordinarily done to a director. I felt it keenly, though we're very close friends... I was looking for something with which to strike him down...." Those two little words, "be better," put Jerry in his place, and in so doing, made history on Radio Row.

Stars Over Hollywood appeared briefly as a television series beginning in September of 1950. The radio production of "My Rival Is a Fiddle" which starred and was directed by Conried, was also filmed for a television broadcast in 1951.

Stars Over Hollywood was a satisfying creative experience for Conried during a time when most network radio programming was in serious decline. The best and brightest from all fields of radio production were jumping ship to television and the lure of more money. The quality of the scripts was slipping, as evidenced in listening to an episode of *Much About Dolittle*. Conried was given his own radio series in the summer of 1950. Normally this would have been an auspicious event, but the show was doomed from the start. Conried portrayed an elderly, henpecked husband by the name of Colonel Lucius Dolitte. Dolittle was a Southern gentleman, but he had a problem with the concept of steady employment. Much of the humor of *Much About Dolittle* is centered on the Colonel's attempts to avoid getting a job. The plots are as thin as rice paper, and there is a dearth of laughter from the live studio audience. Conried does what he can with what he is given, but it's just not enough to raise the show from the dead. The series was cancelled after eight weeks.

It had been about four years since Conried left Japan, and it is easy to imagine that he must have dreamt of the day he would return the moment he set foot on the boat for home. Margaret was a very devoted, patient wife who grew to embrace her husband's new passion, and Conried was eager to share it with her. In the summer of 1950, Conried and Margaret set off for Japan, and spent some time together exploring all the places Conried fell in love with during his Army days. They bought kimonos and lived Japanese style to really absorb the culture. Conried delighted in sharing his love of Japan with his wife. It was a rare chance for the two to be together without any interference or pressures of work, and they talked about starting a family. The following summer would bring the birth of their first child, a daughter Conried named Trilby. Du Maurier's *Trilby* held a strange fascination for him all his life. Years later, Conried explained the timing in starting a family to columnist Hedda Hopper by saying, "Radio died, and I had lots of time at home."

The two films featuring performances by Conried released in 1950 were disappointingly brief appearances that left audiences wanting more. In the Jane Powell vehicle *Nancy Goes to Rio* (MGM), Conried plays the very proper Brazilian butler, Alfredo. The short scene with veteran actor Louis Calhern, where Alfredo teaches his master the finer points of boxing, is the most memorable.

For the Judy Garland musical *Summer Stock*, Conried appeared as the self-centered New York actor Harrison I. Keath. In his rehearsal scene with Gene Kelly as the director of the little summer stock troupe, and Gloria De Haven as his leading lady, Conried had a chance to stretch his acting muscles a bit. Unfortunately, when it came time for him to sing, another actor's voice was dubbed in (very obviously). During one outdoor scene, if you listen carefully, you can hear Conried rehearsing in the background in his real singing voice. The making of this film was not an easy task, as Judy Garland was in poor health due to her substance abuse problems, and shooting around her absences made it difficult for all.

Conried worked with Garland again at the end of 1950 in a special *Lux Radio Theatre* Christmas presentation of "The Wizard of Oz"—an unusual choice for a radio adaptation, considering the amazing special effects that made the 1939 film so memorable. Conried was well cast as the farmhand "Hunk" who would become the Scarecrow in Dorothy's dream. Unfortunately, Conried was the only one in the cast who had his singing dubbed by another actor (again, quite obviously). In spite of any challenges, the production went well, and the live audience enjoyed a very fine performance by all. You can hear some laughter rippling through the audience even before Conried delivers his lines. He couldn't resist mugging a bit to get the extra attention, even if the listeners at home never knew what was so funny.

While listeners tuned in on December 25th to hear Conried on *Lux Radio Theatre*, others were watching him on the first ever Walt Disney television special: *One Hour in Wonderland*. This would be the start of a long association with Walt Disney Productions, and a very lucrative one for Conried. On this groundbreaking television special, he appeared heavily made up as the omnipotent face in the magic mirror. *The Los Angeles Times* would comment in their review, "A magic mirror brings past Disney hits to life for the party with the aid of Hans Conried, the very wonderful voice of the mirror. Hans almost steals the show." It was about this time that Conried was first approached by Disney to be considered as the voice of Peter Pan's nemesis, Captain Hook, as well as the role of Mr. Darling. Disney studios had been toying with the idea to make a feature length, animated film of *Peter Pan* since the late 1930s. The idea was revived around 1949, but it would still take many years to put all of the pieces in place for such an ambitious undertaking.

Whenever Conried was asked which roles he would love to play, he invariably answered Cyrano de Bergerac and Don Quixote. In 1950 Conried would star as both of his two favorite characters, but it would be on the radio. He would, in fact, have a chance to portray Cyrano twice: once on the *Family Theater* program, and again on a broadcast of *The Columbia Workshop*. It is interesting to note that this year would also see the big screen release of *Cyrano de Bergerac* starring José Ferrer. Ferrer would go on to win an Oscar for his role as the love-struck fellow with the unfortunate proboscis.

Conried gave, arguably, the best performance of his radio career as Don Quixote for an adaptation of the classic story for *The NBC University Theatre*. Conried finally had a chance to use his Shakespearean training to its fullest in shaping each melodic syllable of Quixote's speech. His trademark "growl" (Conried could make the words rumble in the back of his throat) was also skillfully used to great effect. Conried's performance ran the gamut of emotions, and gave the listener the rare opportunity to know the great depth he possessed as an actor. There is nothing histrionic or hammy about his Don Quixote, only a finely crafted, robust characterization of a man out of touch with the society of his day who dreamt of a nobler time. Perhaps Conried could readily identify with such a person, and drew from his own experience. Conried was given a chance to portray a Quixote-like character in an episode of the Richard Boone television series *Have Gun Will Travel* in 1963. His performance was a good one, but it is easy to see how difficult it is to play a scene encased almost completely in heavy armor. That is something Conried certainly didn't have to worry about on radio.

Hans, Francis L. Sullivan, and "Corky" in a scene from *Behave Yourself!* (RKO: 1951). The clever canine went on to win a PATSY Award of Excellence for his acting in 1952.

Another outstanding performance can be found in the August 23, 1952, broadcast of the perennial Western series *Gunsmoke*, starring William Conrad. The words written by Anthony Ellis for Conried's character—a pathetic Shakespearean actor—seemed to strangely echo his own personal experience: "My life has been the theater. As a boy, I was a student of Shakespeare. Look at me... Who would accept this face for Hamlet? This ill-shaped body for Romeo? His speech became my speech, but the fools only look; they cannot listen for laughing." The character, Sam Matchett, was an apprentice to a stumbling, drunken sod who "muddled and tore to a tatter the words I should have spoken." Conried was able to convey an aura of dignity to the sense of hopelessness that enveloped Sam after he had killed his master.

As satisfying as some of his radio performances were, Conried was not able to find material of the same quality in the films that were released in 1951. The few noteworthy performances would be in the rarely shown (for good reason) Irving Reis–directed Western *New Mexico* starring Lew Ayres; *Behave Yourself!* with Farley Granger and Shelley Winters; and *Too Young to Kiss* with June Allyson. Conried tested for the part of Orlando Higgins in the United Artist feature *Actors and Sin*. The film was written, directed, and produced by the talented writer Ben Hecht and showcased two of his short stories: "Actor's Blood" (Conried performed in a version of this story on radio for *Suspense* in 1944) and "Woman of Sin" (the script is titled "Concerning a Woman of Sin"). Conried was to be in the second story, which was a comedy about a literary agent who is handling a potentially obscene book written by a nine-year-old girl. Conried carefully underlined the part of Higgins in red pencil, as was his custom, and also noted the clothes he was to wear in each scene, as well as the times he should arrive at the studio. *Actors and Sin* was released in 1952 with Eddie Albert portraying

Orlando Higgins. The part was a substantial one, and would have been a good role for Conried. Unfortunately, he was not quite what Hecht had envisioned for the part.

New Mexico featured Conried as President Abraham Lincoln, in a small, historically farfetched role. Conried used a great deal of restraint, and portrayed Lincoln with the stateliness required of such a character. To his credit, he was barely recognizable in voice or physical appearance. There was some satisfaction in playing this presidential part, as Conried would later comment, "Every tall actor wants to play Lincoln."

Behave Yourself! was a comedy starring the mismatched couple Farley Granger and Shelley Winters. Conried portrayed a sweet natured, but deadly Cockney assassin by the name of Norbert Gillespie—or "Gillie" for short. Gillie was in the employ of a gentleman who went by the moniker of Fat Fred and was splendidly portrayed by character actor Francis L. Sullivan. The connection between the characters was never fully explored, but the main scene between Gillie (who was known as "Gillie the Cherub" in the original script) and Fat Fred, was filmed in the corpulent gangster's luxurious penthouse suite while he was soaking in his swimming pool sized tub. The MPAA censorship board found reason to object to the location of this scene, writing in a letter to the film's producers: "Please have the entire scene between Gillie and Fat Fred located some place other than with Fred in the bathtub. Moreover, there appears to us to be a suggestion of perversion in the relationship between the two men. You realize the Production Code prohibits such perversion or any inference of it." The MPAA must have been sufficiently placated, since the scene was not re-shot.

Even though the premise of *Too Young to Kiss* was too implausible—a mature woman pretends to be a fourteen-year-old girl to win a music competition and catch the eye of a famous music agent—Conried does manage a fine performance as the high-strung director of the youth orchestra that is putting on the competition. *The Citizen News* reported that "after an amusing scene between June Allyson and Hans Conried for *Too Young to Kiss*, in which Hans had some particularly difficult comedy routines to put over, director Robert Z. Leonard had only praise for the radio actor: 'That was great, great, simply great!' enthused Leonard. 'It was nothing, nothing at all,' replied Conried, 'just a little something I picked up to make a living.'"

John Wayne had a hand in crafting a part especially tailored for his friend Conried in his next film: *Big Jim McClain*. The film was made in early 1951, and released in 1952. He named the character Robert Henried. Conried pronounced the name in the French manner so that it didn't actually sound like "Conried." The film was set in Hawaii, and the stars and crew had an enjoyable vacation while making the picture. As Conried remembered, "On *Big Jim McClain* [Wayne] wrote in a character with a name very close to my own, and it was a bizarre, broad character. It was a small part, and he offered me a modest salary; it was a question in my mind, and in my agent's mind, whether it would warrant my going to Hawaii, where it was being shot. In conversation on the telephone, my agent remarked, 'I can't get hold of Conried, I just talked to his wife at home', and the casting director said, 'Tell her she can come to Hawaii too.' So, that evening when I got home, the bags were already packed and waiting in the downstairs hall. It was a very short job, but a very, very pleasant job. We shot it, and I had a mustache at that period; when I came home I had another job, and had to remove the mustache, and have a haircut. Ultimately they re-shot the scene over again in Hollywood with a pasted on mustache to match it. But I remember the warm feeling of camaraderie on the set with Duke Wayne. He engenders a very warm loyalty on the part of his fellows; indeed it is truly a band of brothers. His public façade of being easy-going, and manly, and hearty, is quite factual."

Conried rarely turned down a job, and in 1951 appeared on an obscure, locally produced television quiz show on station KTTV in Los Angeles called *Let's Face It*. Artist Nick Volpe sketched clues for the guest panelists, and they tried to guess what the complete picture would be. Paul V. Coates, who was a reporter for *The Mirror*, had a chance to appear on the show along with actress Ann Rutherford and Conried, and learned firsthand the pitfalls of working with celebrities: "Last Monday, as the show went on, Ann Rutherford leaned over and whispered to me: 'Honey, just sit back in your chair and relax. If we need you, we'll call you.' Volpe sketched the first picture clue. Then he turned to us, 'Got any ideas from this?' he asked. I raised my hand frantically, and caught the camera's attention for a hot moment. 'Say', I said with a sly smile, 'that reminds me of a little story...' Ann stretched languidly, and then adjusted the lilt of her bosom. The camera swerved madly towards her. 'It seems these two fellas...' I said. Conried suddenly spewed forth a burst of broad German dialect. Hilarious. It tore the house down. Ann yawned prettily... Conried waved at some imaginary friend in the audience. Ann snuggled adorably into her chair. 'Pat and Mike,' I continued grimly. Conried sat up and did a pantomime imitation of George Arliss. Rather good, too. Ann sighed and patted her hair. 'And these two fellas met in front of a saloon...' I mumbled, fading sadly."

In 1952, Conried found himself in the Warner Brothers motion picture *Three for Bedroom C*, which was Gloria Swanson's big screen follow-up to her highly acclaimed *Sunset Boulevard*. Conried would recall that making the film was a "pleasant experience," and "it was a picture made to follow up [Swanson's] success in *Sunset Boulevard*, which it didn't. They had a leading man they'd discovered somewhere, a very nice fellow who I think was a shipping clerk; a very nice fellow who was like a stick. We had a marvelously funny scene, in which I was a dyspeptic publicity man from Hollywood, and Fred Clark was an actor's agent; we were in a posh train, and I was being shaved by a nervous barber, played by Gus Schilling. It was the highlight of the picture. It was pretty broad, cheap stuff, but that's the kind of stuff I most enjoy."

The role of Jack Bleck earned him some kind words from the press. *Variety* said in print that Conried's work was the "best performance in [the] picture." *The Daily News* reported, "Conried's slick characterization of a hypochondriac, ulcer ridden movie studio press agent is a gem."

Conried was given a script in 1952 for a comedy-mystery titled, "Dry—with Three Olives." He was the star of the photoplay; a character named Monty Nolan. Bing Crosby Productions filmed the show in November of 1952. The script was a good one, and afforded Conried a rare chance to shine. Nolan was a "tired newspaper reporter," kind of run-down and seedy, who liked to play amateur detective. The cast included Walter Sande, John Hubbard, Phyllis Coates, and Jim Hayward. The 30-minute film was shown on television as part of Bing Crosby's *Rebound* dramatic anthology series. "Dry—with Three Olives" surfaced on television again in 1954. Unfortunately, it was whittled down to a fifteen-minute segment of the *Crown Theatre, Starring Gloria Swanson*. How that script could have been successfully boiled down to fifteen minutes is indeed a mystery.

Before the end of 1952, Conried appeared on two episodes of *I Love Lucy*. It was enjoyable to work with his old friends Jess Oppenheimer and Lucille Ball again. Conried was a used furniture salesman in "Redecorating" shown in November, and then an English tutor the following month.

In "Lucy Hires an English Tutor," Conried is at his best as the fussy elocutionist Percy Livermore. In an effort to thwart Lucy's insistence on learning to speak proper English for their new baby, Desi enlists Mr. Livermore's aid to end the lessons. After all, what the tutor really wants is to be a singer and songwriter, and Desi has promised to introduce him to all the record producers. Returning from a trip to Desi's club, Percy pretends to be so taken with his new friend that his speech suddenly acquires a Cuban accent. At Desi's insistence, Percy launches into a spirited rendition of "Babalu." A disgusted Lucy abruptly cancels the English lessons, much to Desi's delight.

Nineteen fifty-two was also the year Conried began working on a project that would be the biggest film of Conried's career—the film that could have been the big break he was looking for: *The 5000 Fingers of Dr. T.*

6

Peter Pan, The Twonky, *and* Dr. T

The year 1953 was a watershed for Conried, both personally and professionally. This is the year the motion pictures that are widely accepted to be Conried's three major accomplishments in film were released: The animated Walt Disney feature *Peter Pan, The Twonky,* and *The 5000 Fingers of Dr. T.* One other minor film was also released in 1953—*The Siren of Bagdad,* a film Conried described as "shameful."

There is a more ominous significance to 1953 in that it is generally considered to be the year radio died. It was all too clear that the "best of all possible worlds" was gone. Even the old studio system that might have bestowed on Conried a lucrative contract had disintegrated, and veteran character actors were becoming increasingly expendable. It was a time of big stars in big pictures. The rest of the cast seemed to be of little consequence in the overall production.

As noted in a previous chapter, the full-length, animated feature film *Peter Pan* had been in production for many years prior to its release in 1953. Walt Disney's deep pockets meant that he could lavish a large sum of money on his animated works, and he gave his artists and production people the luxury to take as much time as they needed to perfect their work. To aid their efforts, a live action film was made using an unusual size of film that lent itself well to the necessary enlargements needed by the artists to perfect minute details. This film was used as a tool for the animators to study when trying to determine, for example, how the folds of a dress might fall when a character is turning, and a myriad of other fine points. It was made under very harsh lights with a rudimentary set; just a few boards here and there to give an outline of a boat, or the side of a cliff, and so on. The actors were in full costume, most of the time, with Conried dressing the part for the evil Captain Hook and the lovable father, Mr. Darling.

The soundtrack had already been recorded for the film, and the actors were called in to physically perform the movements of the characters to the recording. As Conried noted many years later, this was in contrast to the way he would be called in to dub the voice of a non–English speaking actor for a film: "When you do voice over in a picture, as I used to do ... they'd get a very interesting character man, and he couldn't speak English, then I'd dub whatever he would say in a heavy dialect into a thinner dialect. You then speak your lines coincident with the actor's labile action on the screen. You put the sound to the picture." Conried traveled to the Disney studios for a few days here, or a week there, to complete the soundtrack and film over the course of two and a half years.

This live-action "Peter Pan" was an amazing piece of film, but unfortunately, the prints were destroyed shortly after the animation was completed. There are still photos in existence that show the elaborate measures the Disney company took to ensure the animation was the most lifelike possible. When you watch the animated Captain Hook on the screen, you are actually watching Conried perform. It was his body they used as a model, and of course, his wonderfully wicked voice. Mr. Darling is Conried too—his voice one of a nervous father—but the animated figure has been plumped up considerably. Still there are telltale Conried mannerisms embedded in the artist's strokes.

Conried would later say of Captain Hook, "He's a much maligned character. If you read the lines with any sensibility at all, you must have an animus against Peter Pan who could fly, and took outrageous advantage of this one-armed man. Hook was a gentleman. Pan was not. His behavior was very bad form."

Walt Disney Studios spent nearly four million dollars to produce *Peter Pan*, giving it the distinction of being one of the most expensive films made up to that time. The film has endured as a classic of animation. It has also ensured that Conried—as the voice of Captain Hook—will live on for generations. Conried used no dialect, save for his own affected English accent, to create Hook's speech. The character was played for its broad comedic value, but there is a restrained, almost sympathetic quality to the well-mannered Hook that Conried was adept at instilling in his villains.

The film *The Twonky* also took a long time to complete and reach the theaters, but the reasons behind this are in sharp contrast to *Peter Pan*. The film was the brainchild of former radio genius Arch Oboler. At the time (1950), Oboler had garnered praise for his controversial 1949 science fiction film, *Five*, whose subject was the end of the world

A photograph of Hans, dressed as Captain Hook, taken to aid the animators at Disney to perfect their villain for the animated feature film: *Peter Pan* (1953). From the Hans Conried Collection, Department of Special Collections, Boston University.

due to an atomic holocaust, and the five people left alive: one woman and four men. *Five* bombed during the initial test showings in New York and Chicago. With the help of Hollywood producer Sid Pink, Oboler was able to mount an unusual ad campaign that sparked interested in the film, and packed the West Coast premiere. It went on to become a substantial hit.

Now that *Five* was a financial success (it had been made on a very low budget), Oboler had some clout with Hollywood executives. He had not mellowed in any way from his early days as the difficult "enfant terrible" of radio. Oboler insisted on doing everything his way, would not listen to any criticism whatsoever of his work, and refused to give details of his newest venture. All he would tell the media was that he was working on a revolutionary concept for a science fiction film that would be the first of its kind. The production would be completely independent to rule out any studio interference, but that also made financing the picture more difficult.

Through his lawyer, Jerry Rosenthal, Arch Oboler somehow managed to convince a wealthy businessman, Buddy Nast, to invest the $250,000 needed to begin production on the new film. Nast was a babe in the woods when it came to motion pictures, but loved the idea of being a mogul.

The title of the film was to be *The Twonky*, and it was based on a short story by science fiction writer Henry Kuttner. Oboler had purchased the rights to the story years earlier for possible use on one of his radio shows. He saved it, though, believing it had more potential as a full-length motion picture. Sid Pink would soon come on board as the vice president of Arch Oboler Productions, Inc., and become the film's executive producer.

According to Pink, in his entertaining article about *The Twonky* written for *FilmFax* magazine in 1991, the film was doomed just about from the get-go: "Arch consulted no one. He made the film a truly personal and mysterious project. He played with unworkable camera angles and positions until his crew rebelled. He experimented with the newer forms of sound recording until the sound mixer threatened to quit. He detailed and attempted to do his own special effects until the sight of his wobbling Twonky TV set made him realize how ludicrous it was becoming. He fancied himself a one-man production team, all in the name of making a real 'modern' film... He never permitted any of us to see rushes or to enter the editing room... I watched the shooting on the set, and everyone was uncomfortable without knowing just why. Arch told the actors nothing, allowing them to play the role according to their own whim.

"At least the casting was superb. Again, Arch searched the world of radio for his actors. He hired Hans Conried for the lead, a fine actor equally adept at comedy or Shakespeare, who later became famous on TV game shows. Hans confessed to me he never did understand what part he was playing, and bemoaned the fact he had never read the short story. The female lead went to Joan Blondell's sister Gloria, who was at least as good as her sister. All the rest of the cast came form the world of radio, and they were good. Unfortunately, the great talent was totally wasted, as well as the $300,000 thrown away on this mess.

"On the set, Arch never discussed anything with the actors. He permitted them to do anything they wanted. Not once did Arch ever discuss the script or his intentions with me as his executive producer. I never saw a copy of the script except for the scenes scheduled for each day, and the actors had no idea of who, what, or where they were. Arch kept the secrecy even unto his own film editor. Not one member of the organization saw a complete script until after the picture was made and edited. He made very few takes, and stayed strictly to budget and schedule, but the film remained a mystery. We discovered later that Arch intended to make it a comedy, and felt it would be much more intriguing if his actors didn't know about it. Consequently, all the actors played it literally for horror, per the original short story."

Needless to say, this was not a happy time for Conried. His sense of loyalty to Oboler for having given him a chance as a young radio actor forced him to stay and complete the picture. Conried would arrive for work each day, and do his best, even though he knew the film would be a dismal failure: "*The Twonky* was something in which I was the star. I was the star in that, but I never should have made it. We knew when we were shooting it that it was impossible. I went up and apologized to the backer, a wealthy man from wire manufacturing, and I expressed already my concern, while we were in production! They rented a mansion on Third Street in Los Angeles for $50.00 a day; we didn't even shoot it in a studio. So I expressed my concern to the backer, and he said, 'Don't worry, Hans, I needed a tax write-off this year anyway.' So already we could hear the Angel of Death rustling her wings while we were shooting the picture. Arch Oboler was the first one to make me a star in radio, co-starring with famous artists from motion pictures who would work in radio plays. I remember he picked me to co-star with Bette Davis in 'Beloved Friend'. He is an enormously talented man, but not very strong in comedy."

The actor's attitudes were probably best reflected in the silly publicity photos that were taken for the film showing Conried and Gloria doing the tango, or Conried leering at Gloria from behind his *Passion Through the Ages* book. These stills are probably better than the entire movie. If only Oboler had told his players the picture was intended as a comedy, the talented cast would have been able to rise to the occasion and create something really funny. Without adequate direction or a coherent script, the efforts of everyone involved were wasted. You almost feel sorry for the actors struggling to make their scenes seem viable when you know deep down they haven't a clue as to what it's all about.

There are interesting camera angles, and way-too-close close-ups (Conried overdid it on the eye make-up), but the amateurish special effects make you want to laugh. That is what Oboler wanted, after all, but it would have been a much better idea if he had let the rest of the crew in on his plans. Conried once noted how he needed a "firm, restraining hand" from a director. He was cast adrift with no compass to guide him when making *The Twonky*. As talented as he was, Conried looked lost and bewildered most of the time. This state of affairs probably enhanced his performance as the confused Kerry West, and provided added realism.

The story itself wasn't a bad one, and reflected a mistrustful attitude about television that Oboler identified with and amplified out of proportion for his film. The TV set itself became an evil mechanism designed to control minds and stifle individuality and freedom of speech. The haphazard editing of the film cut out early scenes that would have helped to explain much of Kerry West's attitude towards television and his reasons for not wanting one in the house. He originally has an argument with his wife (played by Janet Warren) over purchasing the TV, and then goes outside to stop the technician from installing the antenna on his roof. The final release just shows a face-

Hans and Gloria Blondell have a little fun mugging for a publicity photograph for Arch Oboler's *The Twonky* (Universal: 1953).

less TV technician hammering at the antenna behind the opening credits, and the film begins with the TV already installed, and the wife leaving for her sister's house. The TV is just explained as the wife's way of keeping her husband company while she's gone. A silly montage is added at the beginning, with Conried doing the narration, to show what a "typical" day it was.

Another Conried managed to get in on the production, though unbilled. It was none other than Conried's infant daughter, Trilby, who played the part of the crying baby. Perhaps she knew the film would be a bomb, just like her Papa did.

According to Sid Pink, preview audiences left the theater in droves. *The Twonky* languished until Oboler's 1952 minor success *Bwana Devil* was produced. As part of the distribution deal, *The Twonky* was thrown in as a second feature, which finally allowed it to be released to the theaters in 1953. Pink thought it might have only been shown three times before it died. It appeared in a few Canadian theaters, also briefly, in a vain attempt to make back a little of the money. TV sales would also prove unprofitable, as the film was considered unworthy even of the small screen. In the past forty-five years, it may have only been on American television once or twice. The reviews in 1953 used phrases such as "dull and gabby," "witless and stumbling," and "unbelievably bad." One reviewer even commented that Conried's acting ability was "overwhelmed by the script." Only one (in the *Los Angeles Times*) had a kind word for *The Twonky*, saying, "It's a sure laugh getter, besides being smartly original." This reviewer also referred to Conried as "handsome." One wonders if the reviewer actually saw the film, or just read the synopsis. A reviewer for *Variety* ended with, "More than once, Oboler has one of his 'Twonky' characters exclaim, 'It's your God-given right to be wrong.' The line can well serve Oboler for seventy-two minutes."

By far the most important film in Conried's career was the Stanley Kramer Productions Technicolor "All New Kind of Wonder Musical"—*The 5000 Fingers of Dr. T*. This was the kind of film Conried had been waiting for, and the one that could have made him a star. He did not receive the top billing, but Conried was given the choice role of the title character.

For Conried, *The 5000 Fingers of Dr. T* would be the most wonderful and the most painful film he would ever work on. According to Stanley Kramer, "It was one of my favorite properties, and one which I very much wanted to direct myself. Columbia Pictures wasn't ready for

A Columbia production shot of filming a scene from *The 5000 Fingers of Dr. T,* with Hans and Tommy Rettig. From the Hans Conried Collection, Department of Special Collections, Boston University.

that yet, and there wasn't enough money to do what should really have been a musical extravaganza. We set the story in a boy's imagination, and the theme in fact becomes imprisonment within that imagination." Conried's old friend, Theodor Geisel (Dr. Seuss), developed the original story and co-wrote the screenplay.

It was Geisel who insisted Conried play the role of the demented, over-the-top piano teacher Dr. Terwilliker for *The 5000 Fingers of Dr. T*, and it gave Conried's movie career the boost it so badly needed. Geisel commented in 1953 that he was inspired by his own childhood experiences: "I took piano lessons from a man who rapped my knuckles with a pencil whenever I made a mistake. I made up my mind I would finally get even with that man. It took me forty-three years to catch up with him. He became the Terwilliker of the movie."

The 5000 Fingers of Dr. T was Geisel's first full-length feature film, and he let his strange imagination loose on the development of the sets, costumes, lyrics, and characters. In short—it was his "baby." Scriptwriter Allan Scott was called in to work with Geisel to rewrite what was at first an unwieldy script. Some of the ideas in this first draft were probably too unusual or just too dangerous to film. For example, Dr. Terwilliker (or "Terwilliger" in the early scripts) was seen as a much darker, violent character who routinely lopped off the heads of his henchmen with a long saber. These unfortunate henchmen didn't die, but continued to serve their master (albeit not very well) without their heads. Dr. T's fondness for Mrs. Collins was also evident in the way he had her placed in a cage that was suspended over his bed.

The early songs, such as the "Massage Opera," contained odd lyrics that would have probably worried the censors. The first draft included more scenes of Mrs. Collins being hypnotized by Dr. T to keep her

A scene from *The 5000 Fingers of Dr. T* that did not make it into the final release. From the Hans Conried Collection, Department of Special Collections, Boston University.

under his power and make her love him. After one treatment, Mrs. Collins is forced to recite how devoted she is to the evil doctor, and says, among other things: "I will be ninety-nine and forty-four hundredths percent pure with you," "I will enjoy the pause that refreshes with you," "I will be antiseptic with you," and "I will luxuriate in the charm of gracious living with you in a form-fit chair."

A source that worked on the original film stated that Stanley Kramer Productions had originally envisioned the film as a big budget vehicle for Danny Kaye—in the role of Dr. Terwilliker—and Bing Crosby as the plumber, Zablodowski. Crosby was unavailable, or possibly uninterested, and Kaye refused to work again with Sammy Cohn and Columbia Pictures. With both major actors out of the running, Stanley Kramer was left holding the bag as production had already begun on the lavish sets and musical score. Hans Conried and Peter Lind Hayes were quickly substituted in the leading roles, and Mrs. Hayes (Mary Healy) would have the only female role. Neither the Hayeses, nor Conried were big enough box office draws to convince Columbia the picture had any chance of success, and Tommy Rettig, though a fairly popular child actor at the time, was not a big enough star to carry an entire picture. Nevertheless, the final draft was submitted and approved, and the filming began.

Notices in the trade papers reported Stanley Kramer had already spent over 2.5 million in production costs by the middle of 1952. The price tag would top 3 million before the film was completed. When released, it was one of the most expensive films ever

A wacky publicity shot of Hans and Mary Healy for *The 5000 Fingers of Dr. T* (Columbia: 1953). At one time during production, Dr. T has a pet toucan.

Decisions, decisions ... Dr. T (Hans) can't make up his mind what to wear for his big day. A publicity photograph for Columbia's *The 5000 Fingers of Dr. T* (1953).

made. How much more Kramer felt would have been necessary to make it the musical he had envisioned is not known.

Because of its big budget and lavish sets, the film received a lot of media attention, and the progress of the production was written up regularly in *The Hollywood Reporter*, *Variety*, *The Los Angeles Daily News*, and other trade papers. The mood on the set was upbeat, and actors and workers from other sets would come by just to watch the filming of the fanciful musical numbers. One often told story was about the day the crew filmed the climactic ending scenes when the 500 little boys gather at Dr. T's enormous, double-decker piano. It seemed a simple enough idea at first, but the logistics of trying to put 500 boys—between the ages of five and nine—all in the same room at the same time and doing what has been scripted proved almost impossible. It was utter chaos. According to a review in *Time* magazine, "Getting '5,000 Fingers' on film posed one momentous problem. That was the rainy day when Stanley Kramer & Co. tried to film the scene where all the small boys play 'Chopsticks' on the double-decker piano monstrosity. By the time the big scene was ready to shoot, the '500' boys (there were actually only about 400) had managed to scatter outside into the rain and gorge themselves at a nearby hot-dog stand. Says Seuss: 'Have you ever tried to get 400 sick, wet boys to play a piano?'" The roughly three minutes of screen time took about five days to shoot. The number of boys used was pared down to around 150 to make things a bit more manageable. In keeping with state law, a classroom had to be established in an adjoining sound stage for the boys, and a teacher employed to make sure their studies were not interrupted. This is also where all the nervous parents waited during the long days of filming.

There were other problems on the set that had to do with a clash of personalities. An article—possibly tongue-in-cheek—appeared in April of 1952 in the *Los Angeles Daily News* describing how an unhappy, nine-year-old Tommy Rettig felt upstaged by the grown-ups: "They claim they've had trouble with me 'cause I'm so little, but that's just a rotten excuse. Wow, oughta see what they do to me every day of the week." Tommy went on to describe Conried as an "eyebrow twitcher": "Every time I'd get a good line to say, old Hans Conried starts waving his eyebrows at me or making silly gestures with his hands." Tommy accused Peter Lind Hayes of using double takes to steal a scene—even triple takes! Mary Healy unknowingly stole scenes too, according to Tommy: "She just stands out there in that pretty dancing costume and the first thing you know everyone on the set is looking at her. I'm afraid the audience will too."

To be fair, Tommy wasn't quite the innocent victim he made himself out to be. Conried is quoted as saying, "[Tommy] was always chewing gum and playing with his yo-yo. The little villain knew every line of dialogue and everybody's lyrics. If another actor blew it, he would correct [them]... He would stand under the camera on second and reflective shots and return lines while playing with that yo-yo." Conried was supposed to have facetiously confided that he had toyed with the idea of having Tommy "sandbagged," "only he was so small, he would have been hard to hit even by the best."

The renowned composer Frederick Hollander, who had studied with Engelbert Humperdinck and Richard Strauss in his native Germany, composed the musical score. Hollander was responsible for the

Dr. T (Hans) being dressed by his five valets while singing his "Dressing Song" ("Do-Me-Do-Duds"). For *The 5000 Fingers of Dr. T* (Columbia: 1953).

music to the German film that launched Marlene Dietrich's career—*The Blue Angel*. In the U.S., he would go on to compose music for many popular Hollywood musicals. *The 5000 Fingers of Dr. T* immediately captured Hollander's imagination, and he enthusiastically told an interviewer in 1952, "This is something altogether new. Children will love it, and their parents will get an equal bang out if it because it's really a wonderfully adult satire as well. The minute I heard the story, I rushed right home and wrote some music. I was so excited. It wasn't 'too' anything, because we didn't even have a script yet, but it just affected me that way." Hollander wrote a total of twenty-four different musical numbers that were filmed in their entirety. Eleven of these numbers would eventually be cut out of the final print of the film in the editing "bloodbath" that followed the disastrous premiere. The lavish, expertly choreographed (by Eugene Loring), and extremely expensive musical number called the "Dungeon Ballet" with its imaginary instruments—all very typically Dr. Seuss—was perhaps the most highly praised element in the film.

The music was inspired, but it was the lyrics written by Geisel that made the songs exceptional, and exceptionally weird. They all somehow passed the MPAA censors, though, without a hitch. Even the bizarre "Dressing Song" was approved. This number is sung by Dr. T as he is preparing himself for his big day—the day the 5000 "happy fingers" of the 500 little boys he has imprisoned will play his gigantic piano on the opening day of his "Institute." Dr. T is also preparing for his wedding, as he has "condescended" to take the widowed Mrs. Collins' hand in marriage (the lucky girl).

Conried—who had never been allowed

The big day has arrived, and Dr. T (Hans) is dressed in all his finery as he prepares to conduct his piano masterpiece: "Ten Happy Fingers." *The 5000 Fingers of Dr. T* (Columbia: 1953).

to sing a song or dance in a film before—did a thoroughly remarkable job as Dr. T, and gave his "villain" a comical, yet subtle, lisp. In the "Dressing Song" we see Dr. T being dressed from his underwear up by a squad of five young valets, whirling around, ever moving, as he sings about his "Do-Me-Do-Duds"—which consist of, with the exception of lavender spats, outlandish articles of women's clothing. All the while, he is actually being dressed in an out-of-this-world, demented rendition of a military outfit with tons of braid and fanciful "medals," and an enormously tall busby (he does get his "lavender spats," though). This scene alone must have taken days to prepare and rehearse, due to the intricacies of the maneuvers between the five valets and Conried. One misstep and the entire scene would have been ruined. It is apparent at the end of the "Do-Me-Do-Duds" scene that Conried was having a terrible time keeping the busby on. It looks like it eventually had to have an invisible string attached to it to keep it upright as Conried marched out of the scene, and it still looked like it was perched very precariously on his head.

Conried would say about *The 5000 Fingers of Dr. T* many years later: "It was a great, beautiful picture. The Americans have never made a really successful fantasy, although, of course, this was a comedic one. The picture was badly cut in fear and anguish of the reappraisal after it was made, even if it was evident to those knowledgeable but inartistic heads of studio that it might have been an artistic triumph, rather than a financial one. But in an attempt to make it [a commercial success], they cut over eleven musical numbers, and re-shot for one whole week. I had never had any such part before, never have since, and probably never will again. We rehearsed for eight weeks before I was engaged to shoot for eight weeks, which was an extravagance that I, as a bit player, had never known. To make this very long and tedious and somewhat tearful story short for me, the picture never made its print money back. It was comparable only to *Wilson* as one of the great money-losers of all time; it would stop conversation for some years thereafter at any Hollywood social gathering. If you mentioned it, people would laugh, and if you were connected with it, you might cough embarrassedly. At any rate, it was a big failure, although it did well and got marvelous reviews in Tokyo, Berlin, Paris, and London. If it had been a success, with my prominent part in the title role, it would have changed my life. The general public thinks of a break as being an opportunity—no. A break is an opportunity that pays off." For the rest of his life, when asked which picture was his favorite, he'd sadly tell the tale of *The 5000 Fingers of Dr. T*, and the big break that wasn't. To Conried, and others associated with the film, it was the hurried, ill-conceived, last minute editing job that ruined the film.

What prompted this hysterical hatchet job was the reaction of the audience at the West Coast sneak preview of the film. According to one witness, the people were filing out of the theater so quickly he thought the fire alarm had gone off! At the end, there was only one little boy left in the seats. He would have left too, but he was waiting for his mother to pick him up. The film was mistakenly marketed as a children's movie; it wasn't. *The 5000 Fingers of Dr. T* is an adult oriented fantasy—something almost totally unheard of in Hollywood. Then as now, the bottom line is money. An adult fantasy film without sex or graphic violence is just not considered a viable property. Maybe if Columbia had gone with the original script showing Mrs. Collins suspended in a cage over Dr. T's bed, and the headless henchmen, it might have given the film more shock value, and hence more box office appeal.

Columbia misguidedly pushed the idea of *The 5000 Fingers of Dr. T* being a children's movie so hard, it even sponsored a first of its kind "Junior Premiere" in Pasadena, California, on October 30, 1953. Tommy Rettig was there, along with Shelley Fabares, George "Foghorn" Winslow, and the Pasadena Boys Band.

Conried felt that it made sense as a story born out of a child's imagination, and any reality should have been kept out. As soon as you had a real piano teacher enter the scene, his broad performance as the Dr. Terwilliker of the boy's dream lost its power, and he felt he just came off looking like a bad, ham actor. He was very much against re-shooting the opening sequence of the film, and thus destroying the pure fantasy element that gave the story its continuity and viability. Conried said that Stanley Kramer took over the directing job for that final sequence, and oversaw the re-editing of the film. Years later, when the film was shown on television for the first time, Conried was again horrified to see it had been even further edited to accommodate the commercials. He lamented that the film had been "mutilated and cut with a broken beer bottle."

The reviews in the U.S. were generally favorable, such as this one by the Southern California Council of Church Women: "Vibrating with the imagination and originality of a Kramer production, this exquisite fantasy holds one spellbound, both through dream sequences and the every-day action." *The New York Times*, on the other hand, took a rather severe view: "The trouble is not in the audacity of those who made the film; it is in the weird confusion and grotesqueness of their fantasy. The nightmarish dreams of the youngster ... are not only lacking in humor but they have a sort of Freudian perversity. The symbolism concocted by Dr. Seuss and Allan Scott is mostly obscure and usually ugly; there are streaks of sheer sadism through the film...." The majority of reviewers were somewhere in the middle of these two opinions. The lack of bankable stars in the film was noted by many, but *The Los Angeles Times* did single out Conried by saying, "Hans Conried is tremendous as Dr. T, his pantomime being wonderful, and his characterization a brilliant blend of fiendishness and tongue-in-cheek."

The film opened in New York on May 29, 1953, at the Criterion on Broadway. A special 1:85 to 1 ratio wide screen and enhanced sound system were installed for the event. The film was screened in Los Angeles for various film critics in early June. Even though the notices from New York were some of the most acid and unmerciful comments printed, the public generally enjoyed the film. It was held over at the Criterion for well over a month. The promotional tour for *The 5000 Fingers of Dr. T* never materialized, no doubt because of financial reasons and the fact that Dr. T himself was unavailable.

Because of the huge financial loss, Kramer did not even like to discuss the film in his later years, and never kept a 35mm print in his collection. Conried noted in a later interview that Columbia Pictures destroyed all 35mm prints, along with the footage that was cut out of the original version of the film. There are a handful of still photographs in existence of some of the cut scenes, and the recordings of the eleven missing songs have been preserved. In 1952, Decca Records had signed a deal with Stanley Kramer Productions to produce a soundtrack album to coincide with the release of the film. Due to the failure of the picture, this soundtrack album was never officially released. There is an album in circulation that purports to be the original soundtrack, but it is a well-made copy produced in the 1970s. It is the only source for the missing musical numbers, however, and very rare.

There were big plans to release many promotional "Dr. T" themed items as well. Kramer Productions had a deal with Macy's department stores to sell "Dr. T" tee shirts, "Happy Fingers" caps (just like in the movie), toy musical instruments, and whimsical jewelry. As may be expected, these items are also very rare, and highly sought after by collectors.

In an attempt to make back a little of the money it lost, Columbia Pictures—in a feckless grab at the new "rock n' roll" craze sweeping the country—re-released *The 5000 Fingers of Dr. T* in 1958 under the title *Crazy Music*. The poster prominently featured Mary Healy and Peter Lind Hayes looking like a giddy couple, and spoke of the "hip" tunes. No one was going to be fooled that *Crazy Music* had anything to do with rock and roll, and the film again failed at the box office.

Luckily, in Conried's lifetime *The 5000 Fingers of Dr. T* became a cult classic, and would even be required viewing in many college film courses. It is interesting to note that the film has frequently been featured at gay film festivals around the country. Dr. Terwilliker has been described as the "first gay villain." Picking up on the comments from earlier reviews, there have been attempts in subsequent years to thoroughly analyze the film from a Freudian perspective—something that gave Conried quite a laugh towards the end of his life. The film was a product of the rich imagination of Dr. Seuss, and succeeds or fails as a pure fantasy. It is unfortunate the film can never be restored to what it once was so audiences today can view it as it was meant to be seen. What is left is miraculous enough to warrant the praise it has received, as it contains Conried's finest performance ever to be captured on film. There are few actors who could have pulled off a character like Terwilliker that demanded such a broad, comical—yet villainous—portrayal, and somehow managed to retain a measure of vulnerability. You almost feel sorry for Dr. T after he was so gloriously ecstatic giving his "This Is My Day!" speech, only to be foiled by Bart and his "music fix" and have all his wonderfully evil plans ruined. Conried's eyes shone with frenzied glee as Dr. T stood on the tall podium before his little victims, and he grandly spoke of how elated he was that 5000 little fingers were "all playing together on *my* piano... Every infinitesimal, microscopic piece of living tissue of those 5000 little fingers cringing and groveling before me... before ME...Dr. Terwilliker!"

The early drafts of the script have Bart shouting "Down with Terwilliker!" near the end of the film, which causes the Twin Guards (who were not killed in this version) to go berserk and strangle Terwilliker with their beard. Dr. T's face goes from white to purple, and "in convulsive agony, writhes on the floor." The final version has Dr. T being dragged off his podium by a group of little boys to an unknown fate.

The failure at the box office of *The 5000 Fingers of Dr. T*, *The Twonky*, and a third film released in 1953—*The Siren of Bagdad*—would leave Conried with an unknown fate career wise. *Siren* was one of those films that, as Conried would put it, "you didn't tell your friends about—when you needed the money." It was produced by Sam Katzman for Columbia Pictures in full Technicolor, and starred an aging Paul Henried as the not-so-dashing magician Kazah the Great. Conried plays his bumbling sidekick, Ben-Ali. Conried recalled it was "a terrible film, the kind we called 'tits-and-sand'—sort of a Western in burnoose. I think in two weeks we had a musical number, the burning of a city, an attack; it was unbelievable." The film was made so quickly, and cheaply, the director didn't even allow a second take to re-shoot when flubs were made (which was often). Conried was never one to purposely let down his fellow actors, but it is evident his heart was not in this one. He has some fun moments, but mostly it is embarrassing stuff. *The Sunday Journal and Star* of Lincoln, Nebraska, noted in its review of the film that working with a live camel has its hazards: "Conried's dromedary charge found the carrot treats, dragged him to the vegetable cache, expectorated a number of times, and could kick with a vengeance." No wonder Conried tried to forget this one.

So, while 1953 was an eventful year for the sheer amount of work by Conried that was released, and the visibility it afforded him with the public, Conried was actually far away from Hollywood in New York appearing in a hit Broadway play. He was not available to attend the West Coast premieres, or work with the media to promote any of the films. Absence does not make the heart grow fonder in Hollywood, and Conried's career was put in jeopardy by his hiatus in the Big Apple.

7

Can-Can *and the Brink of Oblivion*

Amidst all the flurry of film work during the years 1951 and 1952, there were a few radio shows still in production that Conried was able to benefit from as a regular cast member: *December Bride* with Spring Byington and Alan Reed, *My Friend Irma*, and *Life with Luigi*. Parke Levy, the creator of *December Bride* (who also wrote and directed the series), sent Conried an enigmatic telegram on the day the radio series premiered—June 8, 1952—saying, "May your part in *December Bride* do as much for you as *The Twonky*." As fate would have it, that turned out to be a backhanded sort of congratulatory message.

The work seemed plentiful enough for Conried during the early 1950s, but it was unmistakably clear he would no longer be able to make a living primarily through radio. His beloved medium was quickly drying up. Conried was forced to step back and seriously review all his options. The success of the television show *Pantomime Quiz* was boosting Conried's popularity, yet causing him a bit of unexpected embarrassment. Conried admitted to Hal Humphrey in an interview for *The Mirror* in 1952: "I get calls from movie studio executives who are ready to give me parts just on the strength of what I do at a silly party game. They don't know but what I'll fall flat on my face, but they're ready to sign me up. It's gratifying, but a little disconcerting." The article went on to note that Conried was holding out against taking any dramatic parts on television, because that would mean he would only work once a week, and he wouldn't make as much money as he could with comedy roles. In the same breath he admitted to feeling frustrated that he was only a supporting actor doing "low" comedy: "It's just a fancy way of calling us stooges. That's what I am really, just a stooge."

By 1952, most American households owned at least one television. Conried adamantly refused to have one in his house. He justified his decision by saying, "In the house of the hanged, one does not discuss rope." Whether he liked it or not, that little box was becoming an increasingly important source for acting jobs. Conried managed to make a good living, but he was becoming increasingly dissatisfied with the circumstances he found himself in as an actor. Alan Reed discussed the idea with a reporter for the *Los Angeles Times* of having his *December Bride* co-stars get together in a dramatic production as a sort of "holiday" from comedy. Conried enthusiastically commented, "To perform seriously again would, in small part, place a right index finger into the dike withstanding bravely the sea of frustration that ever threatens to engulf the public buffoon."

With the winds of change foreboding

a less favorable climate in Hollywood, Conried welcomed the call from New York producer Lee Sabinson. Sabinson was busy assembling a cast for a musical he was trying to stage, and remembered Conried from working at Columbia Studios many years earlier. Fresh from rehearsing and filming his numbers in *The 5000 Fingers of Dr. T*, Conried felt he was fully prepared to handle another song and dance role. Conried was never too shy to toot his own horn, and had no problem selling himself as something of a rising musical star. Sabinson's production was to be based on the Molière comedy *A Doctor in Spite of Himself*. Coincidentally, this had been one of the first plays Conried performed in after coming out to California in 1935. After a few more telephone discussions, a conference call was set up between Conried in Los Angeles, and the play's producers in New York. He sang the comical song "Titwillow" from Gilbert and Sullivan's *The Mikado*. They thought Conried did a fine comedic performance, and decided he would fit in very well as a member of the cast. Conried, anxious to prove his worth, suggested they listen to tapes of his radio performances with Abe Burrows. In fact, they could even call Burrows and he would be happy to provide a positive reference for his abilities. Sabinson took this suggestion to heart, and asked Burrows—who was casting a production of his own at the time—what he thought of Hans Conried. Burrows was delighted to hear of his old friend, and the idea hit him that Conried was just the actor he was looking for to fill a part in his new Broadway play: Cole Porter's *Can-Can*. Conried, he felt, would be perfect as the eccentric Bulgarian artist Boris Adzinidzinadze. The character's name was such a difficult one, Conried liked to jokingly say that Burrows actually gave him the part because he was the only actor who could pronounce it.

This turn of events worked out well for Conried, as the Sabinson play could not raise enough money to proceed with the production. Conried was unfazed by the loss, as he was beginning to feel there were too many musical numbers for him to handle. *Can-Can* seemed like a good fit for his talents, but accepting the role would require a huge lifestyle change. He wanted to do the right thing for his career, and his family, and would have many heart-to-heart talks with Margaret. The Conrieds were comfortably settled in their Los Angeles home, with their infant daughter Trilby. Doing the play would mean having to live in New York for at least a year, if the play was successful. Margaret knew her husband well, and encouraged Conried to follow his dream of being on Broadway. As an actor in Los Angeles, Conried always felt a twinge of illegitimacy about his work. He still harbored the belief from his youth that *real* actors were on the stage in New York. There was always the question in the back of his mind if he could measure up to their standards. Now, he would have his chance to find out. In later years, Conried made an effort to do a Broadway play now and then "just so I can look New York actors in the eye and say, 'I'm an actor too'—which means you live in a cold water flat and are underpaid."

The Conrieds set up house at the Fifth Avenue Hotel in January of 1953. Their old friends, Burnie and Ruth Craig—fellow Japanophiles, and frequent traveling companions—also came back east with the Conried family to keep them company. Rehearsals were in progress, and the play was being readied for its preview run in Philadelphia in March.

MaryAnn Gibson (née Cohan), who played Gabrielle, remembers Conried fondly as a warm, very funny, and fun loving man who was always a perfect gentleman. She joined the cast in Philly as a replacement for another actress, and only had three days to learn her lines. Her dressing room adjoined Conried's, and when he learned of

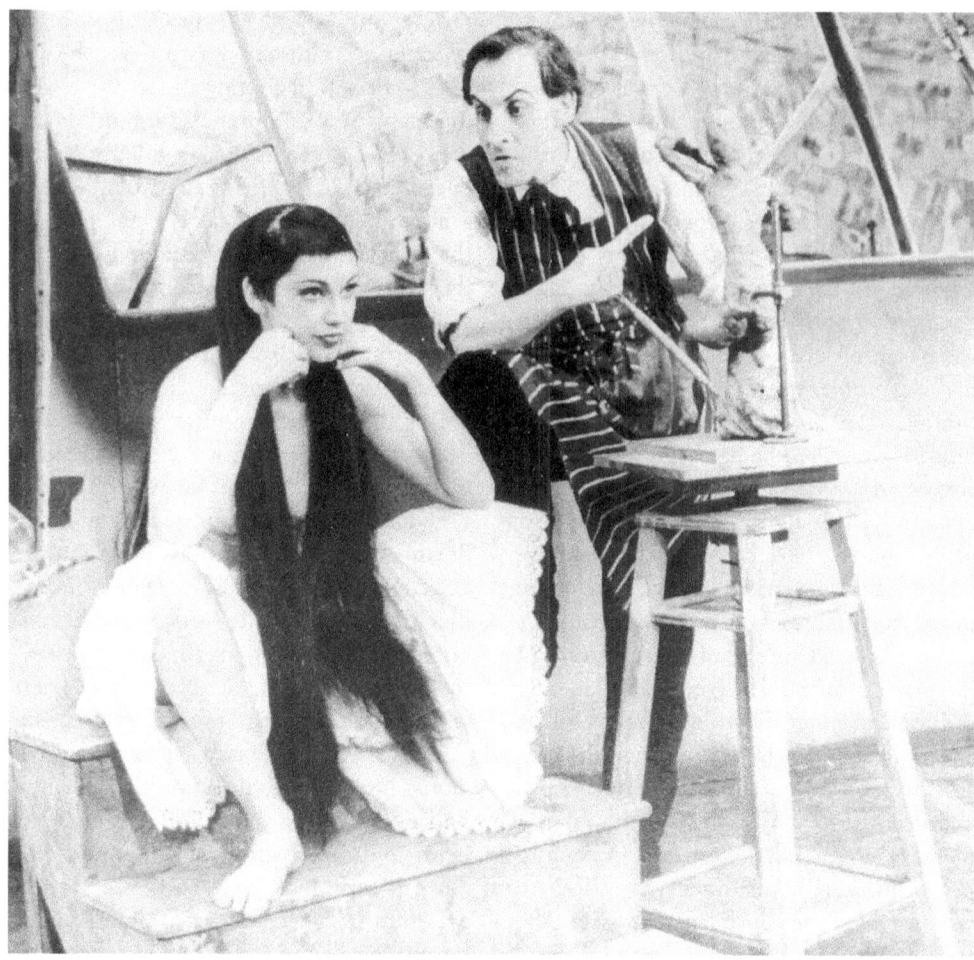

Hans, as the artist Boris Adzinidzinadze, with his model (Ruth Vernon). From *Can-Can* (1953).

her plight, he made a point to talk to her about it and be encouraging. Conried was later "amazed" that she was able to learn her lines in such a short time. MaryAnn especially enjoyed Conried's constant joking, and noted that the lovely young ladies of the cast were his favorite audience.

Producers Cy Feuer and Ernest Martin chose the right time to stage a play like *Can-Can*. With the popularity of the book and 1952 film about the French artist Toulouse-Lautrec, there was a wave of interest in France, especially Paris, of the 1890s. Feuer and Martin hired Abe Burrows to write the book, and also to direct. The very popular, but troubled, Cole Porter wrote the music and lyrics to the show. Porter was recovering from a nervous breakdown in 1951, and the death of his mother. Working on *Can-Can* would prove therapeutic to him, and allow him to channel his energy into something uplifting. It was difficult work for him, though. Porter commented on how in earlier days, the music didn't have to make sense, or match the "book" in any way: "Really, until Rodgers and Hammerstein, if you had to change a scene, a girl could come out in front of the curtain and sing anything or dance anything. But with *Can-Can* I have worked since last June." He was so enthusiastic about the production he wrote ten more songs than could be used. Porter was gratified that the play was shaping up to be such a success, but a little wistful too: "I hate to have the New York curtain go up, then the show is on and the whole thing is over for me. I lose a friend."

Burrows had never set foot in France, so he paid Paris a visit to research the history of the scandalous can-can, and the women who risked arrest to dance it on the stage. Of his experience, Burrows would tell a *New York Times* reporter: "I listened, snooped, really sniffed around. I wanted to feel the geography of the place, I wanted to watch the way people walked. And all of a sudden I was deep in it. I really fell in love. Those people were mugs. They're French, but they're mugs. It's funny; I'm a mug, too. Sinclair Lewis once described me as a mug with a college education."

The French actress Lilo was riding a wave of popularity at the time, and seemed well suited to the starring role in the play as La Mome Pistache, the owner of the club where the can-can is performed. Producers Feuer and Martin watched Lilo perform in

Hans, Gwen Verdon (on his lap), and assorted cast members from the Broadway production of *Can-Can* (1953).

Le Chanteur de Mexico while they were on a business trip to Paris in 1952. They really took notice after seeing the way she was "killing the people every night in a 3,200 seat house." They knew they had their star for *Can-Can*. The producers didn't count on Lilo being upstaged by a virtually unknown actress, Gwen Verdon. Verdon was cast to play one of the dancing girls (Claudine), who is romantically involved with Conried's character, Boris.

The part of the quirky artist given to Conried was broadly comical, and he played it a little like his Dr. T with a Bulgarian accent. Of course, the artist he plays is not villainous, but is a rather spineless sort, with little talent, who tries to survive by sponging off his girlfriend Claudine. One of the comedic highlights of the play is when Boris is pushed into challenging the art critic (and romantic rival) Hillaire to a duel over a bad review. Boris ends up fainting at the mere sight of Hillaire's sword, and gains the sympathy of Claudine once again. She manages to persuade the embarrassed Hillaire to write a glowing review of Boris' so-called art.

Can-Can opened on Broadway at the Shubert Theater on May 7, 1953, after a very successful, six-week preview run in Philadelphia. Normally, preview engagements only last two weeks, but the people of Philadelphia went wild for *Can-Can*, and made a celebrity out of a surprised Burrows. He was routinely stopped in the lobby of the theater, and on the street, by gushing fans who recognized him from his television work. All of this attention, and the huge turnout every night for *Can-Can*, inspired Burrows to work into the wee hours perfecting the show: rewriting, adding, or deleting material as needed. In the early morning hours he would hand his notes to his secretary to type up and distribute to the cast. An exhausted Burrows would then try to get a little sleep so he could make it down to the theater by 1:00 P.M. to rehearse the new material. The day after *Can-Can*'s Broadway premiere, *The New York Daily Mirror* published a glowing review of the show, and took special notice of Conried's performance saying, "[Conried] applies slapstick with just the right amount of pathos, as does every good clown. He had the first nighters rolling in the isles."

Living on the East Coast again was a struggle at first for Conried and his family, who had grown accustomed to the "sedentary, semi–Spanish life" of California. Conried spoke of his experiences in New York in a 1953 interview with William Hawkins: "I have a very young child, and out there we used to open the door and roll him [*sic*] out. Here you have to dress him, put him in a carriage, and wheel him through Washington Square." About *Can-Can* he would say, "I've done good parts, but this is a glamorous thing. The part of a big explosive ham is so suitable. But there's one aspect of this work that never occurred to me. You're up there making crowds laugh. Then you go to a little room and take off the paint. By that time, all the others have gone off. So you walk alone through the dark to the subway. In California, I used to go home for dinner, and still have light and time enough to work in the garden."

While in New York, Conried used his free time to perform in a few television game shows, and on a couple of episodes of *Schlitz Playhouse of Stars*. In the summer of 1953, Conried appeared as a regular on the TV quiz show *I'll Buy That* along with Vanessa Brown, Audrey Meadows, and Albert Morehead. The moderator was a young Mike Wallace—well before his hard-hitting news days. Guests would bring in an object identified only to the audience. The panel would then have to try to find out what this object is by asking questions. A newspaper review recalled one particular show from the 1953 summer season: "A lady of grim visage arrived the other day with an x-ray picture of her stomach. 'If I had the boys over for poker, would they like to see this object?' asked Hans Conried, who, on a modest morning show, has established himself as just about the drollest, brightest fellow to ever sit on a panel. The audience roars at this sort of question, and the panel is expert at asking them. Finally, it was established that the visitor had brought some kind of picture. 'Is it the sort of thing Marilyn Monroe might pose for? An early American calendar, perhaps?' When the object was at last identified, Mr. Conried was in no sense non-plussed. Bowing to the x-ray picture, he told the lady 'It's lovely, and it does you great credit.'"

Conried balanced his time looking for television work during the day and per-

Top: Hans, Vanessa Brown, and an uninvited "guest" taking a break in their luxurious dressing room from taping *I'll Buy That* (CBS: 1953).
　Bottom: The panel of the 1953 CBS summer replacement TV quiz show: *I'll Buy That*: L-R: Albert Morehead, Audrey Meadows, Hans, and Vanessa Brown.

Hans hamming it up as Ben Ali from the disappointing 1953 Columbia Pictures release: *The Siren of Bagdad.*

forming in *Can-Can* at night. Due to his stage commitment, Conried was not able to attend the New York premiere of *The 5000 Fingers of Dr. T.* He did manage to see the film, and so did other members of the *Can-Can* cast. The film role gave Conried, if only temporarily, a little added glamour with his friends in the cast who were in awe of this "movie star." Conried was able to celebrate the opening of the magical film at Eddie Condon's jazz club. A newspaper reporter snapped a picture of Conried sitting at a table with fellow revelers "The Blackburn Twins," with their partner Marion Colby, and Condon himself. Conried looks like he's having a good time, though jazz was not a favorite musical style. Jazz, he confessed, "makes me nervous."

Considering the generally negative tones of the New York reviews, Conried must have had a pretty good idea that his grand hopes and dreams of becoming a motion picture "star" were not going to be realized. When *The 5000 Fingers of Dr. T* opened on the West Coast, his agent sent him regular reports about the film's reception, and they too, sadly, were not promising.

Conried already knew *The Twonky* would go down to defeat, and *The Siren of Bagdad* wasn't anything to write home about. But *The 5000 Fingers of Dr. T* was special. He had placed all his bets on that one horse to win, not just show. He lost it all—maybe not in a literal sense, but considering how low Conried was feeling at this time, he certainly had lost something dear to him.

An actor, by necessity, has to develop a thick skin to survive in a business that seems to delight in ripping careers to shreds. After experiencing the indifference of a large segment of the public, and general panning by the critics, Conried uncharacteristically allowed the failure of *The 5000 Fingers of Dr. T* to bore a hole deep into his heart. He was pleased to hear there were a few critics who praised the work as an "art film," but he knew full well that artsy films do not make big money in Hollywood—this was especially true in the Hollywood of the early 1950s—and that was all the major studios were interested in. Conried's film career was in serious jeopardy, but he was too busy performing on stage to devote much time to his dilemma. *Can-Can* was a phenomenal success, and he was enjoying the moment, with the rest of the cast, each night the curtain went up to a packed house.

By the time it closed on Broadway in late 1954, *Can-Can* would be performed a staggering 892 times. Conried remained with the show for 504 performances before deciding to end his engagement and return home to California. He had been asked to stay on another year, but he was growing a bit weary of the show, and his mind was starting to wander. Conried later recalled that after about the 497th performance, he found himself musing about mundane things while he was in mid-song. Or he would look out over the audience and notice a man was asleep in the second row, or there was an attractive lady with a low cut dress in row three (he was afraid she'd catch cold), and blow a line he'd done flawlessly over 400 times before. It was time to move on. The only question was: Where?

By the end of 1953, Margaret was well into her second pregnancy. The baby was due not long after the start of 1954. This may have been another reason Conried did not want to stay another year in New York. The Conrieds welcomed their first son on February 4, 1954. In keeping with old family tradition, the boy was given his father's name: Hans Georg Conried III. The big baby had his father's long, lanky limbs, but his mother's blue eyes. Trilby was nearly three years old by this time, and used to being the only child. She would have a couple more surprises—thanks to her parents—fairly soon.

The foursome returned to California in the spring of 1954. Finding work again in Los Angeles after being away so long was not proving to be easy. With a growing family, the bills were growing too; Conried needed to find a steady job soon. Radio work had nearly dried up by 1954, but there were still a handful of popular serials being produced. *Lux Radio Theatre*, *The Railroad Hour*, and *Romance* offered Conried consistent employment on the radio, often in well-crafted, dramatic offerings.

Suspense would also continue to provide Conried with an outlet for his dramatic talents. The October 21, 1954, broadcast of "Rave Notice" was a starring vehicle for Conried, and a perfect fit for his craftsmanship as an actor. Conried played the role of Sam, an egotistical ham actor who is cut from a mediocre production by a bloated, self-important director. Not only does he lose a job, but must endure the heartless director's vicious tongue when he callously tells Sam: "You are no actor—you stink!" Sam plots to kill the director and purchases a shotgun, making sure he selects a model that will "shoot through fat." The disgruntled actor does shoot the offending director—in broad daylight—and tries to feign madness to get out of a death sentence. Sam's creation of this new role as a homicidal maniac would provide Conried a lush, verdant field to develop Sam's technique and displays of insanity. Conried succeeded in working himself up to such intensity in this part, he must have been emotionally and physically drained afterwards.

On television, Conried especially enjoyed the work he did for the *U.S. Steel Hour* episode entitled "Presento" (Japanese slang for "gift"), starring Shirley Yamaguchi, Don Taylor, and Jack Klugman. The show had many comedic elements to it, but there was a more dramatic theme involving Taylor as an American journalist who was advocating equal rights for Japanese women. Having a Japanese woman (Yamaguchi) given to him as a "presento" was the source of comedy, and serious commentary, about the role of Japanese women in their society between the journalist, his career girl fiancée, and a French envoy, Jean Pierre Hautcorne (Conried). Larry Tajiri, a reporter for the *Pacific Citizen*, said in his review, "Hans Conried, one of the better TV-radio-movie actors, was splendid in the role of the French attaché who stayed on in Japan to marry a girl named Kimiko, and who served as interpreter between Taylor and Miss Yamaguchi. Conried's handling of the Japanese language probably shamed a lot of Nisei who certainly can't speak it as well as he." Conried certainly did give the impression he could speak Japanese fluently. He couldn't, really, but did understand a great deal of the language, and had a substantial vocabulary.

Candid shot of Hans at home with his new baby son, Hans III, and Trilby (1954).

One of the highlights of this episode was an authentic Japanese tea ceremony. Shirley Yamaguchi and Conried both studied this ancient art from the same teacher: Sosei Matsumoto, of the Ura Senke School in Los Angeles. Conried was reputed to have been an expert in all aspects of this exacting ceremony, and also studied ikebana (flower arranging). Because of "Presento," Conried made the cover of *Scene* magazine, which covered subjects of interest regarding Asian culture for Western audiences. Their review centered on the tea ceremony, and praised Conried and Shirley Yamaguchi for performing the ancient rite so accurately.

The fact that he accurately performed the tea ceremony probably pleased Conried more than any critic's praise of his acting. Not only did Conried collect hundreds of pieces of Japanese art and other Asian works of art, he also actively sought to learn everything he could about the history, culture, and legends of Asia. He would keep adding to his library frequently, and he eventually could boast a collection of books on Japanese art alone that totaled over 500 volumes.

Conried was an avid reader of just about anything he could get his hands on. He would open the cover and enter the date he started reading the volume and the date he ended, just to keep track of it all. "It's kind of a sickness, this compulsion to collect," Conried would say in later life. He described a collector as "someone who is alive, has a lust to possess, organize, and know, and who follows his sickness with passion."

An item that appeared as a full-page advertisement in *Variety* magazine on June 25, 1954, may have been a routine request by an actor for employment offers, but it strikes one as poignant, somehow. After twenty-nine years in the business, Conried found himself in the position of placing an ad that read:

> Hans Conried
> Sometime player in these parts,
> Having just returned from
> New York

HANS CONRIED

SOMETIME *PLAYER* IN THESE PARTS,
HAVING JUST RETURNED FROM
NEW YORK
WHERE THE PUBLICK WAS PLEASED
TO HAVE HIM SHEW HIMSELF IN EXCESS OF
500 PERFORMANCES
AS FEATURED *COMEDIAN* IN THE PLAY YCLEPT
"CAN-CAN"
(STILL UPON THE BOARDS),
DESIRES TO AGAIN LIVE & WORK IN THIS FAIR CITY,
WHERE FOR SOME YEARS PAST
HE BELIEVES HE HAS ENJOYED
A MODEST REPUTATION AS A CRAFTSMAN OF

SOBRIETY, COMPETENCE & VERSATILITY.

HE, THEREFORE, HUMBLY RECOMMENDS HIMSELF
TO ALL THOSE WHO, EMPLOYING PLAYERS, DESIRE TO
FAVOUR WITH THEIR COMMANDS,
THEIR MOST OBEDIENT SERVANT,

HANS CONRIED.

TO BE MET WITH AT THE SIGN OF
SID GOLD
CR. 1-7149

Variety ad that ran on June 25, 1954 asking for work in Hans' flowery, Elizabethan manner. Hans drew the caricature back in the early 1940s. From the Hans Conried Collection, Department of Special Collections, Boston University.

Where the publick was pleased
To have him shew himself in excess of
500 Performances
As featured Comedian in the play yclept
"Can-Can"

(Still upon the boards),
Desires to again live & work in this fair city,
Where for some years past
He believes he has enjoyed
A modest reputation as a craftsman of

Shirley Yamaguchi, Hans, and an unidentified actress on the set of "Presento" in 1954 (*U.S. Steel Hour*, CBS). Hans was intrigued by the Japanese tea ceremony, and studied with a master in Los Angeles to perfect the technique. From the Hans Conried Collection, Department of Special Collections, Boston University.

Sobriety, Competence & Versatility.
He, therefore, humbly recommends himself
To all those who, employing players, desire to
Favour with their commands,
Their most obedient servant,
Hans Conried.

All interested parties were referred to Sid Gold, who was still managing Conried's career.

Times must have indeed been particularly difficult for Conried to place an ad such as this. He was never one to mind blatant self-promotion, but there were certain things—auditions, for instance—that always left a bad taste in his mouth. There was something very cold in the way actors were lined up for auditions while producers and directors looked them over from head to foot. A few would be asked to step forward, and had to give a cold reading on the spot. There was also something cold about an ad begging for work in a trade paper. Desperate times require desperate measures, however, and Conried was willing to do whatever it took to get himself back on his feet in Hollywood.

By the end of 1954, Margaret would discover she was pregnant with their third child. Conried was managing to remain financially solvent in spite of his stalled career, but the timing could have been better. Fortunately, it wouldn't be long before old friends would turn up again and throw Conried a lifeline.

Part III
Jack Paar and the Call of the Road

8

A *"TV Personality" Is Born*

The year 1955 would begin slowly for Conried's career. Radio work was sporadic, and television was not yet providing a stable substitute for the shortfall in his earnings. There was an adversarial atmosphere between the new breed of television directors and actors who had once worked almost exclusively in radio. Conried recalled, "It wasn't easy, having been a radio actor; we were all considered bad actors, you see. And all of the television directors were young men, and I supposed they may have been wary of men who were more veteran than they in years, if not in actual knowledge, and we did not get on. Ex–radio actors did not go gracefully into television." The latter sentiment is eloquently expressed in a statement Conried gave to the press many years later: "I used to be a radio actor, but then television came and killed us all off in one season. The networks devoured their own child in order to give birth to another one. The rose was full-blown, and then, suddenly, it was torn asunder by violent hands." He went on to describe television as "a bird that fouls its own nest." The resentment was strong, but Conried's will to survive was even stronger.

Conried begrudgingly purchased a "twonky" for his home. One can imagine him kicking it a few times when no one was looking. He told a young reporter, who had his own TV show, how he had developed a "morbid fascination" with watching his old movies: "I see a young man of twenty or so, naturally slim with all his hair, who now works for nothing in competition with you on TV."

Walt Disney proved to be a great friend to Conried, and over the years gave him the opportunity to work on a large number of quality projects for his production company, Buena Vista. *Peter Pan* was the first big name project that Conried lent his talent to, but he also worked on a few two-reel animated shorts. The first one, *Ben and Me*, was released the same year as *Peter Pan*, and required the same rigorous work schedule, though on a much smaller scale. Conried was the voice of Thomas Jefferson in the short subject, and also posed for the live action film that helped the animators craft their Jefferson on the screen.

In 1955, Conried worked on the Disney produced *Davy Crockett* series for television. *Davy Crockett at the Alamo* was a three-part special featuring Conried as a dapper, eastern gentleman named Thimblerig who joins the group for their trek to the Alamo (with disastrous results). The show would prove a boon to Conried's career: "It was very popular, of course; and I was suddenly rocketed into great fame among the younger element in America. [My family and I] went on a camping trip at that time with a very close friend of mine, not a fellow theatrically inclined. I was introduced to the others at this camping site, and no one knew me, which was quite all right. I remember overhearing part of a conversation some of them had with my little girl, who was two or three. And one kid said, 'Trilby, your daddy's a movie star!' And she, in all her innocence said, 'No, papa's not that. Papa's an actor.'"

Conried had a little more time around the house in those days, and he enjoyed taking an occasional camping trip—something he would have earlier avoided like the plague. He and Margaret had a wide variety of friends who were not in showbiz at all; many were fellow collectors of Asian art. A small group of them encouraged Conried to "rough it" in the big outdoors, although they didn't stray too far from the well-maintained campsites with all the necessary amenities. Conried was very fond of the outdoors closer to home, and loved to work in his big, beautiful garden whenever he had the chance. Sadly, a good deal of the garden—indeed, almost the entire backyard—would eventually slide down the hillside due to years of erosion and earthquakes.

Radio was going through its painful transformation from a source of quality comedy and drama programming to the purveyor of Top 40 hits and news. Golden Age favorites Edgar Bergen and that loveable little splinter, Charlie McCarthy, managed to hang on to their radio show until 1956. Conried was a frequent guest in a wide variety of roles, including a tree doctor who was called in one day to cure an ailing Charlie.

On November 7, 1955, Alexander Conried was born, a charming fellow with his mother's blonde hair and his father' dark brown eyes. It's a good thing Conried was home a bit more during this period. Poor Margaret had her hands full with a four-year-old, a toddler, and now a new baby. The Conried family was not complete just yet, though. The following summer, Margaret would once again be expecting.

The Conrieds' household expenses must have gone through the roof. Along with his growing family, Conried's elderly parents were still receiving his financial support. He took whatever legitimate job came his way to keep his head above water, which might explain why he accepted a part in the Lewis and Martin film *You're Never Too Young*. As the fussy hair stylist Francois, Conried mainly played the stooge for Jerry Lewis in one short scene near the beginning of the film. This would not be the last time Conried would work for Jerry Lewis. Many years later, when a surprised Conried was reminded of how often he had worked with Martin and Lewis, his only comment was: "I must remember to stay out of those."

Conried had a chance to play a more complex character on the radio series *Romance*. On the December 10, 1955, episode, "The Grasshopper," Conried played a thoroughly despicable artist who is able to charm a married woman into a one-night-stand. The cad callously derides and ridicules her the next day. Here was a chance for Conried to play a serious character who was not at all sympathetic. "The Grasshopper" was loosely based on the Chekov story of the same name.

As a Christmas treat, *The 20th Century Fox Hour* simulcast on television and radio "The Miracle on 34th Street" (a.k.a.: "Meet Mr. Kringle") on December 12, 1955. It was a well-acted, abbreviated version of the well-known story that retained enough of the important elements to be highly entertaining. Conried's role of Mr. Shellhamer, the manager of Macy's toy department, wasn't much to work with, but he made his character believable. Shellhamer was the epitome of the high-strung, over-worked manager trying to cope with the busiest season of the year.

Film roles were becoming increasingly elusive by the mid–1950s, and even when Conried was signed for a part, it didn't always mean his form would grace the big screen. Printed on more than one list of Conried's recent achievements included with the standard publicity kits as late as

1959 was the 1956 MGM feature *Meet Me in Las Vegas*. The picture is a star-studded affair loaded with quirky little cameos by such big names as Peter Lorre and Paul Henried. Conried had his own brief cameo in this over-long film, and was the unfortunate victim of some last minute editing.

Conried was able to find more substantive work in television. One program of note was the 1956 CBS *Ford Theatre* musical program "High Tor" with Bing Crosby and newcomer Julie Andrews. It is a syrupy, half-baked love story, but it afforded Conried a relatively meaty role as an unethical real estate developer. Though the part called for the usual broad comedic brushstrokes, Conried was able to impart a bit more humanity into his characterization than was customary under similar circumstances. Mr. Biggs wasn't just a stooge—there were shades of gray to his character. The ability to bring some creative life to a production that was otherwise devoid of any creativity is a credit to Conried's considerable skill as an actor.

Against his better judgment, Conried signed on to appear in the Joshua Logan directed Marilyn Monroe vehicle, *Bus Stop*. Conried spoke about his experience many years later: "I played the part of Eliot Elisifon, the photographer. It was a walk-on, the tiniest, most modest bit. At the time, I was important enough to refuse such a part, but I was conned by a very famous man named Joshua Logan. He said 'Mr. Conried, I think you're the funniest man in America,' and like a fool I bit. For less money than I should have gotten, and I shouldn't have taken such a lousy part at that stage in life, I went down to Phoenix where they were shooting at a rodeo. And of course, to this day, Mr. Logan has not reiterated, certainly not in my presence (probably that's because I've never been in his presence) that I am the funniest actor in America. You see, even a mature actor can be most ingenuous on occasion." If nothing else, Conried was excited about the free tickets to the rodeo he received as a perk.

Conried's first chance to work on television with his old friend Danny Thomas came in 1954. Thomas had a successful sitcom originally called *Make Room for Daddy* that first went on the air in 1953. (At the beginning of the fourth season in October 1957, the title was changed to *The Danny Thomas Show*.) Though Conried would find fame as Danny's irascible old Uncle Tonoose, one of his other early roles on the show was Margaret's irresponsible cousin Carl. Carl shows up at the Williams' home unexpectedly, and moves in indefinitely. Carl charms the kids, but Danny can't tolerate Carl's mooching ways. It is a delightful performance. Conried would return as an acting coach for Terry, a Cockney con man, and a news reporter before settling into his role as Tonoose.

According to Conried, "This 'Tonoose' character is something of a prototype. Actually, I guess you would say he is the same character as Professor Kropotkin, the role I did on the *My Friend Irma* series—only the name has been changed to protect the guilty...." Tonoose was supposed to be a man in his sixties, with white hair and a prominent stomach. Conried spent long hours in the make-up man's chair being fitted with a large, rubber nose (one that would rival Danny Thomas' schnozz), moustache, and padding for his midsection. Though he towered over Thomas, the make-up made Conried appear as if he really were Danny's Uncle Tonoose, who in real life had been like a father to him.

In 1956, Conried would get his feet wet in the refreshing pool of live theatre; a place he would find himself swimming in often during the next couple of decades. It had been almost sixteen years since he performed on stage. The 1956 production was the light opera *The Student Prince*, and Conried played the part of Johann Lutz, the Prince's valet. The show premiered on July

30, 1956, and ran until August 11th at the Greek Theatre in Los Angeles. *The Citizen News* wrote approvingly that "[Hans Conried] has the gift of taking the lines of any play, and making them his own."

Delighted with the success of *The Student Prince*, and the extra money, Conried was successful in building a relationship with the St. Louis Municipal Opera in St. Louis, Missouri. This arrangement would allow Conried to spend as many summers as he could performing in light opera productions with The Muni. His first appearance in a St. Louis summer production was in a revival of *Can-Can* in 1957, with Conried reprising his role as the artist, Boris Ad-

Conried family portrait taken in the spring of 1957. L-R: Margaret, baby Edie, Hans III, Alexander, Hans, and Trilby.

zinidzinadze. Conried spoke to a reporter about his experience: "In St. Louis we play in a big bowl which seats 12,000. If it rains, we work for an hour; that's so they won't be obligated to give the money back. We just get wet and make our jokes, but the dancers sometimes have trouble."

In his personal life, Conried had to deal with the realities of his father's imminent death and the birth of his fourth child. His mother was not strong enough to handle all of the preparations that needed to be made for Papa Conried, and relied heavily on her son to take care of things. The Conrieds' newest addition to the family, a dark-haired little girl named Edith, after her paternal grandmother, was born on February 5, 1957. Sadly, within a few weeks, Papa Conried passed away. The funeral was a traditional one, which means it was very expensive. Conried was not quite prepared for the reality of how much it would cost to bury his father, and was shocked by the bill. He vowed that his family would never have to go through such a dreadful ordeal when his time came.

The painful experience with his father spurred Conried to find the least expensive and least disturbing alternative to a traditional burial. He came across the idea of donating his body to medical science. Not only would his lifeless body possibly do some good, but also the medical school would take care of cremating his remains, and return them to the family at no cost. He registered with the University of California's Medical School, and made sure to carry his donor card with him at all times. As soon as they were old enough, he sat each of his children down and explained to them exactly what it meant to be a donor. This honesty astounded visitors to the Conried home, who exclaimed that even as young as five years of age the children knew exactly what it meant to donate one's organs and why, and could explain it very matter-of-factly. It is a window into Conried's metaphysical make-up to note that his worldly flesh meant little to him. Though he professed not to be a follower of any particular religious path, his spirituality seemed to lean more heavily towards Eastern philosophies.

Another old friend, Jack Paar, had found his way into television in the early 1950s. At first, Paar worked as a host for a few game shows before being given his own variety show by CBS in 1953. The format of *The Jack Paar Show* would develop into the more recognizable "talk show" style of program with the addition of celebrity guests. After the demise of the CBS show, NBC managed to lure Paar over to their side in 1957. Paar was signed to take over the reigns of *The Tonight Show* after Steve Allen's departure. It proved to be a highly successful move. Conried was one of the old friends Paar gathered around to appear on the first week's broadcasts. *The Tonight Show* featuring host Jack Paar premiered on July 29, 1957.

Paar was well known for his "fanatical loyalty" (as Conried described it) to his old friends, and made sure to hire a group of them to surround him during his maiden voyage as *The Tonight Show* host. "If Paar ever had a show, and there was a cake to be cut," Conried would say, "there was always a slice for me." Though extremely grateful to Paar, Conried never quite understood what motivated this strong sense of loyalty. A befuddled Conried admitted, "I've never thrown myself between him and a mad dog."

Whatever the reasons, Paar had a deep respect for his old friend and would say of him, "Hans adds class to our show; an Elizabethan kind of fun. He's a wonderful talker with that beautiful flowery speech of his ... and Hans has that wonderful wit. He can top most of the so-called wits around here, including me. He has the ability to lie back and wait, for an hour if necessary, to get that barb. Then, *zing!*"

As Conried realized when he first

stepped in front of a television camera, it can be rather disconcerting to be introduced simply as "Hans Conried": "It's quite a change for an actor used to playing characters to be introduced by his own name. I used to say to myself, 'Who am I? What the hell am I playing?' You develop a characterization; you create a personality. You become someone the audience finds witty, and eventually they laugh at anything you say. I wouldn't like to think that sardonic, witty façade is the person my family and friends know ... but I wonder if it's all so insincere and unreal. Good manners and all sorts of 'civilized behavior'—it's in large part a façade, a disguise for natural behavior.... I'm not sure what kind of character Hans Conried is. I wouldn't dare inquire."

Paar was asking Conried to come on his show just as he was: no script to memorize, no dreaded rehearsals. Conried was initially stunned by his friend's offer, and incredulously asked Paar, "You mean, I don't have to do anything?!" Conried recalled that Paar calmly replied, "No, just talk, Hans. You have a big mouth." It was all very loose and informal. In fact, doing any kind of prepared "act," according to Conried, was inviting disaster: "It is very dangerous to perform on the Paar show. The audience is too intimate, and the atmosphere too stark. I remember a famous chanteuse, who shall remain nameless, and her attempt to do the same thing on Paar's show as she does in the swank hotel rooms. She died—it was horrible! It is better to go on cold and just rely on Mother Wit. Jack asks me backstage before the show if I have some new story to tell, and I say no, and he shrugs his shoulders and walks out on stage." The only thing Conried had to remember each night was, "when Jack looks at me the first time I start talking—when he looks at me the second time, I stop."

After appearing each night on *The Tonight Show*—later renamed *The Jack Paar Show*—for a full week, the press was buzzing about this "new" discovery. They referred to Conried as a "personality." Though flattered, Conried was a bit dumbfounded at all the attention he was receiving. His pride was hurt just a little bit too: "After 25 years, I finally found success—by sitting alongside Jack Paar and uttering inanities."

These "inanities" were causing quite a stir, and Conried was being offered a sea of television work (including commercial endorsements), as well as roles in the legitimate theatre. Record companies were also requesting his services for various projects. Conried would say of his changing fate, "Heretofore I was an actor; now I'm a personality. I'm not sure what a personality is, and I hope never to find out, as I like to keep on getting away with it. I attribute my current inflation to my association with Jack Paar. And don't ask me what Paar has because if I knew I'd try to bottle it and sell it. You see, on the Paar show, in the overall roast ham each clove must have its distinction. I suppose I supply something however lethargic, wry, mordant, and warped I may be." Even with all the success, Conried claimed to be relatively unfazed by it all: "I've never worried much about whether I was known as an actor, or as a personality. I just want to stay alive."

Conried did even better than just "stay alive." Paar would ask him back on the show so often he was considered a semi-regular along with Dody Goodman, Jose Mellis, Genevieve, and a select group of Paar faithful. The flush of fame Conried was now enjoying revitalized his career, and allowed him to move in new directions. There was a trade-off, though. Conried was only being offered comedic roles. The idea of Conried as a comedic actor would become solidified by the late 1950s. One major studio's casting director was quoted by *TV Guide* magazine as saying, "When you think of Conried, you think instantly of a comic actor. I would guess that producers feel audiences might have the same reaction, that they would instinctively laugh at the sight of him when they really weren't supposed to." Another casting director said, "I've worked with Conried only twice, and each time he played a comic part. He is the kind of personality that seems to register only in that vein. You look at him and you laugh. He can do Shakespeare beautifully—on radio. But when you see him, the entire aspect is comic."

After reading such remarks, Conried said with an air of resignation, "You do what you are asked to do. Some of the things I am asked to do are a little silly, to be sure, but this is a part of the craft, and you bring to each job the very best you have." Commenting on the same theme a few years later after playing a number of humorous villains on television and the stage, Conried said, "People know I'm up to no good when they see me skulking around ... but I guess I don't have the proper villainous features. They laugh instead of hissing. It's that kind of thing that, were I not so firm in my self-confidence, would make me feel inadequate."

In contrast to the comedy parts he was increasingly being offered, Conried landed the role of an eccentric artist on the crime drama *Dragnet*. The episode—"The Big Howard"—featured only the principal actors on the series, Jack Webb and Ben Alexander, and Conried. All of the action took place during an interrogation in the artist's studio. It was a very tightly woven, psychological drama that Conried found a welcome diversion: "Not that playing an eccentric artist is a new part for me, but this one isn't the putty nose and baggy pants variety. It's a relief to get away from low comedy for a change."

As a result of wowing people with his witty, erudite self on *The Jack Paar Show*, Conried was offered a job in October of 1957 as a regular panelist on the NBC Saturday morning quiz show, *What's It For?* Prior to its first broadcast, Conried told a reporter, "It will be a program dealing with new inventions. Four adult, sober, and apparently sensible people will try to guess, over a period of thirty minutes, what are the purposes of the devices that are brought before them. It will be very light and, I trust, amusing." One of Conried's fellow panelists was old friend, and Broadway producer, Abe Burrows.

His run on *The Danny Thomas Show* as Uncle Tonoose would continue until the show's cancellation in 1971. Even though he only appeared on the show three times during a season, many of the people he met stubbornly identified him with Tonoose: "Since I started this role, people stop me in the street and greet me in Arabic. Since I don't speak Arabic, I usually reply with a cordial 'Gezundheit!' or 'L'chayim', and let it go at that...." Conried eventually learned a few words of Arabic from Danny Thomas. Thomas assured Conried they were friendly words of greeting. An embarrassed Conried later found out the hard way the Arabic words were actually expletives!

Danny Thomas and Conried loved to kid each other on the set. Thomas wrote in his 1991 autobiography: "Hans took great delight in insulting me, and I loved every minute of it. Once, watching my habit of chewing tobacco and using spittoons, which I had set up all over the soundstage, he said, 'I once did a scene with an un-housebroken bear who was neater than you are.' He said terrible things like that with such delightful haughtiness that I could never get mad at him." Angela Cartwright—who played the youngest daughter, Linda, on the show—said recently, "I remember Hans [Conried] very fondly from our days of working together on *Make Room for Daddy*... I was only four when I started the show and to me he was a big man, full of spunk and energy. We filmed the show in front of a live audience every Thursday night with three cameras and there were very rarely any retakes. Hans was always prepared. I would see him backstage before his entrance with intensity and focus reviewing the incredible amount of dialogue he always had in the show." According to Marjorie Lord (the second Mrs. Williams), Thomas used to tease her and Conried constantly for being in the theatre, or as Thomas mockingly pronounced it: "thee-a-tah." His not-so-pleasant experience with the stage actress Jean Hagen, as his first wife Margaret on *Make Room for Daddy*, probably soured him on thespians.

It was gratifying for Conried that Danny Thomas allowed him to play a variety of characters on *Make Room for Daddy* in the early days, and he felt the huge popularity of Uncle Tonoose was bittersweet because of the fact it limited his versatility as an actor. Thomas would no longer allow him to play any other role after a while because of the character's success. When asked about Uncle Tonoose near the end of his life, Conried commented sardonically, "That was one of my early crimes. It's like the mark of Cain. It still follows me around."

In 1957, Conried went to New York to appear in NBC television's special salute to General Motors' 50th anniversary. It was a big extravaganza packed with lots of Hollywood stars. Conried took note of the autograph seekers who surrounded the performers as they left the studio: "There was a crowd of kids outside the Brooklyn studio every day waiting for any autographs they could get. They'd hold books and pencils under my nose and I never turned one down, even though I'm sure they didn't have the vaguest idea who or what I was. Only I didn't sign my right name once, and none of them ever complained. I'd write any name that came to mind; Ramon Navarro, Gypsy Rose Lee—it didn't matter. Once, I even used the name of our pet poodle." Conried wanted to make it clear that his complaint was not inspired by his lack of star status: "Please, don't get the idea that I go around eating my heart out because I am not a big star. But when some clown comes up and asks for your autograph, and you capriciously sign the name 'Milton Sills', and this clown doesn't know the difference, then that hurts!"

Conried was becoming a hot commodity on television, which caught the attention of ad agencies who felt he was the perfect choice to hawk their clients' products. The work was easy for him, and financially quite lucrative, but Conried always had a nagging doubt about doing commercial endorsements: "With residual payments, they can be very attractive. But, there's always a terrible fear that you will destroy yourself—that you will be associated forever, perhaps, with a certain kind of laxative." This fear quickly passed, and Conried went on to ally himself with a large number of commercial clients. One of these clients, *The New York Times*, paid Conried $500 per spot for two radio ads in 1958. This income would soon become a very important part of his yearly earnings.

The largest single advertising contract Conried had in his career was with Seagram, who hired him to sell their gin. His association with Seagram began in 1957 and would continue until late 1959. The contract was for a series of print ads that appeared in a wide variety of publications. The ads consisted of a picture of Conried in some wild get-up, and a few words about Seagram's gin. Conried appeared as a sophisticate in a tuxedo, a beatnik, a World War One flying ace, a snake charmer, a big game hunter, and a dizzying array of other characters.

Towards the end of his association with Seagram, Conried described the relationship to Hedda Hopper: "The deal is on a yearly basis, but how long the association will last I can't say. They're re-using old pictures now. Once a year they bring me to New York and fly a fine photographer in from Paris. We meet for a minimum of 120 exposures while an army of at least twenty

A "TV Personality" Is Born

Magazine ad for Seagram's Golden Gin, circa 1958. From the Hans Conried Collection, Department of Special Collections, Boston University.

crew-cut young advertising cadets and a sprinkling of vice presidents stand by smiling. They all must be paid for something, but I don't know what. I don't drink, but I go to their Christmas parties; they put a glass in my hand and I stand smiling while people tell me they like me on TV."

Conried's revelation that he never imbibed was a sour note to the ears of the marketing executives at Seagram. An "Office Memorandum" was circulated by Seagram's advertising agency stating that contrary to what has been heard, Hans did indeed drink, and was, in fact, a "connoisseur of fine wines." Of course, this was a complete fabrication.

The problem really started on *The Jack Paar Show*. Paar delighted in ribbing Conried about how a non-drinker was trying to entice others to buy alcohol. As a result, Seagram subsequently cancelled Conried's advertising contract. Referring to this lost job, Conried would say good-naturedly, "Paar took good care of that when he began kidding me on the air about my not drinking. As a result, I lost the account. They knew all along I didn't drink, but evidently didn't care until the fact was brought out on the Paar show." Conried's demise as a gin salesman was also hastened after the gossip rag *Hush-Hush* magazine "outed" Conried as a teetotaler in their September 1959 issue.

By the time he spoke to Hedda Hopper in December of 1959, he knew the deal was not going to continue. Hopper wielded enormous influence in Hollywood, and seemed to be genuinely fond of Conried; she had been following his career since the early 1940s. Her published article about Conried filled two large columns, and was uncharacteristically complimentary. Conried was overwhelmed by her kindness, and sent her a glowing letter to express his appreciation for providing him with the "biggest and the best piece of publicity that I've ever enjoyed." With a twist of wicked glee, Conried continued with, "Better than that, however, is the fact that Vincent Price is green with envy; a very good color for the Xmas season."

It must have been somewhat painful for Conried to see his old friend Vincent Price enjoying an increase in popularity in motion pictures around this time. *The 5000 Fingers of Dr. T* put the last nail in the coffin of whatever hopes Conried may have had of ever being a "star" in motion pictures. He abandoned all hope then and there, and concentrated on earning a living as best he could. A reporter asked Conried in 1958 what his ambition was as an actor, and he matter-of-factly replied, "My ambition? To keep working."

Conried was featured in two motion pictures released in 1957. One had actually been filmed in 1949 and 1950. It was the Howard Hughes production of *Jet Pilot* starring John Wayne, and directed by the legendary Josef von Sternberg. When asked about working with von Sternberg many years later, Conried recalled an incident that stood out in his mind: "Mr. von Sternberg, of course, was a great artist; he was the boss on every picture. I worked with him … in *Jet Pilot*, as a Russian officer, much as I'd played German officers before. I made some demurrance about the uniform, which was virtually invented by Mr. von Sternberg for this occasion. The picture was in color, and he redesigned the uniform to be colorful; it was a much more dashing costume than the Russian Army really had. And I made a rather rakish entrance with the coat over my shoulders, the sleeves hanging empty. He said, 'Conried, what are you trying to do, play an officer of the Austrian Imperial Army of 1914? Put your arms in those sleeves!' Well, that dashed my hopes for that scene. Though it was a small scene, with the opulence that Mr. von Sternberg usually demanded, they had not only designed this uniform, but made it, as it were, from the whole cloth, from the boots up, and when I put my arms in the sleeves of the topcoat,

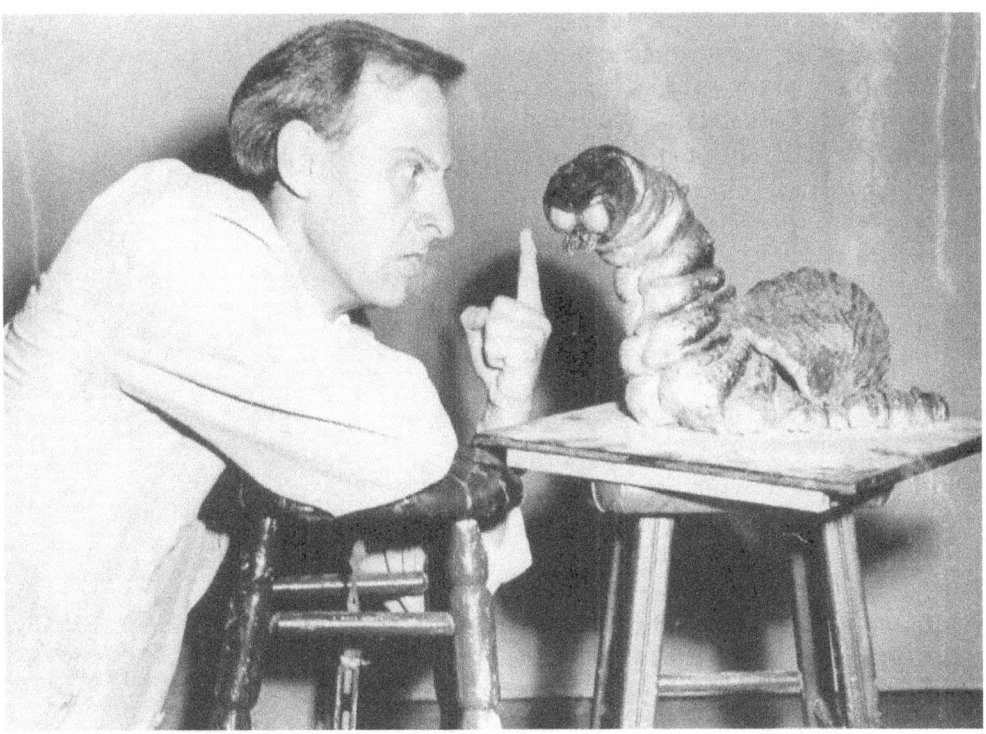

An oddly comical publicity photograph for the United Artists film: *The Monster That Challenged the World* (1957).

the uniform, which probably cost several hundred dollars, could only be seen at the collar."

The other picture released in 1957 was one of the last film roles of any substance Conried would enjoy. He appeared in the overlooked low budget gem *The Monster That Challenged the World*, starring Tim Holt. The film was an entertaining "horror" film that featured a scary, snail-like sea monster and some fairly intelligent dialogue. Conried played it straight as the overworked, and somewhat surly, Dr. Jess Rogers, stationed at the Salton Sea's Navy research lab. He was able to play a dedicated, no-nonsense man of science who wasn't a villain in disguise. Unfortunately, that translated on the screen to a less than thrilling persona, but at least he made it through the whole picture in one piece. Perhaps it was due to the film's lack of funds, but Dr. Rogers wore the same clothes over the course of three days in the film. That may explain why the monster left him alone.

By 1958 Conried's fortunes were changing for the better, thanks in large part to Jack Paar. Conried was able to appear in an increasing number of television roles. One of his most unusual parts can be found in the NBC-produced musical version of *Hansel and Gretel*. The elaborate production was bravely performed for a live broadcast on April 27, 1958. Conried played the wicked witch with a bit more comedic flair than you normally associate with the character. He wore the familiar black dress and pointed black hat, and was fitted with a huge hooked nose and protruding chin. Though not entirely uncommon, it was unconventional to cast a male actor in the role of the witch. The decision to cast Conried served to heighten the comedic value. Conried had a lot of hammy fun with this character, but didn't try very hard to be believable as a female. Even though the cast boasted such popular performers as Red Buttons, Stubby Kaye, and Rudy Vallee, the show was not a hit. The producers piled it a little too high with hokey musical numbers, and asked entirely too much of their audience in accepting a thirty-nine-year-old Red Buttons as a little boy! The ending was also changed to have Conried's witch survive the slip into the oven and promise to change her evil ways.

In keeping with the "live" stage production theme, a cast party was held right after the broadcast to await the first reviews. The general mood started off jovial, but as the negative notices began to roll in, the members of the cast quickly bolted for the door. Conried was left standing there with a glass of soda, wondering what the heck happened.

Conried also appeared on the "What Makes Opera Grand?" segment of the *Omnibus* series hosted by Leonard Bernstein for public television. Conried and the cast helped to illustrate the difference between theatrical and operatic singing. Though he never claimed to be a singer, Conried was able to handle the rigors of light opera with great aplomb. Conried had another chance to display his vocal skills by reading all of the characters for an Audio Book release of Robert Louis Stevenson's *Treasure Island*. The recorded book ended up running over six hours in length. Conried created a unique voice for each character from *Treasure Island*, causing an exhausted Conried to exclaim, "Boy, did I run out of British sailor voices!" Conried obviously enjoyed the adventures encountered by young Jim Hawkins and the treacherous pirate Long John Silver and his crew, and lovingly reads each line. There is not even a whiff of ham in Conried's voice, and his performance is a study of inspired acting in its purest sense. It is as if Conried is having just as much fun reading the story as we are listening to him read it.

Hans dressed as the wicked witch from the live NBC television production of *Hansel and Gretel* (1958). From the Hans Conried Collection, Department of Special Collections, Boston University.

In an ostentatious show of his etymological skill, Conried managed a four-week stint on the ill-fated *$64,000 Question* quiz show in 1958. From all appearances, the show was not rigged in Conried's favor. His winnings were climbing steadily with a long succession of correct answers in the "English Language" category, until one question managed to stump him, and he fell back to the $4,000 level: "The word 'strigine'—owl-like, a Greek derivative—was my Achilles heel... I'll remember that word until death."

Conried's oldest children were at an age when they were beginning to understand what they were seeing on television— something not exactly to their father's liking: "They are becoming aware of my face on the screen and to me, it's unwholesome." Conried was very adamant about separating his public and private lives, and tried to "keep secret what I do for a living." With his increased work load, and the trips to St. Louis to appear with The Muny each summer, Conried felt his children were beginning to think of him as "a rather mysterious person who drops by occasionally." He sought to provide his family with a lifestyle that was financially comfortable and as "normal" as possible. Ironically, in the pursuit of this goal, Conried found himself spending more and more time away from the home he loved. Margaret had to become both mother and father to the children, manage their household, and sometimes be a liaison between Conried and his manager when he was on the road. It was one of those compromises he felt he needed to make to stay alive both literally and figuratively, even though it meant his children would spend a good deal of their formative years without him. Applying for unemployment insurance was a fate worse than death to Conried, and he would do virtually anything to keep working.

As if to prove the point, Conried would again perform with Jerry Lewis in 1958 on a television special that was a live broadcast from the Sands Hotel in Las Vegas, and in the film *Rock-a-Bye Baby*. His role in the film was once again a meager one. Conried played the owner of a TV repair shop, Mr. Wright, who had the ill fortune to employ Lewis' character. One perk Conried enjoyed along with the rest of the cast was due to Lewis' strong devotion to family values. Being a father of six, Lewis made a rule on the set that working hours would be limited strictly to the hours between 8 A.M. and 5 P.M. That meant the cast and crew would be able to go home for dinner with their families each night. The cast also invited a hundred women from the Mt. Sinai Hospital clinic to the set to watch the filming for a Mother's Day treat, and provided them with a delicious luncheon afterwards.

A publicity piece for *Rock-a-Bye Baby* stated that actor Reginald Gardiner, who was also appearing in the film, would soon star on television in 20th Century–Fox's *Mr. Belvedere*. This version of the series never materialized, and Fox would invite Conried to make a pilot for *Mr. Belvedere* the following year.

In addition to all the television and commercial offers Conried received, a substantial number of other interesting bits of work floated his way. One such offer was a short lecture tour of a few places in the Midwest to talk about children's literature. Conried felt well-suited to the task since children's literature was "something I really know, as I've been reading to my kids...." While on the road in Springfield, Illinois, he volunteered to be the local television station's "Principal Master of Ceremonies" for a cerebral palsy telethon broadcast from the Hotel Abraham Lincoln in May of 1958. The town was so smitten with Conried he was named an Honorary Fire Chief.

An item printed in a trade paper in July of 1959 mentioned that RCA Records had wanted to sign Conried to a deal to do a record of Edgar Allan Poe material. It appears that deal never went through. Conried did read excerpts from a Poe story on another record, *America Listens to Literature*, produced by Vocab Records for Scott Foresman and Company. The contract with Vocab is dated March 10, 1959, and specifically mentions the material to be used for the recording: Poe's *The Pit and the Pendulum*, Dickens' *David Copperfield*, and John Masefield's *Spanish Waters*. Conried was to be paid a paltry $180 for his efforts, and was required to sign away his rights to earn any more from the recording. Not exactly a generous offer, but Conried agreed to sign.

Another record deal that Conried did accept—and claimed to have later regretted—was a recording of whimsical musical numbers with a "monster" theme for an album called *Monster Rally*. Today, the record's main claim to fame is the album cover created by noted illustrator Jack Davis. Davis designed a wild cover depicting a mind-boggling array of monsters and ghouls comprising an orchestra of sorts conducted by none other than Dracula himself.

Conried and Alice Pearce (who would later play Gladys Cravitz on the television series *Bewitched*) were the only performers bold enough to use their own names. According to the liner notes, they had been selected to perform on the record due to their "good sportsmanship and courage." Conried may not have been very proud of his efforts on *Monster Rally*, but his rendition of "The Purple People Eater" (or "Eat-ah," as Conried pronounces it) is amazing. When faced with singing lyrics like "pigeon-toed, under-growed, flying purple people eater," Conried couldn't help groaning, "How ungrammatical!"

To kick off the release of *Monster Rally*, Conried and Alice Pearce were guests of honor at a party given at the Round Table in New York. Attendees sipped drinks out of glasses with a skull and crossbones motif, and swizzle sticks sporting tiny skulls perched jauntily on top. The record was received fairly well by the public, and one reviewer made the comment that Conried sounded like a "cross between George Sanders and Zacherley."

Conried filmed an episode of the educational Bell Science series dealing with the creation of language called *The Alphabet Conspiracy*. This installment was first broadcast on television on January 26, 1959. The ubiquitous Dr. Frank Baxter hosted the Bell Science series, which was auspiciously produced under the personal direction of Jack Warner. Dr. Baxter would become well known to generations of elementary school children who had the good fortune to view 16mm prints of the Bell Science films in their classrooms. Conried was perfectly suited to playing the Mad Hatter who stepped out of *Alice in Wonderland*. He could be as big, and bold, and hammy as he wanted to be because, after all, it was just the sort of performance that made kids giggle and pay attention.

Conried found work as a semi-regular on another panel show, the somewhat surreal *Take a Good Look* hosted by the gifted comedian Ernie Kovacs. Kovacs' unconventional, experimental humor was well known to television audiences by 1959. To "help" the panel, Kovacs would provide clues in the form of short skits that had been filmed earlier. They were supposed to relate to the contestant's claim to fame, but were so weird they did more to confound the panelists than clarify. A frustrated Conried wasn't quite used to this kind of thing: "They try to make you look good on the Paar show, but this Kovacs quiz show has so-called clues that are so wild that I believe they are designed to make the panel appear stupid." Kovacs and Conried got along very well, and even socialized a bit, but in an attempt to gain more attention for the show, tried to create some on-camera friction between them. Unfortunately, their "feud" didn't help the show's sagging ratings.

In August of 1959, television audiences watched Conried in the well-publicized NBC comedy special *The Ransom of Red Chief*. Conried co-starred with his old friend William Bendix and Mickey Rooney's young son, Teddy Rooney. The critics blasted the show in print, and showed the elder stars no mercy (though they were kind to Teddy). Conried even found himself taking some of the heat while trying to hail a taxi in New York: "With unbecoming frequency I've been told that wasn't the greatest effort to hit television. As you know, New York cabbies are never loath to advise you on your profession. Well, the day after the show, a New York cabbie expressed it this way: 'Hey Conried, you sure stunk last night!'"

A bad show here or there aside, Conried was creating such a stir on television that he was asked to appear on *The Mike Wallace Interview*. After a few stints as the host of quiz shows—Conried was a panelist on a couple of them—Mike Wallace was quickly making a name for himself as a tough, no-nonsense, go-for-the-jugular in-

William Bendix, Hans, and Teddy Rooney from the television special: *The Ransom of Red Chief* (NBC: 1959).

terviewer. His early efforts with *The Mike Wallace Interview* earned him the brand of "The Terrible Torquemada of the Television Inquisition." What could Mike Wallace possibly want with Conried? Conried was never in any way a controversial figure, or involved in a scandal. He always showed up for work on time, clean-shaven and sober. He had nothing to worry about then, right? Well ... almost right.

Conried was worried, and when it came time to film the interview appeared to be quite uncomfortable, frequently squirming in his seat with arms and legs crossed. For some reason, Mike Wallace went easy on Conried. By 1959, the show's format had changed significantly (there had been some threats of lawsuits), and the questions asked took on a much softer tone. It probably wouldn't have mattered what questions were asked, anyway, as Conried was such an impenetrable fortress there was no way Wallace could get him to open up and say anything that even hinted of controversy— until the second interview, at least. It is amusing to note that as Conried and Wallace were discussing his early radio work, Conried felt the need to remind the viewers that a radio was "a box through which voices came—it's hard to explain it nowadays."

Two complete interviews were taped for *The Mike Wallace Interview*. The tamer, non-confrontational version that ended with Wallace categorizing Conried as a "gentle man" was the one that aired on March 18,

1959. The second interview was much edgier, and veered off into areas Conried did not want to discuss at all: namely, politics. It was brought out by Wallace that some of Conried's "friends" thought of him as an "arch, rabid, reactionary" when it came to politics. Obviously not pleased with where the conversation was going, Conried defended himself, and said he was decidedly a "liberal," and his friends, who were also liberals, were completely wrong (though still friends). Conried's views on politics were in many respects offbeat, and somewhat naïve. For example, this is what he thought of the American system of government: "In many respects, Democracy—Republicanism as we know it—is not successful, and it limps along because we are held back by the many-tongued monster that we are. If you have a vote, and I have a vote, and a Doctor of Philosophy has a vote ... a political scientist has a vote, and the simple man who cannot count without removing his shoes and socks to get beyond ten—we all have equal votes—there is something wrong; that my vote can count out a Doctor of Philosophy, who is probably more worthy and understanding in the matter of what is good for the common weal, and the chap who is having difficulty tying his shoelaces." Conried counted himself about a step and a half above the chap with the shoelace trouble.

Wallace (on a tip from Conried's "friends") asked Conried about his supposed desire to create a monarchy in the U.S., causing the poor fellow to nearly leap out of his chair to proclaim the ludicrousness of that notion, and to assure everyone he had never advocated the violent overthrow of the government. Wallace tried to push him along those lines, but Conried refused to play the game, saying he wouldn't discuss the subject any further: "I don't think publicly, not even as a joke, because I think we'd all be hanged." Noting the increasing level of anxiety Conried was exhibiting, Wallace continued:

MW: You are seriously concerned about speaking your mind...
HC: I always have been. I think as a cheap entertainer; a low clown...
MW: Do you really regard yourself as a "low clown"?
HC: On this occasion I desire to hide behind that shield, yes, I assure you.
MW: Why this fear?
HC: [Actors] are always targets for barbs. We have the equal rights as citizens, surely...
MW: What you're really saying is you're afraid people won't buy tickets to your show.
HC: In effect, Mike, you've hit it precisely and exactly.
MW: And so you are willing to be cowed by...
HC: (Jokingly) By you! Your rudeness—your lack of good taste—your lack of charm on this occasion. Later, when we are in private, I'll probably punch your nose, but here I can do nothing!

The interview ended with Wallace this time categorizing Conried as looking rather like "a devil, who perhaps thinks like a mischievous one too." Conried tried to bolt off the set, but was motioned to sit down so the credits could roll. Behind the credits, you can see Conried reaching over and grabbing Wallace by the collar, and threatening him in a mock aggressive way. Mike Wallace was laughing so hard it looked like he was in danger of falling out of his chair. Conried was probably very happy to finally leave the studio, and even happier that version of the interview did not make it on the air.

The tickets Conried was afraid he would lose were for his hit Broadway play, *Tall Story*, that was playing to packed houses at that time. This was Conried's second opportunity to perform on Broadway, and for the first time in his career he was enjoying a great deal of success as the main star of a legitimate theatrical production. The details surrounding why he chose to leave Hollywood and his flourishing television career behind to do another Broadway play aren't quite clear. It is true 20th Century–Fox was interested in having Conried play the lead in their proposed *Mr. Belvedere* television series, and wanted him to film the pilot. The story goes that he actually flipped a coin to see if he'd do the series, or go to New York. Obviously, Broadway won out.

The television series was by no means a sure thing, and it was seriously doubtful if Fox could find a sponsor. The filming of the pilot was delayed, and he signed with Joshua Logan to star in *Tall Story*. Logan, you may remember, was the one who successfully sweet-talked Conried into his nearly nonexistent role in the film *Bus Stop*. This time, he really had something of substance to offer Conried. Unfortunately, Logan would again disappoint him. Even with the Broadway play going full steam and garnering rave reviews, Logan was already putting together the cast for the motion picture version of *Tall Story* without its Broadway star. Conried was not even in the running. When later asked why Joshua Logan didn't put him in the film version of *Tall Story* Conried replied sadly, "Now you're opening an old wound. I thought it was over. He just didn't see fit to cast me in the picture after I'd done that play." Logan retooled the story for the motion picture to focus more on the basketball star, played in the film by Anthony Perkins, and because of the flexibility of the medium, could include actual basketball games. Conried's character, the middle-aged college professor, who was the focal point of the stage play, ended up with a less important part in the film. Conried summed it up years later by saying, "In my day it wasn't a basketball story; it was about a loveable professor. When they reduced it in content and intellect to the motion picture, they made it a basketball story."

Before its premiere on Broadway on January 29, 1959, *Tall Story* had a trial run at the New Locust Theater in Philadelphia on January 6th. That meant Conried would have to leave before the Christmas holidays to rehearse. Before signing the contract to star, Conried tried to add a clause stating he could remain home with his family for Christmas, and then go east for the rehearsals. His request was turned down, and he signed anyway. It would not be the last holiday that Conried would spend away from his family. Conried left for the rehearsals in early December, and Margaret and the kids followed after the first of the year. Their faithful housekeeper was left behind to watch over the Conried home and make sure the menagerie of animals were well cared for.

While preparing for the opening on Broadway, Conried received congratulatory and encouraging telegrams from friends and family. One in particular from Jack Paar read: "Don't embarrass me by being bad. My good name is at stake. You've got to be a hit!" Conried didn't let his old friend and benefactor down, even though he ended up with a case of laryngitis on the opening night of *Tall Story* in New York.

The reviews were decidedly positive, stating that *Tall Story* was the "funniest comedy of the season." Conried's performance in particular was attracting a lot of favorable attention from the sometimes-harsh New York critics. Bill Slocum of *The New York Mirror* penned an eloquent paean to "hamminess": "In Conried's hands and eyes, hamminess becomes a fine art. His hamminess is not of the ego, but of a professional and skilled actor who gets all there is out of a role that screams for a rococo performance." *The Savannah Morning News* also had some kind things to say about Conried's performance: "Conried's timing is perfect and his face is worthy of constant study—the pale, drawn, concentration; the smiles, never quite free from misgiving, the looks of mingled shyness and disdain down the long nose, the head tossed back in a strange mixture of insecurity and arrogance. It is a superb characterization of its kind." You could almost say they were describing Conried, the man.

Because of the success of *Tall Story*, Conried was recognized everywhere he went in New York: "It has its advantages ... but there are always counterbalances of good and bad. It's a pain in the neck when you have a hot corned beef sandwich in your hand, ready to take a second bite, and a shriveled piece of brown paper is shoved between you and the sandwich with orders to 'write your name again'. Or else you autograph the margins of a newspaper, and the person says 'Who's he?' and crumples it up in high disgust."

While in New York, Conried took a short break from Broadway to co-star with Kitty Carlisle in a play called *Carrie Council*. The play was performed as a benefit for the National Council of Jewish Women at the Hotel Plaza, and had been especially written for the event. Conried also managed to find a little time to talk to a variety of reporters. One asked Conried to give his opinion on whether or not to encourage young people to become actors: "When any young person expresses interest in becoming an actor," Conried replied, "it is the duty of any professional player within earshot to discourage him. If, however, said young person is determined to enter the theatre, then it is wisest to leave him alone. Such youthful purpose is not to be deflected by any advice from any superannuated ham."

Tall Story would end its successful run on Broadway on May 2, 1959, after 109 performances. The producers, Emmet Rogers and Robert Weiner, admitted to the press that the show never had a losing week the entire time it ran at the Belasco; they just felt they should "call it a season while still ahead, before the hot weather sets in." It is unusual that a money making play would have been pulled like this, but it is possible Joshua Logan didn't want the Broadway play conflicting with the release of the motion picture version that was in production at that time.

Conried returned home briefly to film the pilot for *Mr. Belvedere* and enjoy some time at home before heading out on the road with the regional tour production of *Tall Story*. This would be the first such tour Conried had ever attempted. He was buoyed with the success he was having on the legitimate stage, and eagerly agreed to star. Conried was soon discovering one of the joys of the road, which is exploring the best each new city he visited had to offer. His voracious appetite for knowledge led him to seek out all the historical sights and museums he could manage within the limited time he had in any given city. His adventures sometimes led him astray, though, as noted by *The Detroit News*: "Hans enjoyed exploring the sights and sounds of the city, especially a restaurant near his hotel: 'I can walk directly from the hotel to the restaurant in a few minutes, but I can never find my way back. It's like you can't get there from here. Coming back, I find myself blocks beyond the hotel.'"

After the road show of *Tall Story* was over, and Conried was back home in the Hollywood Hills, he had some time to reflect on the radically new direction his career was moving in, and the difficult decisions facing him. 20th Century–Fox was shopping the *Mr. Belvedere* pilot around trying to find a sponsor, and they felt their chances of moving the series into production were very good. At the same time, due to his success on the legitimate stage, Conried was getting offers to do more stock tours, including personal appearances and lectures. If that wasn't enough, Jack Paar wanted Conried to accompany him, and some other Paar regulars, to England for a special trip that would be taped for broadcast on a later Paar show.

For a television actor, finding work in

a series was the best thing that could happen. A series provided some security and a regular paycheck. There were those lean times to get through when the series went on hiatus for the summer, but that sort of thing went along with the territory of television acting. Though Conried longed for a series of his own and the security it would bring, he had to struggle with his other side that resisted any attempt to be categorized, which he felt would limit his flexibility as an actor. To associate himself with one character day in and day out, and possibly be forever linked with the character no matter what he did (remember his love-hate relationship with "Uncle Tonoose"), was not what Conried wanted. Yet he had a wife and four little mouths to feed (not to mention his own large appetite) and a huge house; he would have to find some way to pay the bills.

Conried pondered the idea of having a series, saying, "Naturally it would offer me security. I'd know where I'm going to be next week, but I haven't convinced myself yet that I want it that way… I'm the happiest when I'm doing something different every week." Conried reiterated this point a bit more colorfully a few years later when asked what he felt was the "secret of life": "Not to ever be chained. To be as many people as you want to be, and each as you want to be at the time. To fit on as many saddles as you can with one backside."

It's not too surprising, then, that Conried decided to heed the call of the road. Appearing in the out-of-the-way towns and cities that a tour was often required to play in would allow Conried to swim in a sea of adulation and prestige. His name was above the title on every billboard and marquee. Who cared if it was the same billboard that displayed the dates of the next high school dance. His name was still there in big letters—often misspelled, but there for all to see. As Conried proudly noted, "If the town is small enough, I'm a pretty big star."

The following year, 1960, Conried headed off to England with Jack Paar, gave his first college lecture, and took another former Broadway show on the road. It would be the start of one of the most hectic periods in Conried's career, and probably the most financially lucrative. It was also the start of a very difficult time for his young children, who would rarely get to see their father, and a wife who had to cope as best she could without her husband. Conried was in between that proverbial rock and a hard place, and he did what he felt was best for all concerned. It was not by any means the way he would have wanted it, though: "In life, as in any profession, one falls so far from his youthful goal. Every human being is off target, no matter what he attains. Nothing at this point is anywhere near my high clanking dreams of youth. With necessary compromises, we're all failures, more or less."

Nevertheless, Conried always felt he was on "good terms with himself and his compromises," and forged ahead once again into the new territory of the legitimate stage. After claiming to have had two or three careers shot out from under him, Conried was very pleased to have tenaciously survived long enough in the business to finally find a place where he could be a "star."

9

The Road Show Begins

As the new decade began, Conried dived headlong into his new role as a provincial player and made plans to tour the hinterlands. The bread-and-butter of these stock tours consisted mainly of plays that had already had a successful Broadway run. Conried would joke in later years that he sometimes felt like a vulture sitting on the fence, waiting for a juicy play to die so he could get a piece of it.

In reality, Conried didn't have a lot to say about which parts he did, though he had some preferences. For the most part, he didn't complain, believing his intuition was not the best judge of what was successful: "Any play I think is fine for me doesn't turn out well. If I don't like it, it usually turns out splendid. That's why actors should have agents and directors to guide them." Often, Conried found out what his next project would be while on the road. A letter would arrive from his agent, Sid Gold, informing him bluntly, "You are going to do a show," and name the production. Before long, Sid would make most of the arrangements with Margaret, and Conried would be the last to know. It was probably a relief for Conried to have these details taken care of for him, but it presented a bit of an embarrassment, once in a while, when a reporter knew what show he was going to be doing next before he did. Conried did have a very firm idea what sort of roles he wanted, and when asked the question by a reporter, he animatedly replied: "Why, the kind of roles I want is the kind that will pay the most money, get the best reviews, have the longest runs, require the least amount of preparation and make-up, and the fewest costume changes, and in general, the least amount of exertion."

It is ironic that the role Conried was playing at this time—the part of "Hans Conried," the Paar personality—was the most grueling, time-consuming part he ever had to play. He found it necessary to keep up this performance seven days a week, 365 days a year. The fear of "speaking his mind," as Mike Wallace uncovered, was very real for Conried, and he consciously avoided anything that might tarnish his image in any way. One of the reasons for his avoidance of drugs and alcohol was his anxiety about losing control in public and doing something unseemly. How would people react to this witty, erudite, sophisticated man they saw on TV, falling down drunk and making a fool of himself in public? No, this must never happen, Conried thought, and he diligently guarded his reputation. Perhaps his agent worked hard to protect his investment as well. The vast majority of the roles he played on the stock tours reflected this finely crafted "personality," and never strayed too far from the mold. He no longer played a psychotic killer, a drug addict, or any other type of sociopath on the stage. Conried found himself time and again as the doting father, or the anxious husband, or variations on those themes, in light comedy fare.

Fortunately, his television roles provided a short break now and then from fluffy comedic roles. In 1961 he appeared as the dislikable and dour Dr. Mood on "The Jonah Stone," an episode of *Adventures in Paradise*. Dr. Mood goes mad at the end after losing his precious stone, and Conried had a chance to let loose à la "Banquo's Chair." It is unfortunate that Conried generally did not accept dramatic roles because he felt it would cut into his income. Conried had great depth to his nature, and excelled in serious, dramatic plays. Comedy paid much better at the time, however, and Conried was very sensitive to the bottom line.

The comedic roles he accepted were often of less than stellar quality. A case in point was the *Armstrong Circle Theater* presentation of a show tailored for the talents of Ernie Kovacs and Edie Adams called "Private Eye, Private Eye." It was to be a lighthearted spoof of detective shows, but ended up more of a disappointing and disjointed mess. Conried was billed as co-star with Kovacs and Adams. Inexplicably, this production did not allow Kovacs to write any of the material, except for a small segment featuring the "Nairobi Trio." Without Kovacs' wit and intelligence to back him up, his actual performance was stilted and, for the most part, uncharacteristically unfunny. The best part of the show, ultimately, was the short sketch featuring the three dapper apes—this time there was one very tall ape helping out with a spoof of safe cracking. A small amount of praise should be given to the imaginative opening credits, though. The show began with a street scene in which credits would appear on someone's back; on a letter that was being dropped in a mailbox; on the side of a garbage can, and so on. Conried was gunned down, and as he lay "dying," he managed to find a piece of chalk to scrawl more credits on the sidewalk. Unfortunately, due to his position, Conried was forced to use his right hand to write with, and you barely can make out what he was trying to say.

It may not have been Shakespeare, but Conried was gratified to see the job offers continuing to pour in. The projects before him provided a dazzling array of lucrative career options in a number of different media. Very closely intertwined with the artist in him was a shrewd businessman who never seemed to miss an opportunity to do some personal PR or pick up an extra paycheck. "Remunerative" was one of his favorite words, and he used it to describe any gig that would pay handsomely for his services. As long as they could afford his fee, when Conried had a spare moment on the road he would appear at state fairs, "grand openings," private fund raising lunches, and ladies' "teas." He'd make personal appearances in local department stores (in the men's department), and do radio and TV ads for local businesses. If the fee was right, Conried facetiously boasted, he would even do private parties, as long as "they could provide a 7⅜" lampshade."

It was clear to Conried he would not be able to find enough work to sustain himself if he relied solely on Hollywood: "There's plenty of work for Hollywood actors to do—if they don't just look for it in Hollywood." He could "just sit at home in the hills and wait for a producer to call—or not to call," but he felt that going out to the people was "a good living," and also a consistent one. It was, however, a living fraught with the type of personal demons so familiar to performers. Conried told a reporter of the constant worry actors face when on the road: "[You worry] whether or not you have done the best you could, whether you might have done better, whether you will do better tomorrow. The eight o'clock performance also is a nagging strain—you wonder, in advance, if you will be good enough at the evening performance. The worry even keeps you from a restful nap. That is why, actually, most actors prefer the matinee

Magazine ad for Honeywell thermostats, circa 1961. From the Hans Conried Collection, Department of Special Collections, Boston University.

matic and comedic works to include in his lectures.

Prior to boarding the bus for his first scholastic engagement, Conried accepted Jack Paar's generous offer in March of 1960 to travel with Mrs. Paar; their young daughter, Randy; and funnyman Charlie Weaver to London, England, for a short visit. Paar would shoot some footage at Madame Tussaud's and other tourist locations, to be used on one of his programs later that month. Even though his affected accent gave people the impression Conried had an intimate relationship with Britain, he had actually never set foot on its soil. He was very grateful to Paar for giving him the opportunity to see the land of Shakespeare and the medieval pageantry he loved. Afterwards, he commented, "Now if I had been there only two days I might have emerged as an expert and immediately written a book. But, alas, I was there for two and a half weeks, which is a different matter. Naturally, while over there I talked to many of my fellows in the acting profession. The theatre, it warms my actor's heart to know, is thriving in London. The overhead is low and plays, even when badly reviewed, may run quite a spell. The public may see an actor in a hopeless turkey and say about him, 'He's not good, but isn't he brave?'"

Paar may have been talking about that "hopeless turkey" when he penned this account of a night out with Conried in London for his 1961 book, *My Saber Is Bent*: "Not all the shows are good, of course, and one night, when I went with Hans Conried, the actor, we encountered one which was quite dreary. We sat restlessly through the first act and waited patiently for the intermission so we could escape into the night. When the curtain finally came down, and the lights went up for the intermission, we headed for the door. In the aisle, however, we bumped into Raymond Massey, the distinguished actor, and his wife, whom we

days. It keeps you from your thoughts; you are too busy."

In 1960 Conried would come to grips with the realities of his career and personal situations. He once again had to make the necessary compromises to keep his career and family alive. It would mean the end to whatever was left of his "high clanking dreams of youth," and the beginning of a new journey along a more mature path — one that would at least provide the financial security his large family needed.

Conried and the Boston based promoter Harry Walker inked a deal that would send Conried off to fifty different colleges and universities each year to do his own, unique one-man show. Walker paid him a set salary, plus transportation and housing costs, for seven performances per week. Conried was amazed (and delighted) by the large amount of money he was being paid for these lectures, and set about to collect some of his favorite dra-

knew from the States. They went out with us for a smoke, and we had a pleasant chat through the brief intermission. Then, as the lights dimmed for the Second Act, and the Masseys started back in with the rest of the audience, I saw a chance to flee, and whispered to Hans to join me in my getaway. 'That was a terrible thing to do' Hans said as we headed back to our hotel. 'I know the show was a bore, but it was very bad manners to walk out. What will the Masseys think?' I, too, began having misgivings as Hans repeated gloomily all the way home, 'I wish we hadn't done that. What will the Masseys think?' A few days later, when I was just beginning to get over my remorse over what Hans had insisted was our breach of manners, I got a phone call from Raymond Massey. 'I've been trying for days to get you', he said, 'I wanted to apologize for the other night. My wife and I couldn't stand the show, so we sneaked out right after talking to you. She's been nagging me ever since about our bad manners. She keeps saying, 'What will Jack Paar and Hans Conried think?' I hope you don't think we were rude.'"

Back in the States, Conried packed his bags for the first in what would become a long series of lecture tours booked by Harry Walker. Professor Theodore O.H. Karl of the Pacific Lutheran College in Oregon was the catalyst behind Conried's first lecture there on May 5th. Prof. Karl was an admirer of Conried's work, and called him earlier that year to ask if he would appear on his campus. That one phone call may have been the inspiration for the entire series. The story goes that Conried was reluctant to do that sort of thing, but the persuasive professor was able to convince him to give it a try. The lecture at Pacific Lutheran was a huge success, and this one-man show idea blossomed into a very lucrative cottage industry. Thousands of students would also benefit from their experience with Conried throughout the 1960s. In addition to his academic appearances, Conried also performed "An Evening with Hans Conried" (sometimes "A Morning with...") at various town halls and other venues. Conried's fee was generally $1,500 for one of his lectures. A more established star like Basil Rathbone commanded $2,000. It must have been a thorn in Conried's side if he ever discovered that Harry Walker was paying his old buddy Vincent Price $2,500 for his appearances. Price's career was enjoying a renaissance in the early 1960s, and he was considered a "hot" property.

Conried was "hot" in his own sphere of influence, as he was still riding the wave of popularity generated by his association with Jack Paar: "Listen, since I have appeared on Jack's shows, I no longer have to give auditions or go through casting offices. Being with Jack has given me that added

Picking up a few books for the road while stopping in Indiana during his lecture tour (1964). From the Hans Conried Collection, Department of Special Collections, Boston University.

luster and glamour. I have become a personality ... and in such a capacity, I am allowed to work on the stage—but only in comedy."

Conried felt trapped somewhat by being pigeon-holed as primarily a comedic actor, but he couldn't argue that the newfound prestige didn't have its perks: "It has enabled me to cash a check in a supermarket without having to show any identification." The times were changing, and this time things seemed to be moving in Conried's direction. He reflected on this welcome turn of events by saying: "I came to work sober and clean-shaven, and gave no one any trouble. But the most recognition I had from the public was someone usually saying, 'Oh, gosh, I've seen him before—what's his name?' Now, at least, people misspell my name."

The summer stock offering for 1960 was a successful British import titled *Not in the Book*. It was a pleasant, comedic "who done it," and featured Conried in the leading role as Andrew Bennett. Conried had a chance to see a performance of the play while he was in London starring the talented actor Wilfred Hyde-White. An impressed Conried gushed, "What a performance; so dry. I asked him for some tips. I thought he was terrific. I wish I could play it the way he did."

The cast began rehearsing in April in New York City, and then flew to Toronto, Canada, for the first show of the tour. The actors were still feeling apprehensive about their readiness, and didn't miss an opportunity to rehearse, as noted by a reporter for *The Toronto Telegram*: "Actor Conried turned the Malton Airport restaurant into a rehearsal theatre last night. Between gulps of milk and mouthfuls of steak, he ran through a different scene... Other diners watched with delight. And as the scene ended, an amazed waitress started to applaud. Mr. Conried flew in from New York with the rest of the play's cast, [where he] had been rehearsing the play all week... At 5 p.m. yesterday, [Mr. Conried] and the cast packed up, and boarded the plane. They started rehearsals again—up in the air—and continued them during the eighty-four minute flight to Toronto. At Malton, they stopped for supper, but it was so long in coming that Conried and director Charles Olsen decided to continue rehearsals. 'We want to get the play just right,' Mr. Conried explains. 'So every minute counts.'"

The play premiered in the U.S. in Chicago, and Margaret and the oldest two children were there to help sooth Conried's opening night jitters. The tour was a bona fide success. People were packing the theaters every night, and the show received uniformly favorable notices. With the show being such a big hit, Conried decided to turn down an offer by the Stratford [Connecticut] Shakespeare Company to appear in one of their productions, since it would disrupt the tour.

Reporter Michael Philley of the *Knickerbocker News* (Albany, New York) left us a warm vignette from the tour: "Four curtain calls after the end of the comedy *Not in the Book*... Hans Conried fumbled his way through the heavy blue curtains, and faced the audience. He draped a long calf over the edge of the stage, leaned back on his hands, and told the several hundreds there: 'You can't go home. It's raining. So you might as well listen.' He had the curtain lifted, and asked his fellow actors: 'Please sit down. Don't stand around looking all uncomfortable.' He then turned to the audience, who had loved every second of his performance, and said, 'Thank you. You have thanked us. It is we who should thank you. You have received our play with great kindness.' While the rain teemed down he talked about nothing at all, just anything that came into his head. Then the rain stopped and he said, 'I guess you can go home now.'"

Conried was enjoying what he called a "great egotistical satisfaction" in being able to fill a theater "solely on one's personality." Yes, all the people were there to see this "personality," but it was a double-edged sword: "If I am to judge by the people who come backstage and the people who send me notes, I must come to a conclusion which hurts my professional pride. That lady in the front row did not say to her husband, 'Oh, I see Hans Conried is coming here. I understand he's a splendid actor, absolutely splendid. I wouldn't want to miss him.' What she said was, 'Hans Conried is coming. You remember we saw him on Jack Paar. Let's go see what he looks like in person. I'll bet he looks older.'"

Their reasons for coming to see him aside, Conried must have taken some satisfaction in discovering he was quite popular with the ladies out in the vast fastnesses of America. He was receiving some very flattering fan mail and was invited to speak for a myriad of different women's clubs and organizations. When asked about his lecture tours, Conried told *TV Guide* magazine, "Whenever I'm afraid of over exposure on TV, I hit the road and talk before women's clubs. It's a gold mine! You know how many women's clubs there are in this country? Over 100,000. Know what many of them pay for guest lecturers? From $350 to $1000, and just for an hour's talk. Why, if I'm properly scheduled, I can do two a day."

Conried was a product of his time, and harbored some very old-fashioned ideas about women. He would no doubt be enlightened considerably in the years to come by his two daughters, but in 1961 he was under the impression the ladies he was lecturing to—whom he referred to as "charmingly capricious"—didn't want to hear anything too heavy, or serious: "You've got to keep it light... creamed chicken in a patty shell—maybe some chocolate ice cream... It's nearly always the same... You talk... You answer a few questions... Then you get out of town fast and head for your next stop." The truth of the matter was, though Conried gave his audience a choice of lecture topics that included Shakespeare and modern philosophers, the subject the ladies invariably requested the most was "Hollywood": "All they want me to talk about is Hollywood. So, I read up on the gossip columns and give them a big earful."

One of the stops on what would be known as the "creamed chicken circuit"—speaking engagements for women's functions—was an outdoor fundraising event for about 350 ladies held at a private residence in White Meadow, New York, for the local WML Temple Sisterhood. Conried played it up as the Hollywood star, arriving in a big convertible with his "entourage" (the newspaper account didn't elaborate on who they were). The ladies all fawned over him as he strolled about sipping fruit punch and nibbling a thick slice of salami. All Conried had to do that day was be witty and charming, sign a few autographs, and answer some questions from the adoring crowd. Not a bad afternoon's work.

Events like this were in sharp contrast to the hard work he had to put in for his lectures at colleges and universities. Though no recording of a lecture is known to exist, Maria J. Schenck of *The Oak Ridger* newspaper (Oak Ridge, Tennessee) provided this illuminating firsthand account of Conried's appearance at the Oak Ridge High School Auditorium on February 11, 1962: "Mr. Conried staggered on stage with an armload of books... He admitted frankly that the readings were much more work for him and that he would be quite willing to talk instead. He hinted several times to this effect, but got nowhere with his hard-hearted audience who were fascinated with his readings, which varied from a poem in German dialect to *The Bible* and Shakespeare. Before reading Poe's *The Pit and the Pendulum*, he remarked that Poe was a fine writer, drunk or sober. Looking at the many children in the audience, he explained that the tale he was to tell was 'dreadful, a story of torture,

Hans on the "creamed chicken" circuit, trying valiantly to down one more plate of chicken à la king (Chicago: 1962). From the Hans Conried Collection, Department of Special Collections, Boston University.

but nothing worse than you see everyday on TV.' He preceded his German dialect poem by mentioning the fact that dialects have gone out of style because they often offend people: 'The minorities are so well protected that now the majority needs a champion!'

"Before *Archie and Mehitabel* was read, he gave a little history of the theatrical cat. Pointing out the cat was needed not just as a pet, but for sanitary reasons, 'because in the old days, the theatre was generally dark and dismal and somewhat unclean. Eating, however it might be frowned upon by the management, occurred (no drinking, mind you!), and a cat was needed to keep down the mice.' Following this line of thought, he remarked that acting was growing much more respectable: 'We actors can now be buried in consecrated ground, and our children are legitimized.' Then a wonderful reading from *The Bible*: His interpretation made may people say they wished it could be read in churches that way as he brought the people alive with his voice and mannerisms. He prefaced this reading with these remarks: 'I mean no irreverence at all, but *The Bible* is wonderful for actors—it is actually fun. Listen to this version of the story of the fiery furnace.' He read, 'Oh, peoples, nations, and languages, that when you hear the sound of the horn, pipe, lyre, trigon, harp, bagpipe, and every kind of music...' This phrase alone is repeated four times in the short chapter he read, and when he got through, after each time listing those instruments in a singsong monotonous voice, in contrast to the somber, evil voice he projected onto Nebuchadnezzar, the effect was remarkable! He literally conjured out of air the long-dead sort of half-witted herald singing out 'the horn, pipe, lyre, etc.'

"Of the poem, *John Brown's Body*, he said, 'It's an actor's trap. If you aren't careful of the pronunciation it will issue forth as John's Brown Body!' From that poem he portrayed Lincoln talking to God. When it was completed and produced the sort of reverent applause Lincoln portrayals always get, he said, 'An actor never likes to be on the stage with a child or a dog—or another actor portraying three people: Abraham Lincoln, Napoleon Bonaparte, or Jesus Christ. If the actor comes out with his hand here (he held his hand up in front of him), or here (he held his hand across his right breast), you know you are sunk!'

"After reading some more from *Othello*, he prevailed upon the audience to let him rest by just conversing with him. Many interesting questions were asked. One of which was his opinion of the American theatre. 'The largest and richest country in the world but it cannot afford to subsidize its theatres, and they're going broke. In West Germany there are fifty-eight state subsidized theatres; largely subsidized by money from the United States. But we can't afford to subsidize even one! Figure it out if you can. Oh, I know how you feel about the price of a theatre ticket in New York. When I pay $7.50 for a ticket for an adequate little play with competent actors, I certainly don't feel like I'm getting my money's worth even if I take the leading lady home!'"

What Maria and the rest of the audience didn't know was that Conried relied on those informal chats with the audience at the beginning of his performance to feel out what the group's mood and level of intensity was so he could mentally arrange the readings for that evening. Conried did not as a rule arrive with a set order for his readings, and that is why he had to lug so many books with him. The evening was a great success, and his eager students didn't want to leave. The lecture was to end at 10 pm; at 10:20 pm, a very tired Conried had to say, "Haven't you gotten your money's worth yet?"

Conried had pretty much written off motion picture work during the early 1960s, and in fact, he claimed to have rejected nine out of ten offers for films because they conflicted with his schedule of stock tours and lectures. It's hard to believe he would have really turned down so many. After considering the quality of the films he did make during this period, he could have turned down all ten and posterity would not have suffered for it. The films released in 1963 and 1964 were *My Six Loves*, with Debbie Reynolds; *Robin and the Seven Hoods*, with the Rat Pack; and another embarrassing go around with Jerry Lewis in *The Patsy*. At least Lewis gave him a slightly larger part this time, but it was again only as a stooge for his manic antics.

It was reported in at least two different trade papers that Conried had been signed to "star" in Stanley Kramer's "Decision at Nuremberg" in 1961. This was the working title of Kramer's landmark film *Judgment at Nuremberg*. One article not only said he would star in the film, but went on to say, "[Conried] is to appear with a dozen or more important players in Ben Hecht's *Winkelberg*... and he is reading a script for Allan David's version of *The Emperor's New Clothes*...." The latter was reportedly going to be filmed in Copenhagen and was to include the talents of Basil Rathbone and John Carradine. None of these roles ever came to pass, unfortunately.

Kramer had originally cast Conried as "The Entertainer," and he was listed as a member of the cast on the list the filmmaker was required to submit to the MPAA board along with the synopsis and other required paperwork before filming had begun. It is not known if the footage of Conried as the character of "The Entertainer" was ever filmed, but Mrs. Kramer theorized her husband might have wanted to do that story as a separate film. The incredible true story of the man in the concentration camp who entertained children destined for the gas chambers was a deeply moving, powerful story. One could argue that the scene would have been slightly out of place in *Judgment at Nuremberg*, and because of the film's great length, Kramer wrote the character (and Conried) out of the script. Kramer did not follow through with a separate film, but the idea would be picked up again in 1972 by funnyman Jerry Lewis. Lewis adapted the tragic story for his film *The Day the Clown Cried*. Due to legal problems, the Lewis film was never released.

Producer Allan David was able to interest Conried in one of his productions, if only to lend his voice. *The Magic Fountain* was a live-action tale released in 1961 that combined an odd mixture of fairy tale and fantasy. It was filmed entirely on location in Bavaria, and featured a "great cast of Europe's greatest performers" (according to the promotional piece). Conried, Sir Cedric Hardwicke, and Buddy Baer provided the voices of Otto the owl, the narrator, and a bear, respectively. Since only their voices were required, the three did not get a free trip to the Black Forest.

One project Conried had the good fortune to work on probably helped to wash away the bitter taste some of the other of the jobs left. He was asked by Encyclopedia Britannica to be the host and facilitator for a series they were producing. *Great Voices from Great Books* was a thirteen-week series filmed in Chicago for broadcast on public television. After its first limited run in 1961, the series was syndicated and aired to a larger audience around the country in 1962. Conried was pleased to have been chosen for this series: "I am flattered to be included in conversational exercises with distinguished company, and intrigued by a chance to show off in something I haven't memorized... It will be a different television half hour. No beautiful girls with well formed busts, not a single talking horse, and the quick draws will be mental rather than ballistic." Quite a breath of fresh air, it would seem, for Conried. Each show focused on one particular theme, or influence, of great literature, such as "God"; "The Devil"; "The Fountain of Youth"; "Government"; "Shakespeare," and other thought-provoking topics. For the segment on "Humor," Conried had the chance to spend the show conversing with Steve Allen about all aspects of what makes people laugh.

Conried was almost obsessed with the acquisition of knowledge; he was always on a quest to learn something new, and eager to share it with those around him. He was not motivated by a need to ostentatiously attempt to display his superiority, but rather a heartfelt desire to educate. Chicago reporter Johanna Hafner noticed this trait, and observed: "It just may be that Conried is one of the best examples extant of the possibilities of self-education. He reads the way many men eat—regularly, omnivorously, and of necessity. Wherever he does travel, whether it's within the United States borders, in Canada, or [elsewhere], he misses nothing. But nothing. He can see, hear, and absorb more in a week than most individuals could in a year." Conried was quoted in 1976 as saying, "Books are the only way to stay alive in this business. You travel so much that you have to do something to keep yourself occupied..." Conried seemed oblivious to the other ways in which celebrities were known to keep themselves "occupied."

In 1961, Conried toured with his summer stock troupe in a stage version of *Mr. Belvedere*. The pilot he filmed for a possible television series was still being shopped around, but at this stage of the game, it appeared dead in the water. At least he was already so familiar with the part he could easily slip into the stage role. Rehearsing was not something Conried was particularly fond of, and readily expressed his displeasure when asked his opinion by a reporter: "Does a surgeon enjoy plunging a knife into a patient? But ... it's necessary."

Rehearsing was especially necessary, Conried soon discovered, when playing the huge tent theaters he encountered in some of the towns his shows played in. Conried described a not-so-pleasant experience that occurred in one of those tents during his *Not in the Book* tour: "Your entrances have to be timed to the second, and curious things can happen." He recalled one arena in which a member of the audience laughed at all the wrong moments: "That can upset a performer. I stomp off. I was furious. And on my next entrance, which was very quick, I forgot a very important prop. The actor on stage turned to me, held out his hand, and all I could say was, 'I must have forgotten something,' and go all the way back and get it."

An interesting project for Conried was a deal he made to record material for the Panorama division of the Columbia Record Club. Panorama produced three different groups of educational materials in 1961 for their members; the categories would involve the world of art, foreign travel, and the natural sciences. The works consisted of a large, hardback book, complete with three cards containing thirty-two color slides, and a 7," 33 1/3 RPM record. Different celebrities were enlisted to provide the narration for each "tour," or subject. Conried's voice was used on four offerings covering all three categories. The sleeve for the records sports a picture of Conried and a short biography. The biography included with his tour of the Museum of Sao Paolo, Brazil, noted that Conried had been a student for three years at the Art Students League of New York. The League has no record Conried ever studied with them. Most likely he attended a lecture or two sponsored by the A.S.L., and the publicity people put their spin on it to make Conried sound more like an art expert. Make no mistake, though, Conried possessed an impressive knowledge of art and art history that he acquired solely through self-study.

Being away from home—sometimes for eight to ten months a year—was putting a great strain on Conried's family. As if trying to make this painful fact of life a bit easier to accept, Conried came up with a comforting idea after visiting a whaling museum in New England: "If I'd been born a hundred years ago and been a whaler, I'd have been away from home three years at a time." If you think of it that way, being away ten months at a stretch doesn't seem so bad.

In 1962, his oldest was only ten years old, and the youngest was all of five. Conried remarked rather sadly to a reporter that since embarking on his new career of road shows, Margaret "has to be father, mother, and general manager of the household." The children really didn't understand why their father wasn't home very much anymore. They were too young to have a firm idea what their papa did for a living: "Until recently, none of the children were at all impressed by my method of earning even our precarious living. Though now and then I did detect a note of wistfulness when the boys spoke of jet pilots or Canadian mounted police. I might have gone off each day to the plumbing shop, or a greengrocer's for all it mattered to them—so long, of course, as I made sufficient income to keep them in bubble gum. Now, however, our eldest is approaching the age where she suddenly notices the heroes in movies and television. And she asked me, not long ago, why it was no one ever asked me to play such a part. Ah, it's a sad and disillusioning moment, when you're forced to explain to a daughter that you are no longer the dashing, romantic type. Particularly if that is precisely the way she's always envisioned you."

Around this time, Conried felt Trilby was old enough to tell her stories of his early days in show business: "Just the other morning I was trying to explain to my [oldest] daughter about radio as I knew it; its glories and its grandeur. She said, 'Radio? Oh, I know, daddy, you mean the thing in the car.' I promptly sent her to her room." Conried had fun with the gag about sending Trilby to her room, and used it often when telling stories to his friends. Another one was when Trilby called his magnificent 17th century Japanese painting "neat." Conried may have been reluctant to discuss his family with the media, but he relished the chance to tell stories of his children's antics to friends and cast members—exaggerating them ever so slightly, of course, for effect.

In 1962, the summer stock offering would be *Critic's Choice*. Conried reported he was finally given the role of the comically sardonic theatre critic "after two other actors had taken it and kicked it around a couple of places." The part was well received, and Conried would be able to kick the part around again in a dinner theater setting about ten years later.

Conried's time was largely divided between the summer and winter stock tours and the lectures at colleges and universities. He would find himself invigorated by the highly charged, intellectual atmosphere on the campuses he visited. Conried remarked, "I find this extremely rewarding because most adult audiences want visual humor—what some call 'non-think' humor. College students—with their eager, inquisitive minds—want to be entertained and educated. They savor jokes or remarks that are subtle."

Subtlety was not generally the order of the day in the world of comedy, especially on television, where Conried found himself either appearing with a talking horse on *Mr. Ed*, or working with Red Skelton who "throws milk or chalk or something in my face." In-between the slapstick, there were a few quality shows such as the *U.S. Steel*

Hans recording a promotional radio spot in 1962 for one of his clients while in Chicago. From the Hans Conried Collection, Department of Special Collections, Boston University.

Hour, and continued appearances with Jack Paar. On one Paar show in 1961, Conried actually came out from behind his "low clown" defensive mask to spar with his old friend on the subject of Cuba. Conried was decidedly against Paar's endorsement of the idea to give tractors to the Cubans. A fan who watched the program wrote to Conried to applaud his courage for daring to disagree with his host—an action she felt was dangerous for any guest celebrity.

Paar's friendship with Conried was strong enough to weather a small disagreement like that, but could it survive a family vacation? They would find out in April of 1962, when Paar invited Conried, Buddy Hackett, and their families to join him on a tour of Hawaii, Japan, and Hong Kong.

Waiting for their cue: Hans and Sheri Lewis prepare to go on the CBS television special "Step on the Gas" (*U.S. Steel Hour*, 1960).

As always, there would be some filming done in each location for broadcast on one of Paar's shows. Who could turn down such an offer? Conried eagerly accepted, and prepared for the journey. Alex and Edith were considered too young for such a long voyage, so Margaret would accompany her husband with Trilby and Hans III in tow.

Here is where the problems begin: Trilby was old enough to be on her best behavior, but eight-year-old Hans III was behaving like your average, rambunctious boy. The younger Hans laughed as he remembered his exploits: "I was a bad kid! I was an eight year-old pain-in-the-butt, and I know I stressed the relationship between my parents and Jack Paar." Little Hans was running about the place putting his hand up in front of the camera as they were trying to film a scene, "mouthing off," or generally creating havoc wherever he went. Hans continued, "It was a very interesting trip... A week in Honolulu ... where I proceeded to get second-degree sunburn and was sick. Then a week in Tokyo... I thought that it was an amazing thing that on the top level of every department store was a playground... That was a big, exciting deal... The week after we were in Japan, we were in Hong Kong..." The young Hans was fas-

cinated by the floating restaurant in Kowloon Harbor, and that mysterious fruit he learned was called a mango.

The Conried kids were treated to all sorts of wonderful foods and gifts—Hans noted the miniature reel-to-reel tape recorder he was presented with. Of course, Asian food was not something new to the children. After all, their father was by his own account a "rabid Japanophile" and collector of all manner of Asian art. Hans, the younger, had been exposed to such exotic delicacies as Japanese sushi as a very young boy: "My father had a lot of friends in the Japanese community. In Los Angeles, one of the first Japanese communities was on First Street—"Little Tokyo." We would go down there to the Nisei Week Festival, and picnics."

The footage shot by the Paar crew included a fanciful scene where Conried plays

Top: One in a series of four promotional photos Hans posed for to advertise his appearance in *Critic's Choice* (Florida: 1962). A local reporter did a feature on him for the *Palm Beach Post-Times.* Hans was displaying his disapproval of the reporter's "gross carelessness" in misspelling his name. From the Hans Conried Collection, Department of Special Collections, Boston University.

Bottom: Hans, Jack Paar, and Buddy Hackett in Japan during the spring of 1962. Hans makes the most ungainly geisha, yet manages to look traditionally elegant. From the Hans Conried Collection, Department of Special Collections, Boston University.

a winsome geisha who is fought over by two strapping samurai suitors: Jack Paar and Buddy Hackett. Transforming Conried into a geisha was a time-consuming, elaborate process performed by Japanese artists who were skilled in the Kabuki theatre. The result, though, was rather shocking, as one is not used to seeing a nearly seven foot tall geisha (the wig added even more height).

Later, the three comrades would go to a karate school, where they donned training robes, and were taught a few moves by an expert in the ancient art. Another segment featured Conried—clothed in a small garment that covered the essentials—being given a traditional sponge bath by a lovely, young, scantily clad Japanese woman. The scenes were supposed to give just a hint of impropriety, but with Mrs. Conried watching the entire proceedings (along with the rest of the crew), there wasn't much chance of Conried going astray.

Because Conried had such an erudite aura about him, Buddy Hackett thought he was smug when they first met. That opinion was quickly dissolved by Conried's genuine warmth and friendliness. Hackett would remember Conried as being "a gem of a person; outgoing and helpful." He would be astonished that the Conried children were so matter-of-fact about their father's decision to donate his body after death. They described to Hackett how their father's organs would be used by people who needed them. This candor made a big impression on Hackett, and he was influenced to incorporate this realism into his parenting style.

Back in the U.S., Conried quickly resumed his exhausting schedule of back-to-back lectures, personal appearances, stock tours, recordings, television shows, and many other projects. The glamour of Hollywood seemed very far away.

10

The Business of TV Guest Spots and Jay Ward

Conried, the business man, knew that in order to sell the required amount of tickets to his stock shows and lectures, he had to keep his name in the public eye. The best way to do that was to be seen regularly on television. Television, Conried would tell a reporter, was the "basis of success at this time. Everything else I do depends on television exposure." As a former radio actor, Conried still loathed the entire television industry, but he had to make his deal with the "devil" to keep his career alive.

Beginning around 1963, character actors were finding it increasingly difficult to make a living in Hollywood. Conried was acutely aware of the shrinking market in his adopted hometown: "I have been living in Hollywood for twenty-seven years, but nowadays I have to make my money outside California. For a while, the half-hour TV series gave [character actors] work, but now it has disappeared. Today, a series casts a well-formed young football player, a fellow who works in a gas station, a girl who fits calico snugly, and a bartender who nods. That rounds it out. There's no need for other characters. I tell you, the hour show has been very costly for all of us [character actors]. There are half as many directors working and practically the same figures apply down the line to writers, cameramen, etc."

Films were also using fewer character actors, and followed very much the same formula Conried outlined for television shows. Conried was so disgusted by the sad state of affairs in Hollywood he was quoted as saying, "Picture making is no longer an American craft. Hollywood is now putting out smut for smut's sake to appeal to the teenage crowd."

The stage has never been immune to trends, and very often plays reflect the controversial subjects of their day. Conried was not always comfortable with the risqué subject matter of some of the plays he appeared in, and on occasion would petition a change of dialogue if the script called for something too off-color. Conried was very sensitive to change, and even as early as the 1960s he could feel the changes in the wind for the type of summer and winter stock work that represented the core of his yearly earnings. Broadway was beginning to shift from hosting traditional one or two set dramas and comedies to more lavish musical productions. Conried prophetically said, "I think we'll see the day when Broadway shows are solely musicals. The sensationalism that we've been getting in serious drama lately can be produced much less expensively off-Broadway. Personally, I'd like to see the return to the drawing room comedy sort of thing." The stock circuits relied heavily on the easy to produce, easy to travel with comedy and drama plays that had their first runs on Broadway. Without this steady stream of shows to take on the road, the entire industry would suffer.

There were those who felt Conried's new career on the legitimate stage was a noble endeavor designed to bring culture to the masses, but the true reason was—according to Conried—more down-to-earth: "I'd like to say that I tour in summer stock because I am bringing the theater to America. The truth is that I have a wife and four children and a need for food, and summer stock is very remunerative." Along the same theme, Conried somewhat cynically confessed: "I have no romantic notions whatsoever about the theater. I am an actor because acting is the only way I can make a living... A sense of reality, and a sense of humor, nullified any other avenue of escape."

Still not satisfied with that, some reporters prodded Conried to learn more about how he approached his craft. Was he, for example, a "method actor"? "I certainly am," Conried enthusiastically replied, "My method is to get a job, and then try to please the people who hire me." Another reporter wanted to know how he went about choosing a play: "I have little to do with the choice. There are only a certain number of plays available on the summer circuit. After they have asked a reasonable number of more prominent actors, they ask me. I accept." Conried was aware that his appeal was of a different nature than some other well-known actors of his day: "[Robert] Taylor and [Richard] Burton I ain't. They have a sort of sexual substance about them. I have to be loved for my material, my delivery." Of course, Conried had other factors to consider before signing on the dotted line: "It must be a decent role ... of sufficient size. Because, after all, this is rather connected with the amount they will pay me."

There was a good deal of self-deprecation in many of the comments Conried made to reporters during those hundreds of interviews he gave over the course of his career. Underneath it all, he genuinely enjoyed being on the stage: the star of his very own production. Besides the obvious ego gratification, there was a sincere desire to entertain people and make them happy. Conried spoke of his preference for a live audience: "There's a satisfaction with doing a stage play you can't get anywhere else. It's the only medium in which you have direct contact with the audience; they came and paid money to see you perform. In TV, you work for someone only interested in selling breakfast food. The public has little to say about the success of a performance. Stars are made within the confines of closed rooms. The stage is not that way." Providing entertainment was his calling in life, he felt, and if people wanted him to make them laugh, then he would give them the biggest laugh they ever had. And Conried rarely disappointed his audience.

Conried would describe his many adjustments to the whims of fate as being in tune with the British domestic servant who was "satisfied in the situation to which God was pleased to call him." For the most part, he was content with his life, and that, according to his philosophy, was the root of happiness: "Happiness in its most crystalline, pristine state is contentment. Contentment may not render you breathless, but neither can you be dashed off the pinnacle into bleak despair. I am a contented man, therefore, I consider myself to be a happy man." This contentment, Conried believed, stemmed from the fact that, despite the many ups and downs of his life, he was one of the lucky people in the world who could actually do what they wanted to: "Unfortunately there are those who cannot do what they want. That includes most of the people of the world. I can. That's one reason why I am a contented, even bland, person. And I have horse sense, if I may be permitted to call it that. When there is something I can do nothing about, I accept it." Conried seemed to be a firm believer in knowing your own limits (set by yourself), and staying strictly within those boundaries no matter what. It never paid to push too hard against the current, or in other words, it was best to "go with the flow." The "flow" Conried was riding with was low comedy: "A man must do not so much what he considers ennobling, not what offers him the most recompense, but whatever he can do best. There is nothing else I know in life so well as making a public fool of myself."

Conried's form graced television screens at regular intervals during the 1960s. He was a guest on *The Lucy Show* a couple of times, *Gilligan's Island*, *Burke's Law*, *Dr. Kildare*, and as many other TV shows as he could fit into his schedule. One notable guest appearance was on the 1965 "Dipperful of Water from a Poison Well" episode of *Ben Casey*. This program gave Conried a rare chance to flex his dramatic muscles, and he delivered a gritty, yet sympathetic performance as the head of a tragically dysfunctional family. The lighthearted 1964 *Dr. Kildare* episode titled "Last Leaves on the Tree" provided just the opposite experience, and Conried was in top comedic form in an almost slapstick portrayal of an eccentric (and accident prone) member of an even more eccentric family.

There were also the continued appearances with Jack Paar, and the donning of the fake nose for his Uncle Tonoose on *The Danny Thomas Show*.

Paar would eventually decide to fade out of the television scene altogether in the mid–1960s. Conried was later asked about his friend's departure from the medium that brought him such success: "I don't think Jack Paar should have felt an obligation to go on forever for his public. To what extent does a performer owe his life, or the rest of his life, to the public? He gave a great deal of himself, perhaps more than any man now performing. He gave a good deal of blood, sweat, and several yards of intestines."

Mike Stokey's *Pantomime Quiz* made one final bow during the 1962–1963 season, appearing for the last time in a slightly revamped format under the name *Stump the Stars*. Pat Harrington, Jr., was originally signed to be the host, but was hastily replaced by Stokey in December of 1962. Conried was a seasoned veteran with many years of service under his belt. That last season, though, was one of the toughest he ever had to sit through. The "stumpers" became so complex, and in many cases, lengthy, that with increasing frequency the celebrities could not complete them. Considering a prize had to be given out every time a star was stumped, and the prizes now ranged from a complete set of luggage up to a portable television (remember the cigarette lighters?), the show must have been losing large sums of money. Conried was very competitive, and it was frustrating for him to lose so often. He also endured being accidentally hit in the mouth by an over-excited Beverly Garland on more than one occasion. On one memorable show—in an effort to solve the gag definition of a psychiatrist's couch: "An ad lib id lab"—Beverly got down on her hands and knees trying to imitate a "kid," and crawled up to Conried's lap. She then put her face within inches of his, and kept swatting his nose in a desperate effort to force the word "id" out of him. The attractive Ms. Garland rolling around in his lap became too much for Conried, who could only manage to come up with "libido." Their team lost.

Paar provided Conried with an interesting diversion in 1963 by asking him to dress up as Abraham Lincoln and speak to a group of students at an elementary school in Beverly Hills. The encounter was filmed, and the edited results were shown on Paar's television show. Conried was happy to do it, and remarked, "I tell you; I had to bone up for those kids. Their questions were tough,

Hans dressed as Abe Lincoln for a segment on *The Jack Paar Show* (1963). The event was filmed at an elementary school in Beverly Hills. From the Hans Conried Collection, Department of Special Collections, Boston University.

and they were a much more demanding audience. They are completely apathetic. They do not come to be entertained. Adults want to be taken from reality and it's much easier. But you have to work to get the kids, and it's worth it... I was with those kids dressed as Lincoln for nearly an hour... Everything was going swimmingly until one kid asked 'How would you handle Cuba?'"

Uncle Tonoose was by far Conried's most recognizable character, and he found people throughout the land who knew him from *The Danny Thomas Show*. Finally, in 1964, he had the opportunity to visit the homeland of the fictional Williams clan when one of his college lectures took him to Toledo, Ohio. The press and public showered Conried with attention, and though he was a bit bewildered by it all, he was also very grateful. A few years earlier the American, Lebanese, Syrian Associated Charities—a fundraising organization for Danny Thomas' St. Jude's Hospital—named Conried an "Honorary Lebanese," and presented him with a certificate at one of their fundraising banquets.

Whether or not Conried really felt the Tonoose character was like "the mark of Cain," it did open up the wide, wonderful world of Lebanese food. He became quite a connoisseur of Lebanese and other Middle Eastern food, and would actively seek out restaurants serving such delicacies whenever he was on tour. Conried did not allow himself any of the more obvious vices whatsoever, but he did have an obsession with food that would almost rival his compulsion to collect.

Let's face it: Conried loved to eat! Food was more than just a necessity to him, and he went so far as to describe it once as "the greatest pleasure in the world." Conried was passionate about food, and as often as not, many of the interviews he was obliged to give while on his summer and winter stock tours included a paragraph or two on what he ate for breakfast. Though Conried bemoaned this sort of journalism—feeling it stripped away the "magic" of the theater to know what the actors were like as people—he seemed to wholeheartedly discuss the menu, and freely complained about the sorry state of restaurant bacon: "Most restaurants serve bacon mechanically cut from a pig that has never known love." Though Conried was accustomed to being thin for most of his life, he would find himself steadily gaining in girth as the years progressed. A rude reporter, who was lunching with Conried at the time, once asked if he ever considered going on a diet: "I don't bother," Conried said, ordering a slice of cheesecake. "I believe that everyone loves a fat man."

Voice work was one area of employment in Hollywood that may not have paid extremely well, but it did provide steady work throughout the 1960s and 1970s. Voice acting was the perfect place for many former radio actors—who were, of course, well trained in using their voice as their "instrument"—to find a new niche for their talents. Conried had first heard of the enterprising and ingenious cartoon producer Jay Ward back in 1957. Ward was recruiting cast members for a proposal he was working on with animator Shamus Culhane for a series to be called *Phineas T. Phox, Adventurer*. Ward eventually left the production team due to some conflicts with Culhane, and the project later died. Conried would meet up with Ward again in 1960, and he soon became part of a lively group of creative individuals who comprised Jay Ward Productions.

Jay Ward and the gifted writer and voice actor Bill Scott were two of the most talented people ever to work in the field of animation. The early 1960s were a fertile landscape for pioneers such as Ward and Scott to experiment with their craft in ways that had never been tried before. They didn't have the most elaborate studios or fancy equipment, and their budgets often were laughable, but what they did have in abundance was a rich treasure trove of some of the finest, most talented voice actors in the business at their disposal: William Conrad, Edward Everett Horton, Paul Frees, June Foray, Daws Butler, and of course, Hans Conried. With these actors, and an intelligent, capable writing staff that featured Bill Scott at the helm, Jay Ward was able to produce some of the most memorable cartoon characters of the 20th century: Crusader Rabbit, Bullwinkle and Rocky, Dudley Do-Right, Snidely Whiplash, and Hoppity Hooper.

Conried was first hired by Ward to do the voice of the evil Snidely Whiplash, who was the nemesis of the "stalwart true, with eyes of blue" Canadian Mountie, Dudley Do-Right. Snidely was a comically despicable fellow, with a top-hat, cape, and curling moustache, who enjoyed evicting widows and orphans into the snow, yet somehow gave the impression he wasn't such a bad guy—just misunderstood. In a letter to Margaret after Conried's death, Bill Scott revealed Conried had told him, "I didn't 'do' a voice. I always thought they wrote that part for the 'real' me." Conried would periodically go in to record his Snidely performances in set blocks of time beginning in 1960 through 1964. Conried said at the time, "We have more fun than we should have in the recording sessions... Bill Scott, who writes, is a brilliant man... He can do anything. He's a tremendous actor, but the world will never know about it...."

Also during this period, Jay Ward asked Conried to be the host of a television series he had in mind—something new and revolutionary. It would be a live action show that combined the talents of a genial host (Conried) and a series of short comedy segments that were made out of cannibalized pieces from old silent films, which were spliced together with a new soundtrack. The series would be called *Fractured Flickers*. The results were like nothing that had been on television before. Conried recalled years later, "I didn't exactly have a hand in it, but I had a tongue in it—a helluva lot of jokes. We had an absolute party doing those shows. The lines weren't arcane or obscure, just witty. It was rather a cut above the usual comedy program. But, unfortunately, it wasn't extra popular. And it was very expensive and took a great deal of time."

A pilot show was made in 1960—sans interviews—that featured Conried as a dour character named H. Carleton Fothergill. Fothergill was written as a proud classical actor who was appalled at having to do such a demeaning show. He tried to find a loophole in his contract to get out of his predicament. No loophole could be found with his "Fothergill's Patented Loophole Finder" (a magnifying glass), and he was forced to go on. Conried's characterization created a melancholy man who was a broken shell of his former self, and could now only use his supercilious snarls as a way to get even. Conried's work was expertly done, but it may have been a tad too dark for a comedy show like *Fractured Flickers*. When the show was picked up and put into production in 1963, Conried appeared as himself, and was therefore more warm and fuzzy, though still retaining that "why am I doing schlock like this?" kind of attitude. Twenty-six half-hour episodes were completed in all.

Each show followed a set formula: Conried would come in at the beginning, and somewhere in the middle, and then again at the end. His bits were always funny, and in Ward's characteristic way, often derogatory towards the show. The serious lack of funds was satirized, and many times Jay Ward and his staff became the butt of a "Flickers" joke. The writers even poked fun at Conried. A fine example of this was from an episode where Conried was supposedly reading a letter from a *Fractured Flickers* fan—a "Mr. R. E."—who asked the question: "I noticed every summer you appear as a light comedian in summer stock; every fall you appear on the lecture circuit as a serious actor doing dramatic readings; and every winter you appear on television as a buffoon, or a low Dutch comic. Which is the real you?" Conried cheerfully replied, "None of them, Mr. E. The real me is the one who appears at the unemployment office every spring."

One running gag was the ever-present threat of lawsuits that Conried would allude to now and then in his commentaries. The threat did have an air of reality about it: Lon Chaney, Jr., was extremely unhappy with the way the *Fractured Flickers* staff had mangled his late, great father's *Hunchback of Notre Dame*. After Ward was done with it, Lon Chaney became a cheerleader named Dinky Dunstan.

If the erudite host or the "Flickers" themselves weren't enough to keep the audience's attention, *Fractured Flickers* included a short celebrity interview. The interviews are arguably the best elements in the show. It wasn't always easy to find a celebrity to interview—one good reason for that being they were not paid. Conried would often recruit fellow celebrities from other television shows he was working on at the time, such as *Stump the Stars*. The first guest was Rose Marie, and the last (and one of the best) was Zsa Zsa Gabor. Along the way Conried had fun with Alan Sherman, Sebastian Cabot, Bob Newhart, Gypsy Rose Lee, Ursula Andress, and others. Fabian turned out to be a great foil for Conried, who had fun pretending to be outraged at Fabian's claim of extreme youth. Conried asked Fabian why he kept calling him "sir," and the young man innocently replied, "I call everyone over sixty 'sir', sir." Another youngster, Annette Funicello, also surprised her "aged" host by reminding him, "I'm sort of grown up now, Mr. Conried." Conried looked into the camera and replied, "Never have the words 'sort of' been so fraught with meaning!"

The pace required to produce these shows was mind-boggling, if not a little inhumane. The writers would frequently work round-the-clock, nearly going blind by sifting through numerous reels of old footage, just to get enough material for one half-hour show. Conried would be called in to tape all of his segments in one day: "We never shot shows; we only shot footage. They edited them into shows... I was then on the road a good deal—on the stage—and they would say, 'Listen, we've got six days of shooting. Do you have six days?' and I'd say, 'Sure, I'll be in town six days'. So, we would have then twelve opening introductions. Watch the series. They're all interchangeable bits. They have an introduction ... a closing, and little embracing hooks where you can tie two pieces together. But any two pieces can be tied together by these little shots of me. We had celebrity guests, and they would book an hour with eight guests; one every hour... I'd sit down and talk with Star [#1] at 9 o'clock in the morning, and [Bill] Scott would be in an office typing the interview for Star #4... He'd seldom be an hour or two ahead of his star... They'd give each celebrity a funny hat as a gift. That's about all they got, I think, and a warm handshake, and spoken thanks."

Conried also provided the voice for another Jay Ward–produced cartoon, *Hoppity Hooper*, which first appeared in syndication in 1964. He was the conniving old fox who, in the first episode, befriended the guileless and gullible little frog, Hoppity Hooper. Somehow, the shifty stranger convinced Hoppity he was his long-lost Uncle Waldo Wigglesworth. As hard as that was to believe, Hoppity fell for it, and they became partners in crime (so to speak), along with Waldo's dimwitted sidekick, Fillmore Bear. Bill Scott did the voice for Fillmore in all but the first two episodes, when it was Allan Reed (an old friend of Conried's from Radio Row). One of the ongoing jokes in this series was Waldo's inability to remember Fillmore's name, and the outlandish concoctions he would come up with. Some were inside jokes, like "Feldman" (Conried played Wrongway Feldman in a couple of episodes of *Gilligan's Island*), and "Finster" (the name of a monster created by Snidely Whiplash in an episode of *Dudley Do-Right of the Mounties*). *Hoppity Hooper* didn't quite have as much of Ward's witty polish, and never achieved the "cult" status some of his other creations have been able to engender.

In an effort to spend a little "quality time" with his young namesake, Conried brought his oldest son along to a recording session for *Hoppity Hooper*. The younger Hans remembers the fun he had there, and how strange it was to see two grown men trying to talk like a fox and a bear. He had so much fun that he couldn't quite help making a lot of noise, and talking when he wasn't supposed to. Unfortunately, Hans was ejected from the recording booth, and had to wait for his dad outside.

Even though he was finding an increasing amount of work outside of California, Conried loved Los Angeles: "I don't think I'd want to live anywhere else but Los Angeles. It is a good, balanced life for [my family]... I shall always live there, God willing. My young are born there. My dead are buried there. And though badly scarred, I'm one of the few to survive out there. My comfort, and my second pair of shoes are there."

Part of Conried's strategy for maintaining his sanity throughout the often-grueling schedule of stage performances and personal appearances was to place a very rigid barrier between his personal life and the public persona he displayed for the rest of the world. While on tour, Conried was well known for carrying around a heavy suitcase filled with his stamp collection and other small collectibles. After the evening's performance was done, he would make his way back to his room, and spend a few hours arranging and identifying his stamps. Conried explained, "I'm a stamp collector from way back. I can't bear to throw the most ordinary of them away. I have shoeboxes of them full to the tops. Sometimes, I send them to Japanese students. They are rare over there." He made sure to pack a few books for the road, and he made regular visits to local bookstores to buy more as he passed through each town. The most important part of Conried's evening, though, was his phone call home to Margaret. This call was his lifeline, as he confided to his friend Jerry Hausner: "If I didn't have my darling wife to call every night, this wouldn't be a life at all." He was missing so much of his children's lives, yet he could not find any other option if he hoped to continue with his acting career.

One of the more memorable tours during this period was the summer tour of the successful comedy *Absence of a Cello* in 1965. The cast included a dashing, young actor named James Karen, who would very quickly become firm friends with the play's star: "I had admired Hans' work. I did not know him from stage, I only knew him from television... We went off on the road, and we hit it off, and we had an absolutely wonderful tour... One of the [reasons] we hit it off was when he saw me reading a book one day, and he said, 'What are you reading?' and I showed it to him, and it was a translated Russian novel. He said, 'Uh huh... I haven't seen any actor read that in a long time. Do you understand it?' I said [in a strained voice], 'Yes, Hans, I understand it just fine.' He was impressed. That was early on in our relationship, and we became fast friends."

Karen was pleased to find that Conried "had the graciousness not to take himself too seriously." He recognized the formidable façade Conried showed to the world was merely another part he was playing: "He was a man who played at being an actor of the old school. Hans was definitely not a modern person. He was [more] Victorian, or Edwardian." The Karen and Conried families would become great friends over the years. The Conried kids looked forward to seeing their "Uncle Jimmy."

The humor of *Absence of a Cello* revolved around Conried's character, a nonconformist who found himself in the uncomfortable position of having to hide his eccentricities in order to obtain a coveted job with a large, conservative corporation. There was an element of underlying seriousness to the script that Karen and Conried both commented on, but Conried was reluctant to try to nurture this element during his performances. Karen remembers the play "was a comedy, but it had a serious quality to it too. Hans got an enormous number of laughs in it. One time—we fooled around a lot, because we were just having so much fun, and it was summer stock, it wasn't Broadway—I said, 'Hans, you know you could really play the hell out of this part. You could really play it the way it never has been played before', and he said, 'Well, I don't like to do that... I like to have fun.' I said we ought to play it one time, and I kept at him. When we were in Barnesville, Pennsylvania in a small summer theater on a rainy afternoon—a matinee—and there weren't too many people in the house, Hans suddenly started to play it for real, emotionally, and not covering up with jokes and stuff. And it was one of those performances none of the actors left the stage, they just stood in the wings when they'd get off stage and watch him. When it was over, I went to him and I said, 'Hans, my God!' and he said, 'It was good, wasn't it? I didn't enjoy it. I'll never do that again!' He never played it that way again... [Hans] had tremendous range as an actor. Always lurking behind the comedy was a truthfulness that worked for him. He might get what we call a 'cheap laugh', but there was a reason for it, and there was something that made it work. Hans' problem as an actor was he just loved to amuse people; loved to make people laugh, and he just decided he did not want to be a tragedian, but a comedian. And he could have been a classical actor."

This tour was also special for being one of the few times all four of the Conried kids had a chance to spend some time with their father during their summer break from school. The entire family spent one whole month traveling around New England. Hans III was allowed to fly out to the East Coast ahead of the rest of the family—something unthinkable for many parents today—and remembered the trip as being a "big adventure": "I went a week ahead of the rest of my family to New York, because [the cast was] doing rehearsals in New York City... Normally when [my dad] was out on the road, he would work in the evenings, but during rehearsal week, or the two weeks before, it was during the day. So they were working at a theater, or a rehearsal studio, someplace in downtown New York City, and I, as an eleven-year-old kid, am wandering around New York City by myself... That was the summer that they had the World's Fair there, and I thought it was pretty cool when you'd see all these long lines, and my dad would walk up [and say] 'Come on in!', and you're right at the head of the line. I didn't realize the unfairness of it at the time, but it avoided standing in a lot of long lines."

Margaret disliked airplanes, and decided to take the other three kids with her on the train back to New England. Once there, the Conrieds traveled around in a rented station wagon from gig to gig, enjoying the beautiful New England countryside along the way. During the day, there was time to explore some of the lakes and beaches, and do the sorts of things any normal family would do on vacation. In the evening, Margaret would entertain the kids while her husband readied himself for his performance. Conried remarked to a reporter in Maine: "My oldest son, Hans ... was my dresser during that time. It didn't take a lot of time, so he also butchered candy, and soda pop, and made himself useful backstage. The theater is great on discipline, and it was good for him. I believe in discipline, but I'm not sure I'm always able to enforce it." Hans recalled his stint as a dresser was just a minor thing—usually it involved handing his dad an article of clothing or two—and was designed primarily to keep him out of trouble.

After Margaret and the children returned to California, Conried continued on with the production on the bus with the rest of the cast. A reporter for the *North East Breeze* captured the events of one blustery, sunny day in Pennsylvania as the tour bus decided to stop at the corner of Interstate 90 and Route 20. Almost immediately, a large crowd started to gather for autographs. The reporter noted that "Conried exclaimed, 'I say, we didn't know we were playing here', as he surveyed the crowd, 'Why, we have more customers on the highway than our last stage appearance. We must come to Route 20 again sometime.'" Never one to lose out on a golden opportunity, the reporter heard Conried shout to the cast: "'Get out those Indian blankets and let's go to work! I've never seen such a good market for trinkets!' [The crowd forgot the wind and] traipsed behind Conried like he was 'Mr. Showbiz' himself." One of the autograph seekers in the crowd was a local lady of some prominence who was rather sweet on Conried. She suggestively asked, "What are you doing this evening, dear?" Before Conried had a chance to answer, the lady's husband inserted himself between them, causing a shocked Conried to recoil and gasp, "Give me back my autograph!" The whole scene was played for laughs, of course, and the crowd "screamed in delight."

The *Absence of a Cello* tour finished up in early 1966 in San Francisco. While in town, Conried spoke at length to a reporter about the state of legitimate theatre, and some of the trials and tribulations of being a provincial actor: "People are going to plays. Make no mistake about that. Not just L.A. or the big cities, but across the country. In towns you never heard of. I've played them and I never heard of them. They turn out. They do turn out, by the thousands. It's affluence. Everybody has money. One thing to do is to go to plays. Not that they're really seeing plays until they see them in a real theater. We play these tremendous auditoriums—3,000, 5,000, 7,500 people at a crack. And we're doing an intimate little comedy. How do you expect to get intimacy with 7,500 people? Suppose you raise an eyebrow to make a point, or get the laugh.

Do you think 7,500 people could see you do it? They're lucky if they can see your face!

"Not that it is always the great mobs. We played a little town in Nebraska. It was a beautiful day and when we stepped off the bus I mentioned to a local how nice the weather was. He said we were lucky; it had been raining for two weeks. Now, I'm a provincial player! I said we're doing a matinee on the first sunny day after two weeks of rain. There'll be no one in the theater. Everybody'll be out plowing. They were. They'd sold only eighteen tickets for that matinee and I counted only thirteen people who'd come. I went out, made a little speech and thanked them and said we couldn't really give a performance for so few people. I said they could get their money back but I urged them to exchange their tickets for the night performance. I told them they really couldn't object if we gave no performance because we outnumbered them. Oh ... there are days like that. And nights when you hate to get on that bus and travel six hours. Everything is six hours apart—that's the maximum on the bus and the bookers seem to make sure you go the maximum. Sleep in a different bed every night. Well, I say to myself, perhaps I'm lucky to have a bed at all. This summer will be a joy. Six months at home. I've been going out on tour for eight or nine years now. Last year I was away from home for ten months—hardly knew my children. But between *Cello* and *The [Student] Prince*, I'll have six months in Los Angeles.

"The one mistake people make is to discount the road. That audience is growing very sophisticated. You can't give them the schlock companies they once sent out with bus and truck. You'll die. Now you must cast your play very carefully. Look at this company—we have Ruth McDevitt from the Broadway cast, Donald Buka, Florida Friebus; first-rate people down the line. And me, of course. I never really made it in television but because of Uncle Tonoose and *Fractured Flickers*, I'm a TV personality. And TV personalities sell tickets. I started out to be a Shakespearean actor, but there was really no market for Shakespearean actors. But there was radio. Wonderful radio. Twenty years of radio. Then the bottom fell out, and there I was. Jack Paar transformed me into a television personality. And now here I am—finally on the stage. Out with my company, my name above the title. Not doing Shakespeare, perhaps. But not doing badly."

Conried was able to stay at home for a little while during the summer of 1966. He wasn't just relaxing by the swimming pool, though. As he mentioned to the reporter in San Francisco, Conried accepted a part in the Los Angeles Civic Light Opera's revival of *The Student Prince* that was to open in July. "Actors don't really take vacations," Conried would say, "they only have periods of unemployment between engagements." Trilby remembers that during this period any time they spent with their father outside of California was directly related to whatever job he happened to be doing. There were no organized family vacations. Conried was in a position to include the expenses for his family in his contracts, so it was cheaper and more efficient to have them follow him.

After *The Student Prince*, Conried was back on the road doing his one-man shows at colleges, universities, and on the "creamed chicken" circuit. It was necessary for Conried to be ready for anything, and he had to be prepared to go on under any circumstances. One example of that occurred in Michigan while he was just starting his lecture at the University there. The rain was coming down in sheets, and the violent wind eventually knocked out the power to the school's auditorium. Undaunted, candles were lit, and Conried quipped, "I've always wanted to play Lady Macbeth!"

The next stock production—*Generation*—would bring together Conried and his old friend Jerry Hausner. Conried played the part of a conservative father whose pregnant daughter wanted to deliver her baby at home. Hausner played the doctor Conried smuggles in to stand by in case of trouble. These two colorful characters met back in 1937 while doing a radio show, and quickly became fast friends. Hausner was the older of the two, but noted that on radio, he often was given parts where he played a younger man, while Conried was always pretending to be much older. The infamous "be better" story was a constant source of amusement for Hausner who never lost an opportunity to relive the moment with anyone who would listen. Over the years their friendship would deepen, and they remained very close until Conried's death. The Conried kids knew Hausner as "Uncle Jerry," and he and his family were frequent guests to the Conried home.

Hausner loved to talk about his old friend and his many eccentricities. In 1986, towards the end of his life, Hausner spoke of his time spent on the road with Conried and *Generation*: "[Hans] would carry his mess kit from the Army ... and he'd get up at 5 o'clock in the morning, have his constitutional walk, go into a market, and get a small container of cottage cheese, and a jar of herring, or something like that. Then we would have lunch in a restaurant usually, and he would steal all the crackers and the rolls and put them in the pocket of his overcoat. Then he would save all these things and eat up in his hotel room late at night. That's the way he lived. He would call his wife long distance every night... It's really a terrible life, you know, one-night-stands, because you're in the snow, you're in the rain, you're in strange places and you don't know anybody, and there isn't time to get acquainted."

Worrying about where he was going to find food after a late night performance caused Conried a great deal of anxiety. Sometimes, the mess kit idea didn't work out, and he and Jerry would be left without anything to snack on. In many towns, all the stores and restaurants were closed up tight by 11 P.M. Hausner recalled one such night in Dallas when they walked the streets in search of a bite of food. They finally were directed to a lone candy machine. After a frightful moment where they thought they didn't even have the required dime, they each finally managed to scrounge a nickel out of their pockets. Soon they were the proud owners of a tiny Hershey bar that was skillfully divided in half by Conried. As they were standing there under a street light, eating their chocolate, Conried said, "Now, do you think if we told our wives what a wild time we were having here in Dallas, Texas, do you think they'd believe us?!"

One particularly hot evening during the tour, the mechanically challenged Conried found himself in a quandary, as Hausner would recall: "One night in a hotel [Hans] called me in my room and said, 'Do you know how to turn the air conditioning off? I'm freezing in here!' I said, 'Yes, I'll be right over'. I go to his room, and he was in bed; he had taken the drapes down—it was so cold. He took the drapes off the windows—big heavy drapes—and he had an extra blanket, and he had the drapes on top—he had his overcoat—and he said there's nothing left except a picture of Stonewall Jackson... He said, 'If you can't fix this air conditioning, I'm going to take the picture off the wall and put that on top of this bed!'"

Marietta LaFargue (who was Marietta Frederici then) was the understudy for lead actress Nancy Donohue. The *Generation* tour was her first experience with the life of a traveling actor, and in an interview with the author she remembered her time with Conried very warmly: "Hans was a wonderful 'road dad' and delightful human being... We had been out for quite some time and were very tired. One of the grips [teamsters who drive the trucks and set up scenery] who was from an out of the way town in West Virginia—very poor, coal mine stripped area—asked Hans if we could stop in his hometown for lunch. Hans could refuse no one; he was very generous. We were all grumbling because we just wanted to get where we were going to eat, shower, and get some rest. The bus driver found the town, which at that time of the year, early spring, was very dry, dusty and dead looking. The relatives of this man and most of the town turned out to see us. The place where we ate, a small austere restaurant, was set up for us with the best they had to offer. Not gourmet for sure. Hans was so gracious and charming, talking to the family, signing autographs, answering all questions put to him with such warmth and kindness. He made the rest of us stop, and look around; see the importance of humility and kindness. The man whose town it was beamed with pride. No one had ever done something like this for him I am sure. I know Nancy and I were close to tears, seeing the poverty of the people, even the children had a gray cast to their complexions. It was, for most of the cast, a highlight of our trip. [Many] of us had never witnessed this kind of grinding poverty and malnutrition. For Hans, it was just another day. Nothing special.

"On the lighter side, Tom [Ligon], Nancy, David [Rosenbaum], and I used to play little tricks on Hans. We would pull into a diner on the highway for lunch or dinner, and when Hans and Jerry got situated at their table, we would stand outside the window staring in at them, sometimes with our noses pressed to the window, begging for food. Other times we would tell patrons in the restaurant that we were on a gospel tour with Millard Fillmore, the greatest gospel singer in the world, and point to Hans. Many people would come up and ask who he was: 'Who is that man, I recognize him, he's on TV isn't he?' 'Why yes', we would reply. 'That's Millard Fillmore, and we're with his gospel choir'. Of course they would rush over and ask for his autograph. The joy was in seeing the perplexed look on Hans' face when they called him Mr. Fillmore. One cold night we dragged into a hotel completely exhausted after over eight hours of travel. David, whom we nicknamed 'Snake', because he was such a womanizer, had an awful cold. For some reason we were put in rooms opposite each other in a little cul-de-sac at the end of the hall, cut off from everyone else (usually Nancy and I bunked together, but not this time). When Hans saw where they were putting me, he rushed over and hovered like the protective father he was, shaking his finger at me: 'Tomorrow morning, if you wake up with a cold, I'm calling your mother!'

"Later, on that tour, toward the end when we were all very sick of traveling, and more than sick of being away from our lovers and significant others (Hans for sure) I saw his dressing room door open just a crack and in a low whisper he called to me and Nancy, 'Come here little girls, I have candy…' We both laughed so hard we cried. We knew it was really time to get off the road if 'Hansala' was going over the edge!

"Occasionally we would come to a town where they had a large community theater involvement. Usually we would be invited to dinner or to some kind of reception. Also, someone from this theater group would volunteer to help with the wardrobe, laundry, etc., just to be close to the actors. In one town in Ohio, I think, a young woman offered to do the laundry. I was grateful because this was my job and though small, still not a lot of fun. Hans liked sharp corners on his Oxford cloth shirts and I was a lousy ironer. He was most gracious, though occasionally he would plead with me to try harder not to make creases. Well, this woman said she could do it and would enjoy the job. The company manager decided he would let her wash his shirts too, what the heck. Hans had just had four brand new shirts made at no small expense. The woman poured an entire half-gallon of bleach into the laundry load. When I arrived at the theater to set the wardrobe she greeted me with the shirts in shreds. I almost died, the company manager was hysterical but since he shouldn't have been having his shirts done by us he just swallowed his angst. Hans, however, I thought was going to have a heart attack. He knew it wasn't my fault but he just couldn't figure out what to do with his anger. He kept ranting and raving but saying, 'I know this isn't your fault', etc. I was crying my eyes out, with Nancy supporting me all the way. I ended with promising never to let another person do the laundry again. But I never lived that one down, and poor Hans had two shirts left for the remainder of the tour."

Conried seemed to possess an amazing amount of energy, and managed to handle a heavier than usual schedule. He even found work to do on Sunday, which is traditionally a day off for the cast. Conried once recounted an average week's schedule to a reporter, beginning with doing interviews on Sunday night, "and I have a radio show at 8 tomorrow morning, and a 6 P.M. television show. The curtain goes up at 8:30. It's a long, full day. I have several engagements Tuesday, including one with a firm here which I do television spots for. Wednesday is light, but of course I do two performances that day."

Back in Hollywood, Conried ensured he would be visible for another television season by taping a handful of guest appearances, including *Gilligan's Island* (making another visit as Wrongway Feldman), *Lost in Space*, and *Daniel Boone*. Conried also appeared in 1967 on a special television production of *Kismet*, which starred Jose Ferrer and Barbara Eden. This show is probably best remembered by the cast for an amusing (and somewhat embarrassing) event that took place during a rehearsal. The script required Conried to be ceremoniously carried into the scene by a palace guard: a young actor who stood an imposing 6'8". Though a former football player, and in great physical shape, the actor struggled with his duty of carrying Conried (himself a large man). The guard stumbled into the scene, fell to his knees, and ended up on top of Conried. Fortunately, no one was hurt, and the actor was able to carry Conried through the scene on the next take. Conried was very gracious about the whole thing and laughed it off as the poor actor apologized profusely for dropping him.

The pace of Conried's demanding work schedule continued at its hectic speed well into the 1970s. To his credit, Conried never let the strain on his system show, and he never missed a performance. Something had to give, though, and Conried would soon find himself fighting for his life and livelihood.

Part IV
The Final Years

11

"One with the Gypsies, the Charlatans, the Rogues, the Vagabonds"

Jerry Hausner once said of his old friend: "[Hans] lived in a different world; he had no idea." This simple statement comes the closest to telling the true story of the way Conried approached life. The world was in upheaval around him, but a part of Conried continued to dwell in the sort of world described in his beloved Jeffery Farnol novels of chivalrous deeds and gallantry. In a time of student protests over America's involvement in the Vietnam war; the whole hippy movement with the associated free love and experimentation with drugs; and emerging feminism, Conried seemed relatively untouched by it all. In 1968, the entire world was in shock over the loss of Martin Luther King, Jr., and Robert Kennedy within months of each other. This was also a time of great discovery, when the U.S. was exploring the stars like never before. It was in 1968 that the *Apollo 8* first orbited the moon in preparation for the following year's momentous lunar landing. Conried's first duty, he felt, was to entertain—to take people away from the real world for an hour or two. He wasn't there to preach, or push his political point of view; he just wanted to make people laugh. To that end, he was able to do more good than he ever could have imagined for many people throughout the country. One grateful fan wrote shortly after Robert Kennedy's assassination: "It helps so much to spend an evening in laughter, especially after a week like this one when I couldn't read a newspaper or look at the TV without crying."

What did register in a big way on Conried's cultural radar were the shocking changes happening in the world of theater. It was in 1969 that the world first heard of the controversial *Oh! Calcutta!* which featured full frontal nudity. The enigmatic British playwright and critic Kenneth Tynan put together a series of sketches written by such notables as Sam Shepard and John Lennon. To ensure the audience was thoroughly stunned by their experience, the play included simulated sex acts. *Oh! Calcutta!* enjoyed phenomenal success on the road before beginning its long run on Broadway in 1976.

Conried found *Oh! Calcutta!* appalling, as he did any other play featuring nudity, audience participation of any kind, and four-letter words: "I don't deny being somewhat piqued by the change in standards. What is changed are the good manners; our impulses are the same." He managed to find some consolation in the thought that there were still places left in the country that wanted something more wholesome: "The fare at the moment is not

Hans as Adolphe from the stage production of *Gold Diggers of 1633* (1976). From the Hans Conried Collection, Department of Special Collections, Boston University.

the kind I feel I can sell in Boise, and Cohasset, and Helena, and Medicine Hat. People there want the standard fare; plays during which my clothes never leave my body."

The change in American mores also meant it was harder for Conried to find a vehicle that suited his talents and temperament: "Nowadays I don't know of a play for a clean old man of my years that an audience can relate to. New plays deal with strange, abnormal subjects. A new one on Broadway now has a leading man in love with his pet hog. Come now, St. Louis audiences won't tolerate such nonsense." The problem was actually twofold, in that the plays being written during the late 1960s were dealing with objectionable topics, and there were so few new plays being written at all. "There's a damn acute shortage of product in my business," Conried sadly noted. He felt it was the lure of the big money possible in writing for television that caused so many potential playwrights to give up the legitimate theatre. This in turn produced writers who were forced to work in a very rigid system dictated by egos and deadlines. As a consequence, the quality of television programming suffered as well. A worried Conried told a reporter: "You become jaded when you have to grind out something like a sausage machine. We're in an age when there aren't any more craftsmen... It frightens the hell out of me."

As if to clear the air a bit, Conried eagerly agreed to appear in a revival of the quaint period piece *Rosalinda* with the San Francisco Civic Light Opera Company in 1968 as the slightly mad Prince Orlofsky. Here was an opportunity for Conried to display his talent for offbeat, eccentric characters to the fullest, without having to utter profanities or shed his clothing.

In San Francisco, Conried had a chance to sit down with reporter William Gilkerson, during his stint with the Civic's *Rosalinda*, and discuss a variety of topics. Gilkerson was particularly struck by Conried's wardrobe, and began his article with: "[Conried] is dressed this afternoon in a gray herringbone suit with wide lapels and a purple hanky peeking out of the breast pocket; a pink shirt and a green plaid bow tie that is really tied (no clip-on job), although a little lopsidedly." The conversation quickly turned to the sad state of affairs for character actors, especially in Hollywood. Gilkerson spoke of the industry's tendency to inflate select character actors into stars, to which Conried replied, "My dear boy, this is an age of inflation. Everything is inflated and very little has any value. But the demise of the character actor (he's not dead, mind you, merely less used) is due primarily to a new concept of drama, the day of the anti-hero. Especially in films. The quality of legitimate theater has been maintained somewhat by the relative cost of tickets and the tastes of those who can afford them. But in films — and these comprise the theater of today's youth — the trend for the audience is to identify only with one or two main characters, such as, perhaps, a young man with blue jeans and a leather jacket whose dramatic dilemma is that he can't decide whether he's more in love with his sister or his motorcycle. Where is a man with a noble mien, a classic aura, to work today?"

Conried was asked if growing older makes it any easier to handle bad reviews. Conried candidly confessed, "We are not very mature, we actors. We paint our faces and posture on stages and hope somehow to be loved, so our reactions never become really rational. Whether or not we admit it, we all search the reviews for some reward, some kind adjective." Though he hadn't fulfilled his ambitions as an actor, Conried said he was "happy in my work and with my life. We have a brotherhood, we actors, and—creatures of whim that we are—we need each other, and enjoy one another...."

Gilkerson was inspired by the idea of a brotherhood of actors, and asked Conried a rather fanciful, hypothetical question: What would Conried change or do if he were to be proclaimed the "Absolute Dictator of Theater"? Conried answered as if he'd thought about the idea before: "Do? Well, I would make all modern playwrights, on pain of death, structure their plays. I would demand three acts for the benefit of the play, with two intermissions for the benefit of the audience, and insist that the protagonist be put up in a tree in the first act, get stones and other undesirable things thrown at him in the second, and got down to earth again in the third. Very few people know how to structure a play, and the message or its obscurity is secondary to the structure. Then, before I could make any more edicts, some sensible regicide would assassinate me."

In 1969, Conried performed the title role of a retired chicken farmer in *Spofford!* This light comedy set in modern day Connecticut was the brainchild of veteran theater producer and director (of both stage and screen) Herman Shumlin, who also took the writing credits. *Spofford!* was Shumlin's first effort as a playwright, and he based his story on the novel *Reuben, Reuben*, by Peter deVries. It's possible the title character's name was inspired by one of Shumlin's contemporaries: the theatrical producer, Spofford J. Beadle, who the previous year had helped to produce Conried's *Absence of a Cello* tour. Conried was no stranger to Shumlin, who directed *Tall Story* on Broadway in 1959.

The show played all around the country, and parts of Canada, on a full-blown national tour. What made the long schedule even more tiring for Conried was that his character—Spofford—was on the stage for most of the two hours the play was performed. There was a great deal of memorization required (not a favorite of Conried's), for he not only performed his part, but also provided the narration that was used throughout the play. The separation from his family was difficult, and Conried tried to slip away to visit his home when he could. During a twenty-three-hour break between playing Cleveland and St. Louis, Conried flew home "so my children will have some vague recollection of what their father looks like... If I get there for a few hours on Christmas Eve, that will make a total of fifteen days in the last thirteen months."

A reporter for the *Toronto Daily Star*, Marci McDonald, provided an impromptu character study of Conried while visiting with the *Spofford!* star during the Detroit leg of the tour. Even though the weariness of the road was weighing heavily upon Conried, he could never turn down a request for an interview. He knew very well it was an important publicity tool to help sell tickets, and he allowed Ms. McDonald to conduct the interview in his hotel room: "If all the world's a stage, as Shakespeare had it, certainly no one has his script down more pat than Hans Conried... He looms at you from the sitting room sofa, bigger, puffier, more barrel-chested than the TV cameras make out, but still with the classic supercilious sneer intact. The haughty eagle eyebrows arch and swirl skyward, the beak nose and dry-as-dust mouth purse disapprovingly down to the perennial bow tie. The gestures are extravagant, flamboyant as he greets you. The speech spills florid, flounced and Shakespearean from the sneer—rolling prose a-glitter with $10.00 words and an English accent that never knew Britannia's soil till a two-week visit ten years ago. 'You see me at my most vicious and repulsive', he intones theatrically, eyebrows veering haughtily ever higher. 'Ordinarily, of course, I am charming. Why, I, in my own hand have inscribed on my dressing room door the words, 'Oh Lovable Hans', and dare any soul in the company to disagree on pain of a broken nose.' Whether over-playing his role as the professional Sneer, or under-playing his own achievements, Hans Conried will admit, 'on stage or off, I'm always giving a performance. I'm artificial by nature.'" After speaking at length to Conried about his long career, the reporter takes her leave, and ends her copy with: "And then, suddenly, you have left Hans Conried in his Detroit hotel suite, you realize, without ever really knowing him. Because, after all, the hotel door is closing. The curtain is once more coming down."

The Vietnam War was a full-blown crisis by 1970, and the USO was recruiting celebrities to cheer up the troops injured in battle. Conried and his pal Jerry Hausner were invited to make a seventeen-day tour of military hospitals in the Philippines, Guam, and Japan. Besides the obvious thrill of helping his country, Conried was excited about the idea of going back to San Fernando Pampanga to see the old radio station he was first assigned to during World War II. The idea of going to Japan again was certainly a pleasant prospect as well. The two veterans gladly agreed to travel across the Pacific to do their part for the war effort. Strangely enough, Jerry Hausner confessed later that Conried never confided in him the reason for wanting to go to San Fernando. As soon as they could, though, Conried and Hausner hired a car and hurried off to this place that Conried had to see again. It wasn't until after his friend's death that Hausner was told the full story by Conried's superior at the time, ex–radio actor Jack Kruschen.

The two friends left for the Philippines in May of 1970. A sad event that marred the beginning of this adventure was the passing of Conried's mother, Edith. She had been in decline for many years prior to her death, and eventually suffered a broken hip after a fall at her home in Burbank. She spent a little over a year in the hospital, but never fully recovered from her fall. She passed away on May 2, 1970, at seventy-seven years of age, and was buried with her husband at Forest Lawn.

In the Philippines, the weather was hot, humid, and generally oppressive. Hausner enjoyed making mental notes of his friend's amusing idiosyncrasies: "In the Philippines where it was beastly hot—terribly, terribly humid and hot—Hans would wear a seersucker washable suit, and he always wore a necktie, even in the jungle. He was wearing this necktie, but it was a washable tie, and a washable shirt, and a washable hat. He would say, 'I'm going to take a shower', and he would step into the shower, fully dressed, and he would wash everything out, and then hand it to me outside the shower on a hanger [to dry]."

The high temperatures and humidity may account for the sullen looks on the faces of the two amigos staring back from a photograph taken at some lucky soldier's bedside. The photo was, no doubt, an anomaly, and Conried and Jerry were able to provide plenty of good cheer to the servicemen they met along the way. After the seventeen-day USO tour was over, Conried

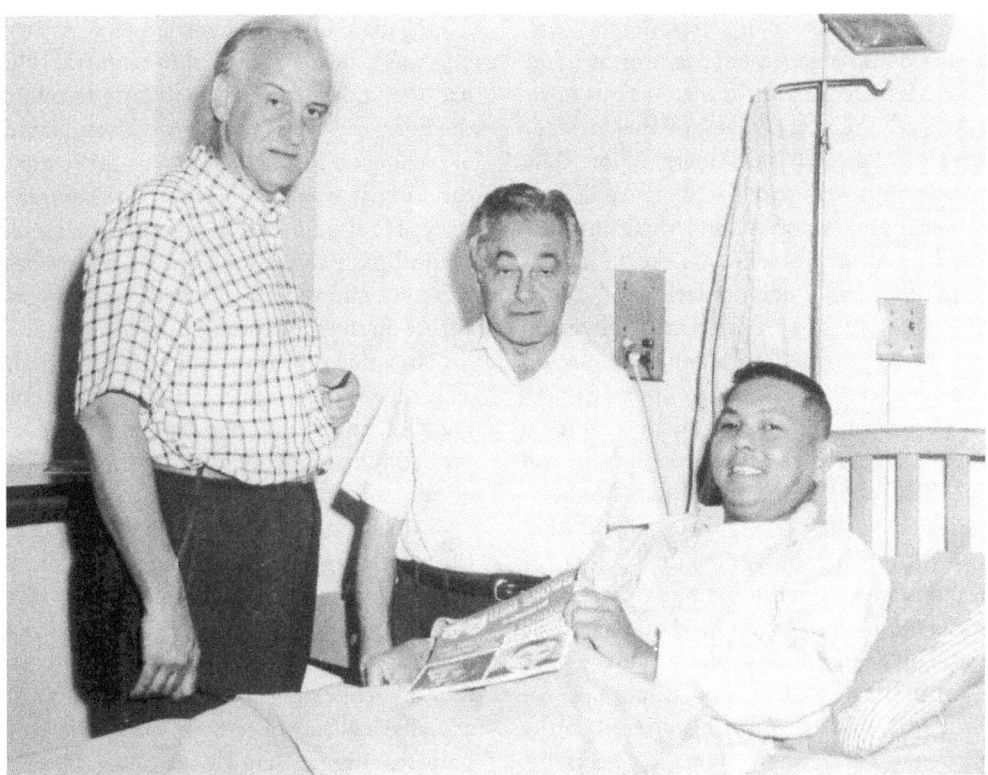

Hans and Jerry Hausner cheering up an unidentified serviceman at a hospital in the Philippines. The two old chums don't look too cheery here, but they successfully entertained the troops for a seventeen-day USO Pacific Hospitals Tour in 1970. From the Hans Conried Collection, Department of Special Collections, Boston University.

and Hausner remained in Japan. Their wives flew over to join them, and the couples were able to stay for two weeks as simple tourists. It was a welcome rest for the two old warriors.

Even with his busy schedule, Conried found time to indulge in his most private passions: food and collecting. Jerry Hausner and James Karen were both part of a "club" informally known as "The Chinese Food Eating Society" put together by Conried and actor Keye Luke. The society was comprised of a small group of actor friends. They would get together every month or so, schedules permitting, to seek out interesting Chinese restaurants in the Los Angeles area, and reminisce about old times. One member of this group was fellow radio actor Elliot Reid, who, though based in New York at the time, would happily join his buddies whenever he was in town. Reid recently recalled his days with Conried: "In later years, after radio had dried up and blown away, and we were all getting older, I was part of a group who met—every few weeks—in various Chinese restaurants. Jerry Hausner, a dear friend of Hans' and a very fine actor, was one of the group—one of the steadies—and others came and went, so to speak. Hans would discover a new restaurant, sometimes a bit of a drive from Hollywood, and off we'd go, to discover, on more than one occasion, that Hans had driven out there the previous day and done all the ordering! He really knew all about it, and we never had cause for complaint. And we enjoyed each other's company most definitely...."

In addition to his restaurant visits, Conried also enjoyed entertaining at home with Margaret serving as the gracious hostess. Over the years, many of their friends were treated to lavish dinners. Elliott Reid recalled his visits to the Conried home: "[Hans] and Margaret and their children lived up near Hollywood Lake in an old house that had a definite feeling of 'castle' about it—the sort of old time Hollywood house that seemed to wander about, on different levels, without any apparent plan to it. I attended many delicious dinners there and much good spirited joshing and fun. The food often featured such Mediterranean favorites as eggplant... Not what you'd probably encounter in Wichita, or Kansas City, but not too exotic either. Hans had a room off the main floor that was close to being a museum—soldiers in every kind of uniform—excellent models too, not just little lead soldiers. Also, his interest in the Orient was everywhere, in many objects, including extremely valuable netsuke...."

Writer and old friend Hal Kanter also picked up the "castle" theme, and said of his visit: "The Conrieds engaged a Chinese caterer to provide a feast elaborate enough to impress an emperor... Hans was an emperor in his house ... and a prince everywhere else." Kanter couldn't help noticing the enormous amount of collectibles Conried had piled in his house, and gleefully confided, "He had the greatest collection of toys this side of Santa's workshop."

James Karen also noticed that "stuff was hidden away everywhere in the house." The younger Hans remembered how his father had to become handy with a power saw and hammer out of necessity; he needed to keep building more and more shelves. Eventually, Conried ran out of spare room in the main house, and boxes had to pile up in the basement. A family friend noted with astonishment during a visit in 1972 that amongst the stacks of unopened boxes in his basement were boxes he had sent home from Japan in 1946! Conried's collecting bug was a sickness he couldn't control. He had the knowledge and good taste to select the finest art pieces, yet he was also capable of picking up some gimcrack at a thrift store thinking it was possibly a priceless "treasure." He also hoarded such mundane items as toothpaste caps—for what reason no one will ever quite know. He had jars of them sitting on the shelf, neatly labeled and waiting for the day they might be needed. Toothpaste caps, zippers, tin foil, books of matches, string; you name it, and Conried probably had a jar of it somewhere in his house.

Conried enjoyed the non-theatrical life, claiming it took his mind off show business, which was, he stressed, "only one side of my life." Conried enjoyed the camaraderie and competitive spirit to be found in collecting, and he went so far as to actually "collect collectors": "As a collector, I possess arcane knowledge and I meet a special circle of idiots—engineers, lawyers, and other non-theatrical types. We argue, trade possessions, cheat each other, and become friends. I collect collectors."

Conried was given the opportunity to write the foreword to a book called *Contemporary Netsuke* (published in 1977), written by Miriam Kinsey. Miriam and her husband Robert were avid Japanophiles, and good friends of Conried. The foreword gives a clear picture as to the insidious nature of the collecting bug: "'Netsuke-itis' is now a common affliction, an intense acquisitive urge that subsides, normally, only with the onset of severe financial insufficiency. Two general categories of the disease emerge: a craving for the old and a craving for the new. Despite the virulent nature of the disorder, it would now seem that sufferers from both varieties can safely share the same ward, and sometimes even the same bed."

There was a downside to Conried's preoccupation with his collections, and at times it strained his relationship with his family: "The collectors meet from time to time, and have marvelous conversations, but it is an awkward time for their wives as I watch them trying to put conversations together. My children do not have my love for collecting. In fact, I believe the children resent the time I spend on my collections."

Margaret was a good sport, and an intelligent woman. She did not have the same enthusiasm level her husband did, though, and often found herself to be one of those ladies struggling to make conversation. The children were growing up, and having the usual difficulties of adolescence. Trilby was in college studying theater arts, while the younger Hans was becoming involved in his high school dramatics. The 6'6" teen directed a production of *Death Takes a Holiday*, though the mechanically inclined Hans admits he was more interested in "cars and girls." Edie was discovering her love of ballet, and Alex was discovering his sense of autonomy by refusing to get a haircut. The Conried kids enjoyed a rather lenient upbringing that spared the rod and invited the proverbial consequences. Though Conried and Margaret were originally followers of the work of Benjamin Spock and his controversial theories of childrearing, Conried confided to a reporter in 1971: "We made a mistake with [Spock's] book; we should have used it differently. We should have hit the kids with it."

Another pilot was made in 1970 for a proposed television series. It was an adaptation of *Barefoot in the Park* with Conried as the Hungarian neighbor, Victor Velasco. Even with the happy news that ABC had picked up the series for their fall schedule, the mood quickly soured when it was discovered the network executives decided to produce the series with an all-black cast. Conried's part of Victor Velaso became "Honey Robinson" when it was taken over by Nipsey Russell. Conried just couldn't seem to get a break when it came to series television. Ten years prior, Conried had been ambivalent about doing a television series. Now, at fifty-three years of age, he would have welcomed a series and the chance for steady work in Los Angeles. The pilot behind him, Conried once more left California for the open road.

To cater to the changing tastes of the audiences, Conried soon found many of the stock productions available to him were, by his standards, of a rather churlish nature. In 1970, Conried agreed to appear in a stock production of *Norman, Is That You?* The play dealt—albeit in a humorous way—with a conservative father (Conried) discovering his son is a homosexual, and his attempts to make him "straight." Along the way, the show also touched on the subjects of adultery and prostitution. One of the father's desperate solutions to his son's "problem" is to hire a hooker to sleep with his son, and thereby transform him into a "normal" man. The son refuses, and dad ends up with the prostitute (he paid her in advance, so why not?). Even though the production tried to deal with homosexuality in a more positive way than in previous years, it was not something Conried felt good about being associated with. He jokingly (it is presumed) told a reporter he was going to change his name and have plastic surgery right after the end of the tour.

A welcome change to the sensationalism that was in vogue in the early 1970s was a chance to co-star with a group of veteran performers in the musical *70, Girls, 70*. The musical was based on a 1958 comedy written by Peter Coke that opened in London as *Breath of Spring*. This play was made into a film in 1960 starring Terry-Thomas and Hattie Jacques called *Make Mine Mink*. The plot of the musical remained essentially the same as the original English play, only this time the gang of elderly fur thieves lives in poverty, instead of relative luxury. Their motivation to steal changes from something to do to make things more exciting, to the more ennobling desire to help out needy seniors. The location of the play was moved to a seedy part of New York City, which provided the opportunity for social commentary regarding the sad living conditions of the city's low-income senior citizens. The musical opened on Broadway on April 15, 1971. The cast included Mildred Natwick, Lillian Roth, Dorothea Freitag, Gil Lamb, and Joey Faye. At only fifty-four years of age (just barely), Conried was the "young lad," considering most of his co-stars were in their seventies and eighties. Conried's thinning hair was by now almost completely gray, and the addition of a full white beard and moustache succeeded in making him look much older than his actual years. Conried told a reporter at the time: "I suppose I should keep my youth a deep dark secret. After all, we're advertised as a stage full of old troupers. I do have a white beard. That should help. However, I'll shave it off the minute the show closes. I'm not trying to be Gabby Hayes. I adore the cast of this musical. They're such a loyal, passionate bunch. And, I'm madly in love with Mildred Natwick. We appeared together in Florida in *Critic's Choice*. She has natural nobility. I took over my role in this musical under very unhappy circumstances. Eddie Foy, an old friend, first had the role, and he became ill. His replacement, David Burns, another dear friend, died on the stage in Philadelphia. It's a helluva way to get a part!"

The character of Harry was originally a former vaudevillian, but this angle was discarded after Conried took over the role. One of the highlights of the show is the gang gathering to hear Harry's strategy for their next caper ("The Caper"). The song involved a good deal of tongue-twisting, and perfect timing, to which Conried added his own manic gesturing.

70, Girls, 70 only lasted a month on Broadway due to generally bad reviews and lackluster ticket sales. The show would find success later in the year when the original soundtrack recording was released. *70, Girls, 70* was revived, and taken on the road in stock productions soon after—without the original cast.

Conried's next project involved a rather uninspiring stock tour of *Murder Without a Trace* in 1972. This was the same Arthur Watkyn play that had been so successful on the road a dozen years earlier under its original title: *Not in the Book*. There were a few changes made to adapt it to the dinner theater environment, and the audiences were inexplicably not as receptive as before. The anemic response didn't alter Conried's hectic schedule, which was just as grueling as always when traveling by bus and truck: "You get in about 2:30 [P.M.], and you've been riding in the bus since 9 [A.M.]. You get something to eat, then talk to the local paper—usually some high school girl doing an interview—take an hour of sleep and get out to the Elk's Club or wherever the the-

Portrait of Hans in 1971. The full beard was a byproduct of his stage role in *70, Girls, 70*, and it was probably shaved off right after this photograph was snapped. Hans jokingly said, "I'm not trying to be Gabby Hayes."

atre is and you go on. After that, if they're not holding a kaffee klatsch for you, you go back to your room and get out your piece of cheese, or whatever you've saved, and you go to sleep. The next morning, you get back on the bus again at 9 and leave for the next town."

In the summer of 1972, Conried traveled to Missouri, as he had for many years, to appear with the St. Louis Municipal Opera in another revival of *The Student Prince*. One of his co-stars, Lynne Stuart, remembers meeting Conried the first day of rehearsal: "When I arrived in my smart red checked slacks and shirt [I] was grabbed by Hans, and flung down over his arm... [He said,] 'I never felt this way about an Italian restaurant before!'" The startled, but amused, young actress felt Conried "run his fingers up and down, feeling my rib cage, and [Hans] said, with wonder in his voice: 'Do you know, I had more for breakfast than you are?!'"

One of the bright spots for the year was a December visit to the San Diego Zoo. Conried was given a special honorary membership by the San Diego Zoological Society. The certificate was handed to Conried by a darling baby orangutan dressed in a Santa suit. Conried bent low and took the gift, saying to the youngster: "I'm glad you're a monkey. I thought I might have to force feed a python to earn this honor." The little redhead let out a happy squeal, even though she was an orangutan, not a monkey.

In early 1973, Conried was approached by his old friend, Arthur Lake ("Dagwood Bumstead"), to work on a project he was putting together involving an animated television series that would help to educate young people about the environment. It was to be called *There Goes Mr. Greenthumb*, and was proposed as a mixture of live-action and animation. The project was almost a one-man crusade, and Lake worked long and hard to convince others of the merit of

CBS publicity photo for the 1971 Dr. Seuss television special: *Horton Hears a Who*.

his idea. Lake had already been able to persuade Mel Blanc to offer his services as the voices of a few characters, and he had hoped Conried would sign on to complete the project. Conried was to be the narrator and to voice some of the group of characters that hailed from an imaginary place called "Wamblonia." It was an ambitious project with an ambitious goal of helping to create pro-environment kids, but it wasn't able to find the funding it needed to get off the ground.

After over ten hard years on the road, living out of suitcases, and being separated from his children for long stretches of time, the stress was beginning to take its toll on Conried. He spoke of the downside of stock touring to a reporter: "We become physically tired. Sometimes we become tired even when the play is going very well and even though we are there, in our childish fashion, to be loved. Sometimes I become aware, even in moments like this, that my feet hurt. So acting is not an orgiastic flight into a nirvana, night after night."

His schedule was frequently packed so tightly he was sometimes required to begin another tour without a full rehearsal with the cast. Problems were occurring much too often, and though Conried was a seasoned pro and knew how to work his way out of a jam, there were occasions when things spiraled out of control. The first performance of *Critic's Choice* in Omaha, Nebraska, in 1973 gave an example of this, as reported by a local newspaper: "Even when the play ground to a halt in Act One because a cue was missed, Conried nonchalantly continued, 'Ladies and Gentlemen. It is opening night. I hope you have enjoyed your dinner. Was it my fault? Just say yes or no.' The answer was negative. The line was picked up by the proper party, and it all continued with the grace and smoothness of Queen Elizabeth in court... And later, in an emotional scene with his [stage] son, when Hans momentarily slipped, he worked his way around with such ease, I'm sure ninety percent of the audience didn't know he missed a beat."

A more serious situation occurred when Conried was signed to appear as Alfred P. Doolittle in a summer stock revival of *My Fair Lady* in Atlanta, Georgia. Conried was handed the script on the night before he arrived in Atlanta, and only had five short days to learn his part before opening night. Through it all, Conried's professionalism never allowed him to complain, except to say he was going to have a massive case of the jitters on opening night. The play's co-star, James Daley, became ill shortly after rehearsals began, and British actor Michael Allison was quickly hired to replace him. Conried wasn't familiar with Allison, but welcomed a seasoned pro: "I've never worked with him, and I've never seen him before, but they say he is so well prepared, and he has done the part so often before, that I expect to be leaning all over him." The play was received very well, and the reviews were generally positive. Conried was not in top form, or rather, he was not up to his high standards due to his lack of rehearsal time. He may not have shown it, but inside he was seething.

John Moore—former host of the *Merry-Go-Round* talk show on WSB Radio in Atlanta, Georgia—had the difficult task of interviewing Conried the day after the opening performance: "I interviewed him the morning after opening night. For background, you should know that opening night was essentially the first time Mr. Conried and the rest of the cast had met each other. I was told that the cast had rehearsed in one city, and Mr. Conried had been on tour or whatever and rehearsed his part separately. On opening night, he blew a line ... badly. The rest of the cast tried to help recover, but things spiraled downward. Even worse, it was a critical line, needed to set up some other bits of 'business'. Finally, they just stopped, went back to where they were, and did it correctly.

"The interview was a nightmare. I felt Hans Conried was mad at himself for blowing the line, mad at the cast for not being able to save him, mad at the audience for being there, and mad at me for getting him up to do what was probably the bazillionth radio appearance of his career. I went through my normal procedures, finished the interview, and saw him out.

"I then threw the reels of tape at Tony Pavone, my editor; told him that I thought this was perhaps the worst interview I had ever done, and that I doubted he could find anything worth using from it, but to see if he could get me an hour's worth of material (that would be about fifteen minutes of usable 'stuff'). I left for the day. Tony called me at home a few hours later and said the material was wonderful! In his judgment, we could easily go a full segment with it. With the memory of that interview fresh in my mind, I had trouble believing him, but told him to go ahead and prep the show. I came in an hour early to listen to the tape, and Tony was absolutely right. Despite those waves of negative emotion I was feeling from the man during the session, absolutely none of it showed in his voice!

"I remain amazed to this day of what that means in terms of Conried's professional control of his 'instrument.' During the interview, I had wanted to crawl under the desk, but on the tape, we were having an interesting, informative discussion about his stage work, radio, and early TV. It was simply incredible."

Conried collapsed during a performance of *How the Other Half Loves* at the Country Dinner Playhouse in Columbus, Ohio, on January 22, 1974. There was no warning, just a sudden loss of consciousness. Thanks to the quick thinking of stage manager Al Grab and other members of the cast, Conried was immediately taken to the intensive care unit at the Mount Carmel East Hospital in Columbus. It was determined he had suffered from a mild stroke, and he was kept for observation and a series of tests. Margaret was in New York City at the time, and flew in the next day to be with her husband. Initially, the only sign of the stroke was a slight speech impairment, which may have seemed relatively minor to the doctors. To a man who made his living by his voice, however, it was one of the most frightening experiences of his life. Conried would later speak of his ordeal: "One night in Columbus, Ohio, about six minutes before the final curtain, my machine stopped, and it was pretty frightening. But I was very lucky, and I recovered to a great extent, and repaired my speech and worked again... For the first time in [my career], I was out for nearly four months." Conried managed to regain enough strength to accept a few small jobs: "Well, I sat on a stool much of the time. A few people out [in Los Angeles], old friends, let me do voiceovers—meaning commercials—just a few in those four months. I had a terrible stammer—had a terrible fear—and a physical inability to project as much as I would like—as much as I had before. But they were patient enough to edit the tape, and let me take long enough to get it together, and I did a very few little pieces. Then I had a call from New York."

In 1954, actor George Irving took over as Boris Adzinidzinadze in *Can-Can* when Conried decided to leave the show. In 1974, Irving was on Broadway playing the role of the flamboyant dress designer Madame Lucy in a production of *Irene*, starring Debbie Reynolds. The show was scheduled to go out of town to tour a few select cities, and Irving did not want to leave New York. The producers remembered how he took over for Conried in 1954, and they thought, why not get Conried to take over for Irving in 1974? Conried seemed a perfect choice for the part, and they phoned his agent to see if he was available. Conried continues: "So they called my agent and [he] said, 'Well, you know, Conried has not been well, ...[though] he tells me on the phone his face [isn't distorted], and he's ready to work.' But when I said I was ready to work, I was half lying to get the job, because I would sit there [when] performing and for ordinary conversations, and I would have my hand over my mouth because I was insecure. So I came out to New York, and we had dinner together, and [the producer] said, 'I don't think your problems are that big.'" Conried was encouraged to give it a try, and he made plans to start rehearsing. In the back of his mind, though, lingered the psychological trauma of his sudden debilitation, and the fear that he just didn't have it anymore: "I had to make up my mind if I was going to ever work again, or whether I was just going to stop and do bits around town—voiceovers—and never appear on the stage again, or whether I was going to try to repair my problems. The miracle was, from the day I started to rehearse, I could notice the improvement. Every day it got easier and easier, and I got a little better... I had to learn to speak again. For an actor, that's a lot."

It was a miracle that Conried was able to recuperate from the stroke so quickly, and be back on the stage. His illness did take a heavy toll on him physically, and he was not able to work the long hours he could before; he found himself tiring more easily. High blood pressure was found to be one of the causes of his sudden collapse, and he was prescribed medication. Conried did not like having to take any kind of medication, and soon found ways to "forget" his medicine. It became the job of conscientious stage managers to assign someone in the company to watch over Conried and make sure he took his medication fifteen minutes prior to going onstage. He resisted, of course, but always ended up taking the stuff whether he liked it or not. The deeper reasons for his stroke were not fully understood at the time. Conried was suffering from severely clogged arteries, though it doesn't appear that any of his doctors recommended further treatment. If they did, Conried kept it to himself, and largely ignored their advice.

Conried had originally accepted a job to appear with theatrical producer Carl Stohn, Jr., on a special tour of London and Paris that was advertised under the name "Curtain Call." The tour was a quick one—only eight days—and promised the travelers a chance to explore the two great cities by day, and enjoy the rich theatre experience by night. Conried and Stohn were to be on hand to answer questions and provide stimulating conversation. The tour was originally set to begin on March 23, 1974, right after the last performance of *How the Other Half Loves*. It was impossible for Conried to honor this obligation, though he decided to use the opportunity to take Margaret and the girls to London. Edie and Trilby went off on their own to experience the lights of Paris, and crossed the English Channel to France. For Conried and Margaret, it was a rare chance to be alone together. Conried needed time to heal and gain his confidence again. The trip did him good, and when he arrived back in the States, he was once again ready to face a live audience. He joined the cast of *Irene* in September of 1974 at the Arie Crown Theatre in Chicago as the troupe headed out on the road. Debbie Reynolds was still the star of the show until late December, when Jane Powell took over for the remainder of the tour.

Work was a vital part of Conried's recovery process, and he was gratified at the opportunities he was being offered to keep earning a living at his craft. Even though he was feeling increasingly stronger as time passed, he still could not shake the nagging doubts that ran through his mind. Doubts, after all, were the stock and trade of an actor's life. When asked by a reporter if he had doubts about returning to the stage, Conried openly said, "Doubts? Every night of the world. You are never without doubts in this glorious and perilous business. A professional actor is one who goes on, regardless, and does his best every night."

Conried finished out the year by touring with a revival of *Don't Drink the Water*. Of his new lease on life, he would say, "It's nice to be employed for one who has devoted his life to being at one with the Gypsies, the charlatans, the rogues, and the vagabonds."

12

Winding Down: The End

By the end of the *Irene* road tour in 1975, Conried's confidence was nearly back to his pre-stroke level. He agreed to continue appearing in stock productions for as long as he was able. With the children getting older, Margaret had more time to join her husband occasionally as he toured the country. Conried rarely shared intimate details of his family life with the press, but confided to a reporter: "Margaret is a pleasant, amiable woman who likes being a housewife; a remarkable woman who manages our home and family well." Though Trilby had graduated from college, Conried was still feeling the financial pinch: "Our other three children are still in school, so it will be a while before I can hang up my masks."

Trilby had graduated from the University of Southern California with a degree in Theater Arts, and was branching out on her own as an actress. As much as her parents tried to discourage her, she was determined to give a career in acting a try. Conried was torn between his fatherly pride and the desire to shield Trilby from the harsh realities of the very difficult road she had chosen. The path was even more difficult, Conried believed, for a woman in show business. The parts available for an actress are frustratingly limited in contrast to those offered their male contemporaries. Conried had been in the business long enough, and had seen his share of tragedies, to know his daughter was setting herself up for heartache: "I don't have the authority my father had, but these are different times, and if she chooses to [be an actress], and is good enough, there is nothing I can say to her. It's a hard life for a woman."

A subject that Conried spoke frequently about in his later years was the difference between the actors who grew up during his time and the new generation of actors. Conried was saddened by the lack of opportunity kids had in the 1960s and 1970s to learn their craft at the side of a more accomplished mentor, as he had done. No one had a college degree in acting when Conried was a young man. He learned by working side-by-side with some of the best in the business. Conried felt the Great Depression, and the necessity to earn a living, positively shaped his character. For Conried, and those like him, the hardships they faced early on helped them to become better actors, and better human beings. By the 1970s, a young person was almost required to have a degree to work in the theater, no matter how talented he or she was. Conried expressed dissatisfaction with this turn of events, and felt the new generation of actors was rather soft: "The kids [of this generation] grew up in opulent times. Actors like boxers do better when they're starving. An actor has to know hunger. It's a good ingredient in the mix. My daughter does well in school, but when she is through there and goes to New York to a cold water flat, it may not be at all feasible."

The father and daughter team was able to work together in 1975 in another run of *How the Other Half Loves* at a dinner theater in Seattle, Washington. Later in the year, Trilby would be in the cast of Neil Simon's *The Sunshine Boys* co-starring Conried. The part required Trilby to do some burlesque humor she wasn't accustomed to, and wear a rather revealing outfit. Conried explained: "I told her this part was not quite worthy of her talents, so she padded her bust and got the job anyway."

Conried thoroughly enjoyed the chance to work with his oldest daughter, and couldn't help saying so to a reporter: "I hope I'll be pardoned for paternal pride, but she was good at it, and it was nice to appear on the stage with her. The comedy skit was quite another sort of part for her because she'd never had that much experience in low comedy and I'd worked, never in burlesque, but with burlesque comedians, and it was a burlesque skit. It was kind of fun to teach her, and she responded well to that particular kind of skill."

The younger children were maturing, and trying to find their own way in the world. Hans III kept an interest in the mechanics of show business—especially film editing—and took a job as a page for CBS Studios in Los Angeles. He worked for a time as a cue card holder for *The Mike Douglas Show*. Hansi's well above average height worked to his advantage; the celebrities on stage couldn't miss him. Alexander was disinterested in school, and preferred to follow the beat of his own drummer. He was artistic by nature, and turned his attentions to the trade of silversmith. Conried was relieved that his two sons "seem to be sensible," and did not wish to follow in their father's footsteps. It was a surprise to Conried that his girls were proving to be more problematic that way.

Edie was finding her dream of becoming a ballet dancer thwarted by her continued increase in height. She would eventually reach nearly six feet—much too tall for a ballerina. Happily, she would soon find another avenue to explore her dancing skills, one where being tall is considered an asset—as a Las Vegas showgirl. Perhaps she had her father's attitude of accepting the compromises of fate, as in his shelving of his youthful dreams of Shakespeare to do low comedy. Edie put aside her dreams of classical ballet to strut her stuff in Vegas.

Jack Paar had long since retired from television, but his legacy remained in the similar talk shows continuing on the air. Johnny Carson (Paar's protégé), Merv Griffin, Mike Douglas, Dick Cavett, and others crowded the channels with their own talk shows in the 1970s. Conried made the rounds of the talk shows when he had time, and appeared as a guest on various television sitcoms. Conried was still amazed at this incredible medium that could reach into millions of homes simultaneously: "It's mildly frustrating to me that if I appear for three or four minutes on a talk show, millions of people will see me sneeze or scratch myself. More people will see me there than have seen me in forty-two years of making up, preparing for a role, and sweating onstage."

The years 1974–1977 were lean for television work, due to Conried's illness and numerous theatrical engagements. His most notable appearance during this time was on an episode of the unusual *Kolchak: The Night Stalker* series entitled "The Knightly Murders."

Conried had a small role in Disney's motion picture *The Shaggy D.A.* released in 1976. This same year, Conried began his theatrical season in April by appearing on stage with Molly Picon in a production of Henry Denker's *The Second Time Around* at a dinner theater in Atlanta, Georgia. The play revolved around an elderly, unmarried couple that agrees to live together to save expenses. Their children are adamantly opposed to the arrangement, and this predicament is the source for most of the comedy.

The show went on the road again in the winter with a new cast, except for the principal players of Conried and Molly Picon, and a new name: *Something Old, Something New*. The winter shows were produced as a prelude to opening on Broadway.

After fourteen previews, *Something Old, Something New* premiered on Broadway at the Morosco Theatre on January 1, 1977, and closed the same day. This would be Conried's last shot at Broadway, and one of his most painful experiences on the stage. It was becoming more difficult every year to try to put a small, one set comedy on Broadway. The ticket prices were so steep that few could afford them, and those who could tended to be elderly people who were too afraid to walk the streets of New York City after dark. The producers were forced to yank *Something Old, Something New* immediately, rather than watch their bank accounts run dry. It was unfortunate for all involved in the production, but money was the primary concern. *Cue* magazine penned an acerbic review of the show, but managed to find a little praise for the two stars: "The first Broadway production of 1977 has come and gone, slunk off in disgrace before most people even knew it was in town. The only observable reason for its existence seemed to have been its co-stars, the indestructible Molly Picon and Hans Conried... Manacled to Henry Denker's asinine comedy ... Conried was called upon to deliver some excruciatingly unfunny lines. It was a joy to watch him play the alchemist and transform dross into richer metal. He turned in a performance that was fresh, vigorous and bristling with technical virtuosity."

After the disappointing Broadway experience, Molly Picon and Hans took the show on the road to Florida in September of 1977 under its original title—*The Second Time Around*—to play a handful of small venues and dinner theaters. Conried found working in dinner theaters a welcome change to one-night-stands: "Working dinner theaters is quite comfortable. The pay is adequate and the accommodations nice. You are located in a city four or five weeks—long enough to send out your laundry. When you do one-nighters you wash everything with you when you take a bath." There was a somewhat unpleasant trade-off, though, in that the average dinner theater audience didn't quite possess the sophistication of a more traditional theatergoer. The fare generally had to be much lighter in a dinner theater environment: "After you have eaten and drunk well ... it's difficult to sit back and watch Ibsen or Strindberg. With a star or celebrity, you need only a telephone book, not a play... The ultimate hope is that people who come to dinner theater will go on to more serious theater."

Actress Lydia Franklin joined the cast of *The Second Time Around* for the winter tour in 1977, and immediately connected with Conried, who played her father on stage. The two actors developed a deep friendship in the short time they worked together. Lydia enjoyed reminiscing about her time spent with Conried on the road. She remembered the first time they met was on her arrival at the hotel in Sarasota, Florida. Somehow, the two actors and the Atlanta Braves were the only guests at the hotel: "I called to [Hans], and he answered over a patch of green, because I was coming out of my hotel room. I introduced myself, and we talked as two veteran actors, not as stars, not as anything, just two veteran actors. Then we had dinner, and we talked far into the night sitting in the pool until our toes got pruney."

Lydia had rented a car, so she offered to drive Conried to the theater for rehearsals each day. This gave them an opportunity to talk about many of the important things going on in their lives: "At that time, I was going through the most horrendous divorce... And I turned to Hans, because by this time Hans was playing my father, and offstage he was very much like my own father. We all went to brunch on a Sunday,

A scene from the 1977 stock tour of *The Second Time Around*: L-R: Hans, Lydia Franklin (standing), and Molly Picon.

when my husband at that time, came up to see the show... Hans went to the table for his fifth helping... and he whispered out of the side of his mouth to me, 'He has a woman'. I was looking at him searchingly [wondering] what he thought was going on, [and I said] 'How do you know?' He said, 'I haven't done a hundred movies, and know people, not to know he's got a woman. Get rid of him.' And that was Hans.

"By the time we got to Miami, Hans was a very big misbehaver. He misbehaved by going to the Hungarian Charda—it was a Hungarian restaurant. You know, Hans had high blood pressure, and he forgot to take his pills on a constant basis. He always got to the theater on time, but you always knew that he had had the most wonderful meal in the world... I was the only one that had influence over Hans...[and] was very concerned... The stage manager gave me the job of seeing to it that he took his high blood pressure medicine every night before the performance... I used to appear at his dressing room door, [and] he would groan: 'There she is, the lady who never forgets!'"

Molly Picon was a veteran stage actress, and a living legend in the Yiddish theater. Though she was in her eighties, she was playing a woman almost twenty years younger. Conried, no stranger to playing older characters, was portraying a man in his sixties. The passage of time wasn't particularly kind to Conried, and physically, he actually appeared to be a man of much greater age than he was. Picon had a reputation of being just slightly difficult at times, but Conried had no trouble winning her over. Lydia continues: "Hans made Molly Picon feel like she was a 'Miss America' contestant. Hans had that facility for really petting her down. Of course, old stars need a lot of attention."

The rehearsals could sometimes be hilarious, as Lydia remembers: "Hans was hysterical. There was [something] in the script about 'simultaneous orgasm', and Molly Picon looked at Robert Turoff [the director], and said 'Bob, what does Henry Denker mean by this?' Hans put one hand on his mouth, and the other one on his crotch, and said 'Oh, I don't know either!'... I ran out of there ... [and] sat in the john till this thing was over... I could not collect myself."

The conversations between Franklin and Conried often turned to more serious subjects, as illustrated by this glimpse into one day during rehearsals: "It was a beautiful shining day... We were both half asleep, and we had a ten o'clock rehearsal. So it was just a little after nine in the morning ... when I asked why we were getting up at 9:00 A.M. to go to a rehearsal. [Hans] answered, 'Don't you know, Lydia? We are God's unhappy children'... I looked at him when he said that to me, and I said 'Hans, it was a terrible battle being what you are, and getting everybody to have faith.' He said 'Yes. For you too?'... We talked about what drew us to the business, and why we were there, and what the situations were with our families ... because other people grow up to be accountants, you know?" Conried confided to Franklin that his father had wanted him to have a "real" job, and didn't think he would be able to make it in a business that prized physical beauty.

During this time, Conried was becoming increasingly bitter about his inability to get the sort of parts he wanted in his career, and told Franklin: "Nothing new ever happens; you're just on replay after fifty." Conried also felt strongly that he had been a failure as a father. There were times, Franklin recalled, when Conried would sit with his head in his hands and moan: "What are you going to do with these kids?" He was especially worried about his boys, but felt all of his children were having a hard time "finding" themselves. They seemed to be moving farther away from him to a place he could not reach, let alone understand. The same could be said about the times Conried lived in as well. He was having difficulty coming to grips with the sweeping changes happening in his private world, and the world around him.

Conried was always able to maintain his graciousness and humor no matter what the strain may have been from his own private troubles. Franklin remembered that "[Hans] never let you sit in a morass. He always pulled you out. He had a solution to every problem, and I think it grew out of Hans' pain... He had the most wonderful sense of humor when it came to anything. He could always flip things, like a record; he would flip it to the other side. His glass was always half full, mine was always half empty because I had been banged around a lot in this business over the years. [The] most important thing was to be a better person... Hans always said, 'Develop [yourself] as a person; the acting will follow. There's no big secret. It's deepening the soul.' That was Hans' credo... Hans was a big believer in inventing yourself minute by minute."

Franklin noted that Conried never complained about anything, even when the weather was sweltering and they had to perform in bulky wool clothes. The young actress soon found out how far a complaint would go around a veteran like Conried: "Every night [Hans] was spiffy, and dressed, and not a hair out of place; I mean he was the most fantastic actor I ever saw. I came out of the dressing room, perspired, and letting my discomfort be known to anyone who would listen, including the stagehands. Hans quietly looked at me, and he said, 'Lydia, we can always get you a job in a nice air-conditioned bank.' That was the last time I bitched and complained about any problems we had."

On one of their free afternoons, the two took a break to see the landmark Steven Spielberg film *Close Encounters of the Third*

Kind. Franklin laughingly remembers having Conried slouch down in the car so people wouldn't recognize him, and sneaking corned beef sandwiches and celery tonic into the theater. Conried was so impressed with the possibility of extraterrestrial life, he and Franklin ended up spending nearly three hours discussing the film. Conried firmly believed we are not alone.

Conried had a lifelong love affair with milk, and he wanted to share his passion with everyone. Unfortunately, Franklin was lactose intolerant, and tried to refuse the glasses of milk Conried regularly offered her. He was under the misguided notion that administering small doses of milk over a given length of time could cure such intolerance. The lack of scientific evidence to support his theory did not deter Conried from spoon feeding poor Lydia milk every day, even though it sent her running to the nearest restroom.

Franklin would eventually have to leave the show prematurely due to a fall during a performance. The time she spent with Conried was one of the best experiences of her career, and she stayed in touch whenever she could. Franklin recalled a poignant comment Conried made to her in reply to a question she asked about what it meant to be an actor: "[Hans] looked at me, and he put his hand up to emulate a candle, and then he blew at his finger [and said,] 'That's an actor. Because once the lights go out we don't exist.'"

Conried was very gratified to be given the opportunity in the 1970s to do something he thought he would never have a chance to do again: perform in a radio drama. There was a small renaissance of interest in radio programming other than the Top 40 hits, and the new programs found eager participants in some of Radio Row's best and brightest who were still in the business. Beginning in 1971, Conried performed in a handful of dramatic radio programs. After 1975, he was heard regularly on *The CBS Radio Mystery Theatre*, *Sears Radio Theatre*, and *Mutual Radio Theatre*. Conried commented on this happy turn of events to a reporter: "Today, of course, anyone who gives work to an old radio actor we regard as someone who feeds the dinosaurs. Now and again, I do radio drama such as *Mystery Theater* and the like. And once or twice a year I do *Heartbeat Theater*, which is sponsored by the Salvation Army—I usually double as a bum and a colonel. But it's nice at *Heartbeat Theater*, for all of us old radio actors to meet again. We put on our spectacles and tearfully embrace each other. 'You haven't died,' one of us will say to the other. And then we all try to play young voices on the air."

The witty Woody Allen play *Don't Drink the Water* would be dusted off again and taken on the road for the summer 1978 season. One of the actors who performed with Conried during the first leg of the tour, George Sanchez, had some fond memories of working with the much admired actor in New Orleans: "When I first met Hans, I was surprised by his appearance, as he looked much older than his years, possibly because of his illness. He did not mingle a great deal, preferring to retire with his stamp collection, and his phone call to his wife in the evenings. He did appreciate dining. As a native New Orleanian, it became my probably self-appointed role to refer him to restaurants. I can still recall that nasal drawl castigating me for what local cuisine did to shrimp: 'A delicate little creature like a shrimp, and you load it up with pepper and spices until you can hardly recognize it.'

"[Hans] was such a pro, and he worked so hard. I can no longer remember the particular line in the show, but there was a spot where he thought a laugh should be, and it was not forthcoming. It was an education in comedy to watch him experiment with timing, pacing, inflection, pitch, gesture, and facial expressions as he searched for it in an effort that was never rushed, harried or egocentric. He simply knew it was there and he was going to work to find it. Need I say he did?

"Hans also had an exquisite internal editor. Our director, Annabelle Weenick, had previously done the show with Shelley Berman. The character has a speech to a sultan which Shelley had apparently really hammered, and which received cheers from the audiences. Annabelle wanted Hans to use the same approach because 'the audience loved it'. Hans demurred on the grounds that while it may have been a jingoistic winner, it wasn't right for the play or the moment. He, of course, never delivered the rant, and I doubt anyone missed it.

"As a person, I never found him to be inconsiderate. He was a gentleman. He was devoted to his craft and never stinted or held back because of his age or health. He tended to be amused by the vagaries of his cast mates and was extremely accepting."

Trilby was also a member of the *Don't Drink the Water* cast, and had been living in New Orleans for a few years after getting married to a young man who was studying medicine at Tulane University. She continued acting in small productions, and did some local television commercials. Trilby managed to pursue a career in acting without having to suffer the discomfort of one of those "cold water flats" in New York her father had nightmares about.

From New Orleans, Conried went to Pittsburgh to appear in their Civic Light Opera's production of *She Loves Me*. Newcomer Dorothy Dybisz (who was known as Dottie Tancredi then) will always remember opening night, and one old veteran's kindness: "I had the pleasure of working with Mr. Conried. He was playing the role of Maraczek, the shop owner, and I was a singer in the chorus, a shop girl. It was my first summer stock experience working with big stars. You could say I was a bit 'green.' It was opening night, time for my big entrance as a shop girl (or so I thought), so I went into the wings to wait for my cue. Much to my confusion, I was the only shop girl out of six in the wings at the time. The set was designed so that a tall circular column, center stage, rotated to reveal different rooms. I saw someone standing upstage, behind this set piece, obviously also waiting for a cue, so I joined him, hoping to find the five missing shop girls. To my horror, this gentleman turned out to be Mr. Conried, the star of the show, about to make his first entrance. I froze! He very calmly leaned down and whispered in the dark: 'My dear, I hope you have something to say, because in a few seconds you will be center stage!' Just then, he positioned himself on the set and it started to rotate. I ran—no, flew—back to the wings just in time, saved by the pro!"

Though Conried had to all outward appearances fully recovered from his stroke, he was not able to keep the rapid pace he knew before his illness. The high blood pressure medication caused unpleasant side effects, and he was forced to face the fact he would have to restrict his intake of rich foods. Conried was experiencing some discomfort eating the foods he loved most, and had to make do with blander fare. All of this conspired to chip away at his good humor, and left him feeling a bit out-of-sorts on occasion. After doing interview after interview over the course of eighteen or more years on the stock circuit, Conried found himself increasingly tired of the platitudes he was required to utter. On more than one occasion he would start the interview with, "And how shall I lie to you today, dear?" Or, to end an interview he would abruptly say, "Haven't you heard enough lies yet?" Conried knew the game well, and he wasn't always interested in playing anymore, as one young reporter found out when Conried was wrenched from an important rehearsal to do an impromptu interview: "While Conried can create elegant sentences with apparent spontaneity, he can also be surprisingly blunt. When a photographer arrived, Conried asked, 'Do you want to get this over with and get the hell out of here?' With a low-key affirmative response, Conried continued, 'As long as we understand each other.'" It was discovered that the reporter and Trilby went to school together at the university in Los Angeles, prompting an amused Conried to say: "When Tril told me she went to school with you, I expected someone to arrive with a big sheet of brown paper and crayons."

The late 1970s were a trying time for Conried's craft. Good roles were becoming hard to find in any medium, and his career seemed to be winding down. Conried was alarmed at the unthinkable prospect of long-term unemployment, but tried to keep as active as possible doing whatever job came his way. The idea of retirement wasn't an option, so Conried struggled to keep working. All the while, Conried couldn't help thinking he was in a very odd business indeed: "You are always conscious of the fact that you are on exhibit. There are times when I have considered quitting—generally in the middle of a performance—but I have this compulsion: It's called hunger. Acting has helped me feed myself and my four children. But it is a strange occupation. Much of what one does in this craft is to memorize. You have to know your lines. And memorization is a drudge. Then there are rehearsals, which for me, at any rate, are times of sleepless nights, anguish, abrasion, and strain. Then come the opening nights and the reviews."

There were some uplifting moments for Conried during 1978. The International Animated Film Society awarded Conried and Jay Ward Productions with an "Annie" for their work in animation. Conried would also have a chance to spend an evening on stage with his old friend and master voice-artist June Foray. He and Foray were asked to appear at the La Jolla Museum of Contemporary Art in California by the animation society ASIFA. They had a chance to talk about their many years in the business, and answer questions from the eager audience. Conried was also honored by his peers by receiving an Emmy for his voice work on the Dr. Seuss animated television special *Halloween Is Grinch Night*. Conried was on the road with *The Sunshine Boys* at the time, and could not attend the ceremony. Margaret stepped up to accept the award for her hard working husband.

Another rather quirky honor Conried received for the year was to be named the Grand Marshal of the Harvest Homecoming Parade in New Albany, Indiana. Conried had the privilege to ride around in a big convertible with a few other local celebrities, and wave to the adoring crowd. Conried was very popular in Indiana, and was the guest of honor at more than one state fair; he would graciously allow himself to be photographed standing next to a cow and a few local dignitaries. On a map of Indianapolis, there is even a "Conried Court."

Conried had a recurring television role on *The Tony Randall Show* as Randall's father, Wyatt Franklin. Randall expressed remorse at not having had the opportunity to have known Conried better during the short time they worked together on the show, but observed that Conried was "shrewd, kind, patient, humorous, and, in all, very good company."

The Walt Disney produced motion picture *The Cat from Outer Space*, starring Ken Berry, was released in 1978. As per the formula, Conried played a grumpy old scientist named Dr. Heffel—a part that prompted Conried to lament: "I play a scientist, and I hate to say it, but he's not even a bad, mad scientist. The villain market has gone to the dogs, and now I'm doing crusty, but loveable, characters." Oh, for those glorious days of playing nasty Nazis sinking hospital ships, and black-hearted—but impeccably dressed—fiends foreclosing the mortgages of helpless widows with good-looking daughters. "Crusty, but loveable" described in a nutshell just about the only kind of character Conried was able to play on the stage or screen for the remainder of his career. Conried explained that "as an actor, one finds oneself playing the same role with different names. One employs the same old tricks."

The opportunity arose for Conried to revive *The Sunshine Boys* for a run at a small dinner theatre in Seattle, Washington. Even though Conried had already done this show a couple times before—first with co-star Lou Jacobi in 1975, and then again with Phil Leeds in 1977—Conried had been hoping to entice his old pal Jerry Hausner out of retirement to do the show one more time. He had actually wanted his best friend to co-star with him ever since he saw the Broadway version of *The Sunshine Boys* in 1975. Hausner explained in 1978: "Hans called me from New York [three] years ago and said, 'I just found the play you and I should do together.'" Even though Hausner was enjoying his retirement, he was not able to resist his friend's entreaty to appear with him when the chance finally came, and agreed to "dust himself off." Since it was dinner theatre, there wasn't the pressure of a road tour, and the two had a chance to enjoy their time together a bit more, and resume the squabbling over their stamp collections. Possibly, Hausner did not enjoy all the time he and his buddy spent together, though. There seemed to be an ongoing problem with Conried's driving habits: "Hans was a terrible automobile driver," Hausner recalled, "but he would always insist on driving whenever we had a car. He never knew where he was going. We would pull into the first gas station, and he would ask directions, and he would never listen… I used to say, 'Look, Spencer Tracy used to say the most important thing for an actor was to listen—listen to what the man said!' Hans said, 'No, no, no… What Spencer Tracy meant was for the visual medium, it was necessary to look as if you were listening!' [Hans] never listened to anything that anybody said on the radio, or on television; he was always acting by himself. He did whatever he wanted to do. So he would ask for directions and didn't hear one word of what the guy said. We were just as lost when we drove out of that [gas station] as [when we drove in]."

Hausner got a laugh when a reporter asked Conried if it was true he was a very frugal man. Conried heartily replied, "Cheap is what I am! That's why my children have the best of everything, but I don't allow myself those luxuries." When he was asked why he denied himself, Conried growled, "My children have a rich father. I don't have a rich father!"

In 1979, Conried spent the summer in Missouri working with the St. Louis Municipal Opera on a production of *A Funny Thing Happened on the Way to the Forum*. Jimmy Roberts was then the assistant conductor and principal pianist for the show, and warmly remembered working with Conried: "Hans displayed tremendous class and polish both on and off stage. There were no ego displays, in spite of his superior talent. He used to sit quietly by himself on the tour bus, though he was always approachable… The particular incident I would like to relate took place during the first week of our performances at the St. Louis Muny Theatre, an outdoor stadium that seated close to ten thousand people and boasted a 45-piece orchestra. Though Hans was word perfect with his lines and even with his melodies, he nevertheless displayed a weakness for singing in tempo. Along with the other male stars—Arte Johnson, John Carradine, and Avery Schreiber—he had to sing a solo verse of the showstopper, 'Everybody Ought to Have a Maid' which tended to bring the house down. Only problem was, whenever his verse came along, he would rush it so much that the conductor and the

Hans in character as Willie Clark from *The Sunshine Boys* (1978 tour). From the Hans Conried Collection, Department of Special Collections, Boston University.

large orchestra would immediately fall out of synch with him. In fact, one night, in desperation, the conductor cut out the entire orchestra for the song, so that I could follow his meandering rhythms on the piano alone (which sounded pretty weak in a stadium-sized theatre!).

"On the final night in St. Louis, I had my own opportunity to conduct the show, since the main conductor had flown ahead to prepare the orchestra in Indianapolis, our next stop. I had studied Hans' performance all week, and was determined to make it work with the orchestra. And I did! When the song in question was to begin, some instinct told me to cue the musicians in with a significantly faster tempo than we had ever played it before. Although there were initial looks of shock on the faces of the orchestra and the other actors, and although the tongue-twisting words were being spat out at a rate beyond the one intended for this song—for the first time, Hans Conried was not rushing! How could he? At last Hans and his fellow performers were in synch, everybody looked good, and the song—though slightly manic—was a resounding success! I was proud of having found the 'solution' and I immediately informed the conductor when we met up in Indianapolis. I never told Hans what I had done, because I don't think he really would have discerned the difference—tempo not being his strong point!"

The politics of television would rear its ugly head once more in 1979 and 1980 with two more failed attempts by Conried to find security in a successful series. At this stage of his life, Conried would have welcomed a steady job close to home. Unfortunately, his time as a "hot" personality had long passed, and it would be even harder now to find a home in the medium that had once been his ticket to fame. In 1979, Conried filmed a pilot for a series that was to be called *Rumple's Last Stand*. The series was geared toward a juvenile audience, and set in a fanciful world of elfin folk and magic. Hans was cast as "Rumple," and dressed in an outlandish costume consisting of black and white plaid pants with red suspenders, and a big red bow tie set against a bright yellow shirt. The series was not able to find a suitable home, and was not developed.

The second pilot Conried worked on had a more promising future, but ended up as a pawn in the Machiavellian world of network television. The series was called *The American Dream*, and was filmed on location in Chicago. It was not a fluffy, "feel good" kind of show, and dealt with some very serious issues facing a suburban working class family. Donna Novak (Karen Carlson) came from a more pampered background, while her husband, Danny (Stephen Macht), grew up on the tough inner-city streets of Chicago. Their cushy, predominantly white, suburban world was creating spoiled children who were insensitive to issues outside of their limited environment. When Donna announced she was pregnant with their fourth child, the family was forced to search for a larger home. The gritty pilot episode established right away the Novak family was not perfect, and the audience watched them wrestle with one difficult situation after another. Danny Novak made the decision to teach his children a thing or two about life, and moved them all to a rough neighborhood in the part of town where he grew up in Chicago.

Conried was cast as the "crusty, but loveable" real estate agent and new neighbor Abe Berlowitz. With the help of Berlowitz, the Novak family was able to settle into a dilapidated old Victorian and begin renovating the place to make it livable. Conried's characterization, while sticking to the familiar formula, was a breakthrough in many ways. Conried said of Berlowitz: "It's the closest thing I've been to a human being in my acting, which is refreshing." There was a delicate understatement to Berlowitz that allowed Conried to show more of his serious acting ability.

ABC picked up the series, and a small number of episodes were filmed on location in Chicago in 1980. The show was slated to appear on the spring 1981 schedule, and the future seemed bright for everyone involved. That was until the in-fighting began amongst the writers, producers, and a whole cast of network characters that earned the sad affair a full chapter in Todd Gitlin's 1983 book *Inside Prime Time*. *The American Dream* became a casualty in a nasty war of words, and was shuffled from one bad time slot to another. Before its early demise, the show ended up slotted between *Charlie's Angels* and *Vega$*. Escapism it was not, and *The American Dream* could do nothing but sink in the ratings until it was yanked altogether. Despite the flood of letters and phone calls from viewers begging the network to give the show another chance, it was shelved permanently. In August of 1981, Conried told a reporter: "The show had marvelous reviews from the *New York Times*, and the trade papers. The reviews were just glowing, but, well, the show had no sex in it; no violence, and we didn't smash cars, so the networks didn't give it much of an opportunity... Now I think it's gone past limbo into oblivion."

The good reviews were not just coming in from the East. Don Freeman of the *San Diego Union* penned this tribute: "The acting honors are taken handily ... by the old pros—Hans Conried as the landlord-neighbor, and John McIntire as the crusty grandpa...There is one quiet scene wherein the two of them ... as wily as two prowling tigers, are seated over a chessboard, eating cheese and sipping wine and exchanging curmudgeonly observations—now there is playing for all the neophytes to study. In that one scene, so beautifully paced, is revealed the acting art so subtle that the art itself is beyond discerning, and how rare that is."

"Subtle" is not a word you'll find in your average television executive's vocabulary, so it was no wonder *The American Dream* didn't stand a chance in 1981. It was unfortunate for all involved, and especially Conried, who finally had a chance to explore a truly human character for a change.

When Conried was asked to comment on his failed television series, he was in Indiana: once again on the road in what would be his last stock tour. The production was ironically titled *Never Too Late* and featured his talented daughter, Trilby, in the cast. Conried told the local papers how he worked so easily with his daughter on stage: "We have an amiable familial relationship. She's well-mannered enough not to resist my direction too much." The play's humor revolved around the consternation of a sixty-year-old man who finds out his wife is pregnant. As Conried had said before, there just wasn't enough good product out there, and actors had to make do with what they could get. The play was a moderate success, but Conried sensed it might be time to think about leaving the road behind.

Conried was able to enjoy an evening of accolades when he was the guest of honor, along with Zsa Zsa Gabor, at the Allegro Ball held in Los Angeles in 1981. The ball was a fundraising event held each year for the California Chamber Symphony, founded by a friend of Conried's, the musician and conductor Henri Temianka.

In December of 1981, Paramount Productions arranged for a special five-day dinner theatre engagement of *Barefoot in the Park* at the Moore Theatre in Seattle, Washington. The production was specifically staged in order to film the show for later broadcast on Paramount's HBO pay-television network. The play starred Richard Thomas and Bess Armstrong, with Conried in his familiar Victor Velasco role. The film of the live performance would unfortunately not be shown on network television until two months after Conried's death.

It is interesting to note that even though Conried was only sixty-four years of age in 1981, the handwriting was already on the wall that his career options were quickly evaporating. Voice work was becoming one of the only avenues of employment still welcoming his services, and that was not sufficient to bring in the kind of income he had been accustomed to. He was by no means in financial straits, but the psychological factor of not being able to find a decent job was weighing heavily on Conried's mind. His children were no longer a significant financial burden: Edie was earning a living in Las Vegas, and Hansi was able to make his own way. Alex was having a harder time of it, but employed, for the most part. Conried was finally able to decide that it was all right to ease up a little, and put an end to his vagabond lifestyle. He would take whatever little jobs he was offered in Hollywood, and spend more time at home with Margaret so, as Conried disturbingly put it, he could "get to know my future widow." Conried had spent most of his life traveling from place to place. It was obvious that he thrived on the variety and intellectual stimulation he found on the road. As much as he loved his home and, above all, his family, could he ever settle down to a sedentary life in Hollywood, and be happy?

Once in a while, though he loathed doing such a thing, it became necessary to audition for a part. Conried was no longer able to just get by on his celebrity, and was considered a "has been" by many narrow-minded young television executives. In late December of 1981, James F. Engelhardt was producing a children's television show called *The Music Shoppe*. Englehardt recalled the events surrounding the development of the series, and his meeting with Conried during an audition: "*The Music Shoppe* was conceived in 1981-82 as a vehicle for the late Gary Crosby... The stories allowed lots of opportunities for guest stars, either dropping in as themselves or playing guest roles. Once the continuing characters were set, we held auditions for a variety of additional parts. As creator and writer, I was present for the auditions. Being an actor as well, I read opposite the actors as a courtesy to the producers. Would that the producers were equally courteous to our guests!

"Russ Tamblyn came in to audition for the part of the father of one of the teens. Not only would he have been wonderful for the role, he was 'between engagements' and affordable. Here was an entertainment legend interested in doing my series. I would have been honored to work with him. But the producers didn't jump at the chance to engage Mr. Tamblyn because he was 'no longer a household name.' Can you imagine? ... A few days later we were auditioning actors for the comic role of a building inspector, who would also have a solo charm song to perform. In strolled the elegant

Hans Conried wearing his signature bow tie to read with me. He brought all his charm to bear on the character, but was somewhat apprehensive about the prospect of what he believed would be his singing debut on a TV show. Once again, the producers were unimpressed by another legend who had come to offer his services. 'Why should we hire that has-been?' they complained. 'He can't even sing, and this is musical show.' This time the director, the late Gene Weed, and I were adamant about hiring the veteran performer. We were like kids awaiting a visit from Santa Claus.

"The day Mr. Conried appeared to shoot his episode was a highlight of my experiences in television in the early 1980s... I believe it was just one week after shooting our 'Building Inspector' episode that we heard the melancholy news of the passing of Hans Conried."

The end came unexpectedly on a Tuesday, the 5th of January 1982, at 11:35 A.M. Two days earlier, on Sunday, the 3rd, Conried had begun to have serious chest pains just after he returned home from having dinner at a restaurant with Margaret and Trilby. An ambulance was called, and Conried was rushed to St. Joseph Medical Center in Burbank. His condition was serious, but would stabilize over the next twenty-four hours. Margaret and a couple of the kids remained by his side almost constantly. It was ironic that the doctors had told the family as late as Tuesday morning that Conried would make a full recovery. He seemed to be responding well to the treatment, and the understanding was that he would be going home soon. There was nothing anyone could do when a final, massive heart attack struck shortly before noon on the 5th. Conried died quickly, thus sparing him any further pain.

Hansi remembered that it was a blessing to the family that, after all the years his father had been on the road for the holidays, 1981 had been a year when the entire family was together for Christmas. There had been no warning Conried was in danger, and the family believed he was in great health for a man of his years. When one considers he neither drank nor smoked in his life (except for pretending to smoke a pipe in his youth), and managed to keep to a regular schedule of light exercise, it is even more surprising that he died young.

The Conried family, and all who knew and loved Conried, were stunned at his sudden death. Conried's final wishes were carried out, and his body was turned over to the St. Joseph's Medical School so that any usable organs could be donated. When their work was completed, they returned Conried's cremated remains to Margaret. The family will keep the remains until her passing, at which time husband and wife will be interred together.

A memorial service was held in the Old North Church at Forest Lawn Cemetery at 3:00 P.M. on Saturday, January 9th. James Karen, Elliott Reid, Frank Nelson, and Henri Temianka all gave eulogies for their dear friend. Later, there was a sort of Irish wake for a group of about forty or fifty of Conried's closest friends in and out of show business, and the Conried family. One of the attendees, Dr. Nathan Rosenbloom, was an avid collector Conried knew from his association with the Japanese Sword Society. Dr. Rosenbloom recalled, "All of the friends came around [after the funeral] as a memorial to him. And the thing wasn't crying and tears; everybody contributed a funny story [about] Hans, with laughter going on like crazy... The people that knew him loved him." The doctor would later have the good fortune to acquire Conried's large collection of Japanese bokuto (ceremonial wooden swords) when they were put up for auction. A substantial part of Conried's netsuke collection, and other selected pieces of Asian art, would be sold at auction within a short time of his death.

Taking stock of his life and career in

Candid portrait of Hans taken at a friend's 50th wedding anniversary in November of 1981.

1980 Conried said, "It has been a very gratifying life. At this point, I'm looking back 45 years, and I'm daring—presuming—to look forward to a very few years more. I've enjoyed acting as much as knowing actors. I like the life; I like the fellowship. They're interesting people—not always honest, not always honorable men, but usually engaging. The life has been a very pleasant one, and I've been very lucky to maintain myself and my family. I'm a survivor...." Indeed, Conried's contribution to the world will survive for many generations to come. All who knew him, and worked with him—all who enjoyed his work on the radio, in films, on television, or on the stage—would be forever enriched by the experience.

Conried was a Hollywood actor who shunned the Hollywood lifestyle. He was a regular guy who just happened to have an irregular job. Then again, he wasn't just a regular guy: Conried fancied himself an English nobleman, and had a rich inner life filled with tales of grandeur and chivalry that was of a much older time. Whatever he may have thought, the truth can be told that he was a gentleman in every sense of the word; an exceptional actor who was as comfortable with Shakespeare as he was with cartoon comedy; a loyal friend, and great companion; and a loving husband and father. Conried never sought the limelight, or pushed himself into the public's attention in an unseemly way to grab a few headlines. Yet, he acutely needed the approval of his audience, and would be gratified to know his work was still being watched and loved by so many.

Conried was honored on February 8, 1960 (the date of the inauguration), with a star on Hollywood's Walk of Fame, located at 6664 Hollywood Blvd. It didn't seem like such a great honor at the time, considering he was asked to put up the money for the star. Even though Conried told them to forget it, the Chamber of Commerce placed his star on the walk anyway. It is ironic, in many ways, that he was recognized for his achievement in television—a medium with which he maintained a rather virulent love-hate relationship. Conried was by far most accomplished as a radio actor, and it would have been fitting for him to be remembered for the work he loved the most in life.

But the world best remembers Conried as Uncle Tonoose, or the voice of Snidely Whiplash, or Dr. Terwilliker, or if they have lived sufficiently long, as that witty "personality" talking late at night to Jack Paar on television. Conried was more than that, of course—more than anyone will ever really know. One thing is certain, though—Conried's work will never fall completely into obscurity. There are too many people who still love him, and are willing ambassadors to spread the word to others who have yet to experience *The 5000 Fingers of Dr. T*, or any number of other wonderful performances.

Thank you, Hans, for all your hard work; the lonely nights on the road with your stamp collection and cottage cheese; the joy of hearing you tell the tale of *Treasure Island*; the wonders of your Dr. Terwilliker, resplendent in his "Do-Me-Do-Duds"; the many thrilling hours you have kept us in *Suspense*; and so many other exquisitely crafted offerings. As you always said, you are a true survivor, and you will continue to survive deep in the hearts and minds of generations of fans to come.

To borrow a saying from the Koran: "He deserves Paradise who makes his companions laugh."

Part V
Appendices

A. Radio Log

This log is designed to give the reader a good idea of the wide variety of radio programs Hans Conried worked on during his long career. Considering the fact he was on over 10,000 radio shows (a conservative estimate), it is unlikely that all performances will ever be accounted for. Supporting actors routinely worked anonymously until some time after World War II, so the identification process often involves educated guesses, and long hours of listening. Many shows did not have titles, and collectors today often refer to them by the show's content. Significant broadcasts—where Conried had a lead role, or was a regular cast member in a series—are highlighted in boldface for easy reference.

1936

January 14—KECA Shakespeare Series, "Othello" (with Lindsay MacHarrie and Mary Jane Higby); *February 11*—KECA Shakespeare Series, "King John"; *March 10*—KECA Shakespeare Series, "Twelfth Night" (with Thelma Hubbard and J. M. Kerrigan); *April 14*—KECA Shakespeare Series, "Coriolanus" (with Conway Tearle); *May 12*—KECA Shakespeare Series, "Richard II" (with Bret Morrison and John Prince); *May 21—It Happened Today*—Conried was a regular for a year on this 5 days-a-week Hal Styles news program; *May 24*—KHJ Radio—"Queen Victoria" (with Lindsay MacHarrie: Hans as "Albert"); *June 17*—KECA Shakespeare Series, "Merry Wives of Windsor" (with Talbot Henderson, Dan Davies); *July 14*—KECA Shakespeare Series, "Julius Caesar"; *August 2—Ports of Call*—"Yugoslavia" (a weekly transcribed travelogue series starring Lindsay MacHarrie broadcast on the West Coast only [beginning in May of 1936]; 38 episodes are known to exist covering such locales as Guinea, Wales, Barbary, Siam, Cuba, Chile, Denmark, Alaska, and Arabia; Conried's dialects got a workout providing the voices of the "locals"); *August 9*—*Ports of Call*, "Austria"; *August 16*—*Ports of Call*, "Central Africa"; *August 23*—*Ports of Call*, "Hungary"; *August 30*—*Ports of Call*, "Germany." *(?)1936*—*Annals of the Ages* [?]; *(?)1936*—*Calling All Cars*—West Coast only: Conried performed on more than one show; *(1936-1937)*—*Saturday Night Party*—popular series that ran October 17, 1936—October 10, 1937; previously untitled, the show became *Saturday Night Party* as of May 23, 1937; Conried performed on at least one episode.

1937

(date unknown)—"The Red Mill" (Victor Herbert story: with Jerry Hausner); *(1937-1938)*—*One Man's Family* (NBC: Conried worked on at least one episode); *January 3*—*Ports of Call*, "Scotland"; *January 10*—*Ports of Call*, "Peru"; *January 17*—*Ports of Call*, "Haiti" (final broadcast of series); *January 27—Thrills*—premiere: sponsored by Union Oil: Conried was a regular cast member for the run of the series, which was broadcast on the West Coast only; the episodes aired on Wednesdays at 6:30 pm until April 27th, when the series moved to Tuesdays at 9:00 pm; the date of the last episode is unknown, but *Thrills* appears to have had at least a year's run; *March 26*— *The First Nighter*, "Spring in Kansas" (with Don Ameche and Barbara Luddy: Conried may have been a regular on the series for one season); *April 2*—KFAC Radio, "Life of Lord Byron" (Conried as a guest performer); *May 7*—*The First Nighter*, "The Lawyer's Dilemma"; *May 31*—KHJ Radio, "Brink of Eternity" (with Lindsay MacHarrie); *June 3*—Short Story Playhouse, "The Specter Bridegroom" (KECA: Conried as Von Altenburg); *June 21*—Streamlined Shakespeare, "Hamlet" (series starred John Barrymore: Conried as Laertes); *June 28*—Streamlined Shakespeare, "Richard III" (Con-

ried as Catesby); *July 5—Streamlined Shakespeare*, "Macbeth" (Conried as Malcolm); *July 5—Thrills*— John Wilkes Booth's brother Edwin's return to the stage after Lincoln's death; *July 12—Streamlined Shakespeare*, "The Tempest" (Conried as Antonio); *July 19—Streamlined Shakespeare*, "Twelfth Night" (Conried as Sebastian); *July 26—Streamlined Shakespeare*, "The Taming of the Shrew" (Conried as Lucentio); *August 30—Moving Stories of Life* (drama series written by Gene Carmen: Conried was on at least one episode); *September 12—John Barrymore Presents*, "Accent on Youth" (with John Barrymore; Conried as "Dickie."); *October 16—* KFWB Radio, "Camille" (Hans as Count DeVarville)

1938

(date unknown)—Signal Carnival (NBC: West Coast only: sponsored by Signal Oil; Conried was on at least one show); *(date unknown)—Hollywood Hotel* (CBS: sponsored by Campbell Soups; Conried was on at least one show); *January 3—* KFAC Radio, "The Life of Lord Byron" (Conried as a guest performer); *March 13—Mickey Mouse Theater*, "The Pied Piper"; *March 22—Preview Tonight*, "Uncle Ivan's Plan" (KECA Radio comedy series); *April 28—*KFI Radio, "Doctor's Husband" (Beatrice Benaderet and Frank Nelson); *May 12—*KFI Radio, "Red Hot Cassidy" (Beatrice Benaderet and Frank Nelson); *August 11—Parents on Trial—*"Are Children People?" (KFI Radio: adapted from real cases from the juvenile court, Conried as neglected 17-year-old son of wealthy parents); *December 14—Texaco Star Theater*, "Twilight Shore" (with Olivia deHavilland)

1939

(date unknown)—The Royal Gelatin Hour (NBC: starring Rudy Vallee; Conried often did dramatic readings emulating his hero, John Barrymore); *(date unknown)—Tuesday Night Party* (CBS: with Dick Powell, as of March 21, 1939, Conried in at least one show); *October (?)—Blondie*, [?]; *October 12—*KNX Radio, "The Chocolate Soldier" (musical: Conried in dramatic part); *December 7—*KNX Radio, "The Prince of Pilsen" (musical: Conried in dramatic part); *December 30—Arch Oboler's Plays*, "This Precious Freedom"

1940

January 13—Arch Oboler's Plays, "The Truth" (with Lou Merrill); *January 14—Gulf Screen Guild Theater*, "This Lonely Heart" (written and directed by Arch Oboler: with Bette Davis); *February 1—* KNX Radio, "Sweethearts"; *February 7—Woodbury's Hollywood Playhouse*, "Cyrano de Bergerac" (with Charles Boyer as Cyrano); *May 6—Once Upon a Midnight* (KECA Radio: series produced tales of Edgar Allan Poe; Conried was a regular on this short-lived series); *June 16—I Was There—* (Conried began as a semi-regular at this time, and would appear frequently through 1944; the series was broadcast only on the West Coast, and featured dramatized true stories of adventure); *June 27—Our Half Hour* (NBC: Hans did a guest spot as a "ham actor"); *July 17—Woodbury's Hollywood Playhouse*, "Romeo & Juliet" (KECA Radio production); *August 8—**The Homer Griffith Show**,* (KECA: Conried was interviewed about his flourishing career); *September 16—Promoting Priscilla*, [?]; *November 14—*"The Great Narration"—quote from nightclub program: "The Victor Hugo Offers: Rudy Vallee & Co. in 'Tonight at 10', a Series of Musical Playlets, Two Nightly, Both Changed Weekly"—Conried, as "The Great Profile," performed an impersonation of John Barrymore; *November 15—Everyman's Theater*, "The Flying Yorkshireman" (directed by Arch Oboler: starring Charles Laughton and Elsa Lancaster); *December 1—The Gulf Screen Guild Theatre*, "Desire" (with Fred MacMurray and Marlene Dietrich); *December 9—Everyman's Theater*, "An American Is Born" (with Elisabeth Bergner); *December 19—The Rudy Valley Show* (Episode #10: "Life of John Barrymore"); *December 20—*KNX Radio, "A Christmas Carol" (w/Lionel Barrymore: Conried as Bob Crachit)

1941

January 2—The Rudy Vallee Show (Conried was among supporting actors to be spotlighted); *February 3—The Lux Radio Theatre*, "Rebecca" (with Ronald Colman); *February 7—Lights Out!*, "Special to Hollywood" (with Joan MacRae and Howard Duff: series was written and directed by Arch Oboler); *February 10—The Lux Radio Theatre*, "The Moon's Our Home" (with James Stewart, Carole Lombard); *February 17—The Lux Radio Theatre*, "Johnny Apollo" (with Burgess Meredith and Dorothy Lamour); *February 22—This Was My Inspiration* (episode about artist Paul Gaugin with Broderic Crawford); *February 23—The Gulf Screen Guild Theatre*, "Altar Bound" (with Betty Grable, Bing Crosby and Bob Hope); *March 17—The Lux Radio Theatre*, "Cheers for Miss Bishop" (with William Gargan and Martha Scott); *March 23—The Silver Theater*, "Lady with Ideas" (with Ann Sothern); *April 7— The Lux Radio Theatre,* "The Stand-In" (with Warner Baxter and Joan Bennett); *April 10— The Rudy Vallee Show* (Conried as John Barrymore's "conscience"); *April 28— The Lux Radio Theatre,* "Wife, Husband and Friend" (with George Brent, Priscilla Lane); *May 26— The Lux Radio Theatre,* "Virginia City" (with Errol Flynn and Martha Scott); *June 27—Hollywood Premiere,* "Blood and Sand" (CBS: hosted by Louella Parsons); *July 7— The Lux Radio Theatre,* "Algiers" (with Charles Boyer and Hedy Lamarr); *August 24— Twenty-Six by Corwin,* #16: "Job" (actually a part of *The Columbia Workshop* series; the program's name was temporarily changed to showcase 26 dramas written by Norman Corwin); *August 31— Twenty-Six by Corwin,* #17: "Mary and the Fairy"; *August 31— The Great Gildersleeve* (premiere episode: Conried was a semi-regular as Oliver Honeywell); *September 15—Orson Welles Theater* (Conried in the sketch: "An Irishman and a Jew"); *September 16— Twenty-Six by Corwin,* #19: "Fragment from a Lost Cause"; *September 29— The Lux Radio Theatre,* "Third Finger, Left Hand" (with Douglas Fairbanks, Jr); *October 26— The Great Gildersleeve* (a visit from Oliver); *November 9— The Great Gildersleeve* (the judge hires Birdie); *November 16— The Great Gildersleeve* (Thanksgiving Dinner); *December 25— The Rudy Valley Show,* (#61: "A Christmas Carol" with Lionel Barrymore; *December 27— The Best of the Week* (Premiere episode of variety series: Conried was a regular)

1942

February 15—Three Sheets to the Wind (premiere of series starring John Wayne; Conried was a semi-regular until the show's merciful death on July 5); *February 15—Gulf Screen Guild Theater,* "Liberty's a Lady" (with Loretta Young); *March 5— The Al Pearce Show* (Conried as J. Herrington Bone); *March 15—American Legion Birthday* (special broadcast with Rudy Vallee); *March 29—Plays for Americans,* "Hate" (Arch Oboler: stars Conrad Veidt); *April 6— The Lux Radio Theatre,* "The Fighting 69th" (with Pat O'Brien); *April 13— The Cavalcade of America,* "A Continental Uniform" (with Basil Rathbone); *April 20— The Cavalcade of America,* "In This Crisis" (with Claude Rains and Agnes Moorehead); *May 25— The Cavalcade of America,* "Young Tom Jefferson" (with Tyrone Power and Gale Gordon); *June 21—Plays for Americans,* "Adolf and Mrs. Runyon" (written and directed by Arch Oboler: Conried co-starred with Bette Davis as an over-the-top Adolf Hitler!); *June 30— Command Performance,* #20: hosted by Spencer Tracy, and featuring Groucho Marx, the show was transcribed for broadcast to the armed forces overseas only; *October 27—Lights Out!* "Mungahra" (series was written and directed by Arch Oboler); *October 31—Radio Canteen,* [?]; *November 9—Ceiling Unlimited,* "The Rulers of the Earth" (premiere: Conried was a regular on this Orson Welles series as one of his "Mercury Theatre" group until Feb. 1, when Welles left the show after a dispute; each episode was 15 minutes in length); *November 15—Hello, Americans,* "The Life of Carmen Miranda" (premiere: as part of Welle's troupe, Conried also performed regularly on his mentor's other Latin American flavored series; the last broadcast was on January 31); *November 22—Hello, Americans,* "The Christ of the Andes" (with Agnes Moorehead); *November 29— Hello, Americans,* "Santo Domingo and Haiti" (with Ray Collins); *December 6—Hello, Americans,* "The Alphabet of the Islands" (Part 1: Conried is not in Part 2); *December 7—Lady Esther Screen Guild Theatre,* "Mrs. Miniver" (with Walter Pidgeon and Greer Garson); *December 13— The Whistler,* "The Accounting" (the series aired on the West Coast only); *December 14—Ceiling Unlimited,* "Espionage Report" (Conried plays Nazi "Operative 23"; one source claims that Conried had a hand in writing the script for this episode); *December 21—Ceiling Unlimited,* "Gremlins" (Christmas episode); *December 24— Mayor of the Town,* "The Christmas Carol" (with Lionel Barrymore); *December 25— The Rudy Valley Show,* #112: "A Christmas Carol" with Lionel Barrymore; *December 27—Hello, Americans,* "The Bad Will Ambassador" (with Orson Welles); *December 28—Ceiling Unlimited,* "A Voyage in Time and Space"

1943

January 3— The Whistler, "The Weakling" (co-starring Conried); *January 10—Hello, Americans,* "Mexico" (with Laird Cregar and Agnes Moorehead); *January 11—Blondie* (Conried as rumba teacher, "Don Rodriguez Jaime Louis Pedro Lopez"; "Dagwood, [the dope!], may call me Carlos!" sighed Conried); *February 2—Lights Out!,* "Until Dead" (with Paul Stewart); *February 21— The Whistler,* "Fool's Gold" (Conried is the star in this well told tale); *February 23—Lights Out!,* "They Met at Dorset"; *March 4— The Bob Burns Show* (NBC: sponsored by Lever Brothers); *March 5— The World We're Fighting For* (audition episode); *March 9—Lights Out!,* "The Ball" (with Jane Morgan and Bea Benaderet); *March 23— Lights Out!,* **"The Flame"** (Conried stars in this melodrama); ***March 23***— *The Silver Theater*, "The Lady with Ideas"; ***March 25***— *The Bob Burns Show*, [?]; ***March 26***— ***The World We're Fighting For*** (series premiere: Conried was a regular in the cast); ***April 13***— *Lights Out!*, "The Archer" (with Claudette Colbert); ***April 20***— *Suspense*, "Moment of Darkness" (starring Peter Lorre: Conried makes his debut on *Suspense* as the train conductor in his episode); ***April 26***— *The Lady Esther Screen Guild Theatre* "Casablanca" (CBS: stars Ingrid Bergman, Humphrey Bogart, and Paul Henried); ***May 3***— *The Cavalcade of America*, "Soldiers in Greasepaint" (with Martha Raye); ***May 6***— *The Bob Burns Show*, [?]; ***May 10***— *The Cavalcade of America*, "Fat Girl" (with Edward Arnold); ***May 25***— *Suspense*, "Sorry, Wrong Number" (with Agnes Moorehead; at the climax of this episode, the actor playing George, the killer [he wasn't identified], was given a miscue and flubs his line; because of this mistake, and the subsequent interest in the outcome of the story by the listeners, this episode was redone on August 21st with Conried in the role of George; a notice about this new production was given at the beginning of "Banquo's Chair"); ***June 1***— *Suspense*, "Banquo's Chair" (with Donald Crisp and John Loder); ***June 12***— *The Whistler*, "Justice"; ***June 15***— *Lights Out!*, "Prelude to Murder" (starring Conried); ***June 24***— ***The World We're Fighting For***, "Furlough" (Conried starred); ***June 29***— *Lights Out!*, "Bathysphere" (co-starring Conried); ***July 6***— *The Judy Canova Show*—Conried was a regular performer on this series; most often heard as the perennial houseguest, Mr. Hemmingway; with the exception of his Army days, Conried performed on-and-off throughout the shows long run that ended on May 28; not all of his episodes appear in the log; ***July 25***— *The Life of Riley* (audition show: Riley plans to build a house); ***August 12***—KFI Radio, "Nazi Spy" (*Conried starred*); ***August 19***— KFI Radio, "Sonata For Remington"; ***August 21***— *Suspense*, "Sorry, Wrong Number" (with Agnes Moorehead; new production to correct an error in the May 25th episode); ***August 31***— *The George Burns and Gracie Allen Show* (with Frank Sinatra: Conried as "Bolingbroke"); ***August 31***— *Lights Out!*, "The Immortal Gentleman" (with Franchot Tone); ***September 14***— *The George Burns and Gracie Allen Show* (with Brian Donlevy); ***September 18***—KFI Radio, "The People March" (Arch Oboler); ***September 21***— *Passport for Adams*, "Tel Aviv" (starred Robert Young); ***October 18***— *The Cavalcade of America*, "The General Wore Calico" (with Harry Bartell and Jane Darwell); ***October 19***— *Suspense*, "Lazarus Walks" (with Orson Welles); ***October 26***— *Suspense*, "The After Dinner Story" (with Otto Kruger); ***November 2***— *Suspense*, "Statement of Henry Wilson" (with Gene Lockhart); ***November 8***— *The Cavalcade of America*, "Joe Dyer Ends the War" (with Beulah Bondi); ***November 9***— *Suspense*, "Cabin B-13" (with Phillip Dorn and Margo); ***November 15***— *The Cavalcade of America*, "Twelve Desperate Miles" (with Edward Arnold); ***November 16***— *Suspense*, "Thieves Fall Out" (with Gene Kelly); ***November 23***— *Suspense*, "The Strange Death of Charles Umberstein" (with Vincent Price); ***November 29***— *The Cavalcade of America*, "The Wise Mad General" (with Warner Baxter); ***December 2***— *Suspense*, "The Black Curtain" (with Cary Grant); ***December 9***— *Suspense*, "The Night Reveals" (with Robert Young and Margo); ***December 16***— *Suspense*, "Wet Saturday" (with Charles Laughton); ***December 19***— *Ceiling Unlimited*, [?] (with Joseph Cotten); ***December 21***— *The George Burns and Gracie Allen Show*, (Christmas Show: with Charles Laughton); ***December 28***— *The George Burns and Gracie Allen Show*, (with John Garfield)

1944

(**date unknown**)— *The Gallant Heart* (Conried as a Nazi spy); (**date unknown**)— *Pabst Blue Ribbon Town*, [?]; (**date unknown**)— *Sherlock Holmes* (Conried performed in a handful of episodes as many different characters, including the dreaded "Moriarty"); ***January 6***— *Suspense*, "One-Way Ride to Nowhere" (with Alan Ladd); ***January 10***— *The Lux Radio Theatre*, "The Constant Nymph" (with Charles Boyer); ***January 13***— *Suspense*, "Dime a Dance" (with Lucille Ball); ***January 16***— *The Life of Riley*—Conried was a regular on this series as "Uncle Baxter" until its demise on June 29 (see 7/25/43 audition show); Uncle Baxter left the show temporarily when Conried went into the Army, but made a triumphant return on the January 31, 1948, show; only select episodes are listed in this log; ***January 20***— *Suspense*—"A World of Darkness" (with Paul Lukas and Ian Wolfe); ***January 25***— *The George Burns and Gracie Allen Show*, (guest: Paul Henreid); ***January 26***— ***Orson Welles Radio Almanac*** (premiere: Conried was a regular on this short-lived series); ***January 27***— *Suspense*, "The Locked Room" (with Virginia Bruce and George Zucco); ***February 2***— *Orson Welles Radio Almanac* (with guest, Lionel Barrymore); ***February 10***— *Suspense*, "Suspicion" (with Charlie Ruggles); ***February 17***— *Suspense*, "Life Ends at Midnight" (with Fay Bainter and Ralph Morgan); ***February 18***— *Great Short Stories*, "The Cask of Amontillado"; ***February 23***— *Orson Welles Radio Almanac* (with Agnes Moorehead); ***February 24***— *Suspense*, "Sorry, Wrong Number" (with Agnes Moorehead); ***February 25***— *Great Short Stories*, "Markheim"; ***March (?)***— *The Whistler*, "Detour to Death"; ***March 2***— *Suspense*, "Portrait Without a Face" (with Phillip Dorn); *March 3*—*Great Short Stories*, "The Necklace"; *March 5*—*The Life of Riley* (Uncle Baxter goes to work); *March 7*—*Everything for the Boys*, "Of Human Bondage" (NBC: Sponsored by Auto-Lite; directed by Arch Oboler; with Ronald Colman and Bette Davis); *March 8*—*Orson Welles Radio Almanac* (with Agnes Moorehead); *March 9*—*Suspense*, "The Defense Rests" (with Alan Ladd); *March 13*—*Sherlock Holmes*, [?]; *March 14*—*The George Burns and Gracie Allen Show* (Conried as "Nigel Bolingbroke"); *March 15*—*Orson Welles Radio Almanac* (with Agnes Moorehead); *March 16*—*Suspense*, "The Narrative About Clarence" (with Laird Cregar); *March 18*—*Don't Believe It* (Conried played Lenin; the Pope; Rudolf Hess, and more!); *March 19*—*Ceiling Unlimited* (Conried reads "Declaration of Independence"; plays three roles); *March 19*—*The Life of Riley*, [?]; *March 19*—*I Was There*, [?]; *March 19*—*Saturday Night Salute* (Conried played a Bulgarian smuggler); *March 22*—*Orson Welles Radio Almanac* (with Agnes Moorehead); *March 23*—*Suspense*, "Sneak Preview" (with Joseph Cotten); *March 29*—*Orson Welles Radio Almanac*, [?]; *April 2*—*The Life of Riley* (Riley's birthday); *April 6*—*Suspense*, "The Woman in Red" (with Katina Paxinou and Ian Wolfe); *April 13*—*Suspense*, "The Marvelous Barastro" (with Orson Welles); *April 20*—*Suspense*, "The Palmer Method" (with Ed Gardner); *April 25*—*Everything for the Boys*, "Death Takes a Holiday" (with Ronald Colman, Ingrid Bergman); *April 27*—*Suspense*, "Death Went Along for the Ride" (with Gene Kelly); *April 30*—*The Life of Riley* (Uncle Baxter goes to New York); *May 2*—*The Judy Canova Show* (Conried as a Shakespearean actor); *May 4*—*Suspense*, "The Dark Tower" (with Orson Welles); *May 11*—*Suspense*, "The Visitor" (with Edie Bracken and Jeanette Nolan); *May 17*—*Orson Welles Radio Almanac* (Welles, as Romeo, reads two of the final scenes of *Romeo and Juliet* with Conried supporting as Count Paris); *May 18*—*Suspense*, "Donovan's Brain" (with Orson Welles; Part 1); *May 25*—*Suspense*, "Donovan's Brain" (with Orson Welles; Part 2); *June 6*—*Columbia Presents Corwin*, "Carl Sandburg" (CBS: with Charles Laughton and Mercedes McCambridge); *June 6*—Special D-Day broadcast by Arch Oboler: Conried co-starred in "Surrender," the first of four stories; *June 7*—*Orson Welles Radio Almanac* (D-Day Invasion Special); *June 8*—*Suspense*, "The Case History of Edgar Lowndes" (with Donald Crisp); *June 13*—*The George Burns and Gracie Allen Show*—Guest: Dinah Shore; *June 15*—*The Birdseye Open House* (a.k.a. *The Dinah Shore Program:* with guest, Phil Harris); *June 15*—*Suspense*, "A Friend to Alexander" (with Geraldine Fitzgerald); *June 25*—*The Life of Riley* (Riley tries to marry off Uncle Baxter); *June 29*—*Suspense*, "The Walls Came Tumbling Down" (with Keenan Wynn); *July 6*—*Suspense*, "The Search for Henri LeFevre" (with Paul Muni); *July 10*—*The Man Called X* (Conried was "Egon, the Chisler," a semi-regular character on series, see Aug. 21st); *July 13*—*Suspense*, "The Beast Must Die" (with Herbert Marshall); *July 19*—*Orson Welles Radio Almanac* (with Ruth Terry); *August 3*—*Suspense*, "Banquo's Chair" (with Donald Crisp: different from 6/1/43); *August 3*—*The Sealtest Village Store* (Hans appeared regularly on this series, and continued when he returned from his stint in the Army; this episode featured Edward Everett Horton and Billie Burke); *August 10*—*Suspense*, "The Man Who Knew How" (with Charles Laughton); *August 10*—*The Sealtest Village Store* (#197: with Edward E. Horton, Billie Burke, and Mel Blanc); *August 17*—*The Sealtest Village Store* (#198: with Joan Davis and Jack Haley); *August 21*—*The Man Called X* (by popular demand, Conried's character, "Egon" becomes a regular in the series); *August 24*—*Suspense*, "Actor's Blood" (with Frederic March); *August 24*—*The Sealtest Village Store*, [?]; *August 28*—*The Man Called X* ("Egon" makes a premature exit; Conried had to report to the Army on August 30th); (**NOTE:** Conried served in the Army ("Our Army the U.S. Army no matter what anyone says") from August 30 to September of 1946; he was stationed first in the Philippines, then Korea, and finally in Tokyo, Japan; the dates presented from August 31, 1944, to May 21, 1945, and May 20, 1946, broadcast are suspect for that reason; they most likely had been transcribed prior to Conried's departure for Ft. Knox); *August 31*—*The Sealtest Village Store* (#199: with Joan Davis, Jack Haley, Si Wills, and Verna Felton); *August 31*—*Suspense*, "The Black Path of Fear" (with Brian Donlevy); *October 13*—*Columbia Presents Corwin*, "Wolfiana" (dir. by Norman Corwin; with Charles Laughton); *October 22*—*The Life of Riley* (flashback to when Riley was married); *October 24(?)*—*The Sealtest Village Store*, [?]; *November 25*—*The Globe Theatre*, "The Distant Future"

1945

April 17—*This Is My Best*, "I Will Not Go Back" (with Orson Welles); *April 19*—*Suspense*, "Pearls are a Nuisance"; *May 21*—*The Lady Esther Screen Guild Theater* "The Desert Song" (with Bruce Cabot and Francia White); *July 25*—Armed Forces Radio Network, "Kilocycle Komics" (produced for Far Eastern Network); *September 15*—Armed Forces Radio Network, "Musical Mailbox" (Conried as DJ on AFRS from the Philippines)

1946

Early 1946—Armed Forces Radio Network,

"Today's Notebook" (produced by Conried for Radio Tokyo); *May 20*— *The Lux Radio Theatre*, "Deadline at Dawn" (with Paul Lukas and Joan Blondell); *October 3*—*Suspense*, "Three Times Murder" (with Rita Hayworth); *October 10*—*Suspense*, "A Plane Case of Murder" (with John Lund); *October 14*— *The Cavalcade of America*, "The Hickory Tree" (with Agnes Moorehead); *October 15*— *The Mel Blanc Show* (ballroom tickets)— Conried became a regular as of this episode; *October 22*— *The Mel Blanc Show* (The songwriter); *October 24*—*Suspense*, "Dame Fortune" (with Susan Hayward); *October 25*— *The Alan Young Show* (Alan's movie career); *October 29*— *The Mel Blanc Show* (community chest fund); *October 30*— *The Jack Carson Show*, [?]; *October 31*—*Suspense*, "Lazarus Walks" (with Brian Donlevy; Conried had the same role as the 1943 production); *November 5*— *The Mel Blanc Show* (Mel breaks the new radio); *November 6*—*Duffy's Tavern*, [?]; *November 10*—*Pacific Story*, "Redemption in Singapore" (melodrama starring Conried); *November 12*— *The Mel Blanc Show* (the lodge invitation); *November 14*—*Suspense*, "The One That Got Away" (with Hume Cronyn); *November 19*— *The Mel Blanc Show* (Mel impersonates Mr. Colby); *November 26*— *The Mel Blanc Show* (the Thanksgiving show); *November 26*— *The Jimmy Durante Show* (Conried as "Anatole" and "Half-Breed Harry"); *November 28*—*Suspense*, "The Strange Death of Gordon Fitzroy" (with Chester Morris); *November 28*— *The Sealtest Village Store* (#347: Jack Haley, Eve Arden, Henry Fonda, and more); *December 1*— *The Fitch Bandwagon* (sponsored by Fitch Shampoo: with Phil Harris and Alice Faye); *December 3*— *The Mel Blanc Show* (the elopement); *December 5*—*Suspense*, "The House in Cypress Canyon" (with Howard Duff); *December 5*— *The Sealtest Village Store* (#348: with Jack Haley, Eve Arden, Frank Nelson, etc.); *December 8*— *The Fitch Bandwagon*, "Musicale at Emily Williams'"; *December 10*— *The Mel Blanc Show* (Betty's Christmas show); *December 17*— *The Mel Blanc Show* (exchanging gifts); *December 19*—*Suspense*, "The Thing in the Window" (with Joseph Cotten); *December 24*— *The Mel Blanc Show* (Mel plays Santa Claus); *December 29*— *The Bob Burns Show*, [?]; *December 31*— *The Mel Blanc Show*, (man of the year)

1947

(date unknown)— *The Jack Haley Show* (Conried played an "egotist"); *January 1*—*A Day in the Life of Dennis Day* (Dennis speaks at a ladies' club); *January 2*—*Suspense*, "Tree of Life" (with Mark Stevens); *January 3*— *The Alan Young Show*, "Napoleon's Descendant"; *January 10*— *The Alan Young Show* (Conried joined the regular cast as ham actor, Jonathan Mildew); *January 14*— *The Mel Blanc Show* (the broken Caruso record); *January 16*—*Suspense*, "Overture in Two Keys" (with Joan Bennett); *January 17*— *The Alan Young Show*, "Clothes Make the Man"; *January 23*— *The Sealtest Village Store* (#355: with Jack Haley, Eve Arden, Charles Ruggles); *January 24*— *The Alan Young Show* (the bear story); *January 28*— *The Mel Blanc Show* (the masquerade ball); *January 31*— *The Alan Young Show* (the return of Jonathan Mildew's ex-wife, Queenie); *February 3*— *The Whistler*, "Seven Steps to Murder"; *February 4*— *The Mel Blanc Show* (Betty's suitors); *February 6*—*Suspense*, "End of the Road" (with Glenn Ford); *February 7*— *The Alan Young Show* (the bank robbers); *February 11*— *The Mel Blanc Show* (Mel's birthday); *February 14*— *The Alan Young Show* (the Valentine's Day gift); *February 18*— *The Mel Blanc Show* (the missing slice of bread); *February 21*— *The Alan Young Show* (the inheritance); *February 25*— *The Mel Blanc Show* (Mel impersonates a movie star); *February 27*—*Suspense*, "Three Faces at Midnight" (with William Bendix); *February 28*— *The Alan Young Show*, "The Kiss Maker"; *March 4*— *The Mel Blanc Show* (Councilman Colby); *March 7*— *The Alan Young Show* (the charity masquerade); *March 11*— *The Mel Blanc Show* (the art critic); *March 14*— *The Alan Young Show* (Alan visits a psychiatrist); *March 18*— *The Mel Blanc Show* (Mel is engaged to two women); *March 20*— *The Sealtest Village Store* (with Vincent Price and Eve Arden); *March 25*— *The Mel Blanc Show* (the "Miss Ugga-Ugga-Boo" contest); *April 1*— *The Mel Blanc Show* (April Fool's joke); *April 8*— *The Mel Blanc Show* (the Easter egg hunt); *April 10*— *The Sealtest Village Store* (#365: with Jack Haley, Eve Arden, Bob Jellison, etc.); *April 11*— *My Friend Irma* (Conried was a regular on this long-running series as the shy old Russian, Professor Kropotkin, who lived upstairs from the two girls: Irma and Jane; the show was on the air until August 23; due to the sheer volume of episodes, only a handful will be listed in this log); *April 15*— *The Mel Blanc Show* (the Colby's society part); *April 18*— *The Alan Young Show* (Alan wants to go into vaudeville); *April 10*— *The Sealtest Village Store* (#366: with Jack Haley, Eve Arden, Victor Moore, etc.); *April 22*— *The Mel Blanc Show* (Mel, the literary expert); *April 24*—*Suspense*, "Win, Place and Murder" (with Richard Conte); *April 27*— *The Play's the Thing*, "Tartuffe" (West Coast "sustainer": Conried was a regular performer); *April 28*—*The Whistler*, "The Black Book" (with Jeanette Nolan); *April 29*— *The Mel Blanc Show* (Mel plays James Mason); *May 2*— *The Alan Young Show*, "The Birth Certificate Mistake"; *May 6*— *The Mel Blanc Show* (Mel buys phony oil stock); *May 9*—

The Alan Young Show, "The Typical American Mother"; **May 13**—*The Mel Blanc Show* (editor of the supermarket journal); **May 15**—*Suspense*, "Death at Live Oak" (with Robert Mitchum); **May 16**—*The Alan Young Show*, "The Big Yacht Race"; **May 20**—*The Mel Blanc Show* (Mel and Betty separate); **May 23**—*The Alan Young Show* (a visit to Updike's ranch); **May 27**—*The Mel Blanc Show* (the interior decorator); **May 29**—*Suspense*, "A Thing of Beauty" (with Angela Lansbury); **May 30**—*The Alan Young Show*, "The Lifeguard Contest"; **June (?)**—*The Play's the Thing*, [?]; **June 3**—*The Mel Blanc Show* (a ghost helps Mel find a place to live); **June 10**—*The Mel Blanc Show* (the Chinese philosopher); **June 12**—*Suspense*, "Stand-In" (with June Havoc and Elliott Lewis); **June 13**—*My Friend Irma* (the fur coat); **June 14**—*Smilin' Ed's Buster Brown Gang* (the young cavalier) (NBC: sponsored by Buster Brown Shoes); **June 15**—*The Couple Next Door* (Episode #7); **June 17**—*The Mel Blanc Show* (the show at Colby's Supermarket); **June 22—The Jack Paar Program** (a spoof on fan magazines—Conried joined the show, and was a regular with Paar until December 24); **June 22**—*The Couple Next Door* (Episode #8); **July 6**—*The Couple Next Door* (Episode #10); **July 13**—*The Jack Paar Program* (spoofing children's adventure shows); **July 22**—*Dark Venture*, [?]; **July 24**—*Suspense*, "Murder by an Expert" (with Lynn Bari and Jack Webb); **July 27**—*The Jack Paar Program* (singing cowboy parody); **July 27**—*The Couple Next Door* (Episode #13); **August 3**—*The Jack Paar Program* (a veteran buys a post-war home); **August 4**—*Suspense*, "The Argyle Album" (with Edmund O'Brien); **August 10**—*The Couple Next Door* (Episode #15); **August 17**—*The Couple Next Door* (Episode #16); **August 17**—*The Jack Paar Program* (guest: Jack Benny; Paar's show was the summer replacement for *The Jack Benny Program*); **August 23**—*Fantasy*, "**Entity From the Void**" (audition recording for unsold series.—Conried introduces and ends the episode, and portrays the title character); **August 24**—*The Couple Next Door* (Episode #17); **August 31**—*The Couple Next Door* (Episode #18); **August 31**—*The Jack Paar Program* (BBC radio parody); **September 7**—*The Jack Paar Program* (breakfast foods parody); **September 14**—*The Jack Paar Program* (interview with a beauty contest loser); **September 14**—*The Couple Next Door* (Episode #20); **September 17**—*The Whistler*, "Death and the Emperor" (with Martha Wentworth); **September 21**—*The Jack Paar Program* ("This Is America"); **September 21**—*The Couple Next Door* (Episode #21); **September 25**—*Suspense*, "The Blue Hour" (with Claire Trevor); **September 28**—*The Jack Paar Program* ("Uncle Jack's" club for kids); **September 30**—*Favorite Story*, "The Mystery of Room 323" (with Janet Waldo); **October 1**—*The Jack Paar Program*, [?]; **October 1**—*Escape*, "The Most Dangerous Game" (with Paul Frees); **October 8**—*The Jack Paar Program*, [?]; **October 15**—*The Jack Paar Program*, [?]; **October 14**—*Favorite Story*, "Bartleby, the Scrivener" (alternative title: "The Strange Mr. Bartleby": Conried as Bartleby, with William Conrad); **October 16**—*The Sealtest Village Store* (a visit to a Hollywood studio); **October 18—The Abe Burrows Show** (CBS: Conried was a semi-regular on this series); **October 19**—*The Charlie McCarthy Show* (a.k.a. *The Chase and Sanborn Program*: Conried and Jane Wyman perform "Aladdin and his Lamp"); **October 22**—*The Jack Paar Program*, [?]; **October 29**—*The Jack Paar Program*, [?]; **October 29**—*Preview Theater of the Air*, "The 13th Juror" (with Otto Kruger); **October 30**—*Maxwell House Coffee Time* (George Burns & Gracie Allen: with Cary Grant); **November 2**—*The Charlie McCarthy Show* (guest: Fred Allen); **November 5**—*The Jack Paar Program*, [?]; **November 8**—*The Abe Burrows Show* (featured song: "The Girl with Three Blue Eyes"); **November 8**—*The People Next Door* (Series 2: Episode 1); **November 9**—*Doorway to Life*, "The Stories of Martin"; **November 12**—*The Jack Paar Program*, [?]; **November 15**—*The Abe Burrows Show* (featured song: "Tokyo Rose"); **November 15**—*The People Next Door* (Series 2: Episode 2); **November 19**—*The Jack Paar Program*, [?]; **November 22**—*The Abe Burrows Show* (featured song: "Naughty Fido"); **November 22**—*The People Next Door* (Series 2: Episode 3); **November 26**—*The Jimmy Durante Show* (guest: Victor Moore); **November 26**—*The Jack Paar Program*, [?]; **November 29**—*The Abe Burrows Show* (featured song: "Act, Little Movie Star, Act"); **November 29**—*The People Next Door* (Series 2: Episode 4); **December (?)**—**Colonel Hoople** (audition show for unsold series starring Conried); **December 1**—*My Friend Irma*, "The Reward"; **December 3**—*The Jack Paar Program*, [?]; **December 4**—*Maxwell House Coffee Time* (starring George Burns and Gracie Allen—guest: Bing Crosby); **December 6**—*The Abe Burrows Show* (featured song: "Muchacha"); **December 8**—*My Friend Irma*, "The Eyes Have Had It"; **December 10**—*The Jack Paar Program*, [?]; **December 12**—*Suspense*, "The Man Who Couldn't Lose" (with Dan Duryea); **December 13**—*The People Next Door* (Series 2: Episode 6); **December 15**—*My Friend Irma*, "Dancing Fools"; **December 17**—*The Jack Paar Program*, [?]; **December 17**—*A Day in the Life of Dennis Day*, "The President of the Ladies Club"; **December 20**—*The Abe Burrows Show* (featured song: "Smile"); **December 20**—*The People Next Door*, (Series 2: Episode 6); **December 22**—*My Friend Irma*, "Double Surprise"; **December 24**—*The Jack Paar Program* (final show of the series); **December 29**—*My Friend Irma*, "Gentlemen Prefer..."

1948

(date unknown)— *The New Adventures of Michael Shayne*, "The Case of the Model Murder" (starring Jeff Chandler); *(date unknown)*— *The New Adventures of Michael Shayne*, "The Case of the Carnival Killer" (starring Jeff Chandler); *(date unknown)*—*Lassie* (Conried was in more than one episode—in particular: "Discipline"); *January 2— The Danny Thomas Show* (Conried was a regular as the unlikely leader of an "all-girl orchestra"; the gimmick bombed; he was fired shortly before the show's early demise); *January 4— The Adventures of Sam Spade*, "The One Hour Caper"; *January 5—My Friend Irma*, "The Great Irma"; *January 7—The Bud Abbott and Lou Costello Show* (Lou wants to be an actor); *January 8— The Maxwell House Coffee Time* (guest: Jack Benny); *January 10— The Judy Canova Show* (Judy is depressed) (with guest, Eddie Cantor); *January 10— Suspense*, "The Kandy Tooth" (with Howard Duff: formerly a two-part *Sam Spade* episode; a shameless rip-off of "The Maltese Falcon"; Conried played three parts: Marvin; Kamidov; and Julius); *January 12—My Friend Irma*, "The Lucky Couple Contest"; *January 12—Point Sublime*, [?]; *January 15— The Maxwell House Coffee Time* (Gracie helps George make out his income tax form); *January 17— The People Next Door* (Series 3: Episode 1); *January 19—My Friend Irma*, "The Book Crook"; *January 26—My Friend Irma*, "The Lonely Hearts Club"; *January 28—Mayor, of the Town*—Conried as "Ambrose Fenimore"—Marilly's boyfriend; *January 31— The Life of Riley* (Uncle Baxter returns); *February 1—Tell It Again,* "Oliver Twist" (Hans as Fagan: with Marvin Miller); *February 2—My Friend Irma*, "The Redhead"; *February 5— The Maxwell House Coffee Time* (Gracie wants a mink coat); *February 9— My Friend Irma*, "Billy Boy, the Boxer"; *February 9—Point Sublime*, [?]; *February 14—Joan Davis Time* (guest: Garry Moore); *February 15— The Private Practice of Dr. Dana* (Episode #38) (series starred Jeff Chandler); *February 16—My Friend Irma*, "The Professor's Concerto"; *February 21— The People Next Door*, (Series 3: Episode 6); *February 22—Tell It Again,* "The Spy"; *March 19— The Adventures of Ozzie & Harriet*, "Who's Walter?"; *March 20—Suspense*, "Wet Saturday" (the first of two stories in hour long format); *March 21— The Whistler*, "The Dark Room"; *March 22—KECA Radio*, "The Clock"; *March 27— The People Next Door* (Series 3: Episode 11); *March 28—There's Always the Guy* (audition show for series created by Hal March & Bob Sweeney, starring H.C: Supposedly two auditions were recorded; even with a sponsor ready to go, CBS did not order more episodes); *April 10— The Judy Canova Show* (Judy gets a parking ticket); *April 11— The Unexpected*, "Fury and Sound" (premiere episode); *April 17—Joan Davis Time* (guest: Rudy Vallee); *April 22— The Maxwell House Coffee Time* (George forgets flowers for Gracie); *April 23—Puppettania* (audition show for unsold series on KFWB Radio; Conried played the "Old Puppetmaker"); *April 27—KFI Radio,* "Treasure Island" (with Alan Reed, and Alan Reed Jr); *May 1—Joan Davis Time* (Joan has amnesia); *May 2—Tell It Again*, "The Legend of Sleepy Hollow"; *May 8— The Judy Canova Show* (Judy interviews Lancelot Buckingham); *May 11—Favorite Story*, "The Gift of Laughter" (Conried was the host of this episode and the star; he sounded like he had a bad head cold, but he managed a fine performance as pantomime actor, Jean Gaspard Deburau); *May 13— The Maxwell House Coffee Time*, [?]; *May 19—Mayor of the Town* (Conried now had a semi-regular role as "Ambrose Fenimore"); *May 23—Hollywood Star Preview* (Conried starred: introduced by Charles Laughton); *May 24— The Amazing Mr. Malone*, "The Charles Morgan Case"; *May 29— The Judy Canova Show* (Judy reads script); *June (?)—It's a Great Life* (Conried was a regular on this West Coast summer series that featured Steve Allen, June Foray, Frank Nelson, and Parley Baer); *June 6—Tell It Again*, "Don Quixote"; *June 12—*[?], "The Duke of Dittendorten" ("Burrows' Operetta"); *June 12—Favorite Story*, "The Mystery of Room 323" (syndicated by ZIV); *June 19—Favorite Story*, "Tom Sawyer" (with Skip Homeier); *June 23—A Day in the Life of Dennis Day* (the telegram); *June 26— Favorite Story*, "Peter Ibbetson"; *June 26—Joan Davis Time* (Episode #38: with Rudy Vallee); *July 3—Favorite Story*, "The Necklace" (co-starring Conried and Heather Angel); *July 4— The Adventures of Sam Spade*, "The Rushlight Diamond Caper"; *July 5—My Favorite Husband*—starring Lucille Ball: Conried would be a semi-regular on this series portraying many different characters from the butcher and milkman, to "Mr. Woods," one of the Cooper's neighbors; *July 17—Favorite Story*, "The Strange Mr. Bartleby" (a.k.a. "Bartleby the Scrivener"); *July 26—Our Miss Brooks*, [?]; *July 31—Jeff Regan, Investigator*, "The Lady with the Golden Hair" (with Jack Webb); *August 1— Johnny Fletcher*, "Music for Murder"; *August 22— The Adventures of Sam Spade*, "The Vaphio Cup Caper"; *August 23— The Amazing Mr. Tutt*, "Liberty of the Jail" (with Ben Wright); *August 27— Dear Miss Ryan* (audition show for unsold comedy series starring Irene Ryan; broadcast on West Coast station KFWB Radio); *August 28—Favorite Story*, "Cashel Byron's Profession" (with Dan O'Herlihy); *September 3— The NBC University Theater*, "Candide" (with Eddie Bracken and June

Foray); *September 5*— *Tell It Again*, "Midsummer Night's Dream"; *September 10*— *My Favorite Husband*, [?]; *September 17*— *My Favorite Husband* (General Timberlake); *September 21*— *Life With Luigi*—Conried was a regular on this series as the crusty old German, "Schultz" until it left the air as of the March 3, 1953, broadcast; only select episodes will appear in this log; *September 23*— *The Dorothy Lamour Show*, "The Love Pact" (with William Powell and Alan Young); *September 24*— *My Favorite Husband* (baby booties); *October 2*— *The Judy Canova Show*, [?]; *October 2*— *My Favorite Husband* (Liz recalls George's wedding proposal); *October 9*— *My Favorite Husband*, [?]; *October 16*— *My Favorite Husband* (Liz returns a dress to the wrong store); *October 23*— *My Favorite Husband*, [?]; *October 23*— *The Edgar Bergen/Charlie McCarthy Show* (Conried as a haughty tramp who teaches Charlie a lesson in "freedom"; not quite the lesson Edgar had in mind!); *October 23*— *The Judy Canova Show* (Mr. Hemmingway gives Judy acting lessons for the charity play); *October 25*— *The Railroad Hour*, "The Student Prince" (with Ken Baker and Dorothy Kristen); *October 30*— *My Favorite Husband*, [?]; *October 30*— *Romance*, "Windward Passage"; *October 31*— *Tell It Again*, "The Legend of Sleepy Hollow"; *October 31*— *The New Adventures of Philip Marlowe* "The Blue Burgonet" (with Alan Reed); *November 6*— *My Favorite Husband* (Katy and Roscoe); *November 9*— *Life with Luigi* (Luigi finds a diamond ring); *November 16*— *Life with Luigi* (the P.T.A. meeting); *November 27*— *My Favorite Husband* (is there a baby in the house?); *December 4*— *My Favorite Husband*, [?]; *December 7*— *Life with Luigi* (the antique mirror); *December 12*— *The Adventures of Sam Spade*, "The Bouncing Betty Caper"; *December 19*— *The New Adventures of Philip Marlowe*, "The Three Wise Guys"; *December 25*— *The Wrigley Christmas Party*; *December 25*— *My Favorite Husband* (numerology); *December 30*— *The Camel Screen Guild Players*, "Pinocchio" (with Fanny Brice and Hanley Stafford)

1949

(date unknown)— *The Hank McCune Show*, [?]; *January 7*— *Ford Theater*, "Talk of the Town" (with Ronald Colman); *January 9*— *Life with Luigi* (Luigi has a big date); *January 14*— *My Favorite Husband* (the piano lesson); *January 16*— *Our Miss Brooks* (Student Government Day: rebroadcast on January 27); *January 22*— *Favorite Story*, "The Man Who Married a Dumb Wife" (with Ronald Colman); *January 25*—KFI Radio, "The Judgment of Paris" (with Alan Reed); *February 4*— *Ford Theater*, "No Time for Love" (with Vincent Price); *February 6*— *Life with Luigi* (the telephone bill]; *February 8*—KFI Radio, "The Magic Shop" (based on the story by H.G. Wells); *February 11*— *My Favorite Husband* (Valentine's Day); *February 19*— *Escape*, "The Orient Express" (with Harry Bartell and Gloria Grant); *February 25*— *My Favorite Husband*, [?]; *February 26*— *Escape*, "Red Wine" (with William Conrad and Edgar Barrier); *February 27*— *The Adventures of Ozzie and Harriet* (trouble over money); *March 4*— *The Ford Theatre*, "The Horn Blows at Midnight" (with Jack Benny); *March 4*— *My Favorite Husband* (George's mother visits); *March 15*— *Command Performance* (with Dennis Day: transcribed for broadcast to soldiers overseas); *March 17*— *The Maxwell House Coffee Time* (guest: Marlene Dietrich); *March 18*— *My Favorite Husband*, [?]; *March 20*— *Life with Luigi* (Luigi's new car); *April 3*— *Life with Luigi* (is Luigi a kleptomaniac?); *April 7*— *Suspense*, "Noose of Coincidence" (with Ronald Colman); *April 8*— *The Eddie Cantor Show* (NBC: sponsored by Pabst Beer); *April 8*— *My Favorite Husband* (the gum machine); *April 10*— *Life with Luigi* (Rosa loses weight); *April 22*— *My Favorite Husband* (the dinner party); *April 23*— *The Thirteenth Juror*, "What Happened to John Wilkes Booth?" (premiere episode with Vincent Price narrating; Conried in fine histrionic form as Booth); *April 24*— *Life with Luigi* (the electric bill); *May 1*— *Life with Luigi*, [The block party]; *May 8*— *Screen Director's Playhouse*, "It's a Wonderful Life" (with Jimmy Stewart); *May 8*— *Life with Luigi* (Luigi's toothache); *May 15*— *Life with Luigi* (the super salesman); *May 22*— *Screen Director's Playhouse*, "Her Husband's Affairs" (with Lucille Ball); *May 29*— *Life with Luigi* (the wedding); *June 4*— *The New Adventures of Philip Marlowe*, "My Unfair Lady" (with Nestor Paiva); *June 5*— *Life with Luigi* (at the race track); *June 11*—KNX Radio, "Exit Linda Davis"; *June 17*— *My Favorite Husband* (the neighbor's television); *June 26*— *Life with Luigi* (the life insurance policy); *July 1*— *My Favorite Husband* (Liz and George reminisce); *July 7*— *Dragnet*, "The Steel Club" (with Jack Webb and Raymond Burr); *July 10*— *Life with Luigi* (the registered letter); *July 17*— *Life with Luigi* (at the beach); *July 24*— *Life with Luigi* (Luigi is homesick); *July 24*— *Chicken Every Sunday* [NBC variety show with Billie Burke, Harry von Zell, Hal March); *July 31*— *Life with Luigi* (X-ray pictures); *July 31*— *Meet Corliss Archer*, [?]; *August 1*— *Young Love* (Episode #5) (series starred Janet Waldo and Jimmy Lydon); *August 13*— *The New Adventures of Philip Marlowe*, "The Indian Giver"; *August 13*— *Favorite Story*, "Enoch Soames"; *August 14*— *Life with Luigi* (the sore thumb); *August 15*— *Young Love* (Episode #7); *August 18*— *Broadway Is My Beat*, "The Silks Bergen Murder Case" (with Anthony Ross); *August 19*—

Screen Director's Playhouse, "Love Crazy" (with William Powell and Gloria Blondell); **August 22**— *Young Love* (Episode #8); **August 28**—*Life with Luigi* (go west, young man); **September 3**—*The New Adventures of Philip Marlowe*, "The Bum's Rush" (with Ann Morrison); **September 10**—*Life with Luigi* (Luigi tries to sing); **September 14**—*The Family Theatre*, "Mademoiselle Fifi"; **September 21**—*Escape*, "The Fortune of Vargas" (with Victor Mature); **September 23**—*My Favorite Husband* (cleaning the attic); **September 30**—*My Favorite Husband* (Liz is elected treasurer of women's club); **October 19**—*The Family Theatre*, "Ivanhoe"; **October 22**—*Favorite Story*, "The Gift of Laughter"; **November 11**—*My Favorite Husband* (Conried as Dr. Schweinkampf, the psychiatrist); **November 11**—*Screen Director's Playhouse*, "Body and Soul" (with John Garfield); **November 15**—*The Fanny Brice Show* (the ruined suit); **November 29**—*The Judy Canova Show*, [?]; **December (?)**—***The Professor and Mrs. O'Reilly*** (audition show for unsold spin-off of "My Friend Irma" series); **December 16**—*Pursuit*, "Murder Is the Cargo" (with Ted de Corsia); **December 17**—*Richard Diamond, Private Detective*, "The John Blackwell Case"; **December 18**—*The Phil Harris/Alice Faye Show* (the Christmas tree); **December 25**—?, "A Christmas Carol" (with Lionel Barrymore)

1950

(date unknown)—*The Hallmark Playhouse*, "Monsieur Beaucaire" (with Douglas Fairbanks, Jr); **January 6**—*Screen Director's Playhouse*, "Magic Town" (with James Stewart); **January 11**—*The Family Theatre*, "A Tale of Two Cities"; **January 15**—*Our Miss Brooks* (Friday, the 13th); **January 19**—*The Hallmark Playhouse*, "Around the World in Eighty Days"; **January 21**—***Stars Over Hollywood***, "Marriage in Heaven" (Conried took over as the director of the series beginning with this episode, and would continue directing on and off for the next few years); **January 21**—*Young Love* (Episode #26); **January 22**—*The Whistler*, "The Go-Between"; **January 27**—*Lassie* (Conried as "Brother Francis"); **January 27**—*My Favorite Husband* (Liz writes a song); **January 31**—*Life with Luigi* (night school class goes on strike); **February 2**—*The Hallmark Playhouse*, "Wine of Youth" (with Ida Lupino); **February 2**—*Maisie*, "Room Clerk" (Episode #11: Conried was a semi-regular on this transcribed series based on the MGM motion pictures starring the vivacious Ann Sothern); **February 7**—*Life with Luigi*, [?]; **February 16**—*Suspense*, "Murder Strikes Three Times" (with Marlene Dietrich); **February 17**—*Screen Director's Playhouse*, "It's in the Bag" (with Fred Allen and Frank Nelson); **February 18**—*The Charlie McCarthy Show*, (Conried in the role of a tree doctor who cures Charlie); **February 24**—*My Favorite Husband* (Liz redecorates the house); **February 28**—*Life with Luigi* (night school class party); **March 2**—*Maisie*, "Maisie on the Farm" (Episode #15); **March 5**—*My Favorite Husband* (women's rights); **March 9**—*Suspense*, "Banquo's Chair" (with James Mason); **March 14**—*Yours Truly, Johnny Dollar*, "The Eighty-Five Little Minks"; **March 16**—*Maisie*, "Chester Drake, the Actor" (Episode #17); **March 23**—*Maisie*, "Jasper, the Lovesick Fan" (Episode #18); **March 24**—*The Halls of Ivy*, "The Vindication of Eddie Gray"; **March 25**—***Much About Dolittle*** (audition show for a short-lived summer series starring Conried as Col. Lucius Dolittle: an eccentric, henpecked, would-be inventor); **March 30**—*Suspense*, "Blood Sacrifice" (with Joseph Cotten); **April 21**—*The Screen Director's Playhouse*, "A Kiss in the Dark" (with Jane Wyman); **April 23**—*The Whistler*, "Returned with the Spray" (with Marvin Miller); **April 24**—*The Railroad Hour*, "The Prince of Pilsen" (with Nadine Conner); **May 12**—*Escape*, "The Rim of Terror" (with Nancy Kelly and Barton Yarborough); **May 21**—*The Phil Harris–Alice Faye Show* (Phil tries to renew his driver's license; Conried as the DMV clerk); **June 1**—*The Hallmark Playhouse* (live broadcast from Kansas City, MO; the program consisted of a story of the city's history); **June 11**—*My Favorite Husband* (Mr. Woods teaches Liz how to swim in her living room); **June 14**—***The Family Theatre*, "Cyrano DeBergerac"** (Conried made a splendid Cyrano, but the production seems rushed: too many commercials); **June 29**—*Maisie*, "Stranded in India" (Episode #32); **July 2**—*Much About Dolittle*, [?]; **July 4**—*Life with Luigi* (the Fourth of July parade); **July 9**—*Much About Dolittle*, [?]; **July 16**—*Much About Dolittle*, [?]; **July 23**—*Much About Dolittle*, [?]; **July 30**—*Much About Dolittle*, [?]; **August 3**—*John Barrymore and Shakespeare*, "Macbeth" (this program first aired on July 5, 1937, as part of the *Streamlined Shakespeare* series; there were five re-broadcasts in all for this short-lived revival); **August 6**—*Much About Dolittle*, [?]; **August 10**—*John Barrymore and Shakespeare*, "Hamlet" (June 21, 1937, *Streamlined Shakespeare* production); **August 13**—*Much About Dolittle*, [?]; **August 15**—*Life with Luigi* (fire insurance); **August 17**—*John Barrymore and Shakespeare*, "Richard III" (June 28, 1937, *Streamlined Shakespeare* production); **August 20**—*Much About Dolittle* (final episode); **August 22**—*Life with Luigi* (the train trip to Buffalo); **August 24**—*John Barrymore and Shakespeare*, "Twelfth Night" (July 19, 1937, *Streamlined Shakespeare*); **August 31**—*John Barrymore and Shakespeare*, "The Tempest" (July 12, 1937, *Streamlined Shakespeare*); **September 5**—*Life* *with Luigi* (Luigi sells ice cream); **September 13—Columbia Workshop,** "Cyrano de Bergerac" (Conried as "Cyrano"); **September 14—Screen Guild Players,** "Ninotchka" (with William Powell and Joan Fontaine); **September 24—NBC University Theatre,** "Don Quixote" (Conried in the role of his career; a masterful performance; Jay Novello and Lou Merrill had supporting roles); **September 28—***Maisie,* "The Nightclub" (Episode #33); **October 3—***Life with Luigi* (Luigi gives blood); **October 8—***The Charlie McCarthy Show* (guest: Jane Wyman); **October 9—***Hollywood Star Playhouse,* "Of Night and the River" (with Joseph Cotten); **October 12—***Maisie,* "Small Town Newspaper" (Episode #35); **October 15—***Our Miss Brooks,* [?]; **October 19—***Maisie,* "The New York Banquet" (Episode #36); **November 23—***Maisie,* "The Birthday Gift" (Episode #41); **December 25—***The Lux Radio Theatre,* "The Wizard of Oz" (unusual production starring Judy Garland; Conried was well cast as The Scarecrow; unfortunately he wasn't allowed to sing!); **December 30—***Stars Over Hollywood,* "The Continental Cowboy" (with Vincent Price)

1951

January 13—My Favorite Husband, "Liz and the Cuckoo Clock"; **January 18—***Maisie,* "The Artist's Model" (Episode #49); **January 19—***The Adventures of Sam Spade,* "The Cloak and Dagger Caper"; **January 25—***Maisie,* "Insurance" (Episode #50); **January 27—***Stars Over Hollywood,* **"My Rival Is a Fiddle"** (directed by and starring Conried); **February 1—***Maisie,* "Duke Johnson" (Episode #51); **February 2—***The Adventures of Sam Spade,* "The String of Death Caper"; **February 15—***Maisie,* "The Napoleon Letter" (Episode #53); **February 22—***Maisie,* "Muscles" (Episode #54); **March 1—***Maisie,* "The Wild West Dude Ranch" (Episode #55); **March 1—***The Hallmark Playhouse,* "Monsieur Beaucaire" (with Douglas Fairbanks, Jr); **March 25—***Amos 'n' Andy* (the stock market); **March 27—***The Damon Runyon Theater,* "So You Won't Talk!" (stars John Brown); **April 5—***Maisie,* "Maisie in Las Vegas" (Episode #60); **April 26—***Maisie,* "Manganese Gold Mine" (Episode #63); **May 3—***Maisie,* "The Hotel Social Director" (Episode #64); **May 10—***Maisie,* "Quackenbush's Universal Elixir" (Episode #65); **May 23—***Stars Over Hollywood,* "When the Police Arrive" (with Joan Crawford); **June 24—***Stars Over Hollywood,* "The Troubled Heart" (with Mala Powers); **June 27—***Rocky Jordan,* [Series 4: Episode 1: with George Raft); **July 1—***Stars Over Hollywood,* "John E. Jones, Vice President" (with Albert Dekker); **July 13—***The Man Called X* (flying trip to Indonesia); **July 18—***Rocky Jordan* (Series 4: Episode 4: with George Raft); **July 25—***Escape,* "The Earthmen" (with Parley Baer and John Dehner); **August 2—***Lineup,* "The Butane Buttonworth Case"; **August 18—***Make Believe Town, Hollywood,* "Another Road"; **August 18—***Rocky Jordan* (Series 4: Episode 7: with George Raft); **August 20—***Meet Millie* (Episode #7: KNX Radio); **August 25—***Make Believe Town, Hollywood,* "Memo on Kathy O'Rourke"; **September 30—***Let's Go, Hollywood!* (West Coast only celebrity news show with George Fisher); **October 15—***The Railroad Hour,* "Martha" (with Dorothy Kirsten); **November 10—***Stars Over Hollywood,* "Short Story" (with Jan Sterling); **November 11—***The Charlie McCarthy Show* (guest: Jussi Björling); **November 24—***Stars Over Hollywood,* "Three Is an Odd Number" (with Rhonda Fleming); **December 1—***Stars Over Hollywood,* "The Perfect Mate" (with Jack Parr); **December 9—***Stars Over Hollywood,* "Round Trip for Cinderella"; **December 22—***Stars Over Hollywood,* "A Christmas Carol" (with Edmund Gwenn); **December 30—***This Is the Story: If Freedom Failed*—AFTRS produced series about what it would be like to live under Communism; Conried was in episode #24: "The Man Who Died Twice": date may not be actual airdate.

1952

January 6—My Friend Irma (Irma's memoirs); **January 12—***Stars Over Hollywood,* "Fog Warning" (with Cameron Mitchell); **January 13—***My Friend Irma* (the Cub Scout speech); **January 13—***Blondie* (a Pasha wants Blondie); **January 26—***The Judy Canova Show* (Judy writes a Wild West play); **January 27—***My Friend Irma* (the lonely hearts club); **February 3—***My Friend Irma* (Irma's gossip column); **February 10—***The Charlie McCarthy Show* (guest: Patti Page); **February 10—***My Friend Irma* (the dictation system); **February 17—***My Friend Irma* (Jane quits her job); **February 24—***My Friend Irma* (the lost friendship ring); **February 26—***Life with Luigi* (civil defense); **March 4—***Life with Luigi* (the little immigrant); **April 1—***Life with Luigi* (April Fool's Day); **April 15—***Life with Luigi* (Luigi goes to work); **April 22—***Life with Luigi* (Luigi has insomnia); **April 27—***Screen Guild Theatre,* "Bluebeard's Eighth Wife" (with David Niven and Diana Lynn); **May 5—***The Dream Team,* "Intellectual Battle of the Century" (CBS panel show: Conried as host); **May 25—***Screen Guild Theatre,* "The Good Fairy"; **June 8—***December Bride*—Conried was regularly heard as the dour neighbor, Pete Porter, in this Spring Byington series; the radio show would be on the air until September 6; *December Bride* would make the transition to television with Spring Byington sans the rest of the radio cast in the fall of 1954; *June 15—December Bride* (Oscar loves Lily); *August 6—Yours Truly, Johnny Dollar,* "The Sidney Mann Matter"; *August 11—The Little Matchmaker* (audition show with Chico Marx and Sheldon Leonard); *August 23—Gunsmoke,* "Shakespeare" (Conried has fine role as a homely actor); *September 2—Life with Luigi* (Luigi at the beach); *September 7—Hollywood Star Playhouse,* "The Tenth Planet"; *September 15—Suspense,* "Sorry, Wrong Number" (with Agnes Moorehead); *October 6—The Lux Radio Theatre,* "The Model and the Marriage Broker" (with Jeanne Crain); *October 19—Escape,* "The Price of the Head" (with Larry Dobkin); *December 8—The Lux Radio Theatre,* "Strictly Dishonorable" (with Janet Leigh and Ted deCorsia); *December 15—The Lux Radio Theatre,* "The African Queen" (with Humphrey Bogart); *December 21—The Hallmark Playhouse,* "A Christmas Carol" (with Lionel Barrymore)

1953

January 1—Bright Star, "The Drama School" (with Fred MacMurray and Irene Dunne)

1954

(date unknown)—That's Rich (Stan Freberg starred in this short-lived series: Conried was a guest performer on at least three episodes); *(date unknown)—The Bob Hope Show* (guest: Jane Wyman; Conried, as a German music teacher, sings a hilarious version of "Glow Worm"!); *February 15—The Lux Radio Theatre,* "Trouble Along the Way" (with Jack Carson and June Haver); *May 21—That's Rich,* "The Movie Producer"; *June 14—The Railroad Hour,* "The Pink Lady" (with Lucille Norman); *June 23—Crime Classics,* "Ali Pasha: A Turkish Delight" (Conried in starring role); *July 24—Romance,* "The Long Way Home"; *July 31—Escape,* "The Night of the Guns" (with Herb Ellis); *August 7—Escape,* "The Price of the Head" (with Ben Wright); *August 28—Romance,* "Silhouette"; *September 2—That's Rich,* "Night Club Act"; *September 11—Escape,* "Carnival in Vienna" (with Barney Phillips); *September 18—Escape,* "The Target" (with Mary Jane Croft); *September 24—Yours Truly, Johnny Dollar,* "The Hamilton Payroll Matter"; *September 25—Romance,* "The Way to the Castle"; *September 28—The Lux Radio Theatre,* "How Green Was My Valley" (with Donald Crisp and Donna Reed); *October 19—The Lux Radio Theatre,* "David and Bathsheba" (with Michael Rennie); *October 21—Suspense,* **"Rave Notice"** (Conried stars as ham actor who kills his cruel director, and feigns madness to escape the death penalty; a tour-de-force performance.)

1955

January 18—The Lux Radio Theatre, "The Awful Truth" (with Irene Dunne and Cary Grant); *February 15—The Hollywood Radio Theatre,* "Five Fingers" (with James and Pamela Mason); *March 29—The Lux Radio Theatre,* "Trouble Along the Way" (with Van Johnson and Joanne Dru); *April 12—The Lux Radio Theatre,* "Stairway to Heaven" (with David Niven and Barbara Rush); *July 31—My Little Margie* (buying a radio station); *October 8—Romance,* "Sir Henry" (Part One) (with Paul Frees); *October 15—Romance,* "Sir Henry" (Part Two) (with Paul Frees); *October 23—The New Edgar Bergen Hour,* [?]; *October 30—The New Edgar Bergen Hour,* [?]; *November 13—The New Edgar Bergen Hour* (Charlie gets a driver's license); *November 20—The New Edgar Bergen Hour,* [?]; *December 10—Romance,* "The Grasshopper"; *December 14—The Twentieth-Century Fox Hour,* "The Miracle on 34th Street" (simulcast with TV broadcast); *December 20—Suspense,* "The Cave" (with John Dehner)

1956

January 21—Romance, "Old Army Buddy"; *February 23—Yours Truly, Johnny Dollar,* "The Bennett Matter" (Part Four: five episodes were broadcast in 15 minute segments over a week's time, beginning on February 20); *February 24—Yours Truly, Johnny Dollar,* "The Bennett Matter" (Part Five); *February 24—The CBS Radio Workshop,* "Colloquy Number One: An Interview with William Shakespeare" with Ben Wright and Raymond Hill; guess who was Shakespeare!); *February 28—Suspense,* "The Diary of Captain Scott" (with Jay Novello); *March 13—Suspense,* **"The Groom of the Ladder"** (starring Conried; with Ben Wright); *April 13—The CBS Radio Workshop,* "Jacob's Hands" (written by Aldous Huxley); *May 11—The CBS Radio Workshop,* "The Enormous Radio" (with William Conrad); *May 25—The CBS Radio Workshop,* "The Little Prince" (with Raymond Burr and Ben Wright); *June 19—Suspense,* "A Sleeping Draught" (with Abraham Sofaer); *July 3—Suspense,* "The Music Lovers" (with Irene Tedrow and Ben Wright); *September 15—Romance,* "The Man from Venus" (Conried as the title character); *November 10—Romance,* "The Log of the Black Parrot"; *November 11—The CBS Radio Workshop,* "Report on the We'uns" (with June Foray and Daws Butler)

1957

(date unknown)—How To... (guest panelists were given a problem to solve); *January 13—The CBS Radio Workshop,* "No Time for Heartaches" (with Sophie Tucker, Daws Butler); *January 20—Sus-*

pense, "Second Class Passenger" (with Sterling Holloway); *January 27—Suspense*, "Freedom This Way" (with Margie Listz); *January 27— Our Miss Brooks*, [?]; *March 3— Yours Truly, Johnny Dollar*, "The Meek Memorial Matter" (#15); *March 17— Suspense*, "The Outer Limit" (with Frank Lovejoy and Barney Phillips); *March 24—Suspense*, "Shooting Star" (with June Lockhart); *April 7— The CBS Radio Workshop*, "Japanese Drama" (with William Conrad and John Dehner); *May 5— Yours Truly, Johnny Dollar*, "The Peerless Fire Matter" (#23); *June 2—Suspense*, "Crossing Paris" (with Ted de Corsia); *July 14—Suspense*, "Flood on the Goodwins" (with Herbert Marshall); *July 14— Yours Truly, Johnny Dollar*, "The Heatherstone Players Matter"; *August 4— The Stan Freberg Show* (Show #4)—Conried in parody of "Lux Radio Theatre"— "Lox Radio Theatre," sponsored by "Lox Soap"— "The only soap that swims upstream."

1958

January 12—Suspense, "The Island" (with John Lund: Conried's last performance on series); *June 5— Whispering Streets* (Episode #1484); *October 5— The Mitch Miller Show* (with guests Bert Lahr and John Huston)

1971

May 30—Heartbeat Theatre, "Dry Guillotine" (Salvation Army production); *October 29— The Devil and Mr. O*, "Ancestor" (written and directed by Arch Oboler); *December 31— The Devil and Mr. O*, "The House is Haunted"

1973

November 22— Crisis, "**The Loophole**" (starring Conried)

1974

June 18—Zero Hour, "The Woman in Black" (written by Rod Serling); *November 7— The CBS Radio Mystery Theater*, "How Mr. Eberhard Won His Wings"; *December 25— The CBS Radio Mystery Theater* (rebroadcast of November 7th show)

1975

September 16— The CBS Radio Mystery Theater, "The Prisoner of Glass"

1976

February 15— The CBS Radio Mystery Theater, (rebroadcast of September 16 show); *March 25— The CBS Radio Mystery Theater* "The Transformation of Joebee"; *August 10— The CBS Radio Mystery Theater* (rebroadcast of March 25th show)

1977

February 21— The CBS Radio Mystery Theater, "Orient Express"; *March 3— The CBS Radio Mystery Theater*, "The Overcoat" (based on the Nikolai Gogol short story); *May 21—Adventure Theatre*, "They Called Him Slim" (a story about Charles Lindbergh); *June 13— The CBS Radio Mystery Theater*, "First Woman in Space"; *June 19— The CBS Radio Mystery Theater* (rebroadcast of February 21st show); *July 3— The CBS Radio Mystery Theater* (rebroadcast of March 3rd show); *October 26— The CBS Radio Mystery Theater* (rebroadcast of June 13th show); *October 27— The CBS Radio Mystery Theater* (rebroadcast of March 3rd show)

1978

June 29— The Adventures of Harry Nile, "Favor for a Friend" (with Jerry Hausner: this episode was not broadcast on this date due to a program change; the program was finally broadcast on December 16, 1990!)

1979

February 9— Sears Radio Theatre, "Choosing"; *February 18—Alien Worlds*, "The Resurrectionists of Lethe, Part 1" (with Corey Burton); *February 25—Alien Worlds*, "The Resurrectionists of Lethe, Part 2" (with Corey Burton); *April 9— Sears Radio Theatre*, "Anne Bonny's Gold"; *May 16— Sears Radio Theatre*, "The Nightmare" (with Vincent Price); *June 13— Sears Radio Theatre*, "The Perfect Hostess"; *June 22— Sears Radio Theatre*, "A Brief Case of Trouble"; *June 29— Sears Radio Theatre*, "Sha-Nama"; *July 2— Sears Radio Theatre*, "The Panther"; *July 6— Sears Radio Theatre*, "Vienna, Three And Four"; *July 17— Sears Radio Theatre*, "The Crown Jewels of Grandomere" (with Andy Griffith); *August 1— Sears Radio Theatre*, "Voodoo Lady"

1980

March 14—Mutual Radio Theater, "North to Marakesh" (with Antoinette Bower); *April 9— Mutual Radio Theater*, "**Last of Scrooge**" (starring Conried); *April 16—Mutual Radio Theater*, "East of Limbo" (with Andy Griffith); *July 22— Mutual Radio Theater*, "Unfinished Concerto" (with Cicely Tyson); *August 1—Mutual Radio Theater*, "Little Tears" (with Lorne Greene); *September 8—Mutual Radio Theater*, "Love Spelled Backwards"

1981

(date unknown)—*Ear Play (National Public Radio)* (Conried starred in an episode directed by Nicholas Meyer); ***May 1981***—*KGGF Fireside Playhouse*, "Breaking Out"

1982

September 27—*Same Time, Same Station*, "A Tribute to Hans Conried" (Radio station KRLA's long-running series paid tribute to one of radio's best loved character actors)

B. Filmography

This filmography is meant primarily as a reference for Conried's work in a particular picture, and not a detailed technical description. The times listed are only approximations, but give a good idea of how long Conried's scenes were in the film. If no time is given, that means I was not able to view the film. Conried's character is shown in brackets.

1938

Dramatic School — MGM — D: Robert B. Sinclair. Luise Rainer, Alan Marshal, Erik Rhodes, Paulette Goddard. [Ramy, a snobbish student, with a good heart].

There are a few substantive scenes with Conried as one of the principal actors. Conried is often included in the background of the schoolroom shots. Ramy is in the crowd at the dressing room door towards the end, but he is not seen leaving with the others. 5 minutes.

1939

It's a Wonderful World — MGM — D: W.S. Van Dyke. James Stewart, Claudette Colbert, Edgar Kennedy, Frances Drake. [The young stage manager (Tony Delmonico?)].

The film is a comedy, but Conried takes his role way too seriously. He is so intense about his first door-opening scene, it looks like his hand is glued to the doorknob. The stage manager is referred to once as "Mr. Delmonico" in the film, but the name is not shown in the credits. Less than 2 minutes.

On Borrowed Time — MGM — D: Harold S. Bucquet. Lionel Barrymore, Cedric Hardwicke, Beulah Bondi, Bobs Watson. [Coughing young man driving a convertible].

Conried is seen only at the beginning asking "Mr. Brink" (Hardwicke) if he'd like a lift. 20 seconds.

1940

More About Nostradamus (short subject) — MGM — D: David Miller. Carey Wilson (Narrator). [A young monk who becomes Pope Sixtus V].

Conried in one brief scene as a young monk who is told of his great future, and one more even shorter scene as the aged Pope Sixtus V (just a flash really). 20 seconds.

Dulcy — MGM — D: S. Sylvan Simon. Ann Sothern, Ian Hunter, Roland Young, Billie Burke. [Vincent Leach, the playwright].

Vincent Leach appears in a running gag about this hapless writer trying to work on his play while in a canoe on the river. Madcap Dulcy keeps disturbing his concentration by dunking him in the drink when she roars by in her speedboat. Conried literally has the last laugh in the final scene of the film. 1–2 minutes.

Bitter Sweet — MGM — D: W.S. Van Dyke. Taken from a Noel Coward play. George Sanders, Felix Bressart. [Young Austrian man at Mama Luden's restaurant].

This film is a vehicle for Nelson Eddy and Jeanette McDonald. If you like them, this film is for you. Otherwise, you have to sit through all of their singing to find 20 seconds of Conried. It is in color, though, and he has one line of dialogue.

1941

Weekend for Three — RKO — D: Irving Reis. Dennis O'Keefe, Jane Wyatt, Franklin Pangborn, Edward Everett Horton, Zasu Pitts. [Desk clerk].

The part was another gift from Irving Reis, but only a walk-on.

Unexpected Uncle — RKO — D: Peter Godfrey. Anne Shirley, James Craig, Charles Coburn, Ernest Truex. [Mr. Clayton].

Maisie Was a Lady — MGM — D: Edwin L. Marin. Ann Sothern, Lew Ayres, C. Aubrey Smith, Maureen O'Sullivan. [George, the boorish, but well-to-do house guest].

Conried plays a rich snob who is one of a group of snobs invited to a weekend engagement party. George is mostly in the background, and has almost no dialogue. There is one funny scene where he imitates the way Maisie walks while at a poolside breakfast party. She retaliates with a put down that sends the crestfallen George head first into the pool (fully clothed!). Less than 2 minutes.

The Gay Falcon—RKO—D: Irving Reis. George Sanders, Wendy Barrie, Allen Jenkins, Arthur Shields. [Herman, the high-strung police sketch artist].

The first of several "Falcon" films with George Sanders that feature Conried in a supporting role. The Falcon's sidekick, Goldie, in his own unique way, is trying to describe a villain while Herman sits on a couch and sketches with a pencil. Conried does his best to milk some laughs with his few seconds on the screen. 90 seconds.

A Date with the Falcon—RKO—D: Irving Reis. George Sanders, Wendy Barrie, Allen Jenkins, Mona Maris. [An oily clerk at the Federal Hotel].

It is fun to see Conried and George Sanders together. While Sanders filled out his suit quite nicely, Conried's suit looked like it was inhabited by a coat tree. Their scene at the hotel front desk, under the angry surveillance of the Falcon's fiancée, is arguably the best part of the film. Less than 5 minutes.

Underground—Warner Bros.—D: Vincent Sherman. Philip Dorn, Jeffrey Lynn, Kaaren Verne, Mona Maris. [Helmut, one of the underground freedom fighters].

Helmut is mostly seen in the background, but he does have a couple lines of dialogue. He was one of the good-guys for a change in this war picture. 45 seconds.

1942

Underground Agent—Columbia—D: Michael Gordon. Bruce Bennett, Leslie Brooks, Frank Albertson, George McKay. [A nasty, scar-faced Nazi spy].

Conried plays one of a group of Nazi thugs bent on their evil mischief.

Portrait of a Genius (short subject)—MGM—D: Pete Smith. Richard Ainlee (da Vinci), Corey Wilson (narrator). [?].

A survey of the life of Leonardo da Vinci, and his many amazing inventions.

Bartolome (short subject)—MGM—(?). [Fabian, a young priest].

Barbee-cues (short subject)—MGM—(?). Max Cullen, Dorothy Morris. [One of the guests at a backyard barbecue].

A funny "How to" type film that purported to show you the right way, and the wrong way, to use a barbeque. It's too bad this short was released just when meat rationing was instituted.

Below the White House (short subject)—Columbia—(?). [Hugo, a patriotic businessman].

A propaganda film centered on the troubles of an honest businessman—Hugo—and the attempts that are made to threaten him into becoming a spy for the Nazi's.

Something to Shout About—Columbia—D: Gregory Ratoff. Don Ameche, Janet Blair, Jack Oakie, Cyd Charisse. [?].

Conried had a very small walk-on in this film, which may have ended up on the cutting room floor.

The Wife Takes a Flyer—Columbia—D: Richard Wallace. Joan Bennett, Franchot Tone, Barbara Brown, Allyn Joslyn. [Hendrik Woverman].

Conried plays Joan Bennett's nutty Dutch husband who is committed to an asylum in order to dry out.

Pacific Rendezvous—MGM—D: George Sidney. Lee Bowman, Jean Rogers, Mona Maris, Paul Cavanagh. [Nazi spy posing as hotel clerk].

Here Conried gets to use his experience as a hotel clerk and Nazi spy in one film! His performance is unfortunately very brief, and routine. His Nazi clerk is a very humorless, unpleasant fellow. 1–2 minutes.

Once Upon a Honeymoon—RKO—D: Leo McCary. Cary Grant, Ginger Rogers, Walter Slezak, Albert Dekker. [Herr Snyder, the Austrian fitter].

Conried has a chance to hold his own in a scene with Cary Grant. Herr Snyder appears in one and a half brief scenes, and has only a couple lines of dialogue (in German). 45 seconds.

Nightmare—U.I.—D: Tim Whelan. Diana Barrymore, Brian Donlevy, Gavin Muir, Arthur Shields. [Hans, a Nazi spy who dresses like Sherlock Holmes].

At this point in his career, Conried could say he worked with the entire Barrymore clan, except for Ethel. Diana was John's daughter, and tragically ended her own life in 1960.

Journey Into Fear—RKO—D: Norman Foster. Joseph Cotton, Dolores Del Rio, Orson Welles, Agnes Moorehead. [A Dutch magician—Though his name is never spoken in the film, the Call Bureau Cast Service list used during production gives the character's name as "Oo Lang Sang"].

Orson Welles directed a portion of this film, but unfortunately, not the one with Conried. The magician's performance is well filmed, and Conried gets a chance to use his dialects to the fullest. 1—2 minutes.

Joan of Paris—RKO—D: Robert Stevenson. Paul Henried, Michele Morgan, Laird Cregar, Alan Ladd. [Shifty Gestapo Agent].

Conried plays an undercover Gestapo agent following Morgan's character around. There is one close-up, and very little dialogue. Less than 2 minutes.

Hitler's Children—RKO—D: Edward Dmytrick. Tim Holt, Bonita Granville, Kent Smith, Otto Kruger. [Dr. Graf—Head of the Nazi Ministry of Education].

An interesting role with Conried dressed in full Nazi regalia. His youth seemed out of place for a man of Dr. Graf's position, though. The moustache didn't help very much. Conried gave Dr. Graf the trademark weakness and instability his Nazi characters usually exhibited. Less than 5 minutes.

Blondie's Blessed Event—Columbia.—D: Frank Strayer. Arthur Lake, Penny Singleton, Larry Simms, Jonathan Hale. [George Wickley, the poor, parasitic playwright].

Finally Conried had a chance to really show what he could do with a comedy role. Dagwood meets Wickley while in Chicago to deliver an important speech to an association of architects. Lured by the free food he sees in Dagwood's hotel room, Wickley offers to write the speech for him (with disastrous results!). Wickley shows up at Dagwood's doorstep, and invites himself for an indefinite stay. Alexander even starts calling him "Uncle George." Of course, Blondie is not at all happy. A wonderful performance in an otherwise mediocre film. 40 minutes.

The Falcon Takes Over—RKO—D: Irving Reis. George Sanders, Lynn Bari, Allen Jenkins, Ward Bond. [Lindsay Marriott].

This time, Conried is the suave, Lindsay Marriott, who tries to lure the Falcon to his death. Of course, Marriott gets it instead. Only a couple of scenes. Less than 2 minutes.

The Big Street—RKO—D: Irving Reis. Henry Fonda, Lucille Ball, Barton MacLane, Agnes Moorehead. [Louie, the headwaiter].

Louie is only on the screen for few memorable scenes. Conried plays him as a rather jaded character with little patience for romantic types. Conried used his experience growing up in New York for the accent. 1—2 minutes.

Saboteur—Universal—D: Alfred Hitchcock. Robert Cummings, Priscilla Lane, Otto Kruger, Alan Baxter. [A butler].

You barely had time to see Conried in this one. He's being berated for his poor service, so he only has a chance to say a couple variations of "I'm sorry, Mrs. Sutton," and then he's off. 20 seconds.

Reunion in France—MGM—D: Jules Dassin. Joan Crawford, Philip Dorn, John Wayne, Reginald Owen. ["Boy" who helps girl on bicycle].

This is one of those "blink and you miss him" roles. Conried is one of the young men who help a girl onto the basket of her boyfriend's bicycle. He's wearing a hat, and it's a long shot, so you can barely tell it is Conried. 10 seconds.

The Greatest Gift—MGM—D: Hal Daniels. (short subject). [?].

The film centered around the famous story of the juggler of Notre Dame, and the yearly adoration of the Virgin Mary.

1943

His Butler's Sister—Universal—D: Frank Borzage. Deanna Darbin, Franchot Tone, Pat O'Brien. [Reeves, one of five butler's courting Deanna Durbin].

His role could have been so much more, but Conried was given next to nothing to work with. This film was a complete waste of Conried's talent, but was very well received in Japan. That helped him greatly when he was stationed there during the Occupation in 1945. Less than 2 minutes.

Crazy House—Universal—D: Edward F. Cline. Ole Olsen, Chick Johnson, Cass Daley, Shemp Howard. [Roco, the eccentric, avant-garde artist].

Conried was popular enough as a radio actor at this time to earn himself a "Special Guest Star" cameo in this Olson and Johnson vehicle. He is seen mainly in the background until the courtroom scene near the end of the film. Finally Conried has a few lines of dialogue. It's too bad his best scenes were left on the cutting room floor. Less than 2 minutes.

The Lady Takes a Chance—RKO—D: Henry Hathaway and William A. Setter. John Wayne, Jean Arthur, Grady Sutton, Grant Withers. [Greg Stone].

If there are four guys interested in Jean Arthur, and one of them is John Wayne, it's not hard to figure out who gets her. Greg Stone was the youngest of the four, and no match for the Duke. He only appears in the early part of the film, and then at the end. 3–4 minutes.

Hostages—Paramount—D: Frank Tuttle. William Bendix, Luise Rainer, Oskar Homolka, Paul Lukas. [Lt. Glasenapp, the lovelorn young Nazi].

Conried has a few scenes at the beginning of the film. His character's troubles spark the melee that results in the capture of the "hostages." A good performance, but the dialogue was unintentionally funny. Less than 10 minutes.

1944

Passage to Marseille—Warner Bros.—D: Michael

Curtiz. Humphrey Bogart, Claude Raines, Sidney Greenstreet, Peter Lorre. [Lt. Jourdain].

Conried is in good company with the all-star cast, but unfortunately the script wasn't worthy of all the talent. Lt. Jourdain thought he was following orders, but ended up getting his neck broken (by George Tobias, no less!) for his trouble. A dark, dreary film. 1–2 minutes.

Mrs. Parkington—MGM—D: Tay Garnett. Greer Garson, Walter Pidgeon, Edward Arnold, Agnes Moorehead. [Mr. Ernst].

A short, but enjoyable part as the elderly Mr. Ernst, who is the nervous manager of the temperamental opera star (Fortunio Bonanova) who is to sing at the Parkington's big soirée. Conried and Bonanova make a good comedy team. Less than 5 minutes.

1947

The Senator Was Indiscreet—Universal—D: George S. Kaufman. William Powell, Peter Lind Hayes, Ella Raines, Allen Jenkins. [Karl, the surly waiter].

Conried gives a very broad performance as the communist waiter with the heavy New York accent. A few good scenes. Less than 2 minutes.

1948

Design for Death (documentary)—RKO—D: Richard Fleischer. Kent Smith ("voice of America"). [The "voice of Japan"].

An interesting piece of propaganda written by Theodor Geisel (Dr. Seuss) and his first wife, Helen. Two voices were used in the narration. An American, and one representing the Japanese. Conried's felt his Japanese accent fit the idea of what the public would expect to hear. The film went on to win an Academy Award.

Variety Time—RKO—D: Hal Yates (with help from Leon Errol and Edgar Kennedy). Frankie Carle, Jack Paar, Leon Errol, Dorothy Granger. [Rudy La Paix].

Conried is in a short comedy skit with pal, Jack Paar. Paar also helped to write some of the material, and was "Master of Ceremonies."

1949

On the Town—MGM—D: Stanley Donen and Gene Kelly. Frank Sinatra, Gene Kelly, Ann Miller, Betty Garrett. [Francois, the headwaiter].

One of those big, Technicolor extravaganzas. Conried's part was embarrassingly small, and another waste of time. 40 seconds.

My Friend Irma—Paramount—D: George Marshall. Dean Martin, Jerry Lewis, Marie Wilson, Gloria Gordon. [Professor Kropotkin].

Conried does the best he can with this one, but it's a lost cause. Kropotkin manages a couple good scenes, but Jerry Lewis and Dean Martin overwhelm the film. Your best bet is to listen to the radio shows. Less than 2 minutes.

Bride for Sale—RKO—D: William D: Russell. Claudette Colbert, Robert Young, George Brent, Max Baer. [Jewelry salesman].

The Barkleys of Broadway—MGM—D: Charles Walters. Fred Astaire, Ginger Rogers, Oscar Levant, Billie Burke. [Ladislav (or "Ladislaus") Ladi].

A vehicle for Astaire and Rogers. Conried is given a tiny part as the well meaning, but clueless avant-garde artist who does an impressionistic portrait of the couple (much to their horror!). 60 seconds.

1950

Summer Stock—MGM—D: Charles Walters. Judy Garland, Gene Kelly, Gloria DeHaven, Phil Silvers. [Harrison I. Keath].

A fine comedic performance as the egotistic New York stage actor who graces the little stock troupe with his presence. It's too bad they wouldn't let Conried sing. Too many people knew his voice, so the vocals appear obviously dubbed. 5 minutes.

Nancy Goes to Rio—MGM—D: Robert Z. Leonard. Jane Powell, Ann Sothern. Barry Sullivan, Carmen Miranda. [Alfredo, the Brazilian butler].

One good scene with veteran actor, Louis Calhern, where Alfredo is giving his master a boxing lesson. Less than 2 minutes.

1951

Too Young to Kiss—MGM—D: Robert Z. Leonard. June Allyson, Van Johnson, Gig Young, Bob Jellison. [Mr. Sparrow, director of the youth orchestra].

Conried gives a fine, controlled, comedic performance as the harried Mr. Sparrow. Less than 5 minutes.

New Mexico—United Artists—D: Irving Reis. Lew Ayres, Raymond Burr, Marilyn Maxwell, Andy Devine. [Abraham Lincoln].

This film is not very convincing as a historical drama, or a western. Old friend Irving Reis gives Conried the plum role of Abe Lincoln, if only briefly. Filmed in "Ansocolor". Less than 2 minutes.

Behave Yourself!—RKO—D: George Beck. Francis L. Sullivan, Lon Chaney, Jr., Elisha Cook, Jr., Allen Jenkins. [Norbert Gillespie, a.k.a. "Gillie the Blade"].

A strange little film that saw fit to pair Shelley Winters and Farley Granger as a loving young couple. Conried's character—Gillie, the Cockney assassin—was a likable sort of guy who just happened to enjoy killing people. A good part that was, again, way too brief. Less than 5 minutes.

Rich, Young and Pretty—MGM—D: Norman Taurog. Jane Powell, Vic Damone, Fernando Lamas, Danielle Darrieux. [A Maitre'd].

Texas Carnival—MGM—D: Charles Walters. Red Skelton, Esther Williams, Howard Keel, Keenan Wynn. [Hotel Clerk].

Another disappointingly brief appearance as a hotel clerk. Conried is not given very much to work with script-wise, but he does get to wear some nifty Western duds. Less than 1 minute.

The Light Touch—MGM—D: Richard Brooks. Stewart Granger, George Sanders, Pier Angeli, Larry Keating. [Leopold, the owner of an antique shop].

The script describes Leopold as being a "sharp-faced Frenchman."

I'll See You in My Dreams—Warner Bros.—D: Michael Curtiz. Frank Lovejoy, Mary Wickes, Jim Backus, Patrice Wymore. [William Rossiter, the president of a sheet music company].

Another strange pairing of Danny Thomas and Doris Day. One good scene and a couple close-ups with Doris Day. Less than 2 minutes.

1952

The World in His Arms—U.I.—D: Raoul Walsh. Anthony Quinn, Gregory Peck, Ann Blyth, Sig Ruman. [Eustace]. Routine role as fussy hotel manager. Less than 10 minutes.

Three for Bedroom C—Warner Bros.—D: Milton H. Bren. Gloria Swanson, Ernest Anderson, Fred Clark, Margaret Dumont. [Jack Bleck].

Conried has a few amusing scenes as a jaded Hollywood publicity man with an ulcer. 2–3 minutes.

Big Jim McLain—Warner Bros.—D: Edward Ludwig. John Wayne, James Arness, Nancy Olson, Alan Napier. [Robert Henried].

Old pal John Wayne wrote a special part for Conried, and flew him and Mrs. Conried out to Hawaii for the filming. The wacky Mr. Henried was indeed tailor-made for Conried's sensibilities, and provided comic relief. Less than 5 minutes.

1953

The Twonky—Universal—D: Arch Oboler. Janet Warren, Ed Max, Gloria Blondell, Billy Lynn. [Kerry West].

Conried finally got his chance to star in a full-length feature film, and it had to be this one! Oboler's maniacal "genius" created a mess of a film that could have been so much more. Conried's Kerry West comes across as a harried, henpecked, philosophy teacher whose life is made a living hell by his wife's gift—a brand new television set. Is *The Twonky* a comedy? Horror film? A witty commentary on modern life? You be the judge. 72 minutes.

Siren of Bagdad—Columbia—D: Richard Quine. Paul Henried, Patricia Medina, Charles Lung, Laurette Luez. [Ben Ali].

A "tits and sand" Technicolor B-movie with an aging Paul Henried as the not-so-dashing magician Kazah. Ben Ali was his not-so-able assistant. Conried had a large role in this one, but the film was hopeless from the start. He must have sensed it early on, because he acts as if he can't wait to get out of the scene. Definitely not one of his best efforts, but pleasant at times. 77 minutes.

The Affairs of Doby Gillis—MGM—D: Don Weis. Debbie Reynolds, Bobby Van, Bob Fosse, Barbara Van Ruick. [Professor Amos Pomfritt].

Conried provides a few hilarious moments as the pompous Professor Pomfritt. His first scene, where he enters the classroom, and you can see him in the background giving the students that weary, withering glance as he skulks up to his podium is priceless. The highbrow tongue-lashing that he gives young Dobey is masterfully handled by Conried. Less than 5 minutes.

The 5000 Fingers of Dr. T.—Columbia—D: Roy Rowland. Peter Lind Hayes, Mary Healy, Tommy Retig, Noel Cravat. [Dr. Terwilliker].

Undeniably Conried's finest cinematic hour. A tour-de-force performance that should have launched him into stardom. Sure Dr. T is a despicable tyrant, but when you see how happy he is with his "Do-Me-Do Duds," and hear Conried masterfully give Dr. T's "This is MY Day" speech, you almost wish things would turn out for the guy. Even though the final film was a pitifully mangled version of the original print, it is still well worth viewing. 88 minutes. Trivia note: The robe worn by Conried at the start of Dr. T's "Dressing Song" scene must have been borrowed from Republic's costume closet. Actor Roy Barcroft—as Retik, leader of the moon men—can be seen wearing the same robe in the 1951 Commando Cody serial *Radar Men from the Moon*. The robe's stylized peacock feather motif seems an odd choice for moon man garb. No doubt it had been used before in a previous, as of yet unknown, production.

Peter Pan—RKO (Animated Walt Disney feature film)—D: Clyde Geronimi, Wilfred Jackson, Hamilton Luske. Voices of. Tom Conway (Narrator), Bobby Driscoll, Kathryn Beaumont, Paul Collins. [Voice of Mr. George Darling and Captain Hook].

Even though this film is animated, you almost feel like you are watching Conried himself perform as Captain Hook. His voice work is unparalleled, and gives credence to the belief that Conried is one of the best voice artists who ever lived. You can hear it all in the kindly Mr. Darling, and the evil, but misunderstood, Captain Hook. 76 minutes.

1955

You're Never Too Young—Paramount—D: Norman Taurog. Jerry Lewis, Dean Martin, Raymond Burr, Diana Lynn. [Francois, the French hair stylist].

Once more, Conried is given very little to do, and ends up as a stooge for Jerry Lewis. Embarrassing. Conried does manage one funny moment. Francois walks away from his barber shop after a run-in with Lewis, throws up his hands, and announces loudly in a voice mixed with frustration, indignation, and resignation. "Ees lunch time!". Less than 1 minute.

Davy Crockett, King of the Wild Frontier—Buena Vista—D: Norman Foster. Fess Parker, Buddy Ebsen, Nick Cravat, Helene Stanley. [Mr. Thimblerig].

A well beloved bit of depressing Americana from Walt Disney. It starts out so happy, and then everybody dies! Conried has quite a few scenes as the spineless gentleman, Mr. Thimblerig, who ends up helping to defend the Alamo. One of the few "action" roles Conried was ever in (probably for the best.). 10—15 minutes.

1956

Bus Stop—20th Century Fox—D: Joshua Logan. Marilyn Monroe, Don Murray, Arthur O'Connell, Eileen Heckart. [Eliot Elisofon, a Life Magazine photographer].

By his own account, Conried was tricked into appearing in this film by Joshua Logan's flattery. One can only hope he received a nice paycheck, because there wasn't much else to show for his effort. What a waste of talent. 20—30 seconds.

The Birds and the Bees—Paramount—D: Norman Taurog. George Gobel, Mitzi Gaynor, David Niven, Reginald Gardiner. (Alternate title. *The George Gobel Story*). [Duc. Jacques de Montaigne]. As the original working title suggests, this film is a vehicle to showcase the obscure talents of George Gobel. The poor, gullible George gets taken by some high-class card sharks and falls in love with one of them—the lovely Mitzi Gaynor. Conried plays a comrade of the lady cheat and her father (David Niven) named "Frenchy." He has found easy pickings in Connecticut (George's hometown), and is calling himself "Jacques, Duc. De Montaigne." Conried's French accent gets a workout, but not very much else. He does hit best with a feeble part: Less than 6 minutes.

1957

The Monster That Challenged the World—United Artists—D: Arnold Laven. Tim Holt, Audrey Dalton, Max Showalter, Marjorie Stapp. [Dr. Jess Rogers]. (Alternate titles: *The Creature from Hell*, *The Krackent*, and *The Jagged Edge*)

Despite the lurid title, this is a pretty good low budget film. Conried has a dramatic role as the dedicated Navy researcher who teams up with Tim Holt's Commander Twillinger to rid the world of the evil snail-like beasties. The budget was so small that Conried wore the same clothes for the entire film, which supposedly took place over the course of three days. 83 minutes.

Jet Pilot—U.I.—D: Josef Von Sternberg—(Originally filmed in 1949). John Wayne, Janet Leigh, Paul Fix, Roland Winters. [Colonel Matoff].

Conried spent more time being fitted for his costume than he did on the screen. He does a good job as the Russian Colonel Matoff, but is given very little to work with. 30 seconds.

1958

Rock-a-Bye Baby—Paramount—D: Frank Tashlin. Jerry Lewis, Marilyn Maxwell, Connie Stevens, Reginald Gardiner. [Mr. Wright, the owner of a TV repair shop].

Another Jerry Lewis vehicle. Conried is allowed one bright moment as a harried Mr. Wright talking on the phone to a disgruntled customer. A few other scenes playing to Lewis. Less than 2 minutes.

The Big Beat—U.I.—D: William J. Cowen. William Reynolds, Andra Martin, Gogi Grant, Rose Marie. [B.J. Carson, a.k.a. "Vladimir Skolsky." A wealthy businessman posing as an eccentric sculptor].

Conried has a surprisingly interesting dual role as the successful, conservative businessman B.J. Carson, and his eccentric alter ego, the Greenwich Village artist Vladimir Skolsky. Critics noted the scenes with Conried and Rose Marie (his romantic interest) as the highlights of the film. One item of interest is a seemingly incongruous bit of dialogue that took place during one of Rose Marie's musical numbers. Conried—as Skolsky—sings, "I should be doing Shakespeare, so talented I am!" to which Rose Marie replies, "No matter how you slice it, boy, it's still a lot of ham." The musical interludes were provided by Fats Domino, Harry James, the Mills Bros., the Del Vikings, the Diamonds, Cal Tjader, and others. Less than 10 minutes.

1959

Juke Box Rhythm—Columbia—D: Arthur Dreifuss. Jo Morrow, Jack Jones, Brian Donlevy,

George Jessel. (Alternate title: *Juke Box Jamboree.*) [Balenko, the junk man who was actually a dress designer].

This film contains some lukewarm musical numbers and a convoluted plot. Conried was given a good-sized role as the poor, Eastern European immigrant, Balenko, who dreams of becoming a great fashion designer. His acting is broadly comical, but still fairly restrained. One notable scene has Balenko being plied with drinks at a cocktail lounge by a scheming seductress while they listen to The Treniers sing their novelty tune. "(Uh oh) Get Out of the Car." Johnny Otis, The Nitwits, The Earl Grant Trio, and a few others were all this "juke box" could manage. Less than 15 minutes

1001 Arabian Nights (a.k.a. *Mr. Magoo's 1001 Arabian Nights*)—Columbia—D: Jack Kinney. Voices of. Jim Backus, Dwayne Hickman, Alan Reed, Daws Butler, Kathryn Grant. [The Wicked Wazir].

A full-length animated feature starring the nearsighted Mr. Magoo as "Uncle Abdul Aziz Magoo." Conried provides the voice for the villain of the piece, the evil Wazir. A fine vocal performance. 75 minutes.

1961

The Magic Fountain—Classic World Distribution—D: Allan David. Helmo Kindermann, Erik Jelde, Osman Ragheb, Greeal Wasson. [Voice of Otto, the owl].

A very odd little film that was a joint European and American project. It features mainly European actors (who were later dubbed in English—very badly, I might add), and was filmed in Germany's beautiful Black Forrest. Cedric Hardwicke is the narrator, and Buddy Baer is the voice of a magical bear. 1—2 minutes.

Everything's Ducky—Columbia—D: Don Taylor. Mickey Rooney, Buddy Hackett, Jackie Cooper, Joanie Sommers. [Voice of a talking duck].

Live action film starring Rooney and Hackett as Navy sailors on furlough. Conried as the voice of a miraculous talking duck.

1963

My Six Loves—Paramount—D: Gower Champion. Debbie Reynolds, David Janssen, Cliff Roberson, Eileen Heckart. [Kingsley Kross, the playwright].

Typical Debbie Reynolds vehicle. Conried has a few good scenes as the controversial playwright who wants to help make Debbie a star. A few more would have made this a palatable picture. 2—3 minutes.

1964

Robin & The Seven Hoods—Warner Bros.—D: Gordon Douglas. Frank Sinatra, Dean Martin, Sammy Davis, Jr., Bing Crosby. [Mr. Ricks, the architect].

A chance for Conried to hold his own with "The Rat Pack." He has a few fun scenes as the shaky architect, Mr. Ricks, who is commissioned to build Frankie's new nightclub (complete with secret hiding places). My favorite moment is at the grand opening of the new nightclub, Mr. Ricks is seen at the bar drinking milk!. 2—3 minutes.

The Patsy—Paramount—D: Jerry Lewis. Keenan Wynn, Peter Lorre, John Carradine. [Professor Mulerr, the voice teacher].

Conried is a stooge again for Jerry Lewis with familiar embarrassing results. He has a little more to work with here, but it is patently unfunny, and difficult to watch. 3—4 minutes.

1969

The Phantom Tollbooth—MGM—D: Chuck Jones, Abe Levitow, Dave Monahan. Butch Patrick. Voices of. Mel Blank, Daws Butler, June Foray. [Voice of Aziz, the Unabridged].

Live action and animated adaptation of the wonderful children's book by Norton Juster. Conried is the kindly Aziz, the Unabridged, who helps the little boy who is bored with school to understand the importance of words. 90 minutes.

1973

The Brothers O'Toole—A.N.E.—D: Richard Erman. John Astin, Pat Carroll, Lee Meriwether, Allyn Joslyn. [Brigadeer Polonius Vandergelt].

Conried is in his element as the flamboyant Vandergelt. His performance may be a bit too broad, but it is the best thing about this otherwise unfunny comedy. Less than 5 minutes.

1976

The Shaggy D.A.—Buena Vista—D: Robert Stevenson. Dean Jones, Suzanne Pleshette, Tim Conway, Keenan Wynn. [Professor Whatley].

By this point, Conried was relegated to the role of a professor, or doctor of some kind. It's pretty much a straight part, and Conried has very little to do. 1 minute.

1977

The Magic Pony—International Film Exchange, LTD—D: Ivan Ivanov-Vano. (Russian produced animated film. Dubbed into English). Voices of. Jim Backus, Erin Moran, Johnny Whitaker, Diana Alton. [Voice of the king's evil groom].

Very nice animation work done by Russian artists (don't let the American artwork on the video box fool you!). Difficult to dub into English, but Conried did a good job as the voice of the King's odious servant. Based on a Russian folk tale by Peter Yershov. 60 minutes.

1978

The Cat from Outer Space—Buena Vista—D: Norman Tokar. Ken Berry, Sandy Duncan, Harry Morgan, Roddy McDowall. [Dr. Heffel].

Conried as the crusty, unimaginative Dr. Heffel. Very little room for Conried to show any of his talent. Less than 2 minutes.

1980

Oh, God! Book II—Warner Bros.—D: Gilbert Cates. George Burns, Suzanne Pleshette, David Birney, Louanne. [Dr. Barnes].

Sadly, Conried has nothing to work with in this film. He's given the tiny part of one of a group of psychiatrists examining the young girl who claims to talk to god. Conried has at most four lines of dialogue delivered while sitting around the table with his "colleagues." Less than 4 minutes.

Below is a list of films Hans Conried has been linked with that he did not appear in.

1939

Never Say Die—Universal—D: Elliott Nugent. Bob Hope, Martha Raye, Andy Devine.

Rumor has circulated that Conried appeared in an unbilled performance as one of the musicians in this film. There is an actor who plays the concertina who bears a striking resemblance to Conried, but he is much older, shorter, and stouter than Conried Nevertheless, he looks enough like Conried to be his uncle! The actor (who has yet to be identified, unfortunately) has a couple lines of dialogue, and seems to have an Italian accent. The bottom line is: Conried was not in this film.

1940

The Great Dictator—U.A.—D: Charles Chaplin.

This film often appears on lists of Conried's work, but I sincerely doubt he is in this film. He may have done a walk-on that was later edited out. The one possibility may be the young man walking down the stairs with a young lady in the background of the scene where two old men are playing chess. After a lot of study, I would have to say no.

Blondie in Society—Columbia—D: Frank Strayer.

Even though this film appears on at least one Hans Conried filmography in print, Conried is nowhere to be found. Possibly his part was cut out of the final print. There is one crowd scene at a dog show with a great deal of chaos going on. After watching that scene frame-by-frame, I came to the conclusion Conried was not one of the faces in the crowd.

1947

Blondie's Big Moment—Columbia—D: Abby Berlin.

I have only seen this title on one Hans Conried filmography, and cannot verify whether it is a real entry or not. There is no corroborating evidence to say Conried appeared in the film.

1956

Meet Me in Las Vegas—MGM—D: Roy Rowland.

Conried's publicity men reported he was in this film until around 1961. After that, the film was deleted from the filmography that was a part of his official press kit. It is unknown if the original theatrical version of *Meet Me in Las Vegas* contained the little cameo that Conried filmed, but it is certain that it was missing from the television and video prints.

1961

Judgment at Nuremberg—U.A.—D: Stanley Kramer.

This film was also listed on the official filmography for a few years. Newspapers ran blurbs saying Conried was in the film, yet there is no evidence to show he ever filmed the scenes for "the entertainer" he and Stanley Kramer had originally discussed. Unfortunately, Conried was either dropped from the project early on, or did not survive the final cut.

B. Filmography

A note about films Hans Conried may appear in.

Conried once said that Irving Reis promised to put him in every film he directed. Considering the number of Reis films Conried does appear in, it is almost certain there are more unbilled performances in other pictures yet to be discovered. For example, in-between *Weekend for Three* (1941) and *The Falcon Takes Over* (1942), Reis directed a film called *Footlight Fever* for RKO (1941). Between *Hitler's Children* in 1942, and *New Mexico* in 1951, Reis directed eight films. With the exception of *Three Husbands* (1950), all could potentially contain a cameo by Conried.

A handwritten list in Conried's scrapbook includes the 1942 film, *Secret Agent of Japan* (20th Century Fox), as being one of his accomplishments. He also listed *The Song of Bernadette*, which he was cut out of, so it's not possible to definitively say he was in *Secret Agent of Japan* without finding a copy to view.

C. Television Log

Animated television series (e.g.: Dudley Do-right of the Mounties, Hoppity Hooper, and The Drak Pack) are listed on the log covering Hans Conried's voice work. The following television log is not definitive, but it is the most complete listing extant.

1948

February 28—*Pantomime Quiz* (Conried was one of the founding celebrity panelists); ***September 2***—*Prime Ribbing* (premiere of short-lived quiz show with Conried as emcee)

1949

March (?)—*Speak the Speech* (KLAC-TV: based on the parlor game, "Manner of the Word": Conried was joined by former radio cohorts John Brown, Lorene Tuttle, Janet Waldo, and Alan Reed); ***September 23***—*Arch Oboler Comedy Theatre* "Ostrich in Bed" (starring Conried), ABC

1950

September 30—*Hamilton the Great* (series pilot: Conried as "Hamilton York": also starring Jerry Hausner); ***December 25***—*One Hour in Wonderland*, first Walt Disney special, NBC

1951

(unknown date)—*Short Story Playhouse*, "My Double and How He Undid Me," NBC; ***October 15***—*Let's Face It* (quiz show: local L.A. produced show: Conried was a regular), KTTV; ***December 25***—*The Walt Disney Christmas Show*, special, CBS

1952

(unknown date)—*Smilin' Ed McConell & His Buster Brown Gang* (Conried in "Gunga Ram" segment), ABC; ***(unknown date)***—*Your Lucky Clue* (panel show hosted by Basil Rathbone; Conried appeared on at least one episode during *Clue*'s short run from July 13th to August 31st); ***July 25***—*Mr. & Mrs. North* "These Latins" (Conried as "Enrique Romero"), CBS; ***November 14***—*Rebound* "Dry, with Three Olives" (Bing Crosby Productions), DuMont; ***November 24***—*I Love Lucy* "Redecorating,"CBS; ***December 29***—*I Love Lucy* "Lucy Hires an English Teacher" (Conried sings "Babalu"), CBS

1953

(unknown date)—*I'll Buy That* (N.Y. based quiz show: Mike Wallace as emcee: regular panelist), CBS; ***February 13***—*Schlitz Playhouse of Stars*, "Mr. Greentree and Friend" (starring Conried), CBS; ***April 24***—*Schlitz Playhouse of Stars*, "Allen of Harper," CBS; ***June 11***—*Take a Guess* (summer quiz show: regular w/Ernie Kovacs until September 10th), CBS

1954

(unknown date)—*Make Room for Daddy* [?], ABC; ***June 27***—*Hallmark Hall of Fame*, "Wife Unto Caesar" (co-starring Conried), NBC; ***July 23***—*The Crown Theatre Starring Gloria Swanson* (a.k.a.: *The Gloria Swanson Show*); "Dry—With Three Olives" (previously shown in 1952 as part of "Rebound" series: cut down to 15 minutes for "Crown Theatre"); ***September 16***—*The Ray Milland Show* [?], CBS; ***December 21***—*U.S. Steel Hour* "Presento," (with Shirley Yamaguchi), CBS

1955

January 30—*Pepsi Cola Playhouse*,"Otto and the Coat," ABC; ***February 23***—*Disneyland* "Davy Crocket at the Alamo," ABC; ***March 10***—*The Ray Milland Show* [?], CBS; ***March 29***—*Make Room for Daddy*, "The Actor," ABC; ***April 28***—*Schlitz Playhouse of Stars*, "The Brute Next Door" (starring

Conried), CBS; *May (?)*, *O. Henry Playhouse* (?), "Man About Town" (Conried as "Clarence"); *May 25—Four Star Playhouse*, "Trudy," CBS; *October 7—San Francisco Beat*, "The Silk Stocking Case," CBS; *October 21—Schlitz Playhouse of Stars*, "The Girl Who Scared Men Off" (co-starring Conried), CBS; *October 25—Cavalcade of America*, "The Swamp Fox," ABC; *December 14—20th Century-Fox Hour*, "Meet Mr. Kringle" (a.k.a. "Miracle on 34th Street"), CBS

1956

(unknown date)—The New Adventures of Charlie Chan, "The Great Salvos," syndicated; *(unknown date)—Bob Cummings Show*, "Bob Escapes Schultzy's Trap," CBS; *January 31—Make Room for Daddy* (Conried as "Cousin Carl"), ABC; *February 15—Walt Disney Presents*, "Our Unsung Villains" (as narrator), ABC; *February 28—Make Room for Daddy* [?], ABC; *March 10—Ford Star Jubilee*, "High Tor" (with Bing Crosby), CBS; *April (?)—NBC Comedy Hour* (variety show: Conried played straight man to Jonathan Winters), NBC; *April 1—Alcoa Hour*, "Finkle's Comet," NBC; *May 23—The Danny Thomas Show*, "Sonnets from the Lebanese," ABC; *October 27—Saturday Spectacular: Manhattan Tower*, musical special, NBC; *September (?)—Schlitz Playhouse of Stars* (?), "My Friends, the Birds" (with Peter Lawford), CBS; *September 29—Code 3*, "The Killer" (Conried was the title character), syndicated; *November 22—Playhouse 90*, "Eloise," CBS

1957

(unknown date)—Red Skelton Show (Conried as guest), CBS; *January 30—Walt Disney Presents*, "All About Magic," ABC; *Spring 1957—Love That Bob*, "Bob Escapes Schultz's Trap," NBC; *April 5—Schlitz Playhouse of Stars*, "Clothes Make the Man," CBS; *July 29—The Jack Paar Show* (premiere of Paar as host of *The Tonight Show*; Conried was considered an "irregular regular"; after Paar's exit from *The Tonight Show* in 1962, Conried was often seen on *The Jack Paar Program* until show went off the air in 1965), NBC; *July 30—The Jack Paar Show* (Dody Goodman tells Conried to "Shut up!"), NBC; *July 31—The Jack Paar Show* (Conried as guest), NBC; *August 1—The Jack Paar Show* (Conried as guest), NBC; *August 2—The Jack Paar Show* (Conried as guest), NBC; *August 20—Meet McGraw*, "Ballerina," NBC; *August 26—The Jack Paar Show* (by popular demand, Conried was back on the show), NBC; *October 11—San Francisco Beat*, "The Honolulu Treasure Case," CBS; *October 12—What's It For?* (Saturday Quiz Show: Conried was a regular until January 4), NBC; *October 18—Climax*, "The Largest City in Captivity," CBS; *October 24—Dragnet*, "The Big Howard" (Conried as "Paul Zavier"), NBC; *November 17—General Motors 50th Anniversary Show* (special), NBC

1958

(unknown date)—The Whirlybirds (Conried appeared as a guest in one episode), syndicated; *(unknown date)—The $64,000 Question* (Conried was a contestant), CBS; *(unknown date)—To Tell the Truth* (quiz show: Conried was a guest panelist), CBS; *January 13—The Jack Paar Show* (Conried as guest), NBC; *January 17—The Jack Paar Show* (Conried as guest), NBC; *January 28—The Donna Reed Show*, "It's the Principle of the Thing," ABC; *February 12—Bell Science Series*, "The Unchained Goddess" (Conried as apothecary: voice only), NBC; *February 18—Jerry Lewis Show* (special: broadcast live from the Sands Hotel in Las Vegas); *March 16—Maverick*, "Black Fire," ABC; *March 19—Walt Disney Presents*, "Magic and Music," ABC; *March 23—Omnibus*, "What Makes Opera Grand?" (Tristan & Isolde), PBS; *April 11—Adventures of Jim Bowie*, "Patron of the Arts," ABC; *April 27—Hansel and Gretel* (live special: Red Buttons; Rudy Vallee; Stubby Kaye), NBC; *May 26—Target*, "The Tattoo Artist," syndicated; *December 9—The Californians*, "The Painless Extractionist," NBC; *December 11—Oscar Levant Show* (on KHJ-TV in Los Angeles: seen only on the West Coast)

1959

January 12—The Danny Thomas Show (Conried as Uncle Tonoose), CBS; *January 26—Bell Science Series*, "The Alphabet Conspiracy" (live-action and animation), NBC; *March 1959—Play Your Hunch* (quiz show: Conried was briefly the emcee), NBC; *March 18—Mike Wallace Interview* (Conried as guest), ABC; *March 26—The Jack Paar Show* (Conried discusses Zen Buddhism), NBC; *June 13—Perry Presents* (Conried was the guest emcee for the premiere episode), NBC; *June 18—The Real McCoys*, "The Actor," ABC; *August 16—The Ransom of Red Chief* (special: with William Bendix and Teddy Rooney), NBC; *August 26—U.S. Steel Hour*, "A Taste of Champagne," CBS; *October 2—Art Carney Variety Show: Small World, Isn't It?* (special), NBC; *October 19—Love and Marriage*, "Child of Capricorn," NBC; *October 22—Take a Good Look* (Ernie Kovacs quiz show: Conried was a semi-regular panelist), ABC; *October 19—Take a Good Look*, ABC; *November 5—Take a Good Look*, ABC; *November 30—The Danny Thomas Show* (Conried as Uncle Tonoose), CBS; *December 4—The Jack Paar Show* (Groucho Marx and Conried as guests), NBC

1960

(unknown date)—*U.S. Steel Hour*, "When in Rome," CBS; *(unknown date)*—*Art Linkletter's House Party*, CBS; *January 16*—*20 Hour Cerebral Palsy Telethon* (live from Albany, New York); *February 8*—*The Danny Thomas Show* (Conried as Uncle Tonoose), CBS; *February 10*—*U.S. Steel Hour*, "The American Cowboy," CBS; *February 25*—*Take a Good Look*, ABC; *March (?)*—*The Charley Weaver Show* [?]—?; *March 4*—*Take a Good Look*, ABC; *March 28*—*The Jack Paar Show*, (tape of London tour with Conried shown), NBC; *April 7*—*Take a Good Look*, ABC; *May 19*—*Take a Good Look*, ABC; *May 27*—*Take a Good Look*, ABC; *June 2*—*Take a Good Look*, ABC; *June 9*—*Take a Good Look*, ABC; *June 16*—*Take a Good Look*, ABC; *June 23*—*Take a Good Look*, ABC; *June 30*—*Take a Good Look*, ABC; *August (?)*—*Celebrity Talent Scouts* (Conried as guest panelist), CBS; *October 19*—*Step on the Gas* (*U.S. Steel Hour* special), CBS

1961

(unknown date)—*The Square World of Jack Paar* (special: footage shown of trips abroad), NBC; *January 29*—*The Islanders*, "Escape from Kaledau," ABC; *February 6*—*The Danny Thomas Show* (Conried as Uncle Tonoose), CBS; *February 13*—*June Allyson Show*, "A Great Day for a Scoundrel," CBS; *March 8*—*Armstrong Circle Theater*, "Private Eye, Private Eye" (Ernie Kovacs / Edie Adams), CBS; *April 3*—*Adventures in Paradise*, "The Jonah Stone," ABC; *April 4*—*The Red Skelton Show*, CBS; *April 5*—*U.S. Steel Hour*, "The Oddball," CBS (live); *July (?)*—*The Jack Paar Show* (Conried crosses swords with Paar about Cuban crisis), NBC; *October 19*—*Feathertop* (special: with Hugh O'Brian), ABC; *October 30*—*The Danny Thomas Show* (Conried as Uncle Tonoose), CBS; *November 1*—*U.S. Steel Hour*, "Little Lost Sheep," CBS; **An Age of Kings** (BBC produced series for public television showcasing Shakespeare's "Kings" plays: Conried as host and commentator; up-and-coming young British actors such as Sean Connery enacted the plays); *November 3*—*An Age of Kings*, "The Hollow Crown" (Richard II, Scene 1,2,3); *November 10*—*An Age of Kings*, "The Deposing of a King" (Richard II, Scene 3,4,5); *November 17*—*An Age of Kings*, "Rebellion from the North" (Henry IV, Scene 1,2); *November 24*—*An Age of Kings*, "The Road to Shrewsbury" (Henry IV, Scene 3,4,5); *December 1*—*An Age of Kings*, "The New Conspiracy" (Henry IV, Pt. II, Scene 1,2); *December 8*—*An Age of Kings*, "Uneasy Lies the Head" (Henry IV, Pt. II, Scene 3,4,5); *December 9*—*Have Gun—Will Travel*, "A Knight to Remember," CBS; *December 15*—*An Age of Kings*, "Signs of War" (Henry V, Scene 1,2,3); *December 22*—*An Age of Kings*, "The Band of Brothers" (Henry V, Scene 4,5); *December 29*—*An Age of Kings*, "The Red Rose and the White" (Henry VI, Pt. 1)

1962

Fall 1962—*Mr. Ed*, "Ed and Paul Revere," CBS; *January 5*—*An Age of Kings*, "The Fall of a Protector" (Henry VI, Pt. II, Scene 1,2,3); *January 12*—*An Age of Kings*, "The Rabble from Kent" (Henry VI, Pt. II, Scene 3,4,5); *January 19*—*An Age of Kings*, "The Morning's War" (Henry VI, Pt. III, Scene 1,2,3); *January 26*—*An Age of Kings*, "The Sun in Splendour" (Henry VI, Pt. III, Scene 4,5); *February 2*—*An Age of Kings*, "The Dangerous Brother" (Richard III, Scene 1,2,3); *February 9*—*An Age of Kings*, "The Boar Hunt" (Richard III–Scene 3,4,5); **Great Voices from Great Books** (erudite syndicated series produced by Encyclopedia Britannica, and first shown on public television in 1961; Conried led discussions of important literary topics); *April 15*—*Great Voices from Great Books*, "Mind" (with Mortimer J. Adler); *April 22*—*Great Voices from Great Books*, "Humor" (with Steve Allen); *April 29*—*Great Voices from Great Books*, "Government" (with Eugene Burdick); *May 6*—*Great Voices from Great Books*, "God" (with Mortimer J. Adler); *May 13*—*Great Voices from Great Books*, "Shakespeare" (with Dr. Bergen Evans); *May 20*—*Great Voices from Great Books*, "Poetry" (with Elden Olson); *May 27*—*Great Voices from Great Books*, "The Devil" (with Jaroslav Pelikan); *June 3*—*Great Voices from Great Books*, "The Fountain of Youth" (with Daniel Posin); *June 10*—*Great Voices from Great Books*, "The Villain of the Piece" (with Dr. Bergen Evans); *June 17*—*Great Voices from Great Books*, "Art" (with Frank Schulze); *June 24*—*Great Voices from Great Books*, "Religious Tolerance" (with Jaroslav Pelikan); *July 1*—*Great Voices from Great Books*, "Mathematics" (with Daniel Posin); *July 8*—*Great Voices from Great Books*, "Education" (with George N. Shuster); *September 17*—*Stump the Stars* (last gasp of "Pantomime Quiz" series: Conried was a semi-regular until the final episode on September 16, 1963), CBS; *December 12*—*The Danny Thomas Show* (Conried as Uncle Tonoose), CBS

1963

(unknown date)—*The Object Is* (quiz show), ABC (?); *January 21*—*The Danny Thomas Show* (Uncle Tonoose needs glasses), CBS; *February 4*—*Lucy Show*, "Lucy's Barbershop Quartet," CBS; *April 29*—*The Danny Thomas Show* (Conried as Uncle Tonoose), CBS; *May 29*—*U.S. Steel Hour*, "A Taste of Champagne," CBS; *September 1963*—**Fractured Flickers** (debut of syndicated Jay Ward

produced series: Conried as host and sometimes narrator: 26 episodes were filmed and shown, off and on, for many years in syndication; the celebrities interviewed by Conried were [in this order]: Rose Marie, Fabian, Gypsy Rose Lee, Allan Sherman, Annette Funicello, Edward Everett Horton, Paula Prentiss, Sebastian Cabot, Roddy McDowall, Vivien Della Chiesa, Connie Stevens, Rod Serling, Connie Hines, Cesar Romero, Diana Dors, Bullwinkle J. Moose [as a puppet], Deborah Walley, Paul Lynde, Anna Maria Alberghetti, Ruta Lee, Barbara Eden, Bob Denver, Pat Carroll, Bob Newhart, Ursula Andress, and Zsa Zasa Gabor); *September 18*—*The Tonight Show* (with Johnny Carson), NBS; *September 22*—*DuPont Show of the Week*, "Holdup," NBC; *September 30*—*Lucy Show*, Lucy Plays Cleopatra," CBS; *November 11*—*The Danny Thomas Show* (Conried as Uncle Tonoose), CBS; *December 23*—*Under Discussion* (Conried was on panel that included actor, Terry-Thomas), KTTV

1964

(unknown date)—*The Willies* (series pilot: George Gobel production); *January 9*—*Truth or Consequences* (Conried appeared as a guest at least once), NBC; *January 31*—*Burke's Law*, "Who Killed April?" ABC; *April 15*—*Made in America* (Conried as emcee of panel show until May 3), CBS; *September 13*—*Happy Birthday, Will* (special: 400th birthday of Shakespeare: Conried narrated, read selections, and did short performances as three different characters), NBC; *October 15*—*Dr. Kildare*, "The Last Leaves on the Tree," NBC; *October 19*—*Harris Against the World* (one segment of series *90 Bristol Court*), NBC; *October 24*—*Gilligan's Island*, "Wrongway Feldman," CBS; *November 15*—*Walt Disney Presents*, "Ben & Me" (animated 1953 short), CBS; *December 9*—*Burke's Law*, "Who Killed 711?" ABC

1965

(unknown date)—*The Celebrity Game* (panel show: Conried was a guest on at least one episode), CBS; *January 27*—*Burke's Law*, "Who Killed Rosie Sunset?" ABC; *February 14*—*The Danny Thomas TV Family Reunion* (special), NBC; *March 1*—*Ben Casey*, "A Dipperful of Water from a Poisoned Well," ABC; *March 13*—*Gilligan's Island*, "The Return of Wrongway Feldman," CBS; *May (?)*—*The Tonight Show* (starring Johnny Carson: Conried was a guest), NBC; *December 31*—*Farmer's Daughter*, "Simple Joys of Nature," ABC

1966

February 11—*Hogan's Heroes*, "The Pizza Parlor" (Conried as "Major Bonacelli"; Vito Scotti would play Bonacelli in the "The Return of Major Bonacelli" which aired on March 15, 1969), CBS; *July 4*—*I'll Buy That* (premiere episode of new version of the 1950s quiz show); *October 8*—*Please Don't Eat the Daisies*, "At Home with the Family," NBC (re-broadcast: 7/1/67)

1967

January 11—*Lost in Space*, "The Questing Beast," CBS; *October 24*—*Kismet* (special: Conried as the "Wazir"), CBS; *November 6*—*Danny Thomas Hour*, "Make More Room for Daddy," NBC; *December 11*—*Danny Thomas Hour*, "The Royal Follies of 1933," NBC; *December 18*—*The Cricket on the Hearth* (animated special with Danny and Marlo Thomas), NBC

1968

January 22—*The Monkees*, "The Monkees Paw," NBC; *February 28*—*The Beverly Hillbillies*, "The Clampetts Fiddle Around" (as the "Great Stromboli"), CBS; *February 29*—*Daniel Boone*, "Orlando the Prophet" (Conried as Orlando), NBC; *November 18*—*The Beverly Hillbillies*, "The Thanksgiving Spirit" (Conried returns as "Stromboli"), CBS

1969

October 14—*Wake Me When the War Is Over* (TV movie: Conried is hilarious as raving ex–Nazi Herman Erhardt; his 6 minutes are the best bits in the film; with Ken Berry and Eva Gabor), ABC; *November 24*—*Love, American Style*, "Love and the Good Deal," ABC

1970

(unknown date)—*Easter Is* (animated special narrated by Conried); *(unknown date)*—*The Debbie Reynolds Show* (Conried was a guest on at least one episode), NBC; *March 19*—*Dr. Seuss' Horton Hears a Who* (animated special), CBS; *August (?)*—*The Merv Griffin Show* (with Conried as guest), CBS; *August 19*—*The Dick Cavett Show* (with Conried as guest), ABC; *September 23*—*Make Room for Granddaddy*, "Make Room for Grandson" (Conried appeared 3 times during the run of this series which ended on September 2, 1971), ABC; *December (?)*—*Christmas Is* (animated special: narrated by Conried)

1971

December 3—*Love, American Style*, "Love and the Tuba," ABC

1972

February 4—*O'Hara, U.S. Treasury*, "Operation: Dorias," CBS; ***February 18***—*Love, American Style*, "Love and the Split Up," ABC; ***August 4***—*The Partners*, "The Magnificent Perception," NBC

1973

September 19—*Here's Lucy*, "Lucy and Danny Thomas," CBS; ***October 15***—*Dr. Seuss on the Loose*, (animated special), CBS; ***December 7***—*Love, American Style*, "Love and the Footlight Fiancée," ABC; ***December (?)***—*The Christmas Visit* (30 min. special describing the meaning of Christmas)

1974

(unknown date)—*Carnival of Animals* (special: Conried reads an Ogden Nash poem), PBS

1975

March 7—*Kolchak: The Night Stalker*, "The Knightly Murders," ABC

1977

(unknown date)—*The Liar's Club* (Conried was a guest panelist on at least one episode), syndicated; ***May 15***—*The Wonderful World of Disney*, "Disney's Greatest Villians," NBC; ***August 22***—*The Match Game* (Conried as guest panelist), CBS; ***August 23***—*The Match Game*, CBS; ***August 24***—*The Match Game*, CBS; ***August 25***—*The Match Game*, CBS; ***August 26***—*The Match Game*, CBS; ***October 1***—*The Tony Randall Show* [?], CBS; ***October 29***—*Halloween Is Grinch Night* (animated special), ABC; ***November 27***—*The Hobbit* (animated special: Conried as "Thorin Oakenshield"), NBC; ***December (?)***—*The Trolls and the Christmas Express* (special)

1978

January 21—*The Tony Randall Show*, [?], CBS; ***February 18***—*The Tony Randall Show*, "Supernatural," CBS; ***February 24***—*Quark*, "May the Source Be with You" (parts 1 & 2: voice of "The Source"), NBC; ***May 5***—*Supertrain*, "Where Have you Been, Billy Boy?" NBC; ***October 17***—*Laverne and Shirley*, "Laverne and Shirley Go to Night School," ABC; ***November 19***—*The World of Disney*, "Mickey Mouse 50th Anniversary Celebration," NBC

1979

January 22—*Fantasy Island*, "The Second Mrs. Winslow," ABC; ***February 10***—*The Love Boat*, "Dream Ship," ABC; ***March 25***—*Alice*, "The Last 'Stow It'" (Part 1: Conried as "Randolph Briggs"), CBS; ***April 11***—*Alice*, "The Last 'Stow It'" (Part 2: Conried again as "Randolph Briggs"), CBS; ***May 12***—*The Return of the King* (special 2 hour animated Tolkien epic), NBC; ***September 14***—*Fantasy Island*, "Goose for the Gander," ABC; ***December 16***—*World of Disney*, "The Adventures of Major Effects," NBC

1980

(unknown date)—*Scruffy* (animated TV movie: Conried as voice of "Tibbles": 60 minutes); ***June 3***—*The Incredible Book Escape* (animated children's special), CBS

1981

(unknown date)—*Faeries* (animated special narrated by Conried based on book by Brian Froud and Alan Lee); ***February 2***—*Fantasy Island*, "A Very Strange Affair," ABC; ***March 27***—*The American Dream*, "Crossing Patterns" (Conried a regular as "Abe Berlowitz"), ABC; ***April 26***—*The American Dream* (official premiere of series), ABC; ***April 27***—*The American Dream*, [?], ABC; ***May 5***—*The American Dream*, [?], ABC; ***May 26***—*The American Dream*, [?], ABC; ***July 26***—*Greatest Heroes of the Bible: Daniel and Nebuchadnezzar* (filmed in 1979), NBC; ***November 11***—*George Burns' Early, Early, Early Christmas Show* (special), NBC; ***December 6***—*Through the Magic Pyramid* (Pt 1: TV movie), NBC; ***December 13***—*Through the Magic Pyramid* (Pt. 2: TV movie), NBC

1982

January 2—*Fantasy Island*, [?], ABC; ***March 21***—*Barefoot in the Park* (special: Filmed live in Seattle in early December of 1981), HBO

1983

(unknown date)—*The Music Shoppe* (Children's show: Conried filmed his scenes in December of 1981); ***August 19***—*Alison Sidney Harrison* (series pilot: filmed in 1981), NBC; ***(unknown date)***—*The Music of the 1930s*, A network special starring Jose Ferrer; probably was broadcast in the early 1970s

D. Stage Work

The list below is designed to give the reader an idea of the variety of work Hans Conried did on the stage after 1950. The dates and places given are for the first performance of the tour. Subsequent dates are also listed for some shows. Typically, the summer and winter tours had different supporting cast members. I have not listed every reading Conried gave at colleges, universities, and women's groups between the years 1960 and 1974. During his heyday in the 1960s, Conried was able to schedule up to 500 readings in a single year in addition to his stage, television, and voice work, and miscellaneous speaking engagements. Conried's character in the play is shown in brackets.

1953

Can-Can—Sam S. Shubert Theatre, New York, NY: May 17 [Boris Adzinidzinadze]: Cast included: Lilo, Gwen Verdon, Erik Rhodes, Phil Leeds, and Peter Cookson.

1956

The Student Prince—Greek Theater, Los Angeles, CA: July 30—August 11 [Johann Lutz]: Cast included: Maria Tallchief, Andre Eglevsky, Brian Sullivan, and Eliane Malbin.

1957

Can-Can—St. Louis Municipal Opera, St. Louis, MO: July 29—August 4 [Boris Adzinidzinadze]: Cast included: Dolores Gray, Norwood Smith, Marcella Dodge, and Ferdinand Hilt.

1958

Lady in the Dark—St. Louis Municipal Opera, St. Louis, MO: July 7—13 [Russell Paxton]: Cast included Dolores Gray, Edmund Lyndeck, Ken Harvey, and Katherine Thomas.

Rosalinda—St. Louis Municipal Opera, St. Louis, MO: July 21—27 [Prince Orlofsky]: Cast included: Jean Fenn, Ralph Herbert, Wilber Evans, and Mia Slavenska.

1959

Tall Story—New Locust Theatre, Philadelphia, PA: January 8—25 [Prof. Leon Solomon]: Cast included: Marian Winters, Robert Wright, Marc Connelly, and Mason Adams.

Tall Story—Belasco Theatre, New York, NY: January 29 [Prof. Leon Solomon]: (same cast as New Locust production)

Song of Norway—St. Louis Municipal Opera, St. Louis, MO: June 22—June 28 [Count Peppi Le Loup]: Cast included: Deni Lamont, Claramae Turner, and Alice Nunn.

Tall Story—Edgewater Beach Playhouse, Edgewater Beach, FL: July 6—19 [Prof. Leon Solomon]: Cast included: Frances Chaney, Ludwig Donath, Joe Ponazecki, and JoAnn LeCompte.

Tall Story—Cass Theatre, Detroit, MI: October 27—November 8 [Prof. Leon Solomon]: Cast included: Will Geer, Jen Nelson, Dermot Cronin, and JoAnn LeCompte.

1960

Not in the Book—New Music Fair/Dixie Plaza, Toronto, Ontario, Canada: June 13—18 [Andrew Bennett]: Cast included: Brook Byron, Francis Compton, and James Valentine.

The Reclining Figure—Edgewater Playhouse Theatre, Chicago, IL: June 26 [?]: Special benefit performance.

Not in the Book—Edgewater Beach Hotel, Chicago, IL: June 27—July 10 [Andrew Bennett]: Cast included: Brook Byron, Francis Compton, and James Valentine

1961

Mr. Belvedere—Drury Lane Theatre, Chicago, IL: April 16 [Mr. Belvedere]: Cast included: Gwen

Davenport, John Himes, Charlene Lee, and Catherine Payne.

The Pleasure of His Company—Westport Country Playhouse, Westport, CT: June 15—July 14 [Biddeford "Pogo" Poole—"International playboy, adventurer, and athlete"]: Cast included: Cornelia Otis Skinner, Hilda Brawner, and Bernard Wu.

1962

Critic's Choice—Royal Poinciana Playhouse, Palm Beach, CA: March 26 [Parker Ballentine]: Cast included: Mldred Natwick, Virginia Gilmore, Ludi Claire, Robert Field. A young Richard Thomas had the role of John Ballantine. He took over from Arthur Norden, who had done the role on Broadway the season before: Winter cast included: Frances Helm, Michaele Myers, Robert Heller, Ethel Shutta, and Don Scardino.

1963

Take Her, She's Mine—Royal Poinciana Playhouse, Palm Beach, FL: January 28—February 9 [Frank Michaelson]: Cast included: Elizabeth Ashley, Ludi Claire, Mary Harrigan, and James Farentino.

Send Me No Flowers—Drury Lane Theatre, Chicago, IL: June 11—July 7 [George Kimball]: Cast included: Norman Barasch, Carroll Moore, and Evelyn King.

Take Her, She's Mine—Mineola Playhouse, Long Island, NY: July 9—20 [Frank Michaelson]: Cast included: Irene Hervey, Heidi Murray, Nancy Gouglas, and Anthony Roberts.

1964

Take Her, She's Mine—Storrowton Music Fair, W. Springfield, MA: June 8—13 [Frank Michaelson]: Cast included: Augusta Dabney, Jean M. Hickey, Linda Lavin, Jon Voight, Jerry Hausner, and Anthony Roberts.

Tall Story—Avondale Playhouse, Indianapolis, IN: September 1—6 [Prof. Leon Solomon]: Cast included: Marilyn Wayne, Anita Bayless, James Harder Don Fenwick, and Tom Adkins.

1965

Absence of a Cello—(National Tour)—Sombrero Playhouse, Phoenix, AZ: January 26 [Andrew Pilgrim]: Cast included: Florida Friebus, Dolores Michaels, Nydia Westman, William Christopher, Julie Parrish, and Dennis Patrick. Summer cast included: Fran Carlon, Micheale Myers, Ruth McDevitt, Robert Rovin, Pamela Dunlap, and James Karen (as "Otis Clifton"). Florida Friebus returned in late 1965 for the winter leg of the tour, and Donald Buka took over as "Otis Clifton." The tour ended in June of 1966.

1966

The Student Prince—Los Angeles Civic Light Opera, Los Angeles, CA: July 26, 1966 [Johann Lutz]: Frank Porretta, Eileen Christy, Walter Cassel, and Irra Petina.

1967

Generation—(5 month tour)—Broadway Theatre League/Veterans Memorial Auditorium: Providence, RI: January 14, 1967 [Jim Bolton]: Cast included: Jerry Hausner, Tom Ligon, Nancy Donahue, David Rosenbaum, and Eric James.

Don't Drink the Water—(Woody Allen play): Parker Playhouse, Ft. Lauderdale, FL: December 30, 1967—January 5, 1968 [Walter Hollander]: Cast included: Fritzi Burr, F. Murray Abraham, Carl Bensen, Dick Van Patten, John Fink, Nancy Pinkerton, William Gleason, and Paul Glaser. Summer 1968 cast included: Dody Goodman, Peter Helm, Joan McCall, John Hallow, and Luke Andreas. The cast as of January 1969 included: Vivian Blaine, Gary Krawford, and Gloria Bleezarde.

1968

Generation—Canton-Fulton Summer Arena, Canton, Ohio: June 4, 1968 [Jim Bolton]: Conried and Jerry Hausner were the only returning members of cast from the 1967 tour.

Rosalinda—Civic Light Opera/The Music Center, Los Angeles, CA: September 3 [Prince Orlofsky]: Cast included: Cyril Ritchard, Phil Leeds, Jean Fenn, and Barbara Meister.

1969

Spofford!—(National tour of the U.S., and parts of Canada): Fisher Theater, Detroit, MI: September 8—Oct. 11 [Spofford—a retired, Connecticut chicken farmer]: Cast included: Edmund Williams, Martha Miller, Mary Cooper, and Linda Parrish. The tour ran through March 21, 1970.

1970

Absence of a Cello—The Wichita Community Theatre, Wichita, KS: October 5—10 [Andrew Pilgrim]: Cast included: Betty Loyd, Connie Wilson, Ruth McCormick, and Robert Williams.

Norman, Is That You?—Playhouse on the Mall, Paramus, N.J.: November 3—15 [Ben Chambers]: Cast included: Alec Murphy, Julie Wilson, Victoria Zussin, and Robert H. Rovin.

1971

Norman, Is That You?—Pheasant Run Playhouse, St. Charles, IL: January 15—Feb. 7 [Ben Chambers]: Cast included: Harmon Dresner, and Rick Plastina.

70, Girls, 70—Broadhurst Theatre, New York, N.Y.: April 15 [Harry]: Cast included: Mildred Natwick, Lillian Roth, Gil Lamb, Joey Faye, and Dorothea Freitag.

Norman, Is That You?—Westport Country Playhouse, Westport, CT: August 16—21 [Ben Chambers]: Cast included: Charlotte Rae, Alec Murphy, Peter Simpson, Judith Jordan.

How the Other Half Loves—Playhouse on the Mall, Paramus, N.J.: October 26—November 7 [Frank Foster]: Cast included: Dorothy Tristan, Michael Levin, Isabelle Farrell, John Stewart, and Olympia Dukakis.

1972

Murder Without a Trace (a.k.a.: *Not in the Book*)—Brown Suburban Dinner Theatre, Louisville, KY: March 28: (5 week run) [Andrew Bennett]: Cast included: Donna Pearson, George Gitto, and Courtney Burr.

The Student Prince (Revival)—St. Louis Municipal Opera, St. Louis, MO: August 21—27 [Johann Lutz]: Cast included: Frank Porretta, Walter Cassel, Lee Beery, and Lynne Stuart.

How the Other Half Loves—Colorado Music Hall Dinner Theatre, Denver, CO: September 20—October 29 [Frank Foster]: Cast included: Diane Deckard, Mary Hennessy, Gary Giem, Daniel Fee, and Susan Holloran

Norman, Is That You?—Off Broadway Theatre, San Diego, CA: November 21—December 17 [Ben Chambers]: Cast included: Jay North, and Fritzi Burr.

1973

How the Other Half Loves—Pheasant Run Playhouse, St. Charles, IL: January 12- February 4 [Frank Foster]: Cast included: Diane Deckard, Marla Friedman, and Jerry Ward.

Norman, Is That You?—New Peachtree Playhouse, Atlanta, GA: February 13—18 [Ben Chambers]: Cast included: Alec Murphy, Natalie Priest, Peter Shawn, and Janet Meshad.

Critic's Choice—Westroads Dinner Theatre, Omaha, NE: April 17—May 20: (Dir. By Carl Stohn Jr.) [Parker Ballentine]: Cast included: Melanie Workhoven, Harriet Olson: Jane McDonough, Phil Laurenson, and Patrick Roddy.

My Fair Lady—Theater of the Stars, Atlanta, GA: July 10—July 16 [Alfred P. Doolittle]: Cast included: Michael Allison, and Gaylea Byrne. Edward Mulhare took over for Michael Allison for the August 7—12 run at the Toledo Masonic Auditorium, Toledo, Ohio.

Norman, Is That You?—Cirque Dinner Theatre, Seattle, WA: *Directed by Conried*: September 25—October 14 [Ben Chambers]: Cast included: Adrian Sparks, Don Sparks, Sally Bouton, and Zoaunne Henriot.

1974

How the Other Half Loves—County Dinner Playhouse, Columbus, OH: January 15-22 (Stroke) [Frank Foster]: Cast included: Gaylea Byrne, Alec Murphy, Diane Deckard, and Stephen Bolster.

Irene—Arie Crown Theatre, Chicago, IL: September 11 [Madame Lucy]: Cast included: Debbie Reynolds, Patsy Kelly, Ruth Warrick, Bruce Lea, Ron Husmann, Bob Freschi, Red Pugh, Penny Worth, and Karen Weeden. The cast performed at the Shubert Theatre, Century City, CA from Oct. 24—December 22. Jane Powell took over in the lead on December 28th at the Denver Auditorium Theater, Denver, CO.

1975

Irene—Music Hall, Houston, TX: January 7—12 [Madame Lucy]: Cast included: Jane Powell, Patsy Kelly, Ron Husmann, and Ruth Warrick.

How the Other Half Loves—Cirque Dinner Theatre, Seattle, WA: April 22—May 25, 1975 [Frank Foster]: Trilby Conried was cast as "Fiona Phillips."

The Sunshine Boys—Showplace Theatre, Chesterland, OH: July 14—July 19 [Willie Clark]: Cast included: Lou Jacobi, Josh Burton, and Darlene Parks. Trilby was a part of the winter tour cast that played the South.

Don't Drink the Water—Midnight Sun Dinner Theatre, Atlanta, GA: November 4—30 [Walter Hollander]: Cast included: Annabelle Weenick, B.G. Fitzgerald, Rick Stokes, and James F. Magee.

1976

The Second Time Around—Midnight Sun Dinner Theater, Atlanta, GA: April 27—May 30 [Samuel Jonas]: Cast included: Molly Picon, Richard Armbruster, and Jane Bergere.

Gold Diggers of 1633—Country Dinner Playhouse, Dallas, TX: August 3 [Arnolphe]: Cast included: Ed Lupinsky, Forrest Rankin, and B.G. Fitzgerald.

Something Old, Something New (a.k.a. *The Second Time Around*)—Shubert Theatre, New

Haven, CT: November 6—13 [Samuel Jonas]: Cast included: Molly Picon, Beryl Towbin, Dick Patterson, Matthew Tobin, and Ahvi Spindell.—NOTE: The show went on to play at the New Locust Theatre in Philadelphia from November 15—December 4; and at the Wilbur Theatre in Boston from December 6—22. Beryl Towbin was replaced by Holland Taylor for the Broadway performance.

1977

Something Old, Something New—Morosco Theatre, New York, NY: January 1st [Samuel Jonas]—(Closed on Broadway after one performance): Cast included: Molly Picon, Holland Taylor, Dick Patterson, Matthew Tobin, and Ahvi Spindell.

Barefoot in the Park—Arlington Park Theatre, Arlington, IL: February 4—27 [Victor Velasco]: Cast included: James MacArthur, Lucy Saroyan, Damon Reicheg, Richard Hutt, and Barbara Britton.

The Sunshine Boys—Midnight Sun Dinner Theatre, Atlanta, GA: August 30—September 25 [Willie Clark]: Cast included: Phil Leeds, David Rosenbaum, and Trilby Conried.

The Second Time Around—Golden Apple Dinner Theatre, Sarasota, FL: September 27—October 2 [Samuel Jonas]: Cast included: Molly Picon, Lydia Franklin, and Philip LeStrange.—NOTE: This cast performed at the Theatre of the Performing Arts in Miami Beach from October 4—9; and the Parker Playhouse in Ft. Lauderdale from October 11—16.

1978

The Second Time Around—Golden Apple Dinner Theatre, Miami Beach, FL: February 14- March 26 [Samuel Jonas]: Cast included: Molly Picon, and Lydia Franklin.

The Sunshine Boys—Griffin Dinner Theatre: Tacoma, WA: April 30—June 3rd [Willie Clark]: Cast included: Jerry Hausner, Bill Buck, Jason West, and Mara Locke.

Don't Drink the Water—Beverly Dinner Playhouse, New Orleans, LA: June 23rd [Walter Hollander]: Cast included: Annabelle Weenick, David Gray, Trilby Conried, and George Sanchez.

She Loves Me—Pittsburgh Civic Light Opera, Pittsburgh, PA: August 15—20 [Mr. Maraczek]: Cast included: John Schuck, Jeanne Lehman, Betty Gillett, and David Holliday.

The Sunshine Boys—Beef & Boards Dinner Theatre, Simpsonville, KY: October 4—29 [Willie Clark]: Cast included: Jerry Hausner, Terry Baker, Thelma Louise Carter, Jerry Sehr, and Janelle Moore.

1979

Barefoot in the Park—Stage West Theatre Restaurant, Edmonton, Alberta, Canada: February 22—31 [Victor Velasco]: Cast included: Jane Kean, Lucy Hutchins, and Joe Hecht.

Funny Thing Happened on the Way to the Forum—St. Louis Municipal Opera, St. Louis, MO: July 2—8 [Senex]: Cast included: Avery Schreiber, Artie Johnson, and John Carradine.

Side by Side by Sondheim—Charles Playhouse, Boston, MA: September 25—October 7 [Conried as the narrator]: Cast included: Joe Masiell, Ann Hodapp, and Cynthia Meryl.

1980: (No stock tours this year).

1981

Never Too Late—The Little Theatre on the Square, Sullivan, IL: August 11—August 23 [Harry Lambert]: Cast included: Trilby Conried, Dude Hatten, and David Gray.

Barefoot in the Park—Moore Theatre, Seattle WA: December 1—5: (Paramount Productions: Filmed for HBO TV broadcast) [Victor Velasco]: Cast included: Richard Thomas, Bess Armstrong, James Cromwell, and Barbara Barrie.

E. Voice Work

This log attempts to encompass all of the live-action short subjects (as narrator only), animated short subjects, cartoons, audio books, phonograph records, and other miscellaneous voice projects Hans Conried completed during his career. There are a number of films he did for corporate clients that are, for the most part, lost. The log should give the reader a good idea of the large variety of voice work Hans Conried performed on. There is a section covering other projects—not limited to voice work alone—that do not fall into a specific category. In the case of phonograph records, only details of the initial release will be given. Some of the material has been reproduced on cassettes or CD's.

Live Action Short Subjects—Conried as Narrator Only

1947 ***Down to Earth***—Columbia—D: Alexander Hall.

1960 ***The Meat Packers***—Privately made short film commissioned by an industrial meat packing company for training purposes.

1960? ***Faces and Fortunes***—Training film produced by Morton and Millie Goldsholl for the Kimberly-Clark Corporation. Conried narrated this look back into history, and the events that shaped the modern corporate mindset. The film hoped that by "simplifying and clarifying corporate identity," all the drones would come together for their own corporate good.

1970 ***Up Is Down***—(Educational film: Privately made.)

Animated Short Subjects and Cartoons

1945 ***Sliphorn, King of Polaroo***—Universal—Walter Lanz Productions—D: Dick Lundy: Conried provided the narration. Released theatrically on March 19, 1945.

1945 ***Woody Woodpecker: Woody Dines Out***—Universal—Walter Lantz Productions—D: James Culhane: Conried provides the voice of the feline taxidermist who wants to stuff Woody for a $100,000 prize from the Natural History Museum. Woody outsmarts him, of course. Conried's voice is so laid-back that it is almost nonexistent. Released theatrically on May 14, 1945.

1953 ***The Emperor's New Clothes***—Columbia—D: Ted Parmelee: Conried narrated this familiar fairy tale. The cartoon was a part of Columbia's "Jolly Frolics" series: 7 minutes.

1953 ***Ben & Me***—Walt Disney Productions—D: Hamilton Luske: Animated 2 reel short released on November 11, 1953: Typical Disney story about an amazing mouse named Amos, and how he was really the brains behind most of Benjamin Franklin's discoveries. Amos even had a hand in writing the "Declaration of Independence." Conried provided the voice of Thomas Jefferson, and was the animator's model for the character. He can also be heard as one of the crooks whispering over a barrel in one scene.

1955 ***The Invisible Moustache of Raoul Dufy***—UPA—Animated short about the life and career of artist, Raoul Dufy. Various examples of Dufy's paintings are shown, and Conried discussed the effect they had on people. Released on video as part of the *Gerald McBoing Boing Presents: Favorite Painters* collection: 12 minutes.

1957 ***The Woody Woodpecker Show***—Walter Lantz Productions—ABC television premiered a show featuring that animated troublemaker, Woody Woodpecker, on October 3, 1957. Each show featured cartoons that had been theatrically released previously, and little connecting bits with Woody, and Walter Lantz in the flesh talking about the art of animation. During this time, Conried was the voice of "Wally Walrus." The series folded on September 25, 1958, but would be resurrected (in a different form) by NBC in 1970, and then again in 1976. In the later incarnations, Paul Frees took over as Wally.

1957 *The Story of Anyburg, U.S.A.* — Walt Disney Productions: Short cartoon attempts to teach about the perils of poor driving on our country's roads. Conried can be heard as the comically anguished plaintiff being arraigned for a driving offense.

1960s *"Peter" series of short cartoons* — Fleetwood Films — Written by Israel Berman — Music by Joseph Kince: Information is scarce about this series of 4.5 minute cartoons that came out in the late 1960s featuring a little boy named Peter, his friend Suzy, and his dog Lucifer. By the look of the animation, these films were probably made in Eastern Europe and dubbed for American distribution. Conried provided the narration for the following titles: *Peter's Merry Space Trip, Peter and the Crystal Ball, Peter at the Zoo, Peter and the Martian, Peter in the Land of Toys, Peter and His Time Machine, Peter and His Mechnical Dog*, and *Peter's Christmas Tree*.

1961 *The Bullwinkle Show [Dudley Do-Right of the Mounties]* — Jay Ward Productions: The first appearance on network television of Jay Ward's legendary moose, "Bullwinkle," and the flying squirrel named "Rocky" was on the Sunday afternoon ABC series called *Rocky and His Friends* that premiered in 1959. This version ended in September of 1961, after which, NBC quickly picked up the characters for another season under the title of *The Bullwinkle Show*. Added to the growing stable of cartoons was a series called *Dudley Do-Right of the Mounties*. Conried had a great time giving life to the dastardly villain, "Snidely Whiplash," who was the bane of young Do-Right's existence. Episodes were included in the half hour show, along with the original titles of *Fractured Fairy Tales, Aesop and Son, Peobody's Improbable History*, and of course, *The Adventures of Bullwinkle and Rocky*. The series effectively ended in September of 1964, but ABC picked up the large amount of accumulated re-runs and ran them at various spots in their schedule until 1973, when the show became syndicated. For more information, please seek out Keith Scott's amazing, everything-you-could-ever-want-to-know book on Jay Ward, Bill Scott, and all of the other geniuses behind the best-loved cartoons of the 1960s.

1964 *Hoppity Hooper* — Jay Ward Productions: This nearly forgotten cartoon series was given a home (temporarily) by ABC television. The show debuted on September 12, 1964, and would run on ABC until September 2, 1967. It would later be syndicated, and was seen sporadically over the years. The main character, of course, was Hoppity, the loveable little frog (voiced by Chris Allen). Conried played a conniving, despicable, yet oddly loveable (in a crusty sort of way), old fox named "Uncle Waldo Wigglesworth." Bill Scott was the voice of Waldo's sidekick, Fillmore, the dim-witted bear who loved to blow his bugle.

1970s *[Training Film]* — Borg Warner Corporation, Cleveland, Ohio: Animated industrial training film. Conried provided the voice of an old, German professor.

1973 *Butch Cassidy and the Sundance Kids* — Hanna-Barbera Studios: NBC Saturday morning television cartoon series that premiered on September 8, 1973. Conried regularly provided his vocal talents until the show went off the air on August 31, 1974. Lucas "Chip" Hand, III was "Butch," and Mickey Dolenz voiced "Harvey."

1977(?) *King Midas/The Salty Sea* — Both are animated short subjects (approx. 7 minutes long) made primarily for distribution to schools. Conried narrated each classic folk tale. They were probably originally released on video around 1977 or 1978. In 1991, a video compilation called *Adventures in Learning: King Midas... and More!* was released by Diamond Entertainment Corp., and included both animated shorts.

1978 *The Youth Who Wanted to Shiver, The Fisherman & His Wife, The Three Golden Hairs, Tom Thumb*, and *Hans in Luck* — Golden Book Video — Bosustow Entertainment Inc. — D: Sam Weiss: Nick Bosustow made frequent use of Conried's vocal talent — often in tandem with June Foray — in the late 1970s. The animation is not of the best quality, but often quite imaginative. Conried provided the narration and voices for all the male characters. The majority of the work Conried did for Bosustow was destined for children's videos marketed by Golden Book Video that did not credit the voice artists on the cover. It is possible that other titles featuring Conried are out there waiting to be discovered.

1980(?) *The Nutcracker* (Russian produced animated short) — Soyuzmult Film Studios: Voice only: This animated film was originally made in 1978, and then a dubbed version was released in the early 1980s in the U.S. Conried is the voice of the evil Mouse King: 26 minutes.

1980 *The Drak Pack* — Hanna-Barbera Studios: NBC Saturday morning cartoon series that first aired on September 6, 1980. The wacky adventures of the "Big D" (Dracula), and his gang. Their evil nemesis was "Dr. Dred," who managed to get around pretty well in his "Dredgible." Conried had some fun with creating the voice for this comical villain.

Phonograph Recordings and Audio Books

1941 *A Christmas Carol*—Decca DA 290 (78 RPM): Ronald Colman stars in this production of Dickens's classic Christmas story. Conried is the voice of the First Ghost.

1947 *A Christmas Carol*—MGM-16—(78 RPM): Starring Lionel Barrymore. Probably the best loved version of this story at the time. Barrymore played Scrooge on the radio every Christmas for many years beginning in 1939. Conried was often Marley's Ghost, but sometimes played Bob Cratchit. MGM re-issued this recording on a 45 RPM EP in 1953 (X16); and as a 33 1/3 LP (E-520) in 1955.

1952 *The Story of a Piano*—RCA EPB 3045 (2, 45 RPM set): Fanciful story created by pianist Andre Previn and told from the piano's point-of-view. Conried is the voice of the piano that tells the story of its origins, and dream to be played at Carnegie Hall. Previn and others provide the musical interludes.

1953 *Can-Can*—Capitol S/DW-452: Original Broadway cast recording made on May 17, 1953.

1958 *The Sounds of Holland*—Capitol T 10133: Conried narrates a travelogue of Holland complete with authentic sounds recorded on location. Conried had to do his work stateside in a recording studio, unfortunately.

1959 *Treasure Island*—Audio Book C-309/6027 (16 RPM): The most wonderful six hours you could ever spend. Conried is delightful as the voice of Jim Hawkins, and everyone else in this Robert Louis Stevenson story.

1959 *America Listens to Literature*—Produced by Vocab Records for Scott, Foresman & Company (LP #3165): The record was made to accompany the book: *Good Times Through Literature*. Both were distributed primarily to schools. Narrated by Richard S. Breen, and featuring Conried and others reading various selections. Conried read from Edgar Allan Poe's "The Pit and the Pendulum."

1959 *Monster Rally*—RCA LSP-1923: One of those frivolous, but fun, novelty albums released in the late 1950s. Conried actually sings: "Flying Saucer," "Not of this Earth," "What Do You Hear From the Red Planet Mars," and the popular (at the time), "The Purple People Eater"—supposedly, the entire album was conceived primarily to capitalize on the success of that one song. Alice Pearce sings four more songs, and then there are a few numbers done by the anonymous "The Creatures." The album was recorded in New York City on August 21st and 28th, and September 4th of 1958. Prized today for its original cover art by illustrator, Jack Davis.

1960s *The First Christmas*—Eva Tone sound sheet—This flimsy, black plastic disc was originally included with a box of cereal. Conried narrates the classic holiday story.

1960 *Peter Meets the Wolf in Dixieland*—Strand 1001: The first release on the enigmatic Strand label. The first side features Conried—who often puts on his best "these people are beneath me" sneer—narrating the classic tale to Pee Wee Erwin's rather mangled Dixieland version of Prokofiev's beloved music. The second side is purely instrumental, and allows Pee Wee and the Dixieland All-Stars to slap around their own versions of some of the familiar themes of the Prokofiev score.

1961 *Panorama Colorslide Programs*—Columbia Record Club (by subscription only): Conried as the narrator on each 7," 33 1/3 RPM disc listed below. The record was included with a hardcover book, and set of 2 cards of 32 color slides:

Holland: Fantastic Land Below the Sea—Columbia ZLP 54129/30

Tour of the Kröller-Müller Museum, Otterlo, Holland—Columbia ZLP 53064/5

Tour of the Museum of Sao Paulo, Brazil—Columbia ZLP 53070/1

The Wonders of the Pacific Shore—Columbia ZLP 52451/2

Camouflage in Nature—Columbia ZLP 53229/30

1961 *Feathertop*—Mars, Inc. LP-232: A limited edition recording made from the October 19, 1961 ABC television special. Conried and Hugh O'Brian sing "Intimate Friends."

1963? *Trilby's Trio*—Prologue Records, Hollywood: Possibly a privately pressed album showcasing the talents of a seven-year-old girl named Trilby Lundgren. Miss Lundgren was something of a child prodigy on the piano, and her "trio" consisted of Beethoven, Bach, and Brahms. Conried can be heard giving some commentary about classical music, and his picture is on the back cover.

His relationship to the Lundgren's is not known, but the young lady's name would have been reason enough to pique Conried's interest.

1964 *An Interview with Henry David Thoreau*—Scott, Foresman & Co. #3178: A record and filmstrip produced for distribution to schools. A student named Arlene Nadel interviews Conried, as Thoreau, in the present day. Conried does a convincing New England accent, and maintains a good control throughout. A fine performance.

1966 *Walt Disney's Peter Pan*—Walt Disney Productions #1206—LP with 11 page booklet: Selections from the 1953 animated film featuring the voices of Conried, Bobby Driscoll, and Kathryn Beaumont.

1967 *Dynamic Denton: in Sound and Music*—Privately issued pressing made by Jodie Lyons: Conried was paid to narrate a special album created to espouse the virtues of Denton, Texas. He shows what a true professional he was by managing to sound thoroughly excited and enthusiastic about a place he'd probably never seen before.

1969 *Dr. Seuss: Happy Birthday to You!*—Caedmon TC 1287: Conried does a fine job of reading the title track, along with, "The Big Brag," "Gertrude McFuzz," "Scrambled Eggs Super!" and "To Think I Saw It on Mulberry Street."

1970s *The 5,000 Fingers of Dr. T*—G.S.F. 1007: Even though the official soundtrack for this 1953 "Wonder Musical" was never released, some enterprising (and very fortunate) soul managed to shanghai the tapes and produce an "unofficial" copy in the early 1970s. What is remarkable about this release is that it contains the 11 songs that were cut from the final version of the film. The quality of the cut songs, as compared to the rest of the album, is often poor, and sound as if they were taken from rehearsal sessions. Nevertheless, they are a marvel to hear for any *Dr. T* buff. Conried singing "My Favorite Note" is especially delightful, and makes one wonder what the original scene would have looked like with Dr. T posturing in front of his gigantic portrait while singing to Mrs. Collins. The cover was well done, and includes informative liner notes and stills from the film.

1971 *70, Girls, 70*—Columbia S-30589: Original cast recording.

1977 *Hardie Gramatky: All the Little Toot Stories*—Caedmon TC 1528: Enjoyable stories of the courageous "Little Toot" the tugboat, and his many adventures on the Grand Canal, the Thames, the Mississippi, and in the San Francisco Bay. Conried reads the stories with affection.

NOTE: Conried's performances were not included on the soundtrack albums released for *High Tor, 1001 Arabian Nights, A Cricket on the Hearth,* and *Summer Stock.*

Live-Action and Animated Commercials

1947 *Ajax Commercial*—Shamus Culhane Productions—Conried was the voice of one of the "Ajax Elves," along with June Foray and Joe Silver in an animated commercial that was made for television. The budget for this tiny masterpiece ran a whopping $5,000.

1955 *Pepsi Cola Commercial*—1:47 minutes: A fun look into the home of your average couple (played by Conried and an unidentified woman) during a break while watching *Annie Get Your Gun*. Conried goes about his business in pantomime while the voice of the commercial announcer (also Conried) follows him from room to room. The husband checks on the kids, and then goes into the kitchen to get a snack. Of course, Pepsi is included.

1958 *New York Times Commercials*: Conried did two radio spots for the newspaper giant, earning a respectable $500. per spot.

1965 *Quisp & Quake Cereal Commercials*—Jay Ward Productions: Beginning in 1965, and continuing until the product's demise in 1973; Conried was often heard as the voice of Snidely Whiplash's doppelganger, "Simon LeGreedy." Bill Scott, William Conrad, Daws Butler, Paul Frees, and June Foray all provided the vocal talent.

1975 *TWA Commercial*—Conried was paid to do a radio spot for the airline.

1981 *Sun Giant Raisins Commercial*—Bozell & Jacobs, Inc.: Live-action commercial featuring a company boardroom with Conried at the helm. This commercial was nominated for an industry award.

Miscellaneous—Including Work That Wasn't Strictly Voice Only

1959 *Sleeping Beauty*—Walt Disney Productions—D: Clyde Geronimi: Conried's voice was not heard in this elaborate, and extravagant animated feature, but his body was seen (in a manner of speaking). Disney once again called upon Conried to appear in a live-action film for the animators dressed in the character of King Stefan. So, the figure you see in the film is modeled after Conried, but his voice was not used.

1961 *The Name's the Game!*—"Invented" by Bob Shanks with pictures by Ann Zane Shanks. Philadelphia: Chilton Company. This is an odd little book that takes full advantage of Shanks' job as talent coordinator for *The Jack Paar Show*. Shanks writes in tongue-in-cheek fashion how essential it is for success to have the right name, and created a party game to facilitate the selection process: "[The authors] are confident that you, emboldened by a good cocktail party, will find the right name, not only for yourself, but for every conceivable occupation." Jack Paar, Conried, Dody Goodman, Genevieve, Jose Mellis, Peter Sellers, and others are pictured in comical poses with a text clue to help partygoers find a good name—e.g.: "German opera star"—Conried dressed in lederhosen, singing, while being inflated with air through a tube in his shirt—Name: Gustof Wind.

1962 (?) *Shakespeare Primer*—Educational film produced for distribution to schools only. Conried is seen and heard reciting excerpts from *Richard III, Romeo & Juliet, Hamlet, As You Like It, The Merchant of Venice,* and *King Lear*. He also has an opportunity to comment on Shakespeare's life and times: 30 minutes.

1963 *Deb Star Ball*—16 MM newsreel footage of Conried as Master of Ceremonies. Many other celebrities are in attendance, including: Walter Pidgeon, Pat O'Brien, Hugh O'Brian, Sal Mineo, Bobby Sherman, Imogene Coca, Gloria Loring, and Ed Wynn: Approximately 10 minutes.

1978 *Outsmarting Crime: An Older Person's Guide to Safer Living*—A public service announcement commissioned by the Attorney General's office of the State of Washington. It was distributed as a slide presentation with a recorded narration performed by Conried The tape was recorded in Tacoma, Washington.

1981 *The Story of the Hotel del Coronado, San Diego, CA*: Conried was commissioned to record a forty-two minute long tape of the highlights of the famous hotel's long history. Guests were supplied with cassette players and headphones, and could listen to the tape as they meandered around the hotel and grounds.

Phonograph Recordings of Previously Broadcast Radio Shows

John Barrymore Reads Shakespeare, Volume 1—Audio Rarities AUR 2280; **John Barrymore Reads Shakespeare, Volume 2**—Audio Rarities RARI 2281—Released in 1950, both volumes contain edited broadcasts from the 1937 *Streamlined Shakespeare* series.

Suspense: "Donovan's Brain"—Radiola (?)—Original broadcasts from May 18th and 25th of 1944.

Suspense: "House in Cypress Canyon"—Nostalgia Lane NLF 1022—Original broadcast from December 5, 1946.

The Judy Canova Show—RCA Camden CAL-662—Excerpts from various shows including the 1948 episode where Mr. Hemmingway gives Judy acting lessons so she can act in the charity play.

The Ford Theater: "The Horn Blows at Midnight"—Radiola MR-1068—Hilarious March 4, 1949 broadcast.

The Lux Radio Theatre: "The Wizard of Oz"—Radiola MR-1109—December 25, 1950 broadcast starring Judy Garland. Conried makes a wonderful Scarecrow, even if he isn't allowed to sing!

The Stan Freberg Show #4—Radiola MR-1166—August 4, 1957 broadcast.

Bibliography

Books

Benny, Jack, and Joan Benny. *Sunday Nights at Seven: The Jack Benny Story*. New York: Warner Books, 1990.

Blanc, Mel. *That's Not All Folks!* New York: Warner Books, 1988.

Brooks, Tim, and Earle Marsh. *The Complete Directory to Prime Time Network and Cable TV Shows: 1946–Present*, 7th ed. New York: Ballantine Books, 1999.

Buxton, Frank, and Bill Owen. *The Big Broadcast, 1920–1950*. New York: Flare/Avon Books, 1966; revised 1973.

Dunning, John. *On the Air: The Encyclopedia of Old-Time Radio*. New York: Oxford University Press, 1998.

_____. *Tune In Yesterday: The Ultimate Encyclopedia of Old-Time Radio*. New Jersey: Prentice-Hall, 1976.

Eames, John Douglas. *The MGM Story: The Complete History of Over Fifty Roaring Years*. New York: Crown, 1976.

Gianakos, Larry James. *Television Drama Series Programming: A Comprehensive Chronicle, 1959–1975*. Metuchen, NJ: Scarecrow Press, 1978.

Gitlin, Todd. *Inside Prime Time*. New York: Pantheon Books, 1983.

Halliwell, Leslie. *The Filmgoer's Companion*, revised. New York: Avon Books, 1978.

Hilmes, Michele. *Radio Voices: American Broadcasting, 1922–1952*. Minneapolis: University of Minnesota Press, 1997.

Inman, David. *The TV Encyclopedia*. New York: Perigos Books, 1991.

Kawai, Kazuo. *Japan's American Interlude*. Chicago: University of Chicago Press, 1960.

Kolodin, Irving. *The Metropolitan Opera, 1883–1966*, 4th ed. New York: Borzoi Books/Alfred A. Knopf, 1966.

Kramer, Stanley, with Thomas M. Coffey. *A Mad, Mad, Mad, Mad World: A Life in Hollywood*. New York: Harcourt, 1997.

Leaming, Barbara. *Orson Welles: A Biography*. New York: Viking Press, 1985.

Maltin, Leonard. *Movie & Video Guide*. New York: Signet Books, 1996.

_____. *The Great American Broadcast: A Celebration of Radio's Golden Age*. New York: Dutton Books, 1997.

Moses, Montrose J. *The Life of Heinrich Conried*. New York: Arno Press, 1977 (reprinted from Thomas Y. Crowell Co. 1916 original).

Oppenheimer, Jess, with Greg Oppenheimer. *Laughs, Luck... and Lucy: How I Came to Create the Most Popular Sitcom of All Time*. Syracuse: Syracuse University Press, 1999.

Paar, Jack. *My Saber Is Bent*. New York: Trident Press, 1961.

Parish, James Robert, and Vincent Terrace. *The Complete Actor's TV Credits, 1948–1988*. Metuchen, NJ: Scarecrow Press, 1989.

Quinlan, David. *Quinlan's Illustrated Directory of Film Comedy Actors*. New York: Holt, 1992.

Scott, Keith. *The Moose That Roared: The Story of Jay Ward, Bill Scott, a Flying Squirrel, and a Talking Moose*. New York: Thomas Dunne Books/St. Martin's Press, 2000.

Schwartz, David, with Steve Ryan and Fred Wostbrock. *Encyclopedia of TV Game Shows*, 3rd ed. New York: Checkmark Books, 1999.

Sheldon, Walt. *The Honorable Conquerors: The Occupation of Japan, 1945–1952*. New York: Macmillan, 1965.

Terrace, Vincent. *Television, 1970–1980*. San Diego: A.S. Barnes, 1981.

_____. *Encyclopedia of Television Series, Pilots, and Specials, 1937–1984, Volume III*. New York: Zoetrope Books, 1985.

Thomas, Danny, with Bill Davidson. *Make Room for Danny*. New York: G.P. Putnam's Sons, 1991.

Vallee, Rudy, with Gil McKean. *My Time Is Your Time: The Story of Rudy Vallee*. New York: I. Oblensky, 1962.

Willis, John. *John Willis' Theater World*. New York: Crown Books, 1971; 1974; 1975; 1977, 1978.

Magazine and Newspaper Articles

Hundreds of different sources were used from a multitude of newspaper articles appearing throughout the United States and Canada. Many of these have been noted within the body of the manuscript. The items listed below represent some of the more important sources.

"The Accent's on Versatility." *TV Guide*, April 23, 1960.

Alexander, Mike. "Hans Conried: Looking Back on Hollywood's Pretty Days." *Dallas Times Herald*, August 25, 1976.

Bigsby, Evelyn. "On Supporting Players: Hans Conried." *Radio Life*, December 13, 1942.

Comar, Ann. "Radio's Most Colorful Actor." *Radio Life*, March 12, 1944.

Conried, Hans. "Friends of 'My Friend Irma'." *Radio and TV Mirror*, March 1952.

Denison, Merrill. "The Actor and the Radio." *Theatre Arts Monthly*, November 1933.

Freeman, Donald. "Conried, The Wandering Player: A 'Dream Series' for Hans." *The San Diego Union*, May 3, 1981.

_____. "Hans Conreid (sic): Paar-Boiled Ham." *The San Diego Union*, May 15, 1960.

Gallagher, Peggy. "Conried: Making a Plum Interesting." *Star-Gazette*, August 20, 1965.

Gilkerson, William. "Hans Conried: A Noble Mien in the Day of the Anti-Hero?" *The San Francisco Chronicle*, (Sunday edition) 1968.

Granger, Bob. "Who's Afraid of Television? Hans Conried!" *Radio and TV Mirror*, October 1948.

Hawkins, William. "'Can-Can' Star Right on Time." *New York World Telegram*, June 27, 1953.

"He Plays Conried to the Hilt." *TV Guide*, August 31, 1963.

Heffernan, Harold. "Conried Discovers 'Gold Mine'." *TV Guide*, February 19, 1961.

Hopper, Hedda. "Conried Returns for Holidays, TV." *Los Angeles Times*, December 15, 1959.

Howard, Cy. "The Blonde I Prefer." *Radio Mirror*, April 1949.

Humphrey, Hal. "Hans Is Efficient and Sober." *The Los Angeles Mirror*, August 18, 1952.

_____. "That New 'Luster' You See on Hans Was Put There by J. Paar." *The Los Angeles Mirror*, March 20, 1961.

Lewis, Emory. "That Youngster Hans Conried Talks of '70, Girls, 70'." *The Record*, May 5, 1971.

Maltin, Leonard. "Hans Conried." *Film Fan Monthly*, May 1970.

McDonald, Marci. "The Actor Who's Performance Never Ends." *Toronto Daily Star*, October 11, 1969.

McManus, Margaret. "Hans Conried Can Smell Out Work." (Newspaper unknown), June (?), 1961.

Panagalos, Mary. "Conried on Theater: 'It's a Living'." *Newsday*, (?) 1962.

Pink, Sid. "*The Twonky*: The Film that Nobody Wants to Love." *FilmFax*, April/May 1991.

"Plenty of Work for Hollywood Actors Willing to Hit the Road: Hans Conried." *Variety Daily*, April 22, 1965.

Roberts, Lynn. "Conried's in 'Civvies'." *Radio and TV Mirror*, 1947.

Saunders, Dudley. "'Generation' Star Conried Puts in a Day's Work Before the Curtain Rises." *The Louisville Times*, February 15, 1967.

Schenck, Maria J. "Intermission: Hans Conried." *The Oak Ridger*, February 12, 1962.

Shanley, J.P. "Hans Conried—Busy Freelancer." *New York Times*, October 6, 1957.

Smith, Cecil. "Hans Conried Out Beating Bushes." *Los Angeles Times*, March 19, 1966.

Smith, Darr. (Column dedicated to Hans Conried). *Los Angeles Daily News*, July 10, 1951.

"Three Wise Men of Radio." *Radio Life*, April 20, 1947.

Wiley, Lib. "Veteran Actor Discusses Work." *Daily Advance*, February 20, 1967.

Witbeck, Charles. "Hour-Long Shows Cut Acting Jobs: Hans Reports on Hard Times." *Saginaw News—TV Key*, March 16, 1963.

Wolters, Larry. "Hans Conried Likes the Word 'Lucrative'." *Chicago Daily Tribune*, July 31, 1961.

Internet Sources

The Internet has been an enormous resource for researchers in all fields of study. I have found a multitude of interesting websites devoted to old radio, television, and films—not to mention fan pages, etc. The sites shown below are selected as the most useful for my purposes, and would benefit anyone interested in the subjects they represent.

Big Cartoon Database—www.bcdb.com: This site has information about just about any cartoon you can think of. (You can't search by voice actor's names, unfortunately.)

Broadcast Information Bureau—www.bibnet.com: A "by subscription only" site.

eBay—www.ebay.com: I realize this is an auction site, but this place was extremely helpful to me. I learned about many Hans Conried related items by either viewing or purchasing them through Ebay.

Epguides.Com—www.epguides.com: A large database of episodes from television series past and present.

Internet Movie Database—www.imdb.com: The most comprehensive site dedicated to film on the

Web. The Database also lists many television shows.

Jerry Haendiges Vintage Radio Logs—www.otrsite.com: Very useful resource for episodic logs of old radio shows. Best used as a reference only, as most are not complete.

Library of Congress—www.loc.gov: Direct access to the library's immense catalog.

Old Time Radio—www.old-time.com: A fantastic resource for anyone interested in all facets of old radio. I was able to read broadcast historian Donna Halpern's excellent essay "History of Early Radio," as well as historian Elizabeth McLeod's "Old Time Radio Moments of the Century."

Yesterdayland—www.yesterdayland.com: A great resource chock full of detailed information about Saturday morning cartoons of the past, as well as prime time cartoons.

Other Sources

I was fortunate to have been able to make use of the following taped interviews:

Sam Frank interview with Conried from 1981.

Chuck Schaden "Those Were the Days" radio interview with Conried, January 19, 1971.

AFRTS Interview with Conried and Jerry Hausner recorded in the Philippines, 1970.

Interview with Jerry Hausner recorded by Larry and John Gassman in 1986.

I feel even more fortunate to have been able to view the two interviews filmed in 1959 for *The Mike Wallace Interview* television show that aired on March 18, 1959. I learned a lot about Conried by watching how he handled himself with Mr. Wallace.

Index

Numbers in **bold** refer to photographs.

Absence of a Cello (1965) 145, 146
Actors and Sin see Hecht, Ben
Adams, Edie 125
Adams, Stanley 57
Adventures in Paradise "The Jonah Stone" 125
The Alan Young Show 56
Albert, Eddie 74
Alexander, Ben 111
Allen, Gracie see Burns, George, and Gracie Allen
Allison, Michael 162
Allyson, June 74, 75
The Alphabet Conspiracy 118
The American Dream (TV series) 1974–175
Andress, Ursula 143
Andrews, Julie 107
Arch Oboler's Comedy Theatre "The Ostrich in Bed" (ABC, 1949) 26, 68
Armstrong, Bess 176
Armstong Circle Theatre "Private Eye, Private Eye" 125
Arnaz, Desi 68, 77
Art Students League of New York 133
Arthur, Jean 36
Astaire, Fred 68
Averback, Hy 59
Ayres, Lew 74

Baer, Buddy 132
Ball, Lucille 34, 42, 68, **69**, 76–77
Barefoot in the Park (HBO TV special, 1981) 176
Barefoot in the Park (TV pilot, 1970) 159
The Barkleys of Broadway (MGM, 1949) 68
Barrymore, John 18
Barrymore, Lionel 22, 37
Bartell, Harry 70
Baxter, Dr. Frank 118
Beadle, Spofford J. 155
Behave Yourself! (RKO, 1951) 3, 74, 75
Ben and Me (Disney animated short, 1953) 105
Ben Casey "Dipperful of Water from a Poison Well" 140
Bendix, William 33, 40, 118, **119**
Benny, Jack 59
Bergen, Edgar, and Charlie McCarthy 106
Bergman, Ingrid 41
Berman, Shelley 171
Bernstein, Leonard 116
Berry, Ken 172
Big Jim McClain (Warner Bros, 1952) 75–76

The Big Street (RKO, 1942) 34–35
Bing Crosby Productions see Crosby, Bing
Binyon, Conrad **40**, 41
Bitter Sweet (MGM, 1940) 24
The Blackburn Twins 98
Blanc, Mel 29, 41, 55, 161
Blondell, Gloria 80, **81**
Blondie's Blessed Event (Columbia, 1942) 3, **28–29**
Bogart, Humphrey 36, 41
Bonanova, Fortunio 36
Boone, Richard 73
Breath of Spring 70
Bressart, Felix 57, 58
Brigham Young 14
Brown, John 57
Brown, Vanessa 96, **97**
Buena Vista see Disney, Walt
Buka, Donald 147
Burns, David 160
Burns, George, and Gracie Allen **61**
Burrows, Abe 58, 93, 94, 95, 96, 111
Bus Stop (20th Century-Fox, 1956) 107, 121
Butler, Daws 142
Buttons, Red 116
Bwana Devil see Oboler, Arch
Byington, Spring 92

Cabot, Sebastian 143
Calhern, Louis 72
California Chamber Symphony, Allegro Ball (1981) 176
Can-Can (Broadway, 1953) 94, **95**; audition for part in 93; Cole Porter's work on 94; decision to leave the show 99, 163; move to New York 93; premiere 96; review 96
Can-Can (revival, 1957) 108
Canova, Judy 41
Carlisle, Kitty 122
Carlson, Karen 174
Carradine, John 131, 173
Carson, Johnny 166
Cartwright, Angela: memories of HC 111
Caruso, Enrico: introduced by Heinrich Conried 9
The Cat from Outer Space (Buena Vista, 1978) 172
Cavett, Dick 166
Cederberg, Carl 47
Chaney, Lon, Jr. 143
A Christmas Carol (1940) 37
Clark, Fred 76

Clayton, Jan 66
Close Encounters of the Third Kind 169–170
Coates, Paul V. 76
Coates, Phyllis 76
Cohn, Sammy 84
Coke, Peter 159
Colbert, Claudette 22
Colby, Marion 98
Colman, Ronald 37
Commerce on the Air 13
Condon, Eddie 98
Conrad, William 74, 142
Conried, Alexander (Alex, son): birth of, 106, **108**, 135, 159, 166, 176
Conried, Alfred (brother) 12
Conried, Edith (Edie, daughter): birth of 109, 135, 159, 164; discusses HC's love of Japan 51, **108**; as Las Vegas showgirl 166, 176
Conried, Edith G. (mother): death of 156; marriage to Hans, Sr. 10; mother's day card **21, 66**
Conried, Edwin (half-brother) 9, 12
Conried, Hans (Hans Georg Conried, Jr.) **11, 12, 16, 45, 66, 68, 108, 160, 178**; as Abraham Lincoln 75, 140–141; acting style of 36, 61, 121–122; ad placed in *Variety* (1954) 100, **101**, 102; at AFRS WlKJ in Fusan, Korea **48**; anxiety over losing control 124; appearance of 3, 13, 18, 20, 27, 49, 154, 155–156; at Armed Forces Radio Station WVTM, The Philippines 46–47; awarded an "Annie" 172; awarded an Emmy 172; on being a provincial actor 146–147; benefit show with Kitty Carlisle 122; birth in Baltimore, Maryland 10; birth of Alexander 106; birth of Edie 109; birth of Hans III 99; birth of Trilby 72; "Busiest man in show business" 43; buying books in Indiana **127**; Christmas cards designed by 38, 48; collections of (art, books, stamps, etc.) 23, 70, 100, 144, 158–159, 177; college lecture described by reporter 129–131; compares life in California and New York 94; on "contentment" and purpose in life 139–140; contract with Seagram (gin) 112, **113**; courtship and marriage to Margaret Grant 29, 31; "creamed chicken" circuit 129, **130**; deal with Vocab Records 117; decision to donate body to science 109; difficulties playing himself on TV 67, 110; difficulty for radio actors getting work on TV 105; on dinner theater 167; as director of AFRS Radio Tokyo, Japan 49–50, 51; the disintegration of the studio system 62; on doing a TV series 123; earning a living outside Hollywood 125; eccentric behavior of 26–27, 34, 41, 48, 50, 148, 156, 173; effect of Army service on career 51–52, 55; female fans of 28, 129; as "Frank Foster 10; as geisha **136**, 137; great love of food 141; HC as "heavy mortar crewman" **45**; Honeywell thermostat ad **126**; host of public TV series 132; house in the Hollywood Hills 70; on HUAC's "gray" list 62–63; impersonation of Barrymore 19; increasing bitterness of 169, 171–172; induction into Army, 42–43; John Barrymore's influence on 18; letter to Norman Corwin 47–48; letter to Orson Welles 44–45; love of Japan 49, 51; as the "mark of Cain" 112; *Monster Rally* album 117–118; move to California in 1935 14; move to New York for *Tall Story* 121; new career of stock tours 124; nickname 13; 1959 TV interview with Mike Wallace 118–120; 1962 publicity photo **136**; 1970 USO tour 156–157; opinion of Jazz music 98; opinion of *Oh! Calcutta!* 153; origin of surname 10; possible role in *Judgment at Nuremberg* 131–132; as "Prof. Kropotkin" (*My Friend Irma*) 56, 58, 107; resemblance to Basil Rathbone 32; resurgence of radio drama in 1970s 170; return to radio in 1946 55; roles as Nazi's 3, 32; separation of public and private life 116, 144, 158; shrinking market for character actors 138, 154–155; on signing autographs 112, 121; solidification as comedic actor 110–111, 128; star on Walk of Fame 178; stress of life on the road 148, 162; stroke and the effects of 163–164, 171; struggles between career and family 123, 126, 133; study of Japanese tea ceremony 100; summing up his career 177–178; support of his parents 21, 70, 106; as teetotaler 114; trip to Asia with Jack Paar (1962) 135; trip to England with Jack Paar 126–127; trip to Japan in 1950 72; trip to London 164; TV "feud" with Vincent Price 64; as TV "personality" 110; as "Uncle Tonoose" (*The Danny Thomas Show*) 3, 107, 111, 141; voice work for *Macbeth see* Welles, Orson; with family on 1965 stock tour 145–146; working on *My Friend Irma* 57; working with Josef von Sternberg 114–115; on working with Trilby 166, 175
Conried, Hans Georg III (Hansi, son): birth of 99, **100, 108**; describes trip to Asia (1962) 135–136; as father's dresser 146, 158, 159, 166, 176, 177; trip to New York (1965) 145–146; visit to *Hoppity Hooper* sound stage 144
Conried, Hans Georg, Sr. (H.G., Papa Conried, father): death of 109; declining health 21; description of 21; early life in Vienna and New York 9; first marriage to Flora 9; interviewed about son's Army career 49, 66; marriage to Edith (née Gildersleeve) 10, **12**
Conried, Heinrich (great-uncle) 3; as Heinrich Cohn 10; life and career 9
Conried, Margaret (née Grant, wife) 6, 29, 31, 50, 63, **66**, 70, 72, 75, 93, 99, 102, 106, **108**, 117, 121, 124, 128, 133, 135, 137, 142, 146, 158, 159, 164, 165, 172, 176, 177
Conried, Trilby (daughter) 18; acting career of 165; birth of 72, 82, 93, 99, **100**, 106, **108**, 133–134, 147, 159, 164; on stage with HC 166, 171, 172, 175, 177
Coogan, Jackie 65, **66**
Cooper, Wylis 39
Corwin, Norman 17, 47
Cotton, Joseph 35
Coward, Noel 24
Craig, Burnie and Ruth 93
Crazy House (Universal, 1943) 35–**36**
Crazy Music see *The 5000 Fingers of Dr. T*
Critic's Choice (1962) 134
Critic's Choice (1973) 162
Crosby, Bing (Bing Crosby Productions) 76, 84
Crown Theatre, Starring Gloria Swanson see Swanson, Gloria
Culhane, Shamus 142
"Cyrano de Bergerac" on *Family Theatre* and *The Columbia Workshop* 73

Daley, James 162
Dandridge, Ruby 41
The Danny Thomas Show (1948) 60

The Danny Thomas Show (Make Room for Daddy, CBS) 107, 111
A Date with the Falcon (RKO, 1941) 3, 29, **30**
David, Allen 131, 132
Davis, Bette 39
Davis, Jack 117
Davy Crockett at the Alamo (Disney) 105
December Bride 92
De Haven, Gloria 72
DeMille, Cecil B. 37
Denker, Henry 166, 167, 169
Design for Death (RKO documentary, 1947) 59
DeVol, Frank **64**
deVries, Peter (*Reuben, Reuben*) 155
The Discovery 15
Disney, Walt (Walt Disney Productions/Buena Vista) 73, 79, 105
Dmytryk, Edward 34
A Doctor in Spite of Himself (Molière) 15, 93
Dr. Kildare "Last Leaves on the Tree" 140
Dr. Seuss see Geisel, Theodor
Donohue, Nancy 148, 149
Don't Drink the Water (1978) 170, 171
Douglas, Mike 166
Dragnet "The Big Howard" 111
Dramatic School (MGM, 1938) 21–22
Dudley Do-Right of the Mounties (as voice of Snidely Whiplash) 3, 144
Dulcy (MGM, 1940) 24–25
Dunning, John 71
Dybisz, Dorothy (Dottie Tancredi) 171

Ebert, Bernie 63, 65
Eden, Barbara 150
Education for Death (book) see *Hitler's Children* (RKO, 1942)
Ellis, Anthony 74
Engelhardt, James F.: on casting HC for *The Music Shoppe* 176
Erlenborn, Ray 26–27

Fabares, Shelley 89
Fabian 143
The Falcon Takes Over (RKO, 1942) 29
Farnol, Jeffery 153
Faye, Joey 160
Ferrer, Jose 150
Feuer, Cy 94, 95
The First Nighter "Spring in Kansas" 18
Five see Oboler, Arch
The 5000 Fingers of Dr. T (Columbia, 1953) 3, 59, 78, 80, 82, 83, 84, 85, 86, 87; Conried discusses changes to film 88; difficulty filming final scenes 85; "Dressing Song" (Do-Me-Do-Duds) 87–88; "Dungeon Ballet" 87; effect on HC 98–99; first draft of script 83; "Freudian" references 89, 90; large budget for 84; "Massage Opera" 83–84; New York premiere 89; original script ending 90; proposed soundtrack album 89; re-release as Crazy Music in 1958 90; reviews of 89; sneak preview 88; soundtrack for 86–87; Theodor Geisel's influence 83; Tommy Rettig's complaint 86
Fonda, Henry 34
Foray, June 142, 172

Ford Theatre "High Tor" 107
The Forest Rose 14
Foster, Norman 35
Foy, Eddie 160
Fractured Flickers (as series host) 3, 142–144
Franklin, Lydia: experiences with HC on stock tour 167, 168–170
Freeman, Don 175
Frees, Paul 142
Freitag, Dorothea 160
Friebus, Florida 147
Funicello, Annette 143
A Funny Thing Happened on the Way to the Forum (1979) 173–174

Gabor, Zsa Zsa 143, 176
Gardiner, Reginald (original choice for *Mr. Belvedere* TV series) 117
Garland, Beverly 140
Garland, Judy 72, 73
Garson, Greer 36
The Gay Falcon (RKO, 1940) 29
Geisel, Theodor (Dr. Seuss): *Design for Death* 59; *The 5000 Fingers of Dr. T.* see *The 5000 Fingers of Dr. T*
Generation (1967) 147–150
Genevieve (*The Tonight Show* regular) 110
Gibson, MaryAnn (née Cohan) 93–94
Gildersleeve, Edith Beyer see Conried, Edith G. (mother)
Gitlin, Todd 175
Gold, Sid (manager) 31, 55, 102, 124
Gold Diggers of 1633 (1976) 154
Goodman, Dody 110
Gordon, Gale 60–61
Gordon, Gloria ("Mrs. O'Reilly") 57, 58
Grab, Al 163
Granger, Farley 74, 75
Grant, Cary 42
Gray, Colleen 66
The Great Gildersleeve 38
The Green Bullet 15
Greenstreet, Sydney 36
Grey, Virginia 22
Griffin, Merv 166
Gunsmoke 74

Hackett, Buddy 134, 136, 137
Hagen, Jean 112
Hale, Alan, Jr. 21
Halop, Florence 59
Hamilton the Great (audition show) 70
Hamlet 13, 16
Hansel and Gretel (live broadcast) 115, 116
Hardwicke, Cedric 22–23, 132
Harrington, Pat, Jr. 140
Hausner, Jerry 60, 70; "be better" story 72, 144, 148; the *Sunshine Boys* tour 173; talks of *Generation* tour 148, 153; USO tour with HC 156, 157
Have Gun Will Travel 73
Hayes, Gabby 160
Hayes, Peter Lind 62, 84, 86
Haymes, Dick 21
Hayward, Jim 76
Hayward, Susan 56

Hayworth, Rita 34, 56
Healy, Mary 83, 84, 86
Hecht, Ben: *Actors and Sin* 74, 131
Henreid, Paul 41, 90
"High Tor" 107
His Butler's Sister (Universal, 1943) 49, 50
Hitler's Children (RKO, 1942) **32**, 33–34,
Hollander, Frederick 86–87
Holt, Tim 33, 115
Hopper, Hedda 3, 72, 112, 114
Hoppity Hooper (as voice of Uncle Waldo Wigglesworth) 144
Horton, Edward Everett 142
Horton Hears a Who (1971 CBS TV special) **161**
Hostages (Paramount, 1943) 32–**33**
House Un-American Activities Committee (HUAC) 62, 63
How the Other Half Loves (1974) 163, 164
How the Other Half Loves (1975) 166
Howard, Cy: on working with HC 57, 58
Hubbard, John 76
Hughes, Howard 114
Hyde-White, Wilfred 128

I Love Lucy 68
I'll Buy That (quiz show) 96–**97**
Irene (1974) 163, 164, 165
Irving, George 163
It Happened Today 17
It's a Wonderful World (MGM, 1939) 22

The Jack Paar Program 59
Jacques, Hattie 159
Japanese Sword Society 177
Jellison, Bob "Jelly" 61
Jergens, Adele **64**
Jet Pilot (U.I., 1957) 114
John Barrymore Presents "Accent on Youth" 18, **19**
Johnson, Arte 173
Jones, Jennifer 42
Journey Into Fear (RKO, 1942) **35**
Judy Canova Show 41

Kaner, Walter 50
Kanter, Hal 70, 158
Karen, James: on working with Hans 145, 157, 158, 177
Karl, Prof. O.H. (Pacific Lutheran College) 127
Katzman, Sam 90
Kaufman, George S. 62
Kaye, Danny 55, 84
Kaye, Stubby 116
Kelly, Gene 68, 72
Kennedy, Robert 153
The Kilocycle Komics 47
King, Martin Luther, Jr. 153
Kismet (TV special) 150
Kolchak: The Night Stalker "The Knightly Murders" (1974) 166
Kovacs, Ernie 118, 125
Kramer, Stanley (Stanley Kramer Productions) 82–83, 84, 85, 89, 131
Kramer, Mrs. Stanley 131–132
Kruger, Otto 34

Kruschen, Jack 46
Kuttner, Henry 80

The Lady Takes a Chance (RKO, 1943) 36
Lady Windermere's Fan 15
LaFargue, Marietta (née Frederici): impressions of HC on *Generation* tour (1967) 148–150
Lake, Arthur **28**–**29**; *There Goes Mr. Greenthumb* 161
Lamb, Gil 160
Lantz, Walter 37
Lee, Gypsy Rose 143
Lennon, John 153
Leonard, Robert Z. 75
Let's Face It (panel show) 76
Levy, Parke 57, 92
Lewis, Cathy 57
Lewis, Jerry 106, 117, 131, 132
Lewis, Sinclair: describing Abe Burrows 95
Lewis and Martin *see* Lewis, Jerry
Life of Riley **40**, 41
Life with Luigi **60**, 68
Lights Out! "The Flame" 39
Ligon, Tom 149
Lilo ("La Mome Pistache") 95–96
Logan, Joshua 107, 121, 122
Lord, Marjorie 112
Lorre, Peter 36
"Lucy Hires an English Tutor" 77
Luke, Keye 157
Lux Radio Theatre: "Rebecca" 37; "The Wizard of Oz" 73

MacHarrie, Lindsay (radio actor) 16
Macht, Stephen 174
MacLaine, Roland 57
The Magic Fountain (Classic World, 1961) 132
Maisie Was a Lady (MGM, 1941) 34
Make Room for Daddy see The Danny Thomas Show
The Man Called X 43
March, Hal 58
Marie, Rose 143
Marshall, George 57
Martin, Ernest 94, 95
Massey, Raymond 126, 127
McCambridge, Mercedes 39
McDevitt, Ruth 147
McDonald, Jeannette 24
McDowell, Roddy 63
McIntire, John 175
Meadows, Audrey **97**
Meet Me in Las Vegas (cut out of film) 107
The Mel Blanc Show 55–56
Mellis, Jose 110
Merry Wives of Windsor: audition for first radio show 16
The Mikado (Gilbert and Sullivan) 93
The Mike Douglas Show 166
Mr. Belvedere (1961) 132
Mr. Belvedere (series pilot) 121, 122
Mr. Ed (CBS, 1962) 56, 134
The Monster That Challenged the World (UA, 1957) 33, **115**
Moore, John (radio show host) 39; interview with HC 162–163
Moorehead, Agnes 26, 41–42

More About Nostradamus (MGM, 1940, short subject) 24, **25**
Morehead, Albert **97**
Mrs. Parkington (Warner Bros, 1944) 36
Murder Without a Trace (1972) 160
Musical Mailbox 51
My Fair Lady (1973) 162
My Favorite Husband 68, **69**
My Friend Irma: film 57; *The Professor and Mrs. O'Reilly* (proposed radio spin-off) 58; radio 57; TV series (1952) 58

Naish, J. Carrol **60**, 68
Nancy Goes to Rio (MGM, 1950) 72
Nast, Buddy 80
Natwick, Mildred 160
The NBC University Theatre "Don Quixote" 73
Nelson, Eddy 24
Nelson, Frank **60**, 61, 177
Never Too Late (1981) 175
New Mexico (UA, 1951) 74, **75**
Newhart, Bob 143
Newhouse, Shelby 47, 50
Nightmare (UA, 1942) **31**, 32
Norman, Is That You? (1970): difficulty with subject matter 159
Not in the Book (1960): rehearsal for and review 128, 133
The Notebook 51

Oboler, Arch: 17, 26, 38, 39, 68, 80, 81; *Bwana Devil* 82; *Five* 79; *The Twonky* see *The Twonky* (UA, 1953)
Olsen & Johnson (*Crazy House*) 35
Omnibus "What Makes Opera Grand?" 116
On Borrowed Time (MGM, 1939) 22
On the Town (MGM, 1949) 68
Once Upon a Honeymoon (RKO, 1942) 42
One Hour in Wonderland (Disney special) 73
Oppenheimer, Jess 68–70, 76
Othello 16
Owen, Bill 70

Paar, Jack: "fanatical loyalty" of 109, 110, 114, 121, 122; as host of *The Tonight Show* (*The Jack Paar Show*) 59, 109; on radio 58; trip to Asia with HC (1962) 134, 135, **136**, 137, 140, 166; trip to England with HC (1960) 126–127
Pantomime Quiz (*Stump the Stars*) 56, 63, **64**, **65**, 67–68, 92, 140
Pasadena Boys Band 89
Passage to Marseilles (Warner Bros, 1944) 36
The Patsy (Paramount, 1964) 131
Pavone, Tony 162–163
Pearce, Alice: *Monster Rally* album 118
Peary, Harold 38
Peter Pan (RKO, 1953) 73; HC on "Capt. Hook" **78**, 105; HC on doing voiceovers 78; live action film for 78–79
Picon, Molly 167, **168**
Pidgeon, Walter 36
Pink, Sid 79, 82
Plays for Americans: "Adolf and Mrs. Runyon" 39; "Hate" 38–39
Plus the Press 14

Porter, Cole 94–95
Powell, Jane 72, 164
Powell, William 62
Price, Vincent 42, **64**, **65**, 114, 127
Prime Ribbing (as emcee, 1949) 65, 67
Promising Priscilla 27

Quillan, Joe 59

Rainer, Luise 21–22, 33
Rains, Claude 36, 37
Randall, Tony 172
The Ransom of Red Chief 118, **119**
Rathbone, Basil 127, 131
Rebound "Dry—with Three Olives" 76
"Redecorating" 76
Reed, Alan 60, 92, 144
Reid, Elliot: on HC and food 157–158, 177
Reis, Irving 17, 29, 34, 74
Rettig, Tommy 84, 86, 89
Reynolds, Debbie 131, 163, 164
Roberts, Jimmy: on HC's trouble with tempo 173–174
Rock-a-Bye Baby (Paramount, 1958) 117
Rogers, Emmet 122
Rogers, Ginger 68
Romance "The Grasshopper" 106
Rooney, Ted (son of Mickey Rooney) 118, **119**
Rosenbaum, David 149
Rosenbloom, Nathan (Dr.) 177
Rosenthal, Jerry 80
Roth, Lillian 160
Rumple's Last Stand (TV pilot, 1979) 174
Russell, Nipsey 159
Rutherford, Ann 76

Sabinson, Lee 93
San Diego Zoological Society 161
Sanchez, George 170
Sande, Walter 76
Schilling, Gus 76
Schnabel, Stephan 32
Schreiber, Avery 173
Scott, Bill 142, 144
The Second Time Around (1976) 166
The Second Time Around (1977) 167–170, **168**
70, Girls, 70 (1971) 159–160
She Loves Me (1978) 171
Sheppard, Sam 153
Shumlin, Herman 155
Sinatra, Frank 68
The Siren of Bagdad (Columbia, 1953) 78; HC's opinion of 90; review of 90–91, **98**
$64,000 Question (quiz show) 116
Skelton, Red 134
Solomon, Leo 59
Something Old, Something New (Broadway premier and closing) 167
Something to Shout About (Columbia, 1942) **30**
Song of Bernardette 42
Sothern, Ann 34,
Spier, William 41
Spock, Benjamin 159
Spofford! (1969) 155
Stars Over Hollywood 71–72

Stewart, James 22, 55
Stohn, Carl, Jr. 164
Stokey, Mike 63, **64**, **65**
Streamlined Shakespeare 18
Stuart, Lynne: first meeting with HC 161
The Student Prince (1956) 107–108
The Student Prince (1966) 147
The Student Prince (1972) 161
Stump the Stars see *Pantomime Quiz*
Sullivan, Francis L. **74**, 75
Summer Stock (MGM, 1950) 72
The Sunshine Boys (pre-1978) 173
The Sunshine Boys (1978) 172, 173, **174**
Suspense (radio series) 41; "Banquo's Chair" 42, 56, 74; "Dime a Dance" 42; "Rave Notice" 99; "Sorry Wrong Number" 41–42
Sutton, Grady 36
Swanson, Gloria 76
Sweeney, Bob 58

Take a Good Look (panel show) 118
Tall Story (Broadway, 1959) 120–122, 155
Tamblyn, Russ 176
The Taming of the Shrew 15
Temianka, Henri 176, 177
The Tempest **14**,16
Terry-Thomas 159
There Goes Mr. Greenthumb see Lake, Arthur
There's Always the Guy (audition shows) 58
Thomas, Danny 60, 107; on working with HC 111–112
Thomas, Richard 176
Three for Bedroom C (Warner Bros, 1952) 76
Three Sheets to the Wind 36
Thrills 18
Tobias, George 37
The Tonight Show see Paar, Jack
The Tony Randall Show 172
Too Young to Kiss (MGM, 1951) 74
Tracy, Spencer 173
Turner, Lana 21
Turoff, Robert 169
20th Century Fox Hour "The Miracle on 34th Street" 106
The Twonky (UA, 1953) 3, 26, 78, 79; Oboler's experimental techniques 80; production difficulties 80, **81**; scathing reviews 82
Tynan, Kenneth 153

Underground Agent (Columbia, 1942) **33**
Unexpected Uncle (RKO, 1940) **25**
US Steel Hour "Presento" 99–100, **102**

Vallee, Rudy 19, 116
Veidt, Conrad 38
Verdon, Gwen **95**, 96
Vernon, Ruth **94**
Volpe, Nick 76
von Sternberg, Josef 114

Walker, Harry 126
Wallace, Mike **97**; *The Mike Wallace Interview* 118–120, 124
Walt Disney Productions see Disney, Walt
Ward, Jay (Jay Ward Productions) 142, 143, 144
Warner, Jack 118
Warren, Janet 81
Watkyn, Arthur 160
Wayne, John 36, 75–76,
Weaver, Charlie 126
Webb, Jack 111
Weed, Gene 177
Weenick, Annabelle 171
Weiner, Robert 122
Welles, Orson 17; gift to HC 44; *Macbeth* (film) 56; radio work with HC 26, **34**, 35, 38, 42, 43
What's It For? (panel show) 111
The Whistler "Fool's Gold" 42
The Wife Takes a Flyer (Columbia, 1942) 34
Wilson, Marie 57
Winslow, George "Foghorn" 89
Winslowe, Paula **40**
Winters, Shelley 74, 75
Withers, Grant 36
Woodbury's Hollywood Playhouse "Romeo & Juliet" 37

Yamaguchi, Shirley 99–100, **102**
Young, Alan 56
You're Never Too Young (Paramount, 1955) 106

www.ingramcontent.com/pod-product-compliance
Lightning Source LLC
Chambersburg PA
CBHW081552300426
44116CB00015B/2853